WELFARE AND OLD AGE IN EUROPE AND NORTH AMERICA: THE DEVELOPMENT OF SOCIAL INSURANCE

PERSPECTIVES IN ECONOMIC AND SOCIAL HISTORY

Series Editors: Robert E. Wright
                   Andrew August

TITLES IN THIS SERIES

1 Migrants and Urban Change: Newcomers to Antwerp, 1760–1860
Anne Winter

2 Female Entrepreneurs in Nineteenth-Century Russia
Galina Ulianova

3 Barriers to Competition: The Evolution of the Debate
Ana Rosado Cubero

4 Rural Unwed Mothers: An American Experience, 1870–1950
Mazie Hough

5 English Catholics and the Education of the Poor, 1847–1902
Eric G. Tenbus

6 The World of Carolus Clusius: Natural History in the Making, 1550–1610
Florike Egmond

7 The Determinants of Entrepreneurship: Leadership, Culture, Institutions
José L. García-Ruiz and Pier Angelo Toninelli (eds)

8 London Clerical Workers, 1880–1914: Development of the Labour Market
Michael Heller

9 The Decline of Jute: Managing Industrial Change
Jim Tomlinson, Carlo Morelli and Valerie Wright

10 Mining and the State in Brazilian Development
Gail D. Triner

11 Global Trade and Commercial Networks: Eighteenth-Century Diamond
Merchants
Tijl Vanneste

12 The Clothing Trade in Provincial England, 1800–1850
Alison Toplis

13 Sex in Japan's Globalization, 1870–1930: Prostitutes, Emigration and
Nation Building
Bill Mihalopoulos

14 Financing India's Imperial Railways, 1875–1914
Stuart Sweeney

15 Energy, Trade and Finance in Asia: A Political and Economic Analysis
Justin Dargin and Tai Wei Lim

16 Violence and Racism in Football: Politics and Cultural Conflict in British
Society, 1968–1998
Brett Bebber

17 The Economies of Latin America: New Cliometric Data
César Yáñez and Albert Carreras (eds)

18 Meat, Commerce and the City: The London Food Market, 1800–1855
Robyn S. Metcalfe

19 Merchant Colonies in the Early Modern Period
Victor N. Zakharov, Gelina Harlaftis and Olga Katsiardi-Hering (eds)

20 Markets and Growth in Early Modern Europe
Victoria N. Bateman

Forthcoming Titles

Female Economic Strategies in the Modern World
Beatrice Moring (ed.)

Policing Prostitution, 1856–1886: Deviance, Surveillance and Morality
Catherine Lee

Respectability and the London Poor, 1780–1870: The Value of Virtue
Lynn MacKay

Narratives of Drunkenness: Belgium, 1830–1914
An Vleugels

Mercantilism and Economic Underdevelopment in Scotland, 1600–1783
Philipp Robinson Rössner

Crime and Community in Reformation Scotland: Negotiating Power in a
Burgh Society
Robert Falconer

Residential Institutions in Britain, 1725–1950: Inmates and Environments
Jane Hamlett, Lesley Hoskins and Rebecca Preston (eds)

Consuls and the Institutions of Global Capitalism, 1783–1914
Ferry de Goey

WELFARE AND OLD AGE IN EUROPE AND NORTH AMERICA: THE DEVELOPMENT OF SOCIAL INSURANCE

EDITED BY

Bernard Harris

Routledge
Taylor & Francis Group

LONDON AND NEW YORK

First published 2012 by Pickering & Chatto (Publishers) Limited

Published 2016 by Routledge
2 Park Square, Milton Park, Abingdon, Oxfordshire OX14 4RN
711 Third Avenue, New York, NY 10017, USA

First issued in paperback 2015

Routledge is an imprint of the Taylor & Francis Group, an informa business

BRITISH LIBRARY CATALOGUING IN PUBLICATION DATA

Welfare and old age in Europe and North America: the development of social
insurance. – (Perspectives in economic and social history)
1. Social security – Europe – History. 2. Social security – North America – History. 3. Older people – Europe – Social conditions. 4. Older people – North
America – Social
conditions. 5. Welfare state – History. I. Series II. Harris, Bernard, 1961–
368.3'009-dc23

ISBN-13: 978-1-138-66161-5 (pbk)
ISBN-13: 978-1-8489-3189-3 (hbk)

Typeset by Pickering & Chatto (Publishers) Limited

CONTENTS

List of Figures   ix
List of Tables   xi
Notes on Contributors   xiii

Introduction – *Bernard Harris*   1
1 Coalminers, Accidents and Insurance in Late Nineteenth-Century
   England – *John Benson*   9
2 The Costs and Benefits of Size in a Mutual Insurance System: The
   German Miners' – *Knappschaften*, 1854–1923 – *Timothy W. Guinnane,*
   Tobias A. Jopp and Jochen Streb   27
3 A New Welfare System: Friendly Societies in the Eastern Lombardy
   from 1860 to 1914 – *Paolo Tedeschi*   47
4 Economic Growth and Demand for Health Coverage in Spain: The Role
   of Friendly Societies (1870–1942) – *Margarita Vilar Rodríguez and*
   Jerònia Pons Pons   65
5 Sickness Insurance and Welfare Reform in England and Wales,
   1870–1914 – *Bernard Harris, Martin Gorsky, Aravinda Guntupalli*
   and Andrew Hinde   89
6 From Sickness to Death: Revisiting the Financial Viability of the English
   Friendly Societies, 1875–1908 – *Nicholas Broten*   107
7 America's Rejection of Government Health Insurance in the Progressive
   Era: Implications for Understanding the Determinants and
   Achievements of Public Insurance of Health Risks – *J. C. Herbert Emery* 121
8 Medical Assistance Provided by *La Conciliación*, a Pamplona Mutual
   Assistance Association (1902–84) – *Pilar León-Sanz*   137
9 In it for the Money? Insurers, Sickness Funds and the Dominance of
   Not-for-Profit Health Insurance in the Netherlands – *R. A. A. Vonk*   167
10 Belgian Mutual Health Insurance and the Nation State – *D. Rigter*   189

Notes   207
Index   257

LIST OF FIGURES

Figure 2.1: Number of Knappschaften by year, Prussia and Bavaria,
1861–1920   32
Figure 2.2: Size distribution of Knappschaften by year, Prussia and Bavaria,
average number of contributors per KV in the respective decile, selected
years   35
Figure 2.3: Average sick days per KV member, Prussia, 1861–1913   39
Figure 3.1: New SMS and total number of SMS in Eastern Lombardy
1860–1914   49
Figure 5.1: Recorded sickness rates among members of British friendly
societies, 1836–97   91
Figure 5.2: Sickness rates in rural areas, towns and cities   93
Figure 8.1: Evolution of annual subsidies compared with membership
figures (1904–35)   150
Figure 8.2: Total income and cost of sick leave (1923–30)   151
Figure 8.3: Evolution of *La Conciliación* member numbers (1903–72)   160
Figure 8.4: Incomes and expenses of *La Conciliación* (1945–69)   162

LIST OF TABLES

Table 1.1: Membership of the Northumberland and Durham Miners' Permanent Relief Fund and the North Staffordshire Coal and Ironworkers'
Permanent Relief Society as a Percentage of Miners Employed 12

Table 1.2: Fatal accidents per thousand employed in the Northumberland,
Durham and North Staffordshire coalfields 14

Table 1.3: Shift earnings (pence) of hewers on piecework in the
Northumberland, Durham and North Staffordshire Coalfields 16

Table 1.4: Colliery owners' payments to the Northumberland and Durham
Miners' Permanent Relief Fund and the North Staffordshire Coal and
Ironworkers' Permanent Relief Society as a percentage of ordinary
members' contributions 24

Table 2.1: Membership development and coverage of Knappschaften in per
cent of Prussia's and Bavaria's population, 1861–1920 33

Table 2.2: Merger and closure activity by decade, Prussia and Bavaria,
1861–1920 36

Table 2:3. The membership structure and social budget of the average
Prussian Knappschaft, selected years 37

Table 2.4: Coincidence of net deficits and KV exit by merger and
closure,Prussia, 1861–20 43

Table 3.1: Members of the SMS in the Eastern Lombardy 50

Table 3.2: Assets, income and expenditure of the SMS existing in the
Eastern Lombardy (in Italian lires) 54

Table 3.3: Data concerning the income and expenditure of the SMS
(in Italian lires) 59

Table 4.1: General charitable institutions in Spain defined by law before
the Civil War 72

Table 4.2: Typology of private charities in Spain 73

Table 4.3: Distribution of insured according to risks covered (percentage) 76

Table 4.4: Expenditure of the Montepío de La Caridad (1901–50)
(percentage of total) 78

Table 4.5: Number of Mutual Insurance Funds (percentage) 80

Table 4.6: Distribution of expenditure in societies in the province of
    Barcelona (current pesetas)   81
Table 4.7: Societies that covered the risk of sickness in the province of
    Barcelona (current pesetas)   81
Table 5.1: Sickness experience among members of the International Order
    of Oddfellows (Manchester Unity), 1891–5   96
Table 5.2: Age distribution of members of the Manchester Unity of
    Oddfellows, 1846/8–1893/7   100
Table 6.1: Court balance sheet summary statistics   112
Table 6.2: Membership Regressions   114
Table 6.3: Sample risk loading estimates   117
Table 6.4: Sample probability of ruin estimates   118
Table 7.1: Median incomes, surpluses, sickness and death expenditures
    and savings rates for US and European households, 1888–90   132
Table 7.2: Median savings rates for US and European households by
    five-year age Group, 1888–90   134
Table 8.1: Spanish wages (1914–1930)   152

NOTES ON CONTRIBUTORS

John Benson is Emeritus Professor of History at the University of Wolverhampton. He has published the results of his research into mining history in journals such as *Business History,* the *Economic History Review,* the *International Review of Social History* and the *Labour History Review,* and in books such as *British Coalminers in the Nineteenth Century: A Social History* (Longman) and (as editor/co-editor) *The Miners of Staffordshire 1840–1914* (Keele University Press), *Studies in the Yorkshire Coal Industry* (Manchester University Press) and the *Bibliography of the British Coal Industry: Secondary Literature, Parliamentary and Departmental Papers, and a Guide to Sources* (Oxford University Press).

Nicholas Broten is a graduate of the University of California, Berkeley, and the London School of Economics. His research seeks to examine the implications of theories of political economy through quantitative analysis of historical data. This will be his first publication.

Herb Emery is the Svare Professor in Health Economics at the University of Calgary with a joint appointment between the departments of Economics and Community Health Sciences. Herb's research has addressed the rise and fall of fraternal sickness insurance, the transition from private voluntary health insurance arrangements to compulsory government health insurance across the twentieth century. He is a co-author (with George Emery) of *A Young Man's Benefit: The Independent Order of Odd Fellows And Sickness Insurance in the United States and Canada, 1860–1929* (Montreal: McGill-Queen's University Press, 1999).

Martin Gorsky is Senior Lecturer in the History of Public Health at the London School of Hygiene and Tropical Medicine. His research interests are in the history of public and voluntary sector health care institutions in the nineteenth and early twentieth century, and health systems within welfare states in the post-war period. He has published widely in these areas, most recently (with John Mohan) *Mutualism and health care: hospital contributory schemes in twentieth-century Britain* (Manchester, Manchester University Press, 2006).

Aravinda Guntupalli is lecturer in Gerontology at the University of Southampton. She joined the Centre for Research on Ageing as lecturer in September 2010 after working at the Medical Research Council, Southampton. Prior to that, she was working as a research fellow at the University of Southampton on the health and morbidity of Friendly Society members in the late nineteenth and twentieth centuries. Her recent work is concerned with life course epidemiology, gender-differentials in well-being, nutritional transition, and reproductive health. Since 2001, she has worked on inequality, welfare and health issues using large scale surveys and historical datasets. Aravinda applies both qualitative and quantitative methods and her interdisciplinary background is reflected in her published work.

Timothy W. Guinnane is the Philip Golden Bartlett Professor of Economic History in the Department of Economics at Yale University. Guinnane's research focuses on the demographic and financial history of Europe and North America in the nineteenth and early twentieth centuries. He is the author of *The Vanishing Irish: Households, Migration, and the Rural Economy in Ireland 1850–1914* (Princeton, NJ: Princeton University Press, 1997), and has published in the *American Economic Review*, the *Quarterly Journal of Economics*, the *Journal of Economic History*, the *Economic History Review*, *Demography*, *Population Studies*, and other journals.

Bernard Harris is Professor of the History of Social Policy at the University of Southampton. He has published on many different aspects of the history of social policy and social welfare. His books include *The Origins of the British Welfare State: State, Society and Social Welfare in England and Wales 1800–1945* (Basingstoke: Palgrave, 2004), *Charity and Mutual Aid in Europe and North America* (edited with Paul Bridgen, and published in New York by Routledge in 2007), and *Gender and Wellbeing in Europe: Historical and Contemporary Perspectives* (edited with Lina Gálvez and Helena Machado, and published in Farnham by Ashgate in 2009). His most recent book (co-authored with Roderick Floud, Robert Fogel and Sok Chul Hong) is *The Changing Body: Health, Nutrition and Human Development in the Western World* (Cambridge: Cambridge University Press, 2011).

Andrew Hinde is Senior Lecturer in the Division of Social Statistics and a member of the Southampton Statistical Sciences Research Institute. His research interests are in demography, and especially the historical demography of England. He is the author of *England's Population: a History since the Domesday Survey*, the only single-volume history of the English population which covers the entire period since 1086, and has written or contributed to numerous articles on the demography of nineteenth-century England and the contemporary demography of developing countries. He is a member of the Editorial Board of the journal *Local Population Studies*, the only English-language journal devoted to population history, and also an Associate Editor of the online journal *Demographic Research*. He was formerly an Associate Editor of the *Journal of the Royal Statistical Society* (Series A).

Tobias A. Jopp is a doctoral candidate in economic history in the Department of Economics at the University of Hohenheim. His dissertation focuses on the German miners' *Knappschaft* insurance since 1854, and especially on the concentration process among the many self-standing *Knappschaft* funds and the question of whether there existed an optimal fund size. Jopp's publications include articles in *Zeitschrift für Unternehmensgeschichte* and *Business History* (both 2011). Forthcoming in *Financial History Review* is the article 'Insurance, size, and exposure to actuarial risk: empirical evidence from nineteenth- and early twentieth-century German Knappschaften'. He is currently working as research assistant at the University of Regensburg.

Pilar León-Sanz is an Associate Professor of the History of Medicine at the University of Navarre. She has also been a Research Fellow at the Wellcome Trust Centre for the History of Medicine at University College, London (2002, 2010), Visiting Scholar at Harvard University (2011), and member of the Steering Committee, Phoenix European Thematic Network on Health and Social Policy (2006–9). Her research interests include topics related to medicine in eighteenth-century Spain and the practices of health care professionals during nineteenth and twentieth centuries. She participates in the Research Group on 'Emotional Culture and Identity', at the Institute for Culture and Society at the University of Navarre. Her recent publications include the books: *Health Institutions at the Origin of the Welfare Systems in Europe* (2010); *La Tarantola Spagnola. Empirismo e tradizione nel XVIII secolo* (2008); *Vicente Ferrer Gorraiz Beaumont y Montesa (1718–1792), un polemista navarro de la ilustración* (with D. Barettino 2007); *La implantación de los derechos del paciente* (2004).

Jerònia Pons Pons is Senior Lecturer in Economic History at the University of Seville. Her research focuses on the economic history of insurance. Her work on industrial accident insurance has been published in the *International Review of Social History*, *Labor History*, *Revista de Historia Industrial*, *Investigaciones de Historia Económica* and *The Appeal of Insurance* edited by Geoffrey Clark *et al.* (University of Toronto Press, 2010). She has published other articles on the Spanish insurance market in the *Revista de Historia Económica*, the *Journal of European Economic History*, the *Business History Review* and a chapter in the collective book edited by P. Borcheid and R. Pearson, *Internationalisation and Globalisation of the Insurance Industry in the 19th and 20th Centuries* (Zurich: Philipps-University, Marburg, 2007).

Danièle Rigter has published on different elements of the history of the Dutch welfare state. She wrote about the role of the department of Labour and about several private organizations. Her latest publications were on the implementation of the Accident Insurance Act (1901) and the Sickness Benefits Act (1930). Her research focuses on the aspects of nationbuilding, democracy and citizenship in the making of the welfare state. She is currently working for the Centre for the History of Health Insurance (Kenniscentrum Historie Zorgverzekeraars) in the Department of Medical Humanities at the VU University Medical Center in Amsterdam where she is, among other things, responsible for its website on the history of health insurance (Erfgoedgids Zorgverzekeraars). More information is available on www.ecade.org.

Jochen Streb is the Professor of Economic History in the Department of Economics at the University of Mannheim in Germany. Streb's research focuses on the innovation history and regulation history of Germany in the nineteenth and twentieth century. He has published in the *Economic History Review*, *Explorations in Economic History*, the *Journal of Economic History*, the *RAND Journal of Economics*, *Research Policy*, and other journals.

Paolo Tedeschi is 'Ricercatore' (Lecturer) in Economic History at the Department of Economics of the University of Milan-Bicocca. His studies particularly concern the following aspects of the economy and society of the Eastern Lombardy during the eighteenth, nineteenth and twentieth centuries: (a) the development of the agriculture and cattle-breeding and the links between the real estate market and the credit market; and (b) the catholic movement from the 'Rerum Novarum' to the rise of fascism, with particular reference to friendly societies and trade unions. His publications include: 'Sale or Gratuitous Transfer? Conveyance of Family Estates in a Manufacturing Village: Lumezzane in the 18th and 19th Centuries', in *Continuity and Change*, 2008, n. 3, pp. 429–55; 'Un rôle nouveau pour les ouvriers au sein des entreprises après la grande guerre: les idées de l'Abbé Pottier et le syndicalisme chrétien en Italie', in M. Dumoulin (ed.), *Italie et Belgique en Europe depuis 1918 / Italië en België in Europa sedert 1918* (Turnhout: Brepols Publishers, 2008); 'Common Land in the Eastern Lombardy during the Nineteenth Century', in *Historia Agraria* (2011).

Margarita Vilar Rodríguez is Lecturer (tenured professor) in Economic History at the University of Corunna. Her research focuses on the labour history and the history of social policies in Spain (nineteenth and twentieth centuries). She has published the results of her research on these topics in journals such as the *International Review of Social History*, *Labor History*, *Revista de Historia Industrial* and *Investigaciones de Historia Económica*, and in collective books such as *Migraciones y coyuntura económica del franquismo a la democracia* (PUZ,

2008) and *Los orígenes del Estado del Bienestar en España, 1900–1945: los seguros de accidentes, vejez, desempleo y enfermedad*, (University of Zaragoza, 2010). She is also autor of *Los salarios del miedo. Mercado de trabajo y crecimiento económico en España durante el franquismo* (Fundación 10 Marzo, 2009).

Robert Vonk is PhD candidate in the field of Medical History and researcher for the *Kenniscentrum Historie Zorgverzekeraars* (Centre for the History of Health Insurance) in the Department of Medical Humanities at the VU University Medical Center in Amsterdam. He is currently writing a dissertation on private health insurance and civil society in the Netherlands during the twentieth century. He has published several articles on the history of health insurance in the Netherlands in various volumes, including: *Tussen volksverzekering en vrije markt. De verzekering van zorg op het snijvlak van sociale zekerheid en gezondheidszorg 1880–2006* (2008). He recently contributed several chapters on health insurance to the upcoming corporate history of Eureko/Achmea (2011).

INTRODUCTION

Bernard Harris

During the last two decades, there has been growing interest in the history of mutualism. This interest has been fuelled, at least in part, by increasing scepticism over the capacity of the state to meet welfare needs, coupled with mounting concern over the seemingly inexorable rise in the costs associated with health care and pension provision. In Britain, this scepticism has been visible on both sides of the political spectrum. In 2010, the self-styled 'Red Tory', Philip Blond, claimed that the growth of the welfare state had 'nationalised a previously mutual society and reframed it according to an individualised culture of universal entitlement'.[1] His 'Blue Labour' counterpart, Maurice Glasman, has also complained that the foundation of the 'classic' welfare state after 1945 caused 'universal benefit ... to replace mutual responsibility as the basic principle of welfare'.[2]

The chapters in this book are designed to help place some of this ferment of contemporary ideas in a more historical context. Almost all the chapters originated as papers which were either presented to a specially organized conference at the University of Southampton in April 2009 on 'Insurance, Sickness and Old Age: Past Experiences and Future Prospects',[3] or during the World Economic History Congress later in the same year. We should like to thank the UK Economic and Social Research Council for supporting the first of these events, and the organizers of the World Economic History Congress for assistance with the second.

In the introduction to his edited collection of essays on *Social Security Mutualism*, Marcel van der Linden defined mutual benefit societies as 'associations formed voluntarily for the purpose of providing their members with financial assistance in case of need'.[4] However, like all definitions, this has its limitations. In the first place, although the majority of such associations were indeed voluntary some, such as the German *Knappschaften*, were not. These are discussed in more detail in Chapter 2 below. Second, although some organizations catered for a wide variety of different financial needs, the majority were particularly concerned with the provision of insurance against sickness, old age and death, and many also provided direct assistance in the form of health care. Third, although the societies' primary functions were economic, many of them also provided access to social and recreational activities. These not only helped to create the bonds of trust which underpinned the societies' economic functions, but also provided members with vital opportunities for fellowship and conviviality.[5]

The chapters in this book examine a number of different aspects of the history of mutual aid in a variety of occupational and national contexts. Although two chapters are particularly concerned with the operation of specialist funds for the support of miners, others deal with more general benefit societies, and whereas some are particularly concerned with the problem of income replacement, others focus more directly on the costs of health care. The chapters also cover a wide geographical range, with three chapters on Britain, two on Spain, and one each on Belgium, Germany, Italy, the Netherlands and the United States. However, almost all the chapters share a common concern, either directly or indirectly, with the relationship between mutual aid and the welfare state. Historians who have examined this relationship in the past have often tended to fall into one of two camps. Some historians have argued that the limitations and deficiencies of mutual-aid organizations paved the way for the introduction of welfare states[6] whereas others argue that the growth of welfare states was at least partly responsible for the death or decline of mutualism.[7] These positions are not, of course, incompatible and both are reflected in a number of the chapters which follow.

One of the central problems for the history of mutualism has been the need to explain why mutual-aid associations developed to a much greater extent in some areas than others.[8] In Chapter 1, John Benson explores this conundrum in relation to the growth of specialist funds for the provision of accident insurance in British coalfields during the nineteenth century. In Durham and Northumberland, the Miners' Permanent Relief Fund was established in 1862, and by the end of the 1880s it had recruited 90 per cent of eligible workers. In North Staffordshire, a Coal and Ironworkers' Permanent Relief Society was founded in 1869, but only one worker in ten belonged to the scheme in 1889/90. Benson argues that miners in the two areas had similar opportunities to join the two funds, faced similar occupational risks and enjoyed similar levels of support from other friendly societies, charities and the poor law. He therefore concludes that the real explanations for differences in rates of growth need to be sought in the culture of the mining communities themselves and in their relationship to their employers. In Durham and Northumberland, miners lived in tightly-knit communities which forged a strong sense of *occupational* solidarity and enjoyed good relationships with the mine-owners. In North Staffordshire, miners were part of the 'ordinary working class' and received much less support from their employers.

In Chapter 2, Timothy Guinnane, Tobias Jopp and Jochen Streb approach the problem of miners' relief from a rather different angle. Their chapter focuses on the operation of miners' general relief funds, or *Knappschaften*, in Germany between 1854 and 1923. As the authors point out, the *Knappschaften* were designed to compensate members for loss of earnings associated with both short-term sickness and with longer periods of chronic illness and invalidity, but they also suggest that these problems did not necessarily lend themselves to the same organizational solutions. The *Knappschaften* needed to be relatively small in order to be able to police short-term claims effectively but they also needed to be large enough to accumulate the resources needed to fund long-term claims. This problem was also familiar to the actuaries who studied nineteenth-century British friendly societies. They argued that the societies needed to grow in order to minimize actuarial risk, but they worried that increases in the size of friendly societies were tending to increase the duration of sickness claims (see Chapter 5).

This means that Guinnane *et al.*'s chapter is interesting on a number of different levels. Their initial aim is to examine the extent to which increases in the size of *Knappschaften* either led to an increase in 'moral hazard' (as reflected in the tendency to make excessive sickness claims) or actuarial efficiency. Their second aim is to estimate the optimal size of *Knappschaften* in relation to each of these issues; and their third aim is to estimate the proportion of *Knappschaften* whose size was 'sub-optimal'. Their overall conclusion is that approximately 50 per cent of societies were too small to deal adequately with the actuarial risks they faced. They argue that this means that the authorities were right to encourage individual *Knappschaften* to form larger organizations, but there was also much less justification – at least in these terms – for the decision to merge all the surviving funds into a single *Reichsknappschaft* at the end of their period.

The next two chapters provide more general accounts of the history of mutual aid organizations in Italy and Spain. In Chapter 3, Paolo Tedeschi explores the development of *societàs di mutuo soccorso*, or 'SMS', in Eastern Lombardy between 1860 and 1914. Although SMS were found in more rural areas, Tedeschi argues that their growth was directly related to the process of industrialization in the region during the second half of the nineteenth century. They differed from the *Knappschaften* in that membership was voluntary and they differed from the majority of British friendly societies in that they were often either overtly confessional, in the case of the Catholic societies, or political, in the case of the socialist societies. They also provided a wider range of benefits than the majority of friendly societies, including unemployment benefits, and were prepared to engage directly in campaigns for the improvement of wages and working conditions. Although they developed in response to the lack of state or other forms of welfare support, they also acted as a bulwark against state interference, and this was why their position became increasingly precarious following the Fascist seizure of power in 1922.[9]

Although research on friendly societies in Spain has generated 'an enormous flow of publications in recent years',[10] Margarita Vilar Rodríguez and Jerònia Pons Pons argue that the value of these publications has been limited by the fact that they often have a highly localized focus. Moreover, they have also tended to concentrate on the role played by the friendly societies in the development of trade unions and as vehicles for the promotion of sociability. Chapter 4 seeks to counter these limitations by examining the development of friendly societies in the country as a whole and by focusing much more closely on what might be regarded as their core insurance-based functions, with particular reference to the provision of health care.

One of the most intriguing questions raised by this history is the role played by the friendly societies in the chronology of state welfare provision. As the authors point out, the state intervened in a number of areas associated with friendly societies, including the provision of insurance against accidents, unemployment, old age and maternity, long before it intervened in the area of health care. It has been argued that this reflected the particular strength of the health care provided by the friendly societies but Vilar and Pons question whether coverage was either as widespread or as comprehensive as this statement might imply. They argue that the state was slow to intervene in the provision of health care because of a 'lack of understanding' between the societies and the state, but they also suggest that this enabled the Franco regime to bypass the societies altogether when a statutory scheme was finally introduced in 1942. This decision had disastrous consequences for the societies, which – in the majority of cases – either collapsed or degenerated into purely recreational associations.[11]

In Chapter 5, Bernard Harris, Martin Gorsky, Aravinda Guntupalli and Andrew Hinde explore two different aspects of the history of British friendly societies. In the first part of the chapter, they re-examine the contemporary debate over the apparent increase in recorded morbidity in the final quarter of the nineteenth century. Although many observers believed that age-specific morbidity rates were increasing, they attributed this to changes in the attitudes and behaviour of society members and in the societies' capacity to police their sickness claims, rather than to any 'objective' change in sickness experience. The second part of the chapter focuses on the societies' attitudes to the introduction of state pensions and national health insurance. Although many members were suspicious of the growth of state intervention, others were more supportive. The chapter explores the reasons for these attitudes and also examines the relationship between the societies and other interest groups, including both the medical profession and the commercial insurance industry.

In Chapter 6, Nicholas Broten also examines the societies' attitudes to the introduction of old age pensions. In a famous paper, the American historian Bentley Gilbert argued that the friendly societies' failure to recruit a larger number of younger members and the increasing longevity of their older members meant that they were threatened by growing insolvency.[12] Broten reassesses this argument with particular reference to one of the largest British friendly societies, the Ancient Order of Foresters. He argues that, even though the society was what George and Herb Emery have called an 'old man's society',[13] its financial situation was nevertheless comparatively healthy. This leads him to conclude that the societies' attitudes to old age pensions cannot be explained by institutional weaknesses, and that more attention therefore needs to be paid to broader political concerns.

In recent years, historians have shown a great deal of interest in the 'failure' of the United States to develop a comprehensive system of national health insurance.[14] This debate has been fuelled by the enormous controversy surrounding Barack Obama's health reform proposals.[15] Herb Emery has explored some of the implications of these issues in a series of papers looking at Progressive attempts to introduce statutory health insurance at the end of the First World War.[16] Many authors have attributed the failure of these proposals either to the poverty of American workers or the power of vested interests, but Emery argues that the real reason was that compulsory health insurance was unnecessary, because US workers were already sufficiently well-paid to make their own provision.

In Chapter 7, Emery uses data from the US Department of Labor's survey of 'The Cost of Living of Industrial Workers in the United States and Europe, 1888–90' to compare the disposable income of US workers with that of their European counterparts. He argues that the savings rate (defined as the ratio of surplus household expenditure to husband's income) of US workers was significantly higher than that of workers in either Belgium or Germany, and that this might help to explain why there was so much more support for compulsory health insurance in those countries. However, his figures also show that savings rates in Britain, France and Switzerland were at least twice as high as their US values, and this leads him to conclude that more attention might also be paid to the impact of changes in savings rates on the evolution of attitudes to health insurance in these countries between 1890 and 1914.

The final three chapters focus much more closely on the history of mutual aid in the twentieth century. In Chapter 8, Pilar León-Sanz provides a detailed history of one particular mutual aid organization in Spain, the Sociedad Protectora de Obreros *La Conciliación*, which was founded in Pamplona in 1902 and remained in existence until 1984. As Leon explains, the society was distinctive because it included representatives of both employers and employees, and provided a labour arbitration service alongside the more traditional activities of providing financial assistance in times of need and access to medical care. In view of its Catholic origins and employer associations, one might have expected *La Conciliación* to have cooperated with the introduction of General Franco's health insurance scheme in 1942 but it declined to do so. However, even though it survived the introduction of Franco's scheme and retained many of its original functions, this did not prevent its eventual decline.

Almost all the organizations which have been discussed in this book are concerned with the provision of either financial support or medical care – or both – to workers and their families. However, in Chapter 9, Robert Vonk takes a rather different approach. This chapter is less concerned with traditional types of friendly or mutual benefit society and more with the operation of not-for-profit organizations providing access to health care for both working- and middle-class members. The main aim of the chapter is to explore the relationship between these organizations and the commercial health sector and to show how the interaction between the two has helped to shape contemporary health policy.

At the end of the nineteenth century, non-profit sickness funds dominated the Dutch health care market. However, as the cost of health care increased, these organizations faced increasing financial pressure, and this gave commercial organizations an opportunity to reenter the market, albeit on a relatively limited basis. Vonk argues that the commercial sector continued to make relatively little progress after the Second World War, and that although some of this can be explained by the sector's own ineptitude, the main reason was the Dutch population's persistent distaste for the association of profit and health care. He also argues that this distaste has continued to shape the development of health policy in the Netherlands during the twenty-first century, even after the Health Insurance Act appeared to offer an important victory to commercial health care providers in 2006.

The final chapter is also concerned with the financing of health care, with particular reference to Belgium. The author, Danièle Rigter, shows how mutual organizations laid the foundations of the Belgian health care system and played a key role in the development of statutory health insurance after 1945. She also demonstrates how the current system has been shaped by a complex web of negotiations between mutual organizations, governments and health care professionals, and explores the extent to which the difficulties associated with these negotiations have been compounded by tensions between Belgium's different national communities. She concludes that it is premature to see Belgium as a model for the development of a single, trans-European health care policy when it is still in the grip of its own complex history.

Taken together, these chapters offer a series of important and fascinating insights into the evolution of mutual aid organizations and the development of a number of different aspects of contemporary health and welfare policy. In particular, the chapters cast some doubt on the assumption that the societies were necessarily moribund and show how they could provide an important defence of worker independence, especially in those countries which eventually succumbed to Fascist dictatorships. However, the chapters also illustrate some of the limitations of these organizations, both in terms of their ability to meet the needs of their existing members and their capacity to extend the benefits of membership to a wider population. In view of this, it may be dangerously premature to suggest that the mutual organizations of the late-nineteenth and early twentieth centuries offer a realistic model for the reform of welfare services in the twenty-first century.

1 COALMINERS, ACCIDENTS AND INSURANCE IN LATE NINETEENTH-CENTURY ENGLAND

John Benson

Historians of the coal industry seem largely unaware of – or uninterested in – coalminers' attempts to insure themselves against workplace accidents.[1] The few scholars who have considered miners' efforts to protect themselves in this way tend to examine financial rather than medical provision, and to emphasize the failings, rather than the benefits, of the schemes which were available.[2] But what is most striking is that they are all inclined to agree that it was the coal industry's combination of high risks and high (if unstable) earnings that explained miners' desire, and ability, to insure themselves and their families against the risks of industrial injury.[3]

It seems odd then that when historians turn their attention to the working class as a whole – including, of course, workers in less dangerous, less well-paid occupations than coal mining – they suggest, some of them, that voluntarism played a greater role in the provision of late nineteenth- (and early-mid twentieth-) century welfare than conventional analysis allows.[4] It also seems odd, to coal mining historians at least, that they have begun to stress the difficulties of determining workers' reasons for deciding to protect themselves and their families by means of insurance.[5] Martin Gorsky, for example, warns against 'monocausal accounts of friendly society growth'.[6] He is at particular pains to counter the view that, in the early nineteenth century at least, either surplus earnings or 'the health risks of industrial labour' provides a complete explanation of increased spending on insurance.[7]

Accordingly, it is the aim of this chapter to explore these issues by examining the reasons that late nineteenth-century English coalminers decided to insure – or not to insure – against the risk of being injured during the course of their employment. It will do so by concentrating upon developments in two coalfields, Northumberland and Durham (about which a good deal is known) and North Staffordshire (which has received much less attention); and by comparing the membership of one form of friendly society, miners' permanent relief funds, with levels of risk, with levels of earnings and with other possible determinants of friendly society membership.[8] It will argue that in order to understand this form of working-class self-help, it is necessary to consider not just levels of risk, levels of earnings and the availability of other sources of relief. It is also essential, it will be suggested, to explore the attitudes and behaviour of both the miners and the miners' employers, the derided and demonized coal owners.

Comparative History

Comparative history promises a great deal. It has the potential, at its best, to confirm or to refute generalizations and explanations which may appear unexceptional or incontrovertible when viewed within a single conceptual, chronological or geographical context. Yet it is a methodology that is hard to establish rigorously and to apply consistently, and it has found a surprisingly limited place in the historiography of British coal mining. Not surprisingly, it has been adopted most often in attempts to understand strike propensity, patterns of unionization and levels of militancy in an industry characterized by what are generally regarded as exceptionally, if not uniquely, poor employer–employee relations. As Royden Harrison explained in the introduction to his edited collection, *Independent Collier*, which was published in 1978, 'This volume was born of the conviction that we need more historical, micro-comparative, studies of coal mining communities if we are ever to return again, with profit, to histories of coal mining trade unionism'.[9] It was a lead which was followed, in Harrison's collection, by historians like Alan Campbell[10] and Pat Spaven.[11] It was taken up, in due course, by scholars such as Martin Daunton,[12] John Benson,[13] Stefan Berger, Andy Croll and Norman Laporte[14] and, most notably and most successfully, by Roy Church and Quentin Outram in their 1998 study, *Strikes and Solidarity: Coalfield Conflict in Britain 1889–1966*. Church and Outram undertook their research, they explained, as 'an important test case for an innovative methodology applied in a historical and comparative analysis'.[15]

This chapter, it is believed, also has some claim to innovation. Not only does it adopt a comparative methodology, but it does so in order to explore the determinants, not of working-class strikes and solidarity, but of cross-class co-operation – indeed what many coal mining historians would regard as cross-class collaboration. Moreover, it does so by examining two coalfields, Northumberland and Durham and North Staffordshire, which, unlike those often chosen for comparative purposes, could scarcely be more different from one another.

Northumberland and Durham was the oldest, largest, most important and best known of all Britain's coalfields. Although its dominance was gradually eroded during the second half of the nineteenth century, it remained home to a fifth of the country's miners and accounted for a fifth or so of the country's coal production. Its industry was characterized by high levels of investment and (particularly in Durham) by large pits and powerful employers. As the coal owners exhausted the region's more easily worked seams, they turned to the more intensive working of existing reserves and the exploitation of more concealed, more difficult and more dangerous deposits.[16] Indeed, it is the industry in Northumberland and Durham (along with South Wales and to a lesser extent Yorkshire) which provides the template upon which, and against which, both popular and academic conceptions of the British coal industry, its workers, its communities and its trade unions have tended to be based.[17]

The North Staffordshire (or Potteries) coalfield was newer, smaller, less important and much less well known. Once the owners had overcome the area's drainage and other geological problems in the late 1860s, the industry grew rapidly, developing from one containing a large number of small owners to one dominated by a few, relatively large undertakings (often associated with the iron industry). Nevertheless, it remained one of the country's less important coalfields, its expansion constrained by a combination of limited local markets and high transport costs. Thus even at the end of the century, when the region was producing over 5.5 million tons of coal a year, its output represented less than 2.5 per cent of the country's total production. North Staffordshire is not a coalfield that has ever impinged significantly upon the consciousness of coal mining historians – and it remains one of the few coalfields unable to boast a trade union history to its name.[18]

The Miners' Permanent Relief Fund Movement

The miners' permanent relief movement had its roots, its leaders explained, in 'the anomaly that while the sufferers by large disasters were generally provided for by public subscriptions, those whose breadwinners lost their lives by accidents causing single deaths, which bore an enormous proportion to great disasters, had no such help'.[19] The first of the societies, the Northumberland and Durham Miners' Permanent Relief Fund, was established in 1862, followed by the North Staffordshire Coal and Ironworkers Permanent Relief Society in 1869, the Lancashire and Cheshire Miners' Permanent Relief Society in 1872 and the West Riding of Yorkshire Miners' Permanent Relief Fund in 1877.[20]

All four societies operated in much the same way. Ordinary members paid a subscription of between two and four pence per week (together sometimes with an entrance fee). If they were injured while at work, they were entitled to payments of between four and ten shillings per week; if they were killed, their families qualified for a funeral grant, a widow's benefit of five shillings per week, and an orphan's benefit of between two shillings and two-and-sixpence per week.[21] Honorary members (who were not entitled to benefits) subscribed in one of three ways. They could either pay an annual subscription of a pound, make a life donation of ten pounds or, if they were an employer of colliery labour, pay an annual subscription equivalent to between ten and twenty per cent of their employees' contributions.[22]

Managed jointly – and efficiently – by their ordinary and honorary members,[23] the miner's permanent relief funds proved increasingly successful in attracting miners to membership. In 1870, just one miner in twenty had joined, but thereafter a larger and larger proportion of the workforce began to enrol. In 1880, a third, and by 1890 more than half, of the country's miners were members of the movement. Indeed, during the final decade of the century, there were as many members of the little-known miners' permanent relief funds as there were of the much better-known mining trade unions.[24]

It is striking, however, that the permanent relief funds – like the trade unions – had a much larger presence in some coalfields than in others. Table 1.1 is most revealing. It shows the membership figures of the Northumberland and Durham Miners' Permanent Relief Fund, which was the most successful, and of the North Staffordshire Coal and Ironworkers' Permanent Relief Society, which was the least successful, of the movement's four bodies in attracting miners to membership. It is true that comparing the figures for the early 1870s (such as they are) may be misleading because only the Northumberland and Durham society had been established for any time. But by the 1880s, both the Northumberland and Durham and the North Staffordshire societies had both been in existence for more than ten years.

Table 1.1: Membership of the Northumberland and Durham Miners' Permanent Relief Fund and the North Staffordshire Coal and Ironworkers' Permanent Relief Society as a Percentage of Miners Employed.

Years	Northumberland and Durham Miners' Permanent Relief Fund	North Staffordshire Coal and Ironworkers' Permanent Relief Society
1859–63	7.0	–
1864–68	13.3	–
1869–73	21.4	0.7
1874–78	48.3	1.4
1879–83	67.5	8.4
1884–88	78.4	11.2
1889–90	90.0	10.2

Source: Central Association for Dealing with Distress Caused by Mining Accidents, *1891 Report*, pp. 50–1.

What is striking is the discrepancy between the popularity of the two organizations. Although the membership density (and membership) of the two bodies grew significantly, the Northumberland and Durham Miners' Permanent Relief Fund was always six times – and was sometimes nine times – as successful as the North Staffordshire Coal and Ironworkers' Permanent Relief Society in recruiting miners to membership. The *Staffordshire Sentinel* was not alone in wondering 'how it was that the Society did not make more way among our underground population'.[25]

Risks

How are such discrepancies to be explained? It is usual, we have seen, for the few historians who have shown any interest in the matter, to explain miners' propensity to insure in terms of the high risks and the high (if unpredictable) earnings characteristic of employment in the industry. But a comparison of developments in Northumberland and Durham and in North Staffordshire suggests that neither of these explanations stands up to serious scrutiny.

The higher – much higher – membership density of the Northumberland and Durham Miners' Permanent Relief Fund cannot be explained by the higher – presumably much higher – risk of working in the north-east of England. In fact, the relationship between behaviour and risk is a great deal more difficult to disentangle than much of the existing literature would lead one to suspect. In this case, it is much easier to enumerate miners' membership of permanent relief funds than it is to quantify the many dangers that prospective members faced during the course of their employment. A full analysis of occupational risk in the coal mining would require, at the very least, an assessment of the incidence of industrial diseases as well as of industrial accidents, and an attempt to delineate the impact, psychological as well as physical, that such diseases and accidents placed upon those working in the industry.[26]

The assessment of occupational risk undertaken here draws only upon industrial accidents. But it is a limitation that can be defended. It is not just that the statistics for industrial accidents are so much fuller and more reliable than those for industrial diseases.[27] It is also that the permanent relief funds insured their members against accidents, but not against diseases. It can be claimed with some confidence therefore that the resulting comparison of occupational risk in Northumberland and Durham and in North Staffordshire, though restricted, is both reasonably reliable and directly relevant to the attempt to explore miners' reasons for enrolling in permanent relief funds.

The comparison is certainly telling. Table 1.2 shows that despite the much greater publicity given to deaths in the north-east of England, miners in Northumberland and Durham were less, not more, likely than those in North Staffordshire to be killed during the course of their employment.[28] It transpires that (with the single exception of Northumberland between 1859 and 1863) death rates from fatal accidents, whether small-scale or large-scale, were lower in Northumberland and Durham than they were in North Staffordshire. (Tables 1.1 and 1.2 also show, in another significant undermining of the conventional model, that in both coalfields, membership density increased as death rates declined). Thus fatal accident rates cannot be used, in this case at least, to explain differences in miners' propensity to insure.[29]

Table 1.2: Fatal accidents per thousand employed in the Northumberland, Durham and North Staffordshire coalfields.

Years	Northumberland	Durham	North Staffordshire
1859–63	3.6	2.4	3.5
1864–68	2.9	2.3	3.4
1869–73	2.1	1.8	2.5
1874–78	1.3	1.5	1.9
1879–83	1.3	1.5	1.8
1884–88	1.1	1.3	1.5
1889–90	1.3	1.2	1.7

Source: See source for Table 1.1 above, pp. 52–3.

Perhaps, it might be objected, it was non-fatal, rather than fatal, accidents which persuaded miners of the need to join a permanent relief fund. The analysis of what has been described as 'colliery disaster in instalments'[30] is particularly complicated. The official returns of non-fatal accidents were, even the mines inspectorate recognized, 'of little value in a statistical point of view'.[31] The best evidence, it has been discovered, comes from the Durham Coal Owners' Association and the miners' permanent relief funds themselves. The extensive experience of these two bodies suggests that during the final third of the nineteenth century the proportion of non-fatal accidents to fatalities from small-scale accidents remained constant, in every coalfield, at almost exactly 100 to one.[32] Thus it is possible to use fatal accident statistics to calculate non-fatal accident statistics. Death rates from small-scale accidents were lower in Northumberland and Durham than they were in North Staffordshire. It follows therefore that injury rates from non-fatal accidents were also lower in Northumberland and Durham than they were in North Staffordshire. The conclusion is clear. It is no more possible to use differences in non-fatal accident rates than it is differences in fatal accident rates to explain miners' willingness to enrol in a permanent relief fund.

Earnings

How then to account for the much greater readiness of the Northumberland and Durham miners to insure with their local permanent relief fund? The solution, according to conventional accounts of the relationship between behaviour, risk and income in the industry, must lie in the fact that wages were higher – presumably much higher – in the north-east of England than they were in the north midlands.

Unfortunately, the assessment of miners' earnings is even more difficult than the assessment of the risks which they faced. It is necessary not only to distinguish between wage rates and earnings and between the earnings of different classes of worker, but also to take account, so far as is possible, of the fluctuations brought about by accident, illness and short-time working – not to mention the desire/need to take a break from what was often a brutally demanding job.[33] Fundamental to miners' standards of living, explains Roy Church, 'was the structure of wages and earnings, affected by geography, function, and grade within the industry, by age and sex, and the trade cycle'.[34] Moreover, 'few generalizations about wages, however restricted and hedged about with qualifications', it has been pointed out, 'are likely to be of much value in an industry with such large differentials between its best and its worst paid workers'.[35]

The best that can be done is to combine contemporary comments on coalfield standards of living with historians' long-run estimates of miners' earnings. When this is done, it becomes clear that, whatever caveats may be entered, miners in Northumberland and Durham did indeed tend to be better paid than those in North Staffordshire. Nevertheless, it must be stressed – and stressed most strongly – that north-eastern miners were not much better paid, and were sometimes less well paid, than their colleagues in the Potteries.

The north-east's high wages probably come as no surprise. It is generally accepted by historians of the coal industry that miners in Northumberland and Durham were the best paid in the country.[36] Not only were their money wages comparatively high but nearly all married workers received a colliery house or a rent allowance in lieu. Miners in the north-east benefited too – and this is obviously directly relevant to this study – from the payment of 'smart money', a system whereby the employers provided assistance to underground workers who were injured during the course of their employment.[37]

Table 1.3 provides a useful, albeit by no means perfect, vehicle for comparing earnings in Northumberland and Durham with those in North Staffordshire. Calculated from data compiled by B. R. Mitchell in 1984, it has obvious limitations: it measures money, rather than real, wages; it records shift, rather than weekly or annual earnings; it takes no account of colliery housing and rent allowances (or deductions for candles and powder);[38] and it applies only to hewers, the most highly paid of all coal mining workers. It is instructive for all that, providing, if nothing else, a consistent set of data from which to explore the relationship between insurance and earnings in the two coalfields.

Table 1.3: Shift earnings (pence) of hewers on piecework in the Northumberland, Durham and North Staffordshire Coalfields.

Years	Northumberland	Durham	North Staffordshire
1859–63	59.1	53.2	48.4
1864–68	63.5	56.6	55.9
1869–73	77.8	65.5	65.0
1874–78	80.8	66.4	64.7
1879–83	61.9	55.3	55.9
1884–88	60.5	56.7	58.4
1889–90	70.7	64.1	72.2

Source: B.R. Mitchell, *Economic Development of the British Coal Industry 1800–1914* (Cambridge: Cambridge University Press, 1984), Table 7.1.

The situation Table 1.3 reveals is more complicated than one might anticipate. There were differences, it is true, between the Northumberland and Durham and the North Staffordshire coalfields. But there were also differences between Northumberland and Durham, and differences too between the years preceding, and the years following, the late 1870s. It transpires that between 1859–63 and 1874–8, miners in the north-east were, as one has been led to expect, better paid than those working in the Potteries. Hewers in Northumberland earned between 12 and 23 per cent more, and in Durham up to 8 per cent more, per shift than those working in North Staffordshire. Thereafter, however, the balance of advantage was reversed. Between 1879–83 and 1889–90, according to the reworking of Mitchell's data, miners working in Durham were paid less, rather than more, than their colleagues in the north midlands. Indeed, by 1889–90, shift earnings in North Staffordshire were 2 per cent higher than they were in Northumberland, and 13 per cent higher than they were in Durham.

So even when the provision of colliery houses and rent allowances is taken into account, the comparison of hewers' earnings in Northumberland and Durham and North Staffordshire undermines, rather than substantiates, the conventional view of the relationship between insurance, risk and income in the coal industry. Permanent relief fund membership density was always between six and nine times higher in the north-east than it was in the north midlands. But hewers' earnings were never more than a twenty-five per cent higher – and were sometimes lower – in Northumberland and Durham than they were in North Staffordshire.

The Poor Law, Charity and the Law

If differences in the density of miners' permanent relief fund membership cannot be accounted for by differences in levels of risk or in levels of earnings, what is the explanation? One obvious way of way of explaining the higher density of permanent relief fund membership in Northumberland and Durham would be to show that injured miners and bereaved families in the two counties had access to, or availed themselves of, fewer other sources of assistance than those working in North Staffordshire. Perhaps poor law guardians, members of the public and/ or the courts in the north-east were less generous than they were in the Potteries.

But this was not the case. There is no sign, for example, that poor law guardians in the north-east of England were less generous than those in North Staffordshire when dealing with the victims of coal mining accidents.[39] The evidence, partial and fragmentary though it is, suggests that boards of guardians in all coalfields were prepared, on occasion, to be more generous than central authority demanded. It was reported in 1894, for instance, that even before the legislation introduced that year permitting guardians to disregard friendly society benefits of up to five shillings a week in their assessment of destitution, boards in many coalfield unions were, 'without sanction of the law', supplementing 'allowances attributable to the thrift of the members of Miners' Permanent Relief Societies'.[40]

There is no sign either that charitable provision by members of the public following industrial accidents was less generous in Northumberland and Durham than it was in North Staffordshire. It is impossible, of course, to quantify the support offered in individual cases by friends, neighbours, drinking companions, concert organizers, *ad hoc* local committees and so on.[41] But what can be done is to quantify the assistance offered by the public disaster funds which were established, in all coalfields, in the wake of major catastrophes.[42]

Here too, however, there is no discernable difference in levels of public generosity, with disasters in both coalfields generating large sums of money. In Northumberland and Durham, for instance, the Hartley fund (of 1862) raised over £81,000, the Seaham fund (1871) £13,000; in North Staffordshire, the Talke fund (of 1866) generated nearly £17,000, the Mossfields fund (1889) in the region of £10,000.[43] The North Staffordshire society spoke for many in the permanent relief fund movement: 'The readiness with which an appeal for a relief fund was responded to has a tendency to encourage the belief that, at least where the loss of life is large, the public will provide'.[44] There seems no reason then for supposing that miners in the north-east were any more – or any less – likely than those in the north midlands to look to charitable intervention rather than permanent relief fund membership to help them in their hours of need.[45]

Nor is there any indication that the courts in Northumberland and Durham were less generous than those in North Staffordshire.[46] Rather the reverse. No miners anywhere, it must be said, secured much by way of legal compensation for industrial injuries. But because mining trade unionism was established earliest and most securely in the north-east of England,[47] the Northumberland Miners' Mutual Confident Association and the Durham Miners' Association were better placed than the North Staffordshire Miners' Federation (and other north midlands unions) to offer their members legal advice and support.

The two north-eastern unions were active even before the passing of the Employers' Liability Act of 1880 (which allowed workers, under certain circumstances, to recover damages when employers or their agents were guilty of the negligence that led to injury).[48] When eight men were killed at the Withymoor colliery in 1864, the leadership of the Northumberland Miners' Mutual Confident Association recommended that its members should contribute three pence each towards the costs of taking legal action.[49] Six years later, the Durham Miners' Association decided that in all cases where it judged a manager responsible for the death of a union member, the matter should be brought before a delegate meeting in order to try to secure compensation.[50]

The two unions took more co-ordinated action in the wake of the 1880 act. Within six months, the executive committee of the Northumberland Miners decided that when it was satisfied that an accident could be traced to the negligence of an employer, the union should bear the cost of any subsequent trial and associated legal expenses.[51] At almost exactly the same time, the Durham Miners' Association decided to impose a quarterly levy of a penny per member in order to finance a defence fund to pursue cases under the new legislation.[52]

Miners in North Staffordshire were left much more exposed.[53] When the North Staffordshire Miners' Federation appealed to other unions in 1881 for financial assistance to enable it to sue the employers of the twenty-five miners killed at the Whitfield colliery, it met with a frosty reaction. The Derbyshire Miners' Association agreed only to refer the question to the lodges for their consideration.[54] The Northumberland Miners' Mutual Confident Association was still less supportive, 'as we are of opinion that a district that cannot itself furnish funds for such a purpose has little claim to the sympathy or support of other districts'.[55] Indeed five years later, the North Staffordshire Federation found itself unable to pay even the relatively small sum of £50 that had already been spent in pursuing the claim of one miner's widow. Eventually, the Federation returned the solicitor's bill unpaid.[56]

Employee Cooperation

Where then should one look for an explanation? The answer is to be found, it will be suggested, in the cultural characteristics – the attitudes and behaviour – of the two sides of the industry in Northumberland and Durham and in North Staffordshire.[57] Such a suggestion, it is true, will probably be met with more than a little scepticism. There is always the temptation, after all, to turn to culture as the explanation of last resort, the factor which, unquantifiable as it is, remains available when all other possibilities have been tried, tested and found wanting.

Nonetheless, it is culture that holds the key to explaining the contrasting experiences of the permanent relief fund movement in the two coalfields under discussion. The miners of Northumberland and Durham had much stronger traditions of mutual co-operation that those working in North Staffordshire. The coal owners of Northumberland and Durham were much more accustomed than their counterparts in North Staffordshire to working – however uneasily – in collaboration with their employees.

Miners in the Northumberland and Durham and the North Staffordshire coalfields drew upon markedly different traditions of mutual co-operation. The 'isolated' pit villages found in many parts of the north-east of England were home, by the end of the nineteenth century, to what has been described as 'almost continuous and enthusiastic activity' (involving everything from concerts and lectures, to picnics and dog-racing, chapel building and shopping with the local co-operative).[58] The result, according to Sid Chaplin, was that, 'each village was, in fact, a sort of self-constructed, a do-it-yourself counter environment, you might dub it. The people had built it themselves'.[59] The settlements of North Staffordshire tended to be less isolated, less dependent upon mining and less inclined, in all probability, towards self-reliance and self-sufficiency. According to Edward Billington, 'The final conclusion must be that in almost all respects, apart from his occupational characteristics, the nineteenth-century miner of North Staffordshire was an ordinary member of working-class society'.[60]

This dichotomy meant, for the purposes of this chapter, that workers in the two coalfields made markedly different efforts to insure against the risks of their work. However, it is a difference that yet again undermines, rather than sustains, the suggestion that the density of permanent relief fund membership was higher where potential members had fewer alternative sources of support. It will be seen that the miners of Northumberland and Durham made more, and more successful, efforts than their contemporaries in North Staffordshire to insure themselves and their families with bodies other than the permanent relief fund. This would mean, one would have thought, that they had fewer, and less compelling, reasons than those in the north midlands for supporting their local branch of the relief fund.

In fact, miners in both coalfields protected themselves, equally so far as one can judge, by taking out policies with the commercial insurance industry. The best evidence, which comes as one might expect in the wake of major disasters, suggests that by the mid-1870s it was common across the country for miners to insure their lives with the market leader, the Prudential. Thus in Northumberland and Durham, over 30 per cent of those killed at Trimdon Grange (in 1882), 15 per cent of those killed at West Stanley (1882), 33 per cent of those killed at Usworth (1885) and 50 per cent of those killed at Elemore (1886) were insured with the Prudential. The figures were not dissimilar in North Staffordshire: 13

per cent of those killed at Apedale (in 1878) and 40 per cent of those dying at Mossfields (1889) had taken out policies with this one company alone.[61]

Otherwise, it was the miners of Northumberland and Durham who were the more likely to insure against the risks of working in the industry. They were possibly more inclined, at least during the early years of the period, to join one of the great affiliated orders of friendly society.[62] They were certainly more inclined to organize quasi-formal collections for workmates killed during the course of their employment. Throughout Northumberland, it was said, miners paid a levy of a shilling per man, and sixpence per boy, whenever a colleague was killed at work.[63] At Durham collieries like Seaham (where the disaster fund raised £13,000 in 1871), adult miners contributed six pence, and the lads three pence, following fatal accidents, a practice which raised about £35 for each bereaved wife.[64] Meanwhile, at nearby Houghton-le-Spring colliery, collections made for the dependants of miners killed at work generally raised in the order of seventy pounds.[65] By the early 1870s, claimed the secretary of the Northumberland and Durham Miners' Permanent Relief Fund, every colliery in the north-east coalfield had a 'slate' club which, in return for a weekly subscription of three pence, paid five shillings per week for the first six months of sickness, and two shillings and sixpence thereafter. A large proportion of any surplus, he noted disapprovingly, was spent on 'jollification'.[66]

Miners in both Northumberland and Durham and North Staffordshire also had access to schemes organized by their trade unions to insure members and their families against industrial accidents.[67] The Northumberland Miners' Mutual Confident Association ran a funeral fund and a non-fatal accident fund. The Durham Miners' Association and the North Staffordshire Miners' Federation each operated a funeral fund, a non-fatal accident fund, along with a widow and orphan fund.[68]

Nowhere in the country, it is true, did trade-union funds relieve a great deal of distress. But unions in the north-east almost certainly insured a higher proportion of the workforce than those in North Staffordshire. Moreover, the funds they organized proved longer lasting and were probably more reliable. So whereas the Northumberland Miners' Mutual Confident Association ran its funeral fund from 1863–78, and again from 1884–97, the North Staffordshire Miner's Federation closed its (much more costly) widows and orphans fund in the late 1870s, less than ten years after it had been opened.[69]

Employer Collaboration

Differences in the density of miners' permanent relief fund membership can be explained too by differences in the culture – the attitudes and behaviour – of the coal owners in Northumberland and Durham and in North Staffordshire.

It is true, of course, that the coal owners (and their agents) can scarcely have received a more hostile press. 'British coalowners', concludes Quentin Outram, 'were widely regarded, and not merely by their employees, as obdurate, stubborn, intransigent, uncompromising, aggressive, vengeful, greedy, tight-fisted, flint-hearted, short-sighted, hide-bound, arrogant and incompetent'.[70]

Yet, the employers, some of them, were perfectly well aware of the ideological and material benefits that might accrue from generous, reliable and/or independently organized systems of employee welfare.[71] The Northumberland and Durham owners were more alert than most. They had a tradition not only of mutual co-operation but also of collaboration, albeit unstable and insecure, with the men whom they employed. In the 1850s and 1860s, claims Roy Church, it was only in Northumberland (and Yorkshire) that the coal owners had 'learned to live with unionism'.[72] During the 1870s, explains Martin Daunton, 'the northern owners welcomed formal procedures in which the union was the sole channel for grievances and the guarantor of acceptance of decisions'. He cites in support of his argument the Durham Coal Owners' Association's 1873 admission that it had, 'in many cases, been indebted to the attention and energy of the Miners' Executive for the repression of unlawful and vindictive action taken unadvisedly by local members'.[73] Both employers and employees hoped that the formalization of the relationship between wages and prices through arbitration and sliding scales would provide a self-acting mechanism that would obviate the need for constant and disruptive wage negotiations.[74]

In fact, employers in Northumberland and Durham, in North Staffordshire – and in other coalfields – did more to help the victims of industrial accidents than is generally recognized.[75] They not only subscribed to the funds that were established following major disasters, but made other provision besides. In 1874, for example, the employers of the fifty-four men killed in an explosion at Dukinfield in North Staffordshire met the cost both of providing coffins and shrouds and of transporting the deceased's bodies to wherever they were to be buried.[76] Eight years later, the Weardale Coal and Iron Company of Durham paid the funeral fees and supplied the coffins and hearses that were required when thirty-seven of its employees were killed at Tudhoe colliery.[77]

Otherwise, employers in Northumberland and Durham did much more than those in North Staffordshire – or in other coalfields – to assist the victims of industrial accidents. Such support meant, one would suppose, that they did much more than employers in North Staffordshire – or in other coalfields – to discourage their employees from undertaking any form of voluntary accident insurance. But this, it has been seen, was far from the case.

Owners in the two counties commonly met the funeral expenses of those killed both singly and in small groups. Of the twenty-three owners providing information to the Northumberland Steam Collieries Defence Association in

1881, five donated a coffin and seventeen both donated a coffin and contributed a pound towards other necessary costs. 'In all cases a man and a horse to go with hearse is supplied by the owners to attend the funerals of workmen'.[78] Moreover, it was said to be the custom across the whole of Northumberland and Durham that whenever a miner was permanently injured, the owner of the pit where the accident occurred would help him purchase a horse and cart or other means of earning a living.[79]

Owners in Northumberland and Durham also provided, we have seen, what was known as smart money. Practice varied across the two counties, and disputes were not uncommon, the employers claiming that the allowance was a gratuity, the men that it was part of their wages.[80] But whatever the status and limitations of smart money, it remained of considerable importance. In 1880, for instance, the owners paid almost 8,000 injured men (7 per cent of those employed) over £6,100 (an average of fifteen shillings each). In 1896, they paid over 14,000 men (9 per cent of those employed) a total of more than £10,300 (again an average of fifteen shillings each).[81] Although the number of recipients was relatively small and the sums they received relatively modest, the existence of smart money presumably discouraged the miners of Northumberland and Durham from subscribing to the permanent relief fund, or at least did nothing to encourage them to do so.

Smart money did not exist elsewhere. In North Staffordshire, as in most other coalfields, many employers compelled their employees, for much of the period, to subscribe to pit clubs, membership of which constituted a condition of employment.[82] These clubs, of course, have been roundly castigated. The employers, it is true, often hoped that the organization of such schemes would restrict the mobility of labour, starve the trade unions of funds, deny subscribers the experience or organizing their own societies, and shift the burden of compensation onto their employees.[83] Moreover, as the permanent relief funds were keen to argue, pit clubs,

> scarcely deserve the name of Insurance Funds. Their operations are confined to one colliery or works, and the area is too small to enable them to deal effectually with the risks they incur ... For these funds to attempt to cope with a large disaster is altogether out of the question.[84]

Yet pit clubs had their advantages, particularly during the early years of the period. Compulsory membership, with subscriptions stopped at the colliery office, meant that at pits with such schemes all workers, whether careful or reckless, provident or improvident, were covered. In return for contributions of between one-and-a-half pence and four pence per week, those employed were entitled to a range of benefits. Provision was least satisfactory after fatal accidents and most satisfactory – though most varied – in the case of non-fatal accidents. Nearly all clubs provided some form of medical treatment, together with an allowance of between five and eight shillings per week, usually for a year.[85] The pit club at the Silverdale colliery, for instance, paid an initial benefit of eight shillings per week, although this was halved after only six weeks.[86] These were substantial benefits, and meant that pit club subscribers in North Staffordshire had something at least to match the smart money that was paid to miners in Northumberland and Durham.

Employers and the Permanent Relief Fund Movement

The employers of Northumberland and Durham were also more likely than those in North Staffordshire to support the efforts of the local branch of the permanent relief fund. Like many other employers, they were keen that their employees should contract out of the provisions of the 1880 Employers' Liability Act. Such action, they claimed, not entirely disingenuously, would provide both them and their employees with a degree of certainty in the wake of industrial accidents.[87] The Steam Collieries Defence Association joined with the United Coal Trade Association in suggesting that the Northumberland and Durham Miners' Permanent Relief Fund should be made the basis of a contracting-out arrangement.[88] The permanent relief fund accepted the proposal but the two major trade unions, the Northumberland Miners' Mutual Confident Association and the Durham Miners' Association, rejected it.[89] The result was that it was rare, though not completely unknown, for collieries in the north-east to contract out of the provisions of the act.[90]

Despite the rebuff, some north-eastern employers continued to look to the permanent relief fund for the certainty they desired. At first, there was considerable opposition to the fund because it 'was regarded as the thin end of the union wedge'.[91] Even employers sympathetic to the movement sometimes felt that its demands for financial support were unreasonably high,[92] and often claimed to be concerned about the way in which it was managed.[93] Thus one employer complained in 1883 that, 'he knew of a colliery at which the owners had ceased to pay their contributions, because they considered that an aged member had been put on the fund when he had no claim to be put on, but it had been done by favour and affection'.[94] However, as Sir J.W. Pease, one of the largest owners in the coalfield, pointed out, 'A man quickly enough found reasons for not paying money if he did not want, and it was an easy thing to lay the blame on the Employers' Liability Bill or bad trade'.[95]

Not all owners were looking for excuses. Some supported the fund from the outset,[96] and a number took up the option of securing honorary membership by adding a fixed proportion (between 10 and 20 per cent) to the subscriptions paid by their employees. The sums involved were not large, but as the *Barnsley*

Chronicle pointed out in 1879, the payment of percentages was important psychologically as well as financially: there could be a direct relationship between the scale of a proprietor's financial support and the number of his employees who joined the local branch of the permanent relief fund.[97]

Table 1.4 shows that between 1869–73 and 1874–8, the Northumberland and Durham owners who paid such percentages added between 10 and 15 per cent to their workers' contributions. However, when they failed to persuade their employees to contact out of the 1880 act, they decided to terminate their support of the society. The owners' payments fell from £5,240 (14 per cent of the men's contributions) in 1880 to £3,171 (7 per cent) in 1881, a decline which was directly attributable to the passing of the act.[98] Two years later, just a quarter of Northumberland owners were paying percentages, and although all but one of the large firms in Durham continued to contribute, many small owners in the county withdrew their support.[99] The result was, as Table 1.4 shows, that by 1889–90 the owners' payment of percentages amounted to less than six per cent of the sum that their workers paid in subscriptions.

Table 1.4: Colliery owners' payments to the Northumberland and Durham Miners' Permanent Relief Fund and the North Staffordshire Coal and Ironworkers' Permanent Relief Society as a percentage of ordinary members' contributions.

Years	Northumberland and Durham Miners' Permanent Relief Fund	North Staffordshire Coal and Iron-workers' Permanent Relief Society
1859–63	–	–
1864–68	7.4	–
1869–73	14.3	–
1874–78	13.2	–
1879–83	7.7	17.0
1884–88	7.0	15.4
1889–90	5.8	15.7

Source: Central Association for Dealing with Distress Caused by Mining Accidents, *1898 Report*.

Much more important – and much less expensive – was the north-east coal owners' practice of deducting permanent relief fund subscriptions at source. Although this gave the owners no formal control over the society, it enabled them, at little cost or inconvenience, to demonstrate their support for the fund, to limit its management expenses and, most importantly, to reduce the possibility of members casually or accidentally falling into arrears.[100] By the mid-1870s, the vast majority of the members of the society had their subscriptions deducted at source,[101] and even towards the end of the century, 'whilst only the few companies subscribed, the vast majority of them helped in managing the Society at much less cost than it could be managed if they were kept outside the colliery offices'.[102] This was crucially important. Although the deduction of subscriptions rarely transmogrified, so far as we know, into compulsion, this form of employer assistance does much to explain the success of the Northumberland and Durham Miners' Permanent Relief Fund.

The employers in North Staffordshire did not offer the same level of support.[103] The situation was complicated by the activities of the Employers' Liability Assurance Corporation, a private company which, like the North Staffordshire Coal and Ironstone Workers' Permanent Relief Society, provided facilities for contracting out of the 1880 Employers' Liability Act. Competition between the two bodies escalated, the corporation's agent speaking locally, the society's secretary responding in the pages of the *Staffordshire Sentinel*.[104] The permanent relief fund was worried, not surprisingly, 'lest the terms offered and the advantages set forth by the Employers' Liability Insurance Association should have weight with mercantile bodies, and lead them to think that they were better and more advantageous than those of the miners' relief societies'.[105]

The North Staffordshire owners did not, as a group, support the permanent relief fund's suggestion that it should form the basis of a mutual insurance scheme whereby collieries would contract out of the provisions of the 1880 act.[106] However, after a great deal of discussion, a small number of owners (chiefly in the north of the coalfield) did participate in a voluntary scheme whereby they paid a larger percentage than normal of their employees' contributions to the permanent relief fund, and in return the men at their collieries agreed to forego all claims under the act.[107] Whatever its merits or demerits, the arrangement did little to stimulate permanent relief fund membership. Although the North Staffordshire employers paid percentages equivalent to over 15 per cent of employee subscriptions between 1879–83 and 1889–90, the sums involved were modest, never amounting to even £1,000 per year.

Nor, more importantly, did the employers of North Staffordshire offer much support by deducting their employees' subscriptions at source. It is true that in the early 1880s at least one colliery insisted upon society membership,[108] and that a few years later the Lancashire and Cheshire Miners' Federation protested, on behalf of its North Staffordshire members, against 'the undue influence and forced coercion by the Employers, which is now brought to bear upon the Workmen to compel them to contract out of the Act'.[109] It is not easy, of course, to prove a negative.[110] But these were isolated complaints and few employers in North Staffordshire, it seems, either deducted contributions to the permanent relief fund at source or made membership a condition of employment.

The inability of the North Staffordshire Coal and Ironstone Workers' Permanent Relief Society to secure more employer support for its scheme of contracting out both reflects, and helps to explain, its failure to recruit more successfully. Its problems during the 1880s resulted from a combination of trade depression, commercial competition, trade-union hostility and, it should not be forgotten, the owners' lack of enthusiasm for mutuality.[111] The coal owners of North Staffordshire were less accustomed than those in Northumberland and Durham to collaborating with their workers and less convinced too of the benefits that might accrue from an independently organized system of employee welfare.

Conclusions

The comparison of miners' permanent relief fund membership in Northumberland and Durham and in North Staffordshire helps us to understand better the determinants of nineteenth-century friendly society membership. The coal industry was unusual both for its high risks and for its high, if unstable, wages. It therefore offers an ideal test-bed upon which to examine the conventional view that, 'Insurance against the catastrophes of working-class life was essential to all families, although that does not mean that all could or did afford it'.[112] If there was one group of workers that had the incentive and the means to insure against industrial accidents it was the coal miners.

The comparison of the Northumberland and Durham Miners' Permanent Relief Fund and the North Staffordshire Coal and Ironstone Workers' Permanent Relief Society during the second half of the century suggests, most obviously, that Martin Gorsky is right to warn against 'monocausal accounts of friendly society growth'.[113] It suggests too that he is right to question the view that workers' – even miners' – friendly society membership can be explained by liability to risk or by level of income.[114] The evidence presented in this chapter shows that the differences in the membership density of the two miners' permanent relief funds cannot be accounted for by differences in levels and risk or in levels of earnings (or indeed by differences in the availability of other sources of relief).

Gorsky goes on to attribute 'the extension of the friendly society form to the changing occupational structure and heightened geographical mobility of the second half of the eighteenth century'. Benefit clubs, he argues, 'were particularly important to young adult migrants, for whom the level of real wages was less significant than the need to recreate the ties and dependencies of the agrarian community'.[115] The hypothesis here is different. The asymmetry of permanent relief fund experience in Northumberland and Durham and North Staffordshire during the second half of the nineteenth century is explained best, it is argued, by the contrasting cultural characteristics of the owners and the miners in the two coalfields.

Acknowledgments

I am grateful to have had the opportunity to present earlier versions of this chapter at the University of Southampton and the University of Wolverhampton.

2 THE COSTS AND BENEFITS OF SIZE IN A MUTUAL INSURANCE SYSTEM: THE GERMAN MINERS' KNAPPSCHAFTEN, 1854–1923

Timothy W. Guinnane, Tobias A. Jopp and Jochen Streb

By the mid-nineteenth century, Prussian miners could rely on their own mutual social insurance system in form of the so-called *Knappschaft*.[1] This institution's historical as well as economic importance stems from its continuous existence as an instrument of occupational provision against the risks of sickness and invalidity for nearly 750 years, and from its status as an influential precursor of the Bismarckian social insurance system.[2] As part of the Prussian mining reform, the *Knappschaft* law of 1854 combined mandatory contributions for all miners with the insurance principle and legal claims, thereby creating one of the few occupational social insurance schemes that co-existed with Bismarck's social insurance later on. The 1854 law standardized for Prussia what miners had already practised before at different locations and with their own sense of mutuality.[3] The reader will associate *Knappschaften* with other prominent institutions of the nineteenth century, especially with British Friendly Societies. However, *Knappschaften* were different in that joining a *Knappschaft* and thus paying contributions was compulsory for workers in covered activities. Membership in Friendly Societies was strictly voluntary in contrast, implying a different, perhaps stronger, sense of solidarity.

This chapter examines a series of arguments concerning the ways in which the size of the *Knappschaften* affected their ability to satisfy their members' needs. As we shall see, the societies' primary functions were to provide different benefits for people experiencing short term illnesses (sickness insurance), long-term or disabling illness (invalidity pensions) or old-age (old-age pensions). It has often been suggested that smaller organizations were more suited to the provision of sickness insurance whereas larger organizations were required to deal with the demands of invalidity pensions and old-age pensions. We intend to explore these questions by testing two different, yet interrelated, hypotheses. The first hypothesis is that moral hazard in the KVs'[4] health insurance was less a problem for smaller funds, that is, that there was a positive relationship between size and moral hazard, and the second is that actuarial risk was less a problem for larger funds, because of a negative relationship between size and actuarial risk. We use data on Prussian and Bavarian KVs to examine these issues.

The chapter includes five sections. In section one, we begin by discussing the *Knappschaften's* medieval origins and their development up to 1854, and the relevant regulatory framework and legal changes between 1854 and 1923. We then go on to examine the argument that the societies were characterized by a fundamental 'design flaw' associated with their size. In Section two, we present quantitative data that are central to our discussion of size as part of an overview of the Prussian KVs' development in general. Section three makes the case for small KVs and moral hazard in health insurance. We first introduce moral hazard theoretically and discuss advantages of small organizations in fighting it. We then present empirical evidence on the relationship between size and moral hazard. The data we use are primarily for Prussia, and to a lesser extent, Bavaria. Section four makes the case for large KVs and actuarial risk. After having introduced the concept and measurement of actuarial risk, we present empirical evidence on the relationship between size and exposure to that risk. This part concentrates on Prussian KVs. Finally, Section five concludes the chapter.

The 'Design Flaw' in the *Knappschaften*

Historical Origins of the Knappschaft

The KV trace their roots to associations created by miners to serve religious purposes, maintain traditions, and to support one another in case of both temporary and permanent income losses due to sickness, injuries and invalidity. Most accounts locate their origins in the medieval ore mining regions in the Harz Mountains (around Goslar) and the Erz Mountains (Saxony). Nineteenth century observes usually assumed that the formation of those voluntary associations reflected the uniqueness of mining at the time and the greater need for financial security because of mining's unprecedented hazard for health and the ability to work. Recent research stresses that association activities of this sort were a widespread phenomenon at the time and not limited to this particular occupation as, for example, the formation of craft guilds shows.[5] We divide the history of the *Knappschaft* from its origins around 1260 to the beginning of our study period into three 'developmental stages'. At first, miners' contributions were voluntary and paid when they were needed, usually after an accident. A fund in the sense of a permanently existing and replenished financial reserve had not yet been established. Accordingly, benefits were needs-tested and not high, and the organizing principle thus was charity. In the second stage, which begins roughly with the first enactments of local mining codes, 1300 (*Kuttenberger Bergordnung*) and 1359 (*Rammelsberger Bergordnung*), the KVs' ability to insure against risks (including survivorship of miners' dependants) improved insofar as associations now demanded regular and obligatory contributions ('*Büchsenpfennig*') from their members. These contributions were used to create and maintain permanent funds. Nonetheless, members were still not formally entitled to a minimum level of payment, not to mention a guaranteed payment. Various mining codes also specified joint financing by miners and mine owners. The Reformation removed much of the KV's religious function.[6] In the third stage, KVs were integrated in the emerging absolutist-mercantilist regime. Around the middle of the eighteenth century, the geographical focus of mining shifted towards Prussia. Frederick the Great and his followers especially ensured that miners came under royal patronage and thereby became an instrument of the mercantilist state's resource policy. The Prussian administration established direct control over minerals' production and every related operational aspect. KVs lost their capacity as self-managed risk sharing communities: charity was replaced with the government's paternalism. This third stage ended in Prussia and soon in all German territorial states with the mining reform between 1851 and 1865. This reform reorganized mining and miners' mutual insurance mechanisms as part of a shift towards a more liberal economic system.[7]

Institutional Features

The all-Prussian *Knappschaft* law of 1854 marks the beginning of the fourth developmental stage in which KVs became organized like modern social insurance organizations. The principles of this law, confirmed and refined by the Prussian general mining law of 1865, soon diffused into most other German territorial states, e.g. into Bavaria, where a new mining law was introduced in 1869. The KVs' social insurance was now characterized by the following regulatory features, which were not all new, of course: (i) KVs were local or regional carriers of *Knappschaft* insurance, limited to a particular mining area or enterprise and operating independently of each other and of financial support by the state; (ii) membership was compulsory for all miners (coal, ores, stone, salt) and for employees in related industries (steelworks and ore processing units) if (i.e. before 1865) their employers had voluntarily decided to join the *Knappschaft*; (iii) KVs insured against the perils of sickness, accident, invalidity, survivorship and – implicitly – old age; (iv) the main benefits included daily sick pay, medical treatment, an invalidity pension (paid until death), and widows' and orphans' pensions (paid until death or remarriage or, respectively, until the age of fourteen), and were usually scaled by seniority and also occupational class (i.e. wages); (v) until 1906 health and pension insurance were neither financially nor institutionally separated, which resulted in one contribution payment per KV member to cover all the risks at once; (vi) insured miners and mine owners jointly financed (both by contributions) and managed KVs but, until 1906, not necessarily on equal terms; (vii) a financing system based on the pay-as-you-go principle and at first modest, but later large, reserve accumulation (viii) cross-KV competition arising only from spatial mobility of insurants (if acquired entitlements were portable), as KVs were not allowed to have branches in the area of another fund.[8] The *Knappschaft* law reform of 1906 included one provision that bore directly on KV size. After 1906, the Prussian mining administration had officially the right to force KVs to merger or closure in order to stabilize the whole scheme. Between

1854 and 1905, we know that the regulators applied verbal pressure to KVs to get them to merge or to close, but we do not know whether they had actually ordered such.[9] Whether mergers were conducted voluntarily or not has important technical implications to bear in mind. As Guinnane and Streb argue, size might have been endogenous to KVs so long as they could decide themselves on mergers.[10]

Of special importance for this chapter is the design of health insurance. Contemporary observers commonly stressed the incentive effects of replacement pay as causal for malingering. Feigning illness or pretending to be ill after cured was perceived to be a serious threat to financing requirements and the idea of mutual insurance in general. The regulation of the mid-19th century specified that daily sick pay was to be paid for a maximum length of eight weeks. The general mining law of 1865 gave KVs the opportunity to establish several smaller sickness funds while still running one large pension fund as before. Actually, only a few KVs took advantage of this provision. Instead, KVs fought malingering by other tactics allowed by the law, including a three-day waiting period before sick pay was paid, and the end of sick pay for Sundays. Under the 1883 sickness insurance law associated with Bismarck, older KVs became a small part of a new German social security system. According to the new rules of this much larger system, KVs had to increase both the amount of daily sick pay and the maximum period it had to be paid to thirteen weeks, since 1905 even to twenty-six weeks.[11]

The Economic Problem

We study the formative period of the German welfare state in the late nineteenth and early twentieth centuries, a period characterized by considerable change of social and political structures. We focus on an economic problem that contemporaries persistently thought to be of substantial importance for a KV's long-term performance. This question was the KV size and whether it was too small to achieve their goals. Because of their historical origins, the *Knappschaft* insurance system was very fragmented by 1854, with a large number of independent funds. In addition, fund size was extremely (and persistently) unequally distributed over the various KVs. This situation persisted, despite a process of concentration and selective survival in the late nineteenth century; only in 1923 were all surviving funds merged into a single *Reichsknappschaft*, the successor organization of the KVs on the national level. As early as 1869, Julius Hiltrop had claimed: 'Of greatest importance for a KV's usefulness and efficiency, however, is its size. The more members a KV has, [...], the more solid will it become in view of granting benefits and overcoming challenges'.[12] Another contemporary, Harry Karwehl, emphasized retrospectively in 1907: 'The German Knappschaft obviously suffers from a cancer: It is the fragmentation into many small funds'.[13]

These comments convey a first impression of how the issue of size was commonly assessed. When contemporary observers discussed the optimal size of single KV, they were asking a basic economic question: What were the economies and diseconomies of scale in this type of insurance provision, and what KV size was, in the end, most efficient? The matter of finding a solution for the size-performance puzzle was even more complicated by the fact that KVs' health and invalidity insurance sections were neither financially nor institutionally separated until 1906. We call this combination of high fragmentation, a very unequal size distribution and the coupling of health and pension insurance the 'design flaw' of the KVs. Again, Hiltrop exemplifies contemporary opinion when saying: 'The basic evil is the preposterous fusion of health and pension insurance; a KV's size is too large for it as provider of health insurance and too small for it as provider of pension insurance'.[14]

Karwehl elabourates: 'All these facts pressure KVs to separate health from pension insurance. A mere financial separation is insufficient; an institutional separation is essential. This is because health funds require a smaller size in order that individual control of members among themselves is possible, which is more effective and cheaper than administrative control by physicians, thereby helping to identify and fight too large additional expenditure. [...]. In contrast, pension funds require many members in order for the law of large numbers to come into effect, [...]. [...]. Only a large number of members helps to identify regularities concerning the invalidity claim process and mortality patterns, and thus to know serves to stabilize the scheme from an actuarial viewpoint'.[15]

Contemporary observers were already well aware of the costs and benefits of size with respect to both health and invalidity insurance, and they thought KVs were troubled by both moral hazard and actuarial risk. Consequently, the KVs 'design flaw' might have made it very difficult to implement the optimal KV size, because minimizing moral hazard in the health insurance section implied small organizations, while minimizing actuarial risk demanded large organizations.

The Quantitative Development of *Knappschaften*, 1854–1923

Our data come from two sources: the *Statistik der Knappschaftsvereine des preussischen Staates*, shortly labelled Prussian KV statistics, and the *Statistik der Knappschaftsvereine im bayerischen Staate*, shortly labelled Bavarian KV statistics. The former was first published in 1854 by the Prussian ministry of trade and commerce and offers annual data for the years 1861 to 1920. The Bavarian KV statistics are available from 1884 at the time of writing, although Bavarian KVs were much older. Both sources compiled the official reports of the KVs operating on Prussian and Bavarian territories by year and district of mining administration. There were five such districts for mine oversight in Prussia, each named after the city in which the administrative office was located, Bonn, Breslau, Clausthal, Dortmund and Halle; and three corresponding Bavarian districts, Bayreuth, Munich and Zweibrücken. We constructed a data set containing KV-level data on many aspects of KV operations such as the number of members and member status (contributor, pensioner), the members' age structure, the amounts of revenues received by category (miners' contributions, employers' contributions, other income sources like interest and various fees), claims costs by category (sick pay, medical treatment and various pensions) and claims incidence. Three points have to be stressed concerning the way data are presented in the original statistical framework and the way we use them: First, the *Knappschaft* law was indeed reformed in 1906, but the KV statistics do not display data separately for health and pension insurance before 1908. This means that we have to treat the period 1861 to 1907 as the pre-reform period. Second, the way data are reported for 1861 to 1907 is not consistent over the whole period; for example, age groups are not reported prior to 1867. Our econometric models use therefore data only from 1867 and later. Third, there are some missing years for some KVs, especially regarding Bavaria.[16]

Number of Knappschaften

We begin our quantitative description by presenting time series on the number of KVs in Prussia and Bavaria. On the whole, the KV statistics list 103 different Prussian and fifty-two Bavarian KVs. By 1852, just before the regulation of the *Knappschaft* was reformed, the Prussian KV statistics records fifty-three KVs under direct control of the mining administration.[17] As Figure 2.1 shows, seventy-one KVs operated on Prussian territories in 1861. In the following, the number increased stepwise and peaked in 1871 at ninety-one, at the start of the German Reich, due to various entries. But since then, the net number of KVs decreased considerably. After 1872, only five 'true' entries, that is KVs not re-established by merger of two more others, are recorded. Accordingly, Prussian KVs faced a marked concentration process towards 1920, when still forty-four KVs were in operation. In 1923, all remaining Prussian KVs were merged into a national fund, the *Reichsknappschaft*. Bavarian KVs ranged lower in number; we know of thirty-eight existing in 1884 (and presumably before) and twelve still operating in 1920.

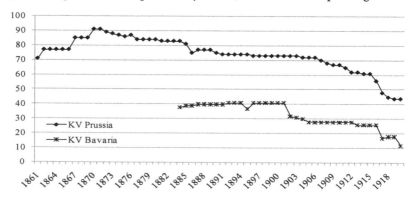

Figure 2.1: Number of Knappschaften by year, Prussia and Bavaria, 1861–1920.

Notes: Data on Prussia are not published before 1861. Bavarian data not available at the time of writing for before 1884.

Sources: Ministerium für Handel, Gewerbe und öffentliche Arbeiten (1859-78), Ministerium für öffentliche Arbeiten (1879-89); Ministerium für Handel und Gewerbe (1890-1922); Oberbergamt München (1884–1920).

Membership

In order to get an impression of the KVs' significance on the national level we need to establish time series on memberships. Table 2.1 displays for Prussia and Bavaria respectively membership series that include contributors, on the one hand, and invalids, widows and orphans, on the other hand, and, as a measure of coverage, the ratio of membership to the total population. Overall membership of Prussian KVs increased from about 140,000 to over 1.3 million, at an annual geometric growth rate of 3.9 per cent. Membership in Bavarian KVs increased at a slightly lower annual rate of 3.45 per cent, from 7,742 to more than 24,000 members. Regarding the scope of the schemes, Prussian KVs provided insurance for a mere 0.37 per cent of the German population in 1861. However, this figure rose to 2.17 per cent in 1920. Coverage of Bavarian KVs always ranged far below 0.05 per cent. In comparison, the coverage of Bismarckian health (accident, invalidity) insurance was about 9.2 (8.0, 22.0) per cent in 1885[18] and 20.2 (43.4, 24.4) per cent in 1913.[19]

Table 2.1: Membership development and coverage of Knappschaften in per cent of Prussia's and Bavaria's population, 1861–1920.

Year	Prussia		Bavaria	
	Members	Coverage	Members	Coverage
1861	139,983	0.57	–	–
1866	189,018	0.74	–	–
1871	275,143	1.04	–	–
1876	328,227	1.18	–	–
1881	376,193	1.29	–	–
1886	438,854	1.45	7,742	0.11
1891	561,189	1.75	9,428	0.13
1896	622,865	1.83	10,730	0.14
1901	793,043	2.16	12,802	0.16
1906	912,680	2.31	14,721	0.17
1911	890,839	2.11	17,147	0.19
1916	1,065,727	2.44	20,189	0.21
1920	1,341567	3.37	24,397	0.29

Notes: Aggregate membership consists of contributors and pensioners (invalids, widows and orphans). After 1907, the number of contributors refers to the pension section. Coverage is members as percentage of each state's population. Based on Rothenbacher's series on the German population, we have recovered the Prussian population per year as (0.64418*German total population) and the Bavarian population as (0.14034*German total population). The constants in the brackets are equal to the mean share of the Prussian and Bavarian populations in total German population as implied by the census population of 1871, 1880, 1890, 1900, and 1910. Sources: See sources for Figure 2.1, above and F. Rothenbacher, *The European Population 1850–1945* (Houndmills *et al.* 2002), pp. 282–90.

Determining how many KVs existed throughout all German territories and, consequently, how many miners were insured at all, is actually not an easy task. Extensive statistical frameworks are only available for Prussia and Bavaria, and also for Saxony. However, these three states certainly account for the vast majority of KVs that existed and miners that were insured. Prussia alone accounted for about 47 per cent of KVs and 88 per cent of members in 1885, and 53 and 90 per cent in 1913; the respective numbers for Bavaria come to 23 and 1.5 per cent both in 1885 and 1913.[20]

Knappschaft Size

The German mining sector's long-term growth in terms of employment combined with the reduction of operating KVs due to mergers and closures led to a continuous increase of the average KV size. In the following, we measure KV size by the number of contributors per 31 December. We exclude pensioners to get an idea about the true financing power a KV had. In order to illustrate the annual size distribution for Prussia and Bavaria, Figure 2.2 reports deciles of KV size.

From the start, contributors were very unequally distributed over KVs, thereby reflecting the high degree of fragmentation of the mining areas. With regard to Panel A, Prussia, ten per cent of KVs persistently operated with fewer than 52 contributors. The largest ten per cent of KVs increased their share of contributors steadily towards 1907. The share amounted to sixty-two per cent in 1861, seventy-two per cent in 1884 and seventy-nine per cent in 1907; towards 1920, their share decreased to seventy-four per cent. The average number of a KV's contributors in the fifth decile is equal to the median size, a measure suggested by the literature as a practical approximation of the minimum efficient size (MES) in an insurance market. MES may be considered as the size beyond which no further economies of scale exist that could be exploited. Another suggested measure is mean size, which amounted to 1,675 (1861), 4,087 (1884), 11,221 (1907) and 23,044 (1920) contributors regarding Prussia; the numbers for Bavaria are 140 (1884), 443 (1907) and 1,713 (1920). The difference between average and median size indicates the heavy left-hand skewed distribution.[21]

Panel A Prussia

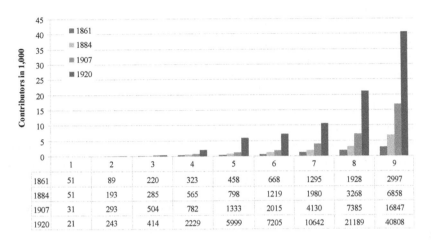

	1	2	3	4	5	6	7	8	9
1861	51	89	220	323	458	668	1295	1928	2997
1884	51	193	285	565	798	1219	1980	3268	6858
1907	31	293	504	782	1333	2015	4130	7385	16847
1920	21	243	414	2229	5999	7205	10642	21189	40808

Panel B Bavaria

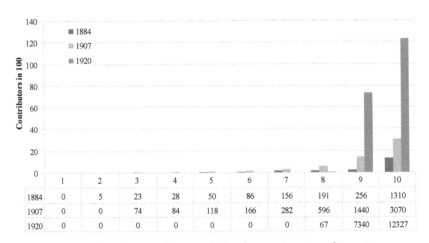

	1	2	3	4	5	6	7	8	9	10
1884	0	5	23	28	50	86	156	191	256	1310
1907	0	0	74	84	118	166	282	596	1440	3070
1920	0	0	0	0	0	0	0	67	7340	12327

Figure 2.2: Size distribution of Knappschaften by year, Prussia and Bavaria, average number of contributors per KV in the respective decile, selected years.

Notes: Displayed are deciles of size. Size is measured in terms of active, i.e. contributing, miners. Regarding Prussia, the tenth decile is not depicted because of the values' magnitude (1861: 18,895, 1884: 70,124, 1907: 327,989, 1920: 411,585). The zeros in Panel B, Bavaria, stem from the fact that the Bavarian KV statistics reports some, later many, KVs still to exist, but to have no contributors; we cannot figure out actually, whether those KVs had truly none or did simply not report the number to the government.
Sources: Own calculation based on sources for Figure 2.1, above.

In addition, Table 2.2 reports the number of mergers and closures conducted as well as the number of different KVs involved in the mergers by decade. In all, twenty mergers were conducted in Prussia. Against this, mergers were less common in Bavaria, which saw only four of them. Yet the proportion of closures was much higher with respect to Bavaria where twenty-one KVs were closed (Prussia: twenty-two cases). For both Prussia and Bavaria, about half of all closures happened during war time and shortly after war. This phenomenon might be explained by the fact that many KVs suffered from temporary losses of contributors who were enlisted in military service, while the number of sick cases and pensioners (invalid soldiers, soldiers' widows and orphans) to be financed even increased. Almost every KV that was closed or absorbed by another fund during war experienced zero or negative growth in size.

Table 2.2: Merger and closure activity by decade, Prussia and Bavaria, 1861–1920.

Decade	Prussia			Bavaria		
	Number of mergers	Number of KVs involved in the mergers	Number of closures	Number of mergers	Number of KVs involved in the mergers	Number of closures
1861–1869	1	2		–	–	–
1870–1879	7	13	4	–	–	–
1880–1889	3	10	2	–	–	–
1890–1899	1	3	2	–	–	–
1900–1909	4	8	2	3	15	4
1910–1919	4	15	12	2	14	–
1920	–	–	–	1	6	1

Sources: Own calculation based on sources for Figure 2.1, above.

The Average Knappschaft

Finally, we introduce some financial data by looking at the characteristics of the average Prussian KV in the years 1867, 1890 and 1913. We constructed the average KV per year as the sum of non-weighted averages per variable. Table 2.3 reports a set of basic variables on membership structure, costs and revenues. Presented are absolute values in persons, per cent or marks, and indices where 1867 equals one hundred. All financial quantities are displayed in prices of 1913; we used Hoffmann's (1965) price series on private consumption to deflate. Furthermore, various series on annual net wages were used to calculate the cost shares of pension and other benefits regarding a miner's annual gross labour earnings (i.e. inclusive of contributions to the KV).

Table 2.3: The membership structure and social budget of the average Prussian Knapp-schaft, selected years.

	1867	1890	1913	1890	1913
		(absolute)		(1867 = 100)	
Number of contributors (1913: pension section)	2,050	5,529	12,102	270	590
Number of pensioners	385	1,699	3,458	441	898
Invalids per 100 contributors	4	9	11	225	275
Survivors per 100 contributors	15	22	18	147	120
Total invalidity pensions (marks)	15,592	132,456	434,021	850	2,784
Total survivorship pensions (marks)	17,416	97,123	198,921	558	1,142
Total sick pay (marks)	12,328	59,185	269,342	480	2,185
Total health care (marks)	13,296	56,772	323,456	427	2,433
Total miscellaneous benefits (marks)	5,239	9,385	28,209	179	538
Average annual invalidity pension (marks)	148	220	319	149	215
Pension cost per contributor as percentage of average gross labour earnings	2.07	3.15	3.53	152	171
Average daily sick pay (marks)	0.21	0.45	1.71	214	814
Health cost per contributor as percentage of average gross labour earnings	1.23	1.74	2.37	141	193
Employers' share in contributions as a percentage of total contributions	39.5	43.5	50.0	110	127
Administrative overhead per contributor (1913: pension section, marks)	2.00	2.44	2.42	122	121
Assets per member (1913: pension section, marks)	51	104	240	204	741

Notes: Monetary figures are in prices of 1913. Regarding figures for 1867, when the currency unit was still thalers, we converted one thaler into three marks.

Sources: Own calculation based on Ministerium für Handel, Gewerbe und öffentliche Arbeiten (1859-1878); Ministerium für öffentliche Arbeiten (1879-1889); Ministerium für Handel und Gewerbe (1890-1922), W.G. Hoffmann, *Das Wachstum der deutschen Wirtschaft seit der Mitte des 19. Jahrhunderts* (Berlin 1965), pp. 598–600, p. 461 and pp. 468–70, Ministerium für öffentliche Arbeiten (ed.), 'Statistische Mitteilungen über die beim Bergbau Preußens gezahlten Arbeitslöhne und erzielten Arbeitsleistungen', *Zeitschrift für das Berg-, Hütten- und Salinenwesen im preussischen Staate*, 33-37 (1885-1889); Ministerium für Handel und Gewerbe (ed.), 'Statistische Mitteilungen über die beim Bergbau Preußens gezahlten Arbeitslöhne und erzielten Arbeitsleistungen', *Zeitschrift für das Berg-, Hütten- und Salinenwesen im preussischen Staate*, 38-70 (1890-1922); and R. Banken, *Die Industrialisierung der Saarregion 1815–1914* (Stuttgart 1997).

In 1867, the average Prussian KV had 2,435 members – 15.8 per cent thereof were pensioners – and provided insurance benefits to a total amount of about 64,000 marks in prices of 1913. Reported expenditure data enable us to derive the functional division of claims costs of the early average KV's compound insurance scheme. Of those costs, 24.4 per cent were spent on invalidity pensions, 27.2 per cent on survivorship pensions, 19.3 per cent on sick pay and 20.8 per cent on health care benefits (physician costs, medicine); the remaining 8.3 per cent of miscellaneous benefits can be further aggregated into funeral pay and such benefits that did not belong to the set the regulator prescribed by law, e.g. education subsidies for the miners' children and charitable payments to members. The two single most important benefits were the invalidity pension, granted if a miner was judged permanently incapacitated for work for fifty per cent or more (i.e. in his physical state the miner would no longer be able to earn half the wage he had earned before) and sick pay per day on leave.[22] The former amounted to 148 marks per year; for reasons of comparison note that the average Bismarckian invalidity pension of 1891 (1913) was worth 136.4 marks (195.4 marks) in prices of 1913.[23] Daily sick pay amounted to a mere 0.21 marks at the start of the system. At the mean, the contributor of the average 1867 KV had to bear a financing burden of 3.3 per cent of his real gross labour earnings, taking into account pensions and sickness-related costs; a burden rather low compared to what today's average contributor has to bear in the German social security system. The data also show that mine owners initially did not pay half of total contributions on average, as the new *Knappschaft* law of 1906 later required (and as is required today), but about forty per cent. Administrative overhead per contributor ranged around two marks. Although this quantity might appear small, it is actually not because it corresponds for the average KV to about six per cent of the real per capita contribution (inclusive of employers' payments). Finally, assets per contributor amounted to just fifty-one marks; even if the average KV had reserves, they were arguably not sufficient to fund future liabilities, especially from pensions.

Reported indices draw a picture of long-term growth in almost every aspect. The average KV's contributor base increased enormously, but not as rapidly as the number of financially dependent pensioners. The growth of claims costs, in turn, outperformed membership growth, thus indicating rising costs per capita. Especially costs as a percentage of a contributor's annual labour earnings rose, on the one hand, reflecting rising generosity and system dependency and, on the other hand, implying financing challenges quite similar to those of today. The implementation of Bismarckian social insurance after 1883 pushed those percentages further up because miners were now also integrated into the statutory workmen's insurance, thus had to pay mandatory contributions to two systems.

The Case for Small *Knappschaften*: Minimizing Moral Hazard

The existence of information asymmetries as the necessary precondition for adverse selection and moral hazard problems is a central issue to any sort of insurance scheme. While, in contrast to the Friendly Societies, adverse selection of risks was not a problem for KVs because of compulsory membership (every risk, good or bad, had to be insured), moral hazard, that is malingering, was claimed to be an important and persistent problem in the health insurance. Since a miner was usually better informed about his actual health status than was the organization, he had a margin for opportunistic behaviour; that is to rake in insurance benefits without being sick or by exaggerating the duration of his sickness. Clearly, the more miners were willing to spend leisure time at the expense of their KV the more were KVs overwhelmed with non-functional costs. The strongest incentive for malingering was arguably sick pay per sick day – provided that the probability of being exposed as a *Simulant* was judged to be rather low. To fight malingering, KVs could either decrease the incentives to do so by lowering the sick pay or increase the probability of disclosure by closely monitoring miners who claimed to be sick. Contemporaries claimed that monitoring was easier and more effective in small KVs. If this claim was true malingering was less common in small KVs. Figure 2.3 provides descriptive evidence on average sick days per KV member by size class. We distinguish here three size classes: small (up to 200 contributors), medium (between 200 and 4,999 contributors) and large (more than 5,000 contributors). Small KVs show both the lowest sick days per KV member in many years and the greatest fluctuation. Averaged over the whole period, small KVs faced 6.13 sick days per member, while medium and large KVs faced 7.03 and 7.50 sick days per member. These quantities give rise to the assessment that KV size really mattered.

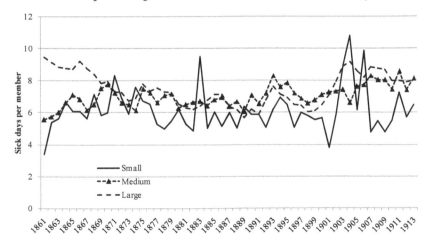

Figure 2.3: Average sick days per KV member, Prussia, 1861–1913.
Notes: Averages within size classes are unweighted.
Sources: Own calculation based on sources for Figure 2.1, above.

Measuring Moral Hazard

To analyze the relationship between KV size and moral hazard in more detail we test the following hypotheses:

Hypothesis 1: Rheumatism cases per KV member are positively related to KV size.

Hypothesis 2: Reported sick days, cases of sickness and the duration of sickness per KV member are positively related to KV size.

Our first hypothesis is based on the idea that some illness can be better verified than others. In contrast to well identifiable contusions, for example, a malingering-prone miner could have used rheumatism as a cover to get sick pay. As contemporary observers claimed, rheumatism was, indeed, a kind of catch-all-term for all those health problems whose cause could not be identified by medical practitioners at the time.[24] Our second hypothesis follows the usual approach in the literature to check for the effects of various controls on sick days paid, reported cases of illness and the duration of sickness. The basic idea here is that if illness is real, it will not respond to variations in the source of KV financing. We use fixed effects estimation in combination with an instrumental variables approach. The fixed effects estimation cleans out unobserved hetero-geneity on the KV-level, and the instrumental variable approach deals with the endogeneity of average sick pay; our instrument is the firms' share in costs per member. For a detailed discussion of this econometric approach, we refer the reader to Guinnane and Streb.[25]

The case for small KVs turns on the claim that small groups are better at disciplining members who might abuse the system. In small groups, members (and therefore also the organization) have low-cost access to information about abusers because everyone knows each other and has an eye on his fellows' (mis) behaviour. This control mechanism will be undermined by growth in member-ship as greater numbers and more dispersed membership reduce interactions among members. This is precisely what happened to KVs as they grew larger. Reductions in personal contact eroded the sense of solidarity that made the smaller KV work. Members found it easier to abuse an impersonal organization than to draw directly from their fellow-members' pocketbooks.[26]

Other arguments concerning the rise of malingering have nothing to do with KV size itself. First, the regulations following the introduction of the Bismarck-ian social insurance system required that KVs raise daily sick pay and extend the benefit period. These regulatory changes increased the benefits of malingering considerably. What is more, health insurance might also have been used as sub-stitute for the non-existent unemployment insurance at the time. Miners' wages varied over the business cycle, and so did the replacement rate of the sick benefit. As daily wages decreased during an economic downturn, relative income replacement increased since sick pay was set at a fixed rate.

Empirical Results

Here we briefly summarize the main findings of Guinnane's and Streb's (2010) analysis of moral hazard in the KVs' health insurance. Our controls at the KV level include (instrumented) sick pay per sick day, the mine owners' portions of costs, overall membership and membership per production unit. Furthermore, we control for Reich regulation of 1887 and 1905, which required raising sick pay and extending the benefit period, by use of dummy variables:

1. *Difference in reported rheumatism and contusion cases per KV member:* Because of data limitations, we can evaluate the difference in causes of illness only for the period 1867–84. First, we find a generally higher mean incidence of annual rheumatism cases per member compared to contusion cases (0.1 and 0.06), and also a higher standard deviation of the former compared to the latter (0.11 and 0.05). Second, we find evidence that the incidence of rheumatism depended positively on daily sick pay. Especially for stagnant KVs, those with an average annual rate of less than the median of 1.8 per cent, an increase in the mine owners' share in costs also implied a significant increase in rheumatism over contusion cases. KV size itself, measured by total membership, was not significantly related to the difference in causes of illness.

2. *Sick days per KV member:* We again divided the population of KVs into those growing at a higher annual rate than median growth and those growing at a rate below. Our models suggest that the stagnant KVs did not suffer from moral hazard at any size level. For the rapidly-growing KVs, however, we find three important effects. First, the more costs were financed by employers, the higher were reported sick days per member; obviously, miners adjusted their malingering behaviour to who was actually paying. Second, an increase in KV membership overall did not affect malingering, but increases in the number of workers per production unit did. Third, the Reich regulations of both 1887 and 1905 had a notable positive effect on sick days.

3. *Cases of illness per KV member:* Focusing on cases of illness allows us to approximate the times a simulation-prone miner bore the costs of the waiting period before receiving sick pay. We find two significant effects. First, cases of illness increased if membership per production unit increased. Second, in contrast to our expectation, the Reich regulations of both 1887 and 1905 affected reported cases of illness negatively. This implies that KVs compensated for increasing sick pay and the extension of the benefit period by controlling more rigorously for malingering.

4. *Length of illness per KV member:* Finally, we considered the influence of controls on the mean length of illness, which is the number of sick days per case

of illness. Two variables have significant explanatory power. The length of illness is positively related to the mine owners' share in costs, just as we found for sick days. In addition, the Reich regulation of 1905 led to prolonged illness, but the effect is not as large as we have expected. Obviously, KVs managed to reduce cases of illness at the expense of length of illness. KV size measured by either overall membership or membership per production unit does not play a statistically significant role here.

To conclude, some size effects were present: KVs with larger production units definitely experienced more sickness claims. But these effects are slight compared to the impact of more generous sick pay, especially when that sick pay was funded by the mines' owners. That is why our statistical results provide only mild support for contemporaries' view that malingering increased considerably with KV size. Social control mechanisms were either not relevant for moral hazard in health insurance or did not lose much of their power in larger KVs.

The Case for Large *Knappschaften*: Minimizing Actuarial Risk

An insurer produces insurance coverage by making conditional promises to pay a certain benefit if a certain event occurs, e.g. if the insurant becomes sick or permanently incapacitated. KVs operated according to the principle of collective equivalence that demands that total annual contributions (plus other revenues and assets) had to settle total annual claims costs. There might be a considerable difference between effective (or historical) claims costs per year, observed in retrospect, and what the KV management had expected *ex ante*. Since KVs required contributions to be paid in a given time interval in advance, they were subject to the actuarial risk of under-estimating future costs. Contemporaries made the case for large KVs on the basis of the Law of Large Numbers that assumes that the variance of the average claim (that is, the actuarial risk) decreases with a growing number of insurants. If at the end of a period revenues did not match costs, a KV had to draw on accumulated reserves. From the available sources we cannot really say how much sophisticated actuarial expertise the KVs employed in their calculations. However, Table 2.4 gives some indication of whether a closure or a merger might have been decided as a direct consequence of a net deficit or sequence of recent deficits.

Table 2.4: Coincidence of net deficits and KV exit by merger and closure, Prussia, 1861–1920.

	Exits by merger	Exits by closure
1861–1907: Compound insurance		
Number of KVs involved	24	10
Thereof deficit in the last year of operation (% of KVs involved)	4 (17 %)	5 (50 %)
Thereof deficit in the last two or more years of operation (number of consecutive years on average)	1 (3 years)	2 (3 years)
Exit without deficit in the final year of operation	20	5
1908–20: Pension and sickness section		
Number of KVs involved	13	12
Pension section		
Thereof deficit in the last year of operation (% of KVs involved)	4 (31 %)	7 (58 %)
Thereof deficit in the last two or more years of operation (number of consecutive years on average)	3 (3 years)	5 (2 years)
Sickness section		
Thereof deficit in the last year of operation (% of KVs involved)	6 (46 %)	8 (66 %)
Thereof deficit in the last two or more years of operation (number of consecutive years on average)	2 (2 years)	4 (3 years)
Exit without deficit in any section in the final year of operation	7	3

Sources: Own calculation based on sources for Figure 2.1, above.

Table 2.4 reports data separately for the two time periods 1861–1907 and 1908–20. In the former period, just seventeen per cent of the KVs absorbed reported a net deficit in the pre-merger year; only one KV experienced a sequence of three deficits before the merger took place. The coincidence of exit by merger and having reported a net deficit was notably higher in the latter period. Of thirteen KVs absorbed into another, 31 and 46 per cent, respectively, experienced a deficit in the pension and sickness insurance sections. The picture for closures is different. Half of KVs closed before 1908 saw a net deficit in their final year of operation. In the second period, fifty-eight per cent of closed KVs show a deficit in the pension insurance section and 66 per cent in the health insurance section; only three KVs remained open after reporting a deficit in either section. Historical evidence suggests that closures were indeed correlated with an immediate financial shock due to inaccurate prediction of the claim costs.

Measuring Actuarial Risk

More formally, we follow the insurance literature and measure actuarial risk as the ex post variance of the average claim to be financed by one contributor. We test the hypothesis that the variance of the average claim (to be financed by one contributor) decreases with an increase in KV size.[27]

We define the ex post variance of the average claim to be $\{Z-E(Z)\}^2/N^2$ where Z denotes historical aggregate claims costs, $E(Z)$ the unknown expected value and N the KV's size; the corresponding average claim to be financed by each KV policy is Z/N. Testing for the supposed negative relationship between our measures of actuarial risk and KV size requires estimating $E(Z)$. We calculate $E(Z)$ following the approach used by Emery and Emery (1996, 1999) and Broten (2010).[28] We estimate aggregate claims distributions for five claims categories: invalidity, widows' and orphans' pensions, sick pay and miscellaneous health care costs. Aggregate claims for a given year and category are modeled as a function of various control variables accounting for the KVs' risk structure. These variables include age group shares, subsector employment shares, the pensioners-to-contributors ratio and sick pay-to-contributors ratio, the employers' share in costs and location. Jopp (2010) contains a detailed technical overview and the results outlined below.[29]

Empirical Results

We estimated the relationship between the variance of the average claim and KV size separately for five size classes (1–199, 200–999, 1,000–4,999, 5,000–9,999 and 10,000 and more contributors), and within each size class separately for the pension and health insurance sections. Again, this procedure examines the problem of variance separately from the other issue contemporaries stressed, that of moral hazard. For the pension insurance section, we find a significantly negative statistical relationship between variance and KV size in the two smallest size classes, i.e. up to 999 contributors. In the first case (1–199 contributors), an increase in KV size by one per cent reduces the variance by 61 per cent; in the second case by 32 per cent. Of course, the variance itself is largest in the smallest size class. For a KV size beyond 1,000 contributors, we cannot reject the hypothesis that the relevant coefficients are zero. Hence, our findings suggest that there existed no scale economies in pension coverage with respect to exposure to actuarial risk beyond a KV size of 1,000 contributors. We therefore propose a KV size of about 1,000 contributors to be a first approximation of the minimum efficient size of a KV. For the health insurance sector we find a higher minimum efficient size of about 5,000 contributors. A significant negative relationship is found in size classes 200–999 and 1,000–4,999 contributors. This result probably reflects the strong impact of unpredictable fluctuations in claims due to influenza or hookworm epidemics on the costs in health insurance.[30] In any case, it suggests that if the KV's only problem was the variance of health claims, that it should have been much larger even than was required for pension coverage.

Given the low median size of the Prussian KVs, especially in the 19th century, our statistical analysis suggest that about half of all Prussian KVs were too small to deal adequately with the actuarial risk of an unexpected increase in the claim costs in the health and invalidity insurances. That is why the increasing political pressure on small KVs to merge with larger ones was indeed justified. However, as the economies of scale diminished after a KV reached its minimum efficient size which was somewhere between 1,000 and 10,000 contributors the implementation of one nation-wide *Reichsknappschaft* cannot be explained by the need to minimize actuarial risk.

Conclusion

The *Knappschaft* was a mutual association through which German miners insured themselves against accident, illness, and old age. In the late 19th century, contemporary observers criticized two shortcomings of this occupation-based social insurance system: First, *Knappschaften* were limited to a particular mining area or even to a single enterprise, which led to a highly fragmented system characterized by many independent insurance organizations. Contributing miners were also very unequally distributed over the different KVs. Some organizations had more than 10,000 contributors, while the median KV had fewer than 1,000 active members. Second, KVs' health and invalidity insurance funds were neither financially nor institutionally separated until 1906. This basic organizations' feature seems especially important in making it difficult for KVs to realize the optimal size. Minimizing moral hazard in the health insurance section required a smaller organization, while minimizing actuarial risk demanded large organizations.

We tested this claim in two consecutive steps. First, we analyzed whether the problem of malingering was more severe in large KVs' health insurance. Small KVs, we find, were not systematically better in avoiding moral hazard in the health insurance than larger ones. KVs with larger production units definitely experienced more sickness claims, claims that do not seem to reflect a greater danger in the larger units. But these effects were slight compared to the impact of more generous sick pay, especially when that sick pay was funded by the mines' owners. Second, we tested the hypothesis that larger KV funds were necessary to minimize actuarial risk. Our findings support contemporary observers' claim that larger KVs faced smaller variance in the average claims of the insurants, even though these scale economies diminished after the KVs had reached a minimum efficient size. Our results imply that merging the small Prussian KVs into larger organizational units, each with at least 5,000 contributors, would have captured all the scale economies available for actuarial problems. To conclude, the 'design flaw' of *Knappschaften* was doubtlessly troublesome, especially for small-sized KVs, but its quantitative impact on the KVs' finances was overestimated by contemporary observers.

3 A NEW WELFARE SYSTEM: FRIENDLY SOCIETIES IN THE EASTERN LOMBARDY, 1860–1914

Paolo Tedeschi

The aim of this chapter is to illustrate the development of the Friendly Societies (or Mutual Aid Organisations which in Italy were called 'Società di Mutuo Soccorso', hereafter SMS) in the Eastern Lombardy (particularly the area including the provinces of Brescia and Bergamo) from 1860 to the start of World War 1.[1]

This chapter is based on the analysis of the statutes of the SMS and the collection of the data concerning the censuses of the Italian SMS which was conducted from 1862 to 1904 by the Ministero d'agricoltura, industria e commercio (that is the Department for Agriculture, Industry and Trade, hereafter Maic). These sources allow scholars to verify a variety of aspects of the structure and activity of the SMS in the Eastern Lombardy.[2] In particular, this chapter is concerned with the different types of the SMS and the benefits they granted to their members. Moreover, it presents evidence that in the Eastern Lombardy the SMS created a 'new welfare system' while the Italian state did not engage in the provision of welfare support until the twentieth century. In this sense, the SMS in the Eastern Lombardy also represented an important example for the other SMS existing in Northern Italy (again, mainly for the Catholic ones). During the same period they allowed the Catholic and socialist movements to increase their popularity among workers, peasants and craftsmen. Furthermore, this chapter illustrates the difficult relations existing between the SMS (particularly the Catholic and socialist ones) and the Italian state government, which was disposed to finance the SMS only if it had a wide control on their activity. The chapter also provides a professional, gender and age profile of the members of the SMS, while looking at the assets at the disposal of the organizations. The benefits which the SMS granted to its members can aid identification of the diseases and accidents they suffered.

The dimensions and characteristics of the provinces of Bergamo and Brescia frame this chapter: in 1901 they accounted for 3 per cent of the Italian population of approximately 33,500,000. The SMS analysed here accounted for 4 per cent of the almost 1,000,000 Italian SMS members at the end of the nineteenth century. Besides that, in the Eastern Lombardy the Catholic movement always had the support of a large proportion of the population and this was an exception in the context of the industrialized provinces of Northern Italy. In the Eastern Lombardy all the anti-Catholic associations related to the socialist movement or the parties supporting the government had to deal with the popular catholic idea of 'welfare'. This means that the catholic SMS in the Eastern Lombardy were surely an important example and encouraged the birth and the development of new catholic SMS in the other provinces. In the same time, however, they do not represent a perfect paradigm for the wider Italian history of SMS. This is particularly true of areas where the Catholic movement was a minority.

Despite these limitations, this chapter is one of only a few about SMS in Lombardy, one of the most industrialized Italian regions and one where the SMS had the highest average dimension and assets and were in a position to grant substantial benefits to members. This analysis shows that the SMS in Lombardy were among the best organized in Italy and were successful in creating a new welfare system in a society which was quickly changing because of industrialization and related demographic growth. Between the end of the 1880s and the beginning of World War 1 SMS in the Eastern Lombardy began the renewal and enlargement of the existing small proto-industrial textile (cotton, silk, wool and linen) and iron manufactures and, at the same time, many new factories operating in the mechanical and chemical and cement and electrical sectors were founded. Thousands of peasants moved from the countryside to find work in the factories situated in urban Bergamo and Brescia and the other industrial towns and villages of the two provinces.[3] This obviously modified social relations in the Eastern Lombardy and simultaneously increased the welfare needs of families who could no longer benefit from the traditional aid provided by landlords and local charitable associations.[4] From this perspective, this chapter can enhance our knowledge and understanding of the relevance of the SMS during the very early stages of Italian industrialization. As it examines how the Italian SMS financed themselves and the benefits they granted, this chapter also allows scholars to make some comparisons with other European countries and regions where there existed mutual aid organizations which operated in a similar social and economic context.[5]

The Different Types of SMS

SMS were associations aiming to 'promote the material well-being and intellectual and moral development of their members through mutual help and mutual aid': in the second half of the nineteenth century they in fact represented the most developed and organized Italian associations which could meet the welfare needs of a wide part of the population. During the period analysed the number of SMS existing in the Eastern Lombardy greatly increased: at the start of 1860 there were seven SMS and in 1914 they were 494 (see Figure 3.1).

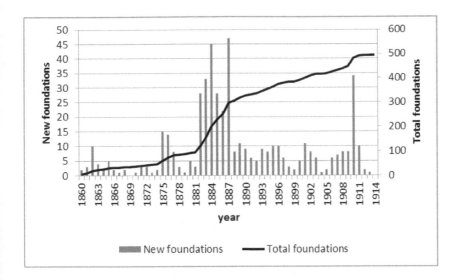

Figure 3.1: New SMS and total number of SMS in the Eastern Lombardy, 1860–1914.
Note. Before 1860 there were five SMS in the Eastern Lombardy: they were founded in
1809, 1811, 1845, 1853 and 1859.
Sources: See the censuses and the bibliography and the other documents quoted in note 2.

During the 1880s the number of SMS increased threefold: the great agrarian
crisis and the start-up of the first factories made the foundation of new associations helping peasants and workers indispensible. The increase continued, but at
a reduced rate (50 per cent from 1890 to 1914) because the SMS by then already
had a presence in many of the main villages (see also Figure 3.1). Therefore, it
started the 'phase of strengthening', i.e. the increasing the number of members
in existing branches and the diffusion of new branches into small villages. There
was no news concerning the permanent closure of a branch of the SMS because
of administrative or financial problems: if the public authorities closed an
SMS for 'reasons of public policy' (this particularly concerned the socialist and
Catholic SMS when there were some political demonstrations banned or strikes
prohibited), the members normally reopened it after some months or, rarely,
more than a year. It is also important to underline that there were no newspaper reports of the definitive closure of an SMS: since neither the Catholic nor
socialist newspapers (nor even the pro-government ones) gave any account of
an event with great propaganda potential, the most probable scenario is that no
SMS permanently closed down in the Eastern Lombardy during the period of
the study. Finally, it is important to note that when an SMS had some financial
problems, it was normally helped by other SMS or the political movement to

which it belonged: the 'managers' were substituted, but the SMS stayed 'alive' and this solution maintained the trust of people in the 'system of SMS'.[6]

In the same years the membership of the SMS increased from 3,500 to more than 37,000 (see Table 3.1) and it is important to note that this is the 'official figure' which is surely underestimated because several SMS were not correctly registered by the census and some others, because they wanted to avoid the government's control, gave no data concerning their members and assets. The Italian censuses only identified 241 SMS in the Eastern Lombardy, that is less than 49 per cent of the existing ones. Analysing every individual census it is also possible to note that, before the 1880s, the registered SMS represented from 60 to 75 per cent of the total, but in the following years the number of unidentified SMS increased: in 1885 the registered SMS amounted to only 38 per cent of the actual figure and in 55 per cent in 1895, while in 1904 the proportion was 43 per cent.[7] It is also impossible to know the real level of membership of Italian SMS. However, analysis of the data concerning the SMS linked to the Catholic movements in the Eastern Lombardy makes it clear that there were at least 37,000 ordinary members in the 1890s and the first decade of the twentieth century because they had either declared their status to the public authorities or there were other sources indicating their membership, e.g. newspapers articles. Considering all available sources on the Catholic and socialist SMS, including police documents written by prefectures, it seems reasonable to suggest that, at a conservative estimate, there were 45,000 ordinary members of the SMS in Brescia and Bergamo in the years before the World War 1. In the same time the honorary ones were almost 1,500 even if their official number was lower because many of them did not declare their adhesion to catholic and socialist SMS.[8]

Table 3.1: Members of the SMS in the Eastern Lombardy.

Census	Ordinary M.	Honorary M.	Total members	A	B	C	D
1862	4,043	486	4,529	10.7%	15	20	75.0%
1873/8	3,680	951	4,631	20.5%	27	44	61.4%
1885	17,070	1,318	18,388	7.2%	92	229	40.2%
1897	34,026	42	34,068	0.1%	282	380	74.2%
1904/10	37,242	102	37,344	0.3%	267	481	55.5%

Notes: Data included the Catholic SMS which were registered in 1910; A) Share of honorary members; B) Number of the SMS which gave some data concerning their members; C) Numbers of the SMS existing; D) share of the analysed SMS (B/C).
Sources: See sources for Figure 3.1, above.

In the Eastern Lombardy there were many types of SMS and the differences could concern their aims, their dimension and assets, the benefits which they could offer, the ideology of their founders and leaders, and their eventual links to economic institutions and political movements and other associations. The SMS could be related to a particular factory. This was possible when the owners of that factory decided to create an SMS grouping all the workers to help them and their families. This normally happened when owners had religious motivations or followed philanthropic aims or simply wanted to keep the 'social peace' in their factory (this might be described as the owners having paternalistic aims) but it was also designed as a method by which to maximize the productivity of their human resources. Whatever the owners' reasons it is evident that a part of the factory income financed an SMS and it was obviously possible that owners could also give some money to an SMS which was established by other people: in this case they normally financed an SMS which was based in the community where their factory operated. There were only nineteen SMS which were related to only one factory: their social relevance was probably higher than their number: even if the census gave the data concerning only six SMS which were strictly related to a factory, it is worth noting that these SMS could have hundreds of members and that their dimensions could significantly increase during the period concerned.[9]

Other SMS could include workers of a factory who decided to establish an association without owners' financing or might also include people working and/or living in the same community without considering their profession. In the first case the SMS was normally related to the Catholic or socialist movement: this also happened when the SMS included only one professional category of workers who normally arrived from factories operating in the same branch of industry. In the second case the SMS could be formed by workers of the same sector (that is they could include only peasant workers including sharecroppers and owners of small plots, or only steelworkers, or only musicians, or only barbers etc.) or, particularly in the villages, the SMS could be 'mixed' (i.e., they included all the resident people working in the factories and in the farms and they could also include sharecroppers and craftsmen and small landowners).

The 'mixed' SMS represented the majority of SMS existing in Eastern Lombardy: there were 312 of them and their number increased as a consequence of the diffusion of the SMS in the small villages where it was normal to aggregate people of varying professions. There were 116 which only included workers, and only a few which included only other professions: there were nine dedicated to craftsmen, six composed only by peasants and twenty-two grouped other professions such as teachers, journalists, secretaries, attendants, nurses, employees, tailors, shoemakers, cooks, waiters, manservants, members of a choir or an orchestra, public clerks etc. Finally, some SMS grouped war veterans: they received a state pension, but they normally needed further welfare services (and also a place in which they could meet together and remember their war experiences).[10] In these cases (or in some other particular cases such as that of SMS grouping people coming from Mantua and living in Brescia) only the existence of welfare benefits for the members distinguished the SMS from a club where members could meet friends and have a drink with them or read a newspaper or a book in a comfortable library room or buy some food and clothes at a discounted price (these were the 'other services' granted by the best SMS).

It is also interesting to underline that in the SMS grouping workers and peasants there could sometimes exist a special section dedicated to the improvement of work conditions and wages. These sections were normally created to obtain more stable workplaces and contributions from companies towards SMS. When these sections asked employers to make payments towards the welfare needs of their workers, they obviously interfered with the contractual clauses concerning real wages and so they became different from the mutual aid organizations: so, in the first decades of the twentieth century, all these sections parted from the SMS and became local sections of Catholic or socialist trade unions. So an SMS could be related to the catholic or socialist movements and its section was called 'Lega di Resistenza' or 'Camera del Lavoro' (for the socialist trade union) or 'Unione del Lavoro' (for the Catholic trade union): to join these SMS, people had obviously to agree with the Catholic religion or socialist ideology.[11] In the first decade of the twentieth century there were 282 Catholic SMS, that is they represented the majority of SMS existing in the Eastern Lombardy. However, they significantly increased in number during the last decade of the nineteenth century, that is after the publication in 1891 of the papal encyclical letter *Rerum Novarum*. There were only four SMS linked to a liberal party while there were officially also only four socialist SMS: however, the real number of SMS which were linked to socialist movement were surely much greater. Their members did not declare their ideology and so the SMS were formally neutral because they wanted to avoid the control and, in the 1890s, the closure of many SMS ordered by the government or the prefecture for the maintenance of 'public order' (that is after prohibited strikes or demonstrations).[12]

This explains why many SMS were 'independent', that is they were not linked to the trade unions or any political movements: there were 204 such SMS and their aim was 'simply' to grant benefits to their members and they did not deal with some difficult problems such as wages and work conditions. Not all the SMS were 'independent' because their members did not want to declare their political ideology: many SMS were really not linked to other associations. This usually happened when the members were solely artisans (bakers and butchers) or artists (musicians playing in an orchestra) or very specialized workers (marble cutters): these SMS were often the 'heirs' of the guild (which had been abolished by Napoleonic laws) and so the 'new' SMS was the 'old' guild with a new name and some variations of the original statute. This also explains why these SMS were normally the oldest in the Eastern Lombardy: they could not, as they had in the past, make the rules concerning their profession, but they guaranteed the welfare of their members and they became 'lobbies' to maintain at least a part of their former political influence.

Finally, SMS were sometimes related to local economic and cultural institutions such as small cooperative banks or small cooperative insurance companies for cattle breeding or societies organizing vocational training for peasants and workers. In some cases these institutions were created by the members of the SMS and so they were strictly linked to the SMS.

Concerning the 'nature' of members, it is important to note that the SMS could also include some 'honorary members', that is wealthy people such as owners or managers of factories, great landlords, notaries, lawyers, doctors etc.) who financed the SMS and obviously had no right to receive subsidies or other benefits. In supporting the SMS these benefactors wanted to keep the 'social peace', that is they had the same aim as the owners of the factories who created an SMS. They sometimes wanted to link an SMS to their political movement or to make sure that an SMS could not be related to socialist or catholic trade unions. This explains why some honorary members also helped with the organization and the activity of the SMS (that is they became 'managers' of the SMS), and why they could support many SMS (but there were few cases). The relevance of the honorary members progressively declined: they represented an important share of the total members of the SMS only until the 1880s. During the following years, that is the period of the great development of the SMS in the Eastern Lombardy (see Table 3.2), the great increase in the number of ordinary members obviously reduced the share of the honorary ones whose number remained about the same.

Concerning the localization and the dimension of the SMS, we observe that in the Eastern Lombardy the strongest SMS were in the towns (that is in Bergamo and Brescia where there were ninety-nine SMS) and, in general, where there were many factories. In both Bergamo and Brescia the Catholic movement also created the Provincial Federations grouping all the Catholic SMS. It is important to note, however, that many SMS were also founded in the rural villages where they grouped peasants and craftsmen: the 'rural' SMS could have many members, but many of them involved only a few people. This usually happened at the Catholic SMS: in fact, thanks to the priests who were often the founders and leaders, the Catholic SMS had a capillary distribution (in the small communities they always had their office in parish buildings) and in the same time many of them were obviously small and sometimes represented only a local section of a main SMS. Some small SMS only had 10–15 members, while main SMS had 1,300–500 members: the main SMS normally managed the financial assets of the small SMS which simply had to collect the subscriptions and produce propaganda to increase the enrolments. The small size of an SMS did not imply that it was not important for the relevant movement: the 'rural' SMS often represented the greatest and most influential association existing in the village (in many cases it was the only one) and so an efficient SMS could guarantee the Catholic and socialist movement the inhabitants' support (i.e., many votes at the municipal and general elections when, after the new electoral law of 1882, a portion of male peasants and workers could vote).[13]

Table 3.2: Assets, income and expenditure of the SMS existing in the Eastern Lombardy (in Italian lires).

Census	Assets	*	Income	Expenditure	*
1862	89,147	14	41,753	14,268	13
1873/8	453,481	27	75,593	43,374	27
1885	1,116,434	84	215,052	137,232	84
1895/7	590,614	42	36,726	38,075	5
1904/10	2,707,302	193	381,962	319,270	174

Notes: Further information concerning the income and the expenditure are indicated in the Table 3.3, below; *indicates the number of the SMS which gave data.
Sources: See sources for Figure 3.1, above.

The census (and also the statistics concerning the Catholic SMS) did not give sufficient data from which to correctly calculate the total value of assets of the SMS existing in the Eastern Lombardy: however, Table 3.3 indicates some figures concerning the value of their assets and their income and the expenditure. As the SMS which declared their data were not the same in all censuses it is not possible to make particular comparisons, but it is evident that the increase in the number of the small SMS during the 1890s and the first decades of the twentieth century progressively reduced average assets and that income was normally higher than expenditure (the data concerning the census of 1895–7 represented an exception linked to a temporary problem of cash in one SMS). Besides that, it is important to note that during the assemblies grouping the representatives of the SMS from the 1890s to World War 1, many relations explained that total assets of SMS and their incomes and expenditure increased, that is there was an expansion in the economic and social relevance of the SMS in the Eastern Lombardy.

The Benefits Granted to their Members by SMS

The different types of SMS offered different forms of assistance to workers and their families. The best SMS could provide a real welfare system. In fact, they provided their members with employer's liability insurance, a sickness and disablement subsidy, the dole for 'involuntary unemployment', the pension for retirement and life annuity for widows, free medicals (which were made by a doctor chosen by the SMS). The pension and life annuity rates were fixed, that is they did not increase following the rate of inflation. In many cases, the pension accrued was very low and so one lump sum was paid when the worker retired.

Some special subsidies were also provided for pregnant women at full-term and for a four-week period thereafter. This normally applied to industries with a high proportion of female employees, such as in textile factories. While this only happened in thirty SMS, they were the first associations helping women at work in a context where the first laws in favour of female employees were promulgated only at the start of the twentieth century.[14] The SMS could not help women to increase their wages (which were always inferior to those of men because the female work was considered subordinate to male work) or to reduce their working hours, but they could allow women to reduce the risk for their babies. This also explains why many SMS grouping both men and women were divided in two sections, one male and one female: again, this was designed to protect the health of mothers and their babies, i.e., the female section granted subsidies and free medicals in hospital to pregnant women, when they gave birth and during their puerperium (and also for the newborn babies). It is not possible to indicate the number of female members of the SMS because relevant figures were not communicated by the SMS: without supporting information from newspapers it is only possible to definitively establish that women were members of an SMS if its statute indicated the existence of a female section or if it included some particular subsidies for women or, obviously, if it declared that the SMS grouped women exclusively. The existence of distinct male and female sections also depended on traditional customs which maintained a gender division 'to guarantee the protection of the female virtue', as was particularly common in the Catholic associations.

Furthermore, an SMS could make some contributions to their members' funeral expenses. Members could only receive benefits from the SMS if they regularly paid their subscriptions and if they had been in the SMS for more than a year: the retirement pension was reserved for older members who had paid their subscriptions over an extended period (five or more years depending on the strategies of the SMS and in many cases the members had to be sixty-five years old). People could join an SMS only after having a medical examination which certified that they were healthy. It is also important to consider that most SMS did not accept new members who were more than forty-five years old: this means that 'old' people could not work enough to save money for their pension and it is important to note that old members paid more than young members for their admission fee and regular contributions.

It is evident that some SMS gave more benefits to their members than others and were able to fully meet the welfare needs of their members. This 'ability' depended on the cash available to the friendly society and this was related to the number of members paying their dues and also depended on existing links to other institutions. So the SMS including 'honorary members' were normally richer than others and could guarantee more benefits. The SMS linked to the socialist or Catholic movements could also be helped by other like-minded organizations. They normally belonged to the socialist or Catholic provincial federation of the friendly societies: they gave the federation part of their money and received strong support in return. The Catholic SMS were also helped by the funds raised in the churches and other ecclesiastical institutions. Furthermore, they sometimes received money from the Catholic banks (which usually financed all Catholic associations) and they also received other money through donations. The members of the Catholic SMS could also take advantage of the other benefits granted by the Catholic institutions such as low interest loans from cooperative Catholic banks or free or low-cost lodgement in a nunnery for unmarried women who had to work far from their home. In contrast, every socialist SMS relied solely on disposal of its assets and the funds raised in the socialist movement (the other SMS, the sections of the labour party, the trade unions and the cooperatives): socialist SMS did not usually receive any money from other socialist organizations and it was more probable that SMS helped trade unions and gave money and food to the families of striking workers.

It is evident that the 'independent' SMS and the ones which were only financed by workers' subscriptions had less money to spend: however, an SMS which replaced a guild could use its knowledge. It is also important to consider that an SMS including workers normally had to pay out more benefits because there was a greater likelihood of being taken ill or injured while working up to sixteen hours a day in an unventilated, steam saturated and dusty factory than in a farm where there were also more opportunities to have a break.[15] Furthermore, it was obviously less dangerous and more financially rewarding to teach in a school or to play in an orchestra, and in such cases the SMS were usually organized to provide for pensions and sickness more so than labour accidents.

Some SMS granted other benefits which improved their members' 'quality of life': for example, they organized evening classes and light reading or recreational meetings (like a dance or a performance). They sometimes lent money to their members 'sull'onore': the borrower only 'gave his word', that is he promised to pay the debt at the deadline and there were no other securities. There were twenty-six SMS which declared in their statutes that they would lend money to their members, but many other SMS also did this: in their statutes they usually indicated that their aim was to give their members 'a full assistance' and this included credit to those who urgently needed some money.

It was also possible that the SMS organized their members as in a cooperative which produced goods or provided services. This officially happened in only six SMS, but there were other SMS that created a separate cooperative in which a section of their members worked: at the end of the nineteenth century and also during following years the Italian government provided tax concessions to cooperatives and this obviously promoted the birth of new cooperatives.

Some SMS could also create a factory shop where their members could purchase food or clothes at a low price: there were only four SMS which declared this function in the Eastern Lombardy, but many others did the same using a cooperative (whose associates were members of the SMS) or through links to a shop which granted discounts to the members of the SMS.

It is evident that some benefits did not concern the welfare system, but workers and peasants particularly appreciated them and this obviously promoted the growth of membership of the SMS. In fact these benefits allowed members of the SMS to save money and to increase their quality of life: when the SMS operated with the aim of improving the quality of life of members, the objective was to put a welfare system into practice.

Thanks to the benefits they granted, SMS represented an important 'answer' for peasants, workers, craftsmen and artists' welfare needs. The SMS helped the people living in the Eastern Lombardy during the first step of industrialization. As they were non-profit organizations, the SMS could offer better conditions than other types of life or sickness insurance: this means that their members paid less and received more benefits. Most members of the SMS kept an acceptable quality of family life: so the benefits granted by the SMS guaranteed the 'social peace' in most of the communities involved. Moreover, for most of the families the benefits received from the SMS substituted the welfare state, particularly for children who often worked in the same factory or farm as their parents and often fell ill.[16]

Until the end of the nineteenth century social security and pensions were provided by the state for government officials and soldiers only; thanks to SMS these benefits were also granted to the working classes at a low price. Besides that, it is important to underline that members of the SMS had more possibilities than others to obtain new work when they became unemployed and to secure a council house for their family, and, for peasants, to borrow money from the 'Casse Rurali' (small country savings banks). Furthermore, the SMS existing in the Eastern Lombardy (particularly the Catholic ones) were very well organized and had some strong financial resources: they had no financial problems and their members never lost their money. So the welfare system created by the SMS attracted many people working in factories and farms and, at the same time, their efficiency represented an example for people creating or managing an SMS in other provinces in Northern Italy.

To verify the social relevance of the SMS it is important to know their income and particularly their expenditure in favour of their members. However, this cannot be deduced for all SMS because the relevant data (census data or other) is not extant for all the registered branches. The fluctuations in numbers of SMS branches over time also create problems in terms of comparing census data. This also means that data only helps to know how the SMS financed themselves and the benefits they preferred to grant and which issues they tended to pay for.[17]

To understand the relevance of the benefits granted by SMS in Lombardy it is also important to indicate the number of members who received subsides dedicated to illness and what proportion of subsidies the SMS actually declared, whether in census records or Catholic records. However, a few SMS communicated data about the number of the subsides they granted and their amount: so while it is possible to observe that SMS normally granted many subsides, it is not possible to identify how the increase in the number of members influenced the number of subsides awarded.[18]

Some SMS indicated in their records the ailments which most regularly affected their members. The flu was the most frequent but it was sometimes only the first symptom of a more serious illness such as pneumonia or tuberculosis or 'brutti mali' (the dialectal word normally used to define all types of cancer): in all these cases the subsides 'covered' the members of the SMS for only two months, after which point people depended on the help of ecclesiastical and charitable institutions. Some subsidies were usually set aside to deal with the typical diseases suffered by members who operated in a loud or wet working environment. These included deafness and rheumatoid and degenerative arthritis: subsides only applied when diseases prevented workers from working. Other subsides related to the excessive consumption of wine: people with diseases such as cirrhosis of the liver were subsidized, but there were no help for workplace accidents involving drunken workers. Finally, there were few subsidies for people who had pellagra, that is the disease linked to lack of niacin, or vitamin B3: there were many cases of pellagra, but they normally affected jobless peasants and fell under the remit of other institutions.[19]

Data concerning expenditure gave further information on the benefits granted by the SMS and showed that the most important expenses were obviously related to the cases in which the members were ill or victims of workplace accidents (see Table 3.3). The dole for involuntary employment was rarely indicated because in many cases jobless workers received food for their families directly from the SMS and so in the balance the related cost became a 'running cost'. Very often, these members did not remain jobless for a long time: they found other work or they were obliged to emigrate because the SMS could only grant the dole for between two and six weeks (depending on the cash available for this aim). In fact the SMS could include and help only people who were temporarily unemployed. Those who could not find work (in the Eastern Lombardy or elsewhere) in the long term were helped by the ecclesiastic and charitable institutions and did not receive subsidies from SMS.

Table 3.3: Data concerning the income and expenditure of the SMS (in Italian lires).*

Years / Income	A	B	C	D
1862	8,433	3,695	27,811	1,814
1873/8	2,182	3,234	43,887	26,290
1885	**	8,389	147,860	58,803
1895/7	**	174	23,529	13,023
1904/10	**	5,292	251,418	125,252
Years / Expenditure	E	F	G	H
1862	7,742	**	6,145	381
1873/8	27,678	1,089	9,755	4,852
1885	87,039	**	24,171	26,022
1895/7	27,077	**	5,997	5,001
1904/10	240,094	**	79,176	**

Notes: * See nn. 17 and 18 concerning the number of SMS which communicated their data: ** Sources gave no data. A) money receiving as new members' 'admission fee'; B) contributions paid by the honorary members; C) contributions paid by the ordinary members; D) other money received by the SMS as settlements or interests on financial investments; E) expenses for illness or injured members; F) expenses for temporarily jobless members; G) running costs for administration; H) expenses for pensions and other benefits as contributions for women during puerperium or loans to members.
Sources: See sources for Figure 3.1, above.

Finally, it is important to emphasize that the expenditure included many benefits the cost of which progressively declined because of the creation of national funds dedicated to certain welfare needs (see next paragraphs). So the SMS only had to transfer the contributions of their members to these funds and, when it was necessary, they helped the ill (or injured or disabled workers, or the pregnant women or the retired people etc.) to receive money from national funds: this reduced the expenses of the SMS related to the welfare of their members, but it did not decrease the social relevance of the SMS. They remained the link between the people and public institutions and they were fundamental, particularly for their less educated members, in the solution of all bureaucratic problems concerning the money that the members had to pay or received.

It is also possible to easily verify the economic and social relevance that SMS assumed in the Eastern Lombardy if we consider that 45,000 members represented a very important social group in two provinces where the population was approximately 1,020,000 in the first years of the twentieth century. In fact, a family normally included four or five people in the towns and more than six in country villages: so, even if we only consider the official data (concerning 37,000 members), we obtain a 'minimum rate' of 3.5 members for 100 inhabitants. Considering an average family including five people (and this is evidently an underestimate because it 'excluded' most rural families) we see that one family in six was related to an SMS; if we calculate on the basis of 45,000 members and an average family including six persons, we find almost one family in four being members of an SMS. This clearly explains the social and economic importance of the SMS in the Eastern Lombardy and these figures have a few reduction even if we consider the existence of almost 10 per cent of families in which both the father and the mother (and/or sons and daughters) worked and joined two or more different SMS. Furthermore the relevance of SMS is confirmed by the financial involvement of almost 1,500 families of honorary members.

Difficult Relations between SMS and the Italian Government

Until the end of the nineteenth century moral and ecclesiastical institutions helped poor and often unemployed people and gave them money and free treatments, while SMS granted benefits to people who worked or were occasionally unemployed. The local administrations partially financed institutions helping poor people, but they gave no money to the majority of SMS. The Italian government wanted to save money and so it delegated the welfare of families to moral institutions and SMS; at the same time it wanted to control them because it was evident that people appreciated the benefits granted by the SMS and followed the ideology of their managers. However, many SMS (particularly the Catholic and socialist ones) did not welcome the control of the government on their balance sheet or their rules and statutes. The SMS were disposed to accept the financial help of the State, but not government interference concerning their administration. Furthermore, the Catholic and socialist SMS, which did not agree with all Italian governments during the nineteenth century, did not want to give the public authorities any information concerning their members and their assets. In fact, they feared the repressive measures operated by the Italian government against all organizations belonging to the opposition. They also thought that their success depended on their independence and on their opposition to the politics of 'laissez faire' operated by the Italian government from the 1880s until the early twentieth century.

The National Fund for Insurance concerning 'workplace accidents' (called 'Cassa Nazionale di assicurazione contro gli infortuni sul lavoro') was created by a law of 8 July 1883, but this insurance became compulsory only by a new law of 17 March 1898 and did not concern all professional categories and, particularly, did not include peasants.[20] The National Fund for Social Security concerning 'illness and old-age' (called 'Cassa di previdenza per la malattia e la vecchiaia') was created by a law of 17 July 1898 but workers were not obliged to enrol themselves until the end of World War 1. It is evident that people receiving low wages did not pay contributions to these institutions and they preferred to become members of an SMS and avail of its benefits.

The Italian government did not take particular measures in favour of the working classes when the process of industrialization started and so the welfare needs of the people working in the new factories increased.[21] It also took few measures when, at the same time, there was an increase in the vulnerability of peasants' crops to diseases concerning the silkworm, viticulture and cattle breeding and the fall of corn prices. So the SMS substituted the State during this particularly difficult economic period for the Eastern Lombardy and for the Italian economy in general. The SMS organized all aspects concerning workers' insurances (labour accidents and sickness), pensions and doles: they were also supported by all organizations linked to the SMS as part of cooperative societies. Many people joined the SMS: they paid low prices and received 'complete welfare' for their families. The great success of the SMS allowed the Catholic and socialist movements to increase their support among the working classes: besides that 'neutral' SMS also increased in number and in 1901 the Federazione Nazionale delle SMS (that is the National Federation of the SMS) was created. It is evident that the growth of the social and economic relevance of the SMS, particularly the catholic and socialist branches, created some problems for the government and obliged it to change its attitude concerning the welfare state.

After the 1880s the average number of members per society fell, but this was not symptomatic of a problem. In fact, there are two main reasons which explain this trend: a) the first SMS were born in the towns and grouped a lot of workers and craftsmen; b) the creation of new factories and the diffusion of the socialist and catholic movement in the rural villages favoured the increasing of the number of SMS and their capillary distribution in the territory (particularly the Catholic ones which were born in most of parishes), but this implied that the average scale of societies fell because it was possible to create a new SMS including only ten to fifteen members and strictly linked to the provincial SMS for all aspects concerning subsides and doles the financial administration of the raised money.

The case of the Eastern Lombardy is very important because in this area the creation of its SMS represented for the Catholic movements the first step of their intervention in the social problems linked to the start of Italian industrialization: the choices made in the Eastern Lombardy represented the example to follow for the rest of the Italian catholic movement. At the same time the very positive results obtained by the SMS obliged the Italian government (which wanted to stop the growth of the number of the adherents to the Catholic and socialist movements) to create a new welfare state: so it was their success, rather than their weaknesses, which provoked the State intervention.[22] As the increase in the number of people joining the Catholic and socialist associations also happened in other provinces of Northern Italy, the Italian government partially changed its policies concerning welfare early in the twentieth century: e.g. it financed the 'Cassa Nazionale di assicurazione contro gli infortuni sul lavoro' and encouraged the enrolment of the members of the SMS; besides that, in 1910 it created the National Fund for the Maternity Insurance and Leave (called 'Cassa nazionale di maternità obbligatoria'). However, relations between the public authorities and the Catholic and socialist SMS did not improve: the communities and the provincial administrations started to finance the SMS without obtaining control over them, and at the same time the Italian government did not agree with the first important strikes promoted by the catholic and socialist trade unions (which were linked to the SMS). The Italian government wanted to reduce the 'social power' of the SMS and the strength they granted to the Catholic and socialist movements, but this could be possible only if it enlarged the welfare state. So the SMS created in Northern Italy a new welfare system and, in the process, obliged the Italian government to change its policy concerning the provision of welfare assistance: in any case the SMS (particularly the SMS operating in the Eastern Lombardy) maintained full control of their welfare system until World War 1.

In the provinces of Bergamo and Brescia, at the first election with universal male suffrage after the war (that is in 1919), the Catholic party won and the socialist party obtained an excellent result: it was evident that only organizations answering the workers and peasants' welfare needs could have a large popular support in the Eastern Lombardy. This also explains why fascism destroyed most of the institutions promoted by the Catholic and socialist movements, but it maintained the SMS and the structures coordinating their activity (the 'old' leaders were obviously substituted by members of the fascist party) and it progressively created new institutions to enlarge the Italian welfare state.

Conclusion

The SMS developed a new welfare system in the Eastern Lombardy during the second half of the nineteenth century: they provided for their members employers' liability insurance, the sickness and disablement subsidy, the dole for 'involuntary unemployment', the pension for the retired and some other benefits which reduced costs of medicals, food and clothing. They granted to their members the social security and the pension which the Italian State only reserved for government officials and soldiers. So, during a difficult economic period, the SMS met the welfare needs of the families of many workers and peasants: the SMS provided a measure of protection against negative contingencies and, at the same time, they granted benefits which allowed to their members to save money and improve the quality of their life. In the Eastern Lombardy membership of SMS increased significantly: moreover, the Catholic and socialist SMS had great success among the working classes. As these SMS were in opposition to the social policy operated by the Italian government, the government tried, but failed, to control them. In the first decade of the twentieth century, the increase in the dimension and social relevance of the SMS obliged the Italian government to adopt new welfare measures, but the SMS (particularly the socialist and Catholic ones) maintained full control of their welfare systems until World War 1.

4 ECONOMIC GROWTH AND DEMAND FOR HEALTH COVERAGE IN SPAIN: THE ROLE OF FRIENDLY SOCIETIES, 1870–1942

Margarita Vilar Rodríguez and Jerònia Pons Pons

The roots of the phenomenon of mutuality stretch way back in time, emanating from associations of a religious character such as the confraternities or brotherhoods of medieval origin, and from the guild networks typical of the Old Regime.[1] From the nineteenth century onwards, both in Europe and America, the old formulas of solidarity were expanded and reinvented in order to protect a large part of the population, mainly workers, from the uncertainty arising from the risks of sickness, death, industrial accidents or old age, in view of the passivity of the liberal state. It is difficult to determine common patterns of behaviour for this international phenomenon, which was conditioned by the political context and the growth rate of each country and by the diversity of the type and extent of coverage offered, and there is also a lack of statistics for some countries. Some basic common traits of the friendly societies, however, do exist. These include their limited capacity of coverage, especially the scant value and limited duration of benefits; the limited diversification of risk, as they were often dealing with workers of the same trade; the absence of actuarial techniques and extreme sensitivity to economic cycles due to the limited nature of their reserves.[2] Generally speaking, their heyday was between the end of the nineteenth century and the beginning of the twentieth century.[3]

Research on friendly societies in Spain has generated an enormous flow of publications in recent years. Paradoxically, Spanish historiography has little knowledge of the overall role played by these societies in the country as a whole, their territorial importance or the different types of organizational forms. The main problem lies in the fact that the majority of studies respond to a fragmented vision from an excessively micro perspective. That is to say, they study friendly societies in a limited geographical area or emphasize a single, small-scale society with only local influence, which makes it difficult to obtain overall patterns of behaviour. Some publications have tried to overcome these deficiencies and have enabled great quantitative progress to be made in studies on friendly societies in

Spain in the last two decades.[4] As a result of this effort, there are over a hundred works where the focus of study is this formula of solidarity, especially among workers. A substantial part of these studies are concentrated in four collective works that encouraged research on this topic. The first, *Solidaridad desde abajo*, edited by Santiago Castillo in 1994, compiled thirty-one works that largely concentrate on the creation of these societies in different regions of Spain. Along the same lines, and edited by Santiago Castillo and José M. Ortiz de Orruño, the book *Estado, protesta y movimientos sociales* brought together twelve works on associationism in Spain from a historical point of view. A few years later, in 2003, a new collective volume was added to this analysis: *Asociacionismo en España contemporánea*. One of the more recent works, published in 2009 and entitled *La Previsión social en la Historia*, includes the main advances achieved in this line of research in recent years.[5]

The majority of works on the subject have made their analysis from the perspective of social and political history and within the study of the working-class movement. In some of the articles, the role of the friendly societies as associations that propelled the development of modern trade unionism is studied. In others, research was based on studies of sociability.[6] By concentrating on this perspective, the numerous definitions and classifications of these organizations that have been elaborated have centred on the study of their members and the internal rules and regulations which controlled their functioning. The most classical classification in terms of the kind of members was expounded by Castillo in the introduction to the collective work *Solidaridad desde Abajo*. In this classification, the societies were divided into popular societies, defined as those that did not take into account social class or occupation; professional ones, which did consider these aspects; and workers' societies, in reference to those comprised, in general, of paid workers. These, in turn, were divided into general and territorial, depending on whether they accepted workers from a specific geographical area or not; those organized by guild or trade, if they were only comprised of workers of the same profession; and, finally, those related to workshops or companies.

On the other hand, we find classifications that have concentrated on internal functioning. In this case, the historiography has divided the typology of societies into autonomous, when their members acted as managers, or 'protected' societies (sociedades *asistenciales*), under the tutelage and control of external patrons, who provided them with economic support, to a greater or lesser extent. This welfare mutualism has in turn been the object of study, and sub-classified according to the type of patronage received. That is, whether such patronage was merely an economic subsidy at the time the society was founded; if technical advice was given without financial support; whether patrons participated in some way in the management; or whether the original initiative or the principal financing depended on them.[7] Catholic mutualism, described as an 'overprotected' model, achieved greater importance within this welfare mutualism.[8] Catholic mutualism was inspired by the *Rerum Novarum* and had an anti-liberal and anti-socialist outlook.[9] The importance and propagation attained by the friendly societies in terms of social protection also had an influence on the internal organization of trade union organizations, which introduced the multiple base system. The introduction of the multiple base system entailed the extension of trade union activity from the traditional struggle over pay and working conditions to the establishment of some of the types of assistance (sickness, unemployment, disability, etc.) typical of friendly societies. Under this system, contributions from trade union members opened the door to two types of coverage, which were distributed equally: the strike fund and the relief fund.[10]

The creation and diffusion of these classifications is to a large extent upheld by the original statistical sources, both governmental and those issued by bodies such as the Institute for Social Reform (*Instituto de Reformas Sociales* or IRS), which in turn complied with the political considerations and interests of the time.[11] In other words, contemporary classification was a result of distrust, and responded to the authorities' attempts to control and identify workers' societies, in a context where the state feared that the labour movement could put the success of the liberal state at risk. In this climate, Spanish legislation concerning workers' societies in general, and friendly societies in particular, was ambiguous during the nineteenth century, and this conditioned the development of the right of association at that time.[12] After the abolition of the guilds in 1834, the free association of professional societies oriented towards mutual support in case of accidents and sickness was permitted (1839). Later, a circular of 1841 limited the scope of activities of workers' associations to welfare provision and mutual protection. In the following decades, the creation of societies that were non-political and did not assert workers' rights was tolerated, until the first specific law of association, which included the friendly societies in a generic fashion, was passed in 1887. So, in spite of their demands, friendly societies remained in this legal limbo and the state never offered a specific legal framework to regulate the functioning of these solidarity-based organizations.

In the first decades of the twentieth century the authorities limited themselves to establishing the legal frontiers between charitable welfare organizations and profit-making ones. Thus, the insurance law of 14 May 1908 exempted mutual associations without a fixed subscription that only operated on a local, municipal or provincial scale. Generally speaking, these were friendly societies and *montepíos* (similar to friendly societies) that continued to function as simple associations until the Civil War. Later, under the Franco dictatorship, the law on mutual societies of 1941 was passed, which regulated the functioning of the welfare mutuals with the aim of differentiating some profit-making societies that had taken on the mutual form of organization.[13]

In general, Spanish historiography defines friendly societies as 'associations whose purpose lies, fundamentally, in insuring their members'.[14] Although the majority of authors specify that insurance is their basic function, generally speaking the analyses do not focus on the insurance function but rather nearly always on their members or their internal functioning. On the other hand, some authors point out that the associative formula, that is, mutuality, is not only used by workers.[15] In Spain, above all in the nineteenth century, friendly societies were used by the owners to defend and insure their business interests. Thus, friendly societies were created to insure against fire or death of livestock, or to obtain life annuities in the form of tontines. Employers also used the formula of mutual solidarity to create employers' industrial accident mutuals from 1900 onwards, when the Dato Law established employers' responsibility for the industrial accidents of their workers.[16]

Nevertheless, personal risk insurance societies (sickness, old age, unemployment, accidents, disability and death) were most widespread in Spain through the formula of mutual aid. This model was used by workers, and also by professionals and the middle classes, to cover new needs arising from the changing industrial society, where the traditional social protection models of the Old Regime had become obsolete. More than 50 per cent of these societies offered sickness coverage, which often included the risks of maternity or death. Paradoxically, as it was the risk most feared by the workers, and the protection most in demand, the health care coverage offered by the friendly societies has barely been studied in Spanish historiography, and has remained in the background compared with studies dedicated to analysing the role of friendly societies in the formation of trade unionism and sociability.

Of the hundred or so works published in Spain, very few offer information about the development of medical coverage and the incorporation of specialities; about monetary compensation and pharmaceutical costs; or about the incorporation of medical advances and the accompanying financial situation.[17] Evidently, the type of sources used, mainly official statistics or documentation generated by civil governments, has conditioned the lack of studies from this perspective. The fact that friendly societies survived until the middle of the twentieth century, either autonomously or linked to workers' or Catholic unions, is related to the persistence of their social objective, in other words, the need for coverage against sickness, maternity, old age, unemployment or industrial accidents. Later, as the first social insurance programmes were being drawn up and the state progressively took over this coverage in Spain, these societies ceased to be necessary and rapidly entered into decline.[18]

This chapter aims to reflect on research into friendly societies in Spanish historiography, and propose a change of focus in the analysis of these societies, concentrating on the principal friendly societies that offered different kinds of health coverage (sickness, health care provision, maternity, pharmaceutical and in case of death). The objective is to analyse the type of coverage, the provisions that were offered, their evolution and the factors that were influential in the changes that took place. To complement this, it is intended to explain the stages of their geographical and chronological expansion, relating these stages to regional economic development.

Traditionally, a series of stages has been established for the evolution of friendly societies in Spain, based mainly on political factors.[19] These stages could be modified to some extent if more importance were given to economic and social aspects. Initially, the friendly societies were concentrated in industrial areas. A qualitative analysis of the historiography allows us to concentrate their development in the areas of greatest economic development: on the east coast (Catalonia and Valencia), in the north of Spain (the Basque Country) and in and around Madrid. In order to establish the spread and evolution of the friendly societies, it is indispensable to have overall statistics for the entire territory, but unfortunately the few that are available are unreliable. The official data published for 1887 established that the provinces with the greatest concentration were Girona (143), Tarragona (141), Valladolid (51) and A Coruña (45), which accounted for more than 57 per cent of the friendly societies registered in Spain. Nevertheless, it is obvious that the source was deficient because it did not include societies for Barcelona or Guipúzcoa, which, due to local studies, we know existed, and this fact impaired the real geographical distribution of these societies.[20] At the beginning of the twentieth century, the greatest number of members per 100,000 inhabitants was concentrated in Barcelona (11,782), Girona (8,707) and the Balearic Islands (4,613).[21] Figures are skewed due to the varying availability of information, depending on the region.

In general it can be established that in areas of greater economic development, this type of society spread first of all in urban areas and then later the model was exported to rural areas, where generally speaking small and medium-sized family concerns predominated.[22] The technological advances in the cities must be taken into account, and the success of many businesses coexisted with the brutal poverty of the industrial proletariat, subjected to harsh working and living conditions. Besides the problems of overcrowding, hygiene and sanitation, workers had to confront the economic insecurity stemming from sickness, old age, industrial accidents or unemployment, any of which could prevent them from earning a wage, their only source of survival. As a result, workers unable to work fell into a situation of helplessness and exclusion, giving rise to new categories of poverty for which the traditional category of *vagrants and crooks* now no longer served.[23]

However, in the context of nineteenth-century Spanish agriculture, life in the country underwent fewer changes. The old formulas of solidarity inherited from the Old Regime endured for longer and there was dependence on a monetary wage. In these circumstances, and in the style of traditional societies, the family guaranteed both the availability of labour and social protection in cases of sickness, old age or incapacity for work of one of its members. Consequently, the majority of peasants and livestock farmers chose to protect their main source of livelihood, the harvests or the livestock of their farms, through different formulas of solidarity. Nevertheless, the structure of the ownership of the land, very heterogeneous in the Spanish countryside, played a key role here. In fact, the welfare model based on friendly societies barely took root in the regions of the centre-south such as eastern Andalusia, Extremadura and Castile-La Mancha.[24] The limited success in these regions was undoubtedly linked to the dominant type of property, that is, important landowners with large estates, who kept their workers isolated within the estate itself and where the landowner exercised a strong paternalism and control, which prevented any form of association. On the contrary, in the north, where small and medium-sized family farms were the norm, we find associative formulas that were adapted to the needs of the peasant families.

With regard to the chronological stages, these varied according to the region and its economic development (industrial and agricultural). What can be established is the early development of fraternal societies of guild or confraternity origin (the so-called 'hermandades de socorros' and 'montepíos'), adapted to the new capitalist legal framework, which started to develop in the 1830s as a vestige of the Old Regime. These were followed by workers' and popular societies which took off especially from 1870 onwards, while in the last decades of the nineteenth century and at the beginning of the twentieth century the societies of Catholic influence, or those run by employers, increased. These employers' societies were sponsored or at least maintained by the large mining, iron and steel and electric companies, and banks.[25] The participation of public companies (transport, tobacco, shipbuilding, etc.) during this last stage should also be noted. Their workers created *montepíos* that, as well as offering retirement, widows' and orphans' pensions, also provided aid for the sick.[26] So economic growth, the advance of industrialization with the incorporation of companies typical of the Second Industrial Revolution, and the changes taking place in family-based agriculture all had an influence on the evolution of the friendly societies. Within this context, the society's ideology lost importance, and its main function took on greater importance: the coverage of risk, especially that of sickness. However, before analysing the coverage offered by these societies, we will consider the deficiencies of the other alternatives that were available, offered by the state and by the market.

Forms of Sickness Risk Coverage in Spain: State and Market

The breakdown of the Old Regime and the establishment of the liberal state in nineteenth-century Spain required the construction of a new legal and administrative framework. The sale of Church lands by the governments of Charles IV, in 1798 and 1808, provoked a crisis in the hospitals and in charitable institutions. As the majority up to this time were in the hands of the Church and *Obras Pías* (religious charities), they were left without economic resources. Spain's system of public finances during this period was conditioned by classical financial orthodoxy, and assigned very limited funds to charitable causes. The main objective of public charity was to fight against poverty, not so much to protect social rights but rather to defend the security of the urban oligarchies, maintain public order and contain epidemics.[27] The liberal legislative framework of nineteenth-century Spain defined charity as a combination of provisions that the state and private donors offered those incapable of providing for themselves, and expressly prohibited both private and public charitable institutions from admitting poor or beggars who were fit and able to work.[28]

With regard to legislative changes, the most important were the charity laws of 1822 and 1849 and the Madoz legislation of 1855 promoting the secularization of Church lands, which transferred social welfare from the religious sector to the public authorities. Within this context, the state took responsibility for providing aid in cases of permanent need, through a limited number of institutions, the majority of which were located in Madrid. The municipalities offered aid in cases of a temporary nature in the form of refuges and shelters, and the provincial councils provided support in a variety of cases of mixed character, through maternity and children's homes, charitable institutions known as '*casas de misericordia*', hospitals and hospices. In order to fulfil its protective role of providing for the different charitable institutions, the government created various auxiliary bodies such as the '*Juntas de beneficencia*' (charity committees) or the '*Juntas de señoras*' (women's committees) that took responsibility for visiting, supervising and reporting on the functioning of the charitable institutions paid for by the state, the province or the municipality. Later, the Regulation of 1852 and the General Instructions for Charity of 1885 and 1889 were intended to promote private initiative, while they conceived of state welfare as a mere complement to, and a stimulus for, private action in social matters.

Table 4.1: General charitable institutions in Spain defined by law before the Civil War.

Name	Locality	Speciality
Hospital de la Princesa	Madrid	Acute non-infectious disorders. Both sexes
Hospital de Jesús Nazareno	Madrid	Disabled and incurable women
Hospital de Ntra. Señora del Carmen	Madrid	Disabled and incurable women
Hospital de Toledo	Toledo	Infirm and blind of both sexes
Hospital Manicomio Sta Isabel	Leganés	Insane of both sexes
Hospital Hidrológico de Carlos III	Guadalajara	Care for the sick
Colegio de Sta Catalina de los Donados	Madrid	Shelter for blind children
Colegio de Huérfanas La Unión	Aranjuez	Care for orphan minors
Patronato Nacional de las Hurdes	Cáceres	Remedy the region's needs
Instituto Oftálmico Nacional	Madrid	Care of the sick
Instituto de inválidos del trabajo	Madrid	Professional re-training
Manicomio Ntra. Señora del Pilar	Zaragoza	Insane
Asilos de S. Juan y Sta María de El Pardo	Madrid	Boys' and girls' homes
Asilo de Hijos de Lavanderas	Madrid	Children's home
Patronato Nacional de protección de ciegos	Madrid	Education of the blind

Sources: Based on data from the Gazeta de Madrid (later, official state gazette -*Boletín Oficial del Estado*-) and A. Marin de la Barcena, *Apuntes para el estudio y la organización en España de las instituciones de beneficencia y previsión* (Madrid: Rivadeneyra, 1909).

The limited number of state institutions comprising part of general charity, and their geographical location, heavily concentrated in and around the capital, meant that public charitable works in the provinces were left in the hands of the provincial, city and town councils. But charity at the provincial level was almost totally lacking in innovation, as it was limited to attending the oldest, traditional sectors of the poor in a precarious manner.[29] Their main efforts were concentrated on providing food, clothing and hospital attention for the poorest families, and on the confinement of the old, vagrants and foundlings in hospices and children's homes. Their income came from three main sources: their budgets, private donations and state aid, while some of those who were taken in by these charitable institutions were charged for their stay, either in money or in kind.[30] Such meagre resources limited spending possibilities, which was obviously detrimental to the quality of the charitable services offered.

Private charity coexisted alongside this official organization, proceeding from religious, philanthropic or political institutions. Private charitable institutions hardly improved the situation, as the majority had very limited budgets coming from private donations. Only 15 per cent of these institutions attended to the sick, the majority of whom had infectious diseases (yellow fever, tuberculosis, cholera or scabies), which caused a high death rate in Spain at this time. The poor standard of living of a predominantly agricultural population played a decisive role in the spread of these epidemics. A society that to a large extent barely survived at subsistence level, with a low cultural level and poor standards of hygiene, coincided with a shortage of doctors, and there was little demand for their services from a population that in many cases considered mortality as something natural and unavoidable.[31] Dependent on living conditions, infectious diseases were present as typical social diseases in nineteenth-century Spain. The inexistence, or ineffectiveness, of any public intervention to help combat these diseases further contributed to strengthening the discriminatory character that distinguishes them. Infections wreaked havoc among the lower classes, yet they usually respected privileged sectors of the population more.

Table 4.2: Typology of private charities in Spain.

	Religious	In favour of the poor	For the sick	Economic social	For dowries and pensions	Of an educational nature	Various or unknown ends
1915	802	2,003	1,630	389	1,722	1,626	2,966
1926	821	2,108	1,702	428	1,745	1,632	3,027
1930	826	2,160	1,726	451	1,752	1,633	1,658
1933	829	2,212	1,751	459	1,765	1,635	3,078

Source: *Anuarios Estadísticos de España* (1915), pp. 492–3; (1920), pp. 49–50; (1925–6), pp. 596–7; (1930), pp. 648–9; (1934), p. 805.

The organic law on health of 1855, in effect until the 1940s, established the obligation of municipalities to provide medical and pharmaceutical care for the poorer families of the area, creating the post of Medical Officer to provide this service and to attend to matters of public hygiene.[32] The General Instruction of Public Health legislation, decreed on 12 January 1904, contemplated the following as minimum obligations of town and city councils: measures to improve sanitation; supervision of hygiene in schools; inspection of food and drinks; a calendar of vaccinations; and improvements in the hygiene of homes and child care. But the real impact of these measures was practically nonexistent. From a practical point of view, charity was considered to be an inefficient way of attending to the health care needs of the population.[33] In the majority of cases it only meant care, with scant resources and antiquated facilities, for people with an official certificate of poverty, victims of a vicious circle of poverty and sickness.

Charitable medical care had even less impact in the towns and villages where 70.7 per cent of the population lived in 1900 and 63 per cent still lived in 1930.[34] In rural areas, health care remained linked to the doctors who had established practices in these areas. These doctors, besides taking responsibility for the medical attention of those included in the census of the poor, also offered private cover to the rest of the population in return for payment by means of a system of *igualas*.[35] The system of *igualas* consisted in a kind of private insurance that the neighbours contracted with the local doctor and pharmacist, by virtue of which the clients paid a modest periodic fee and the doctor and the pharmacist agreed to provide them with their services when needed. This system, however, did not include monetary compensation or care in medical and surgical specialities.[36]

In Spain at the beginning of the twentieth century, there were 183 provincial charitable institutions and 363 municipal ones that offered 66,014 beds, which was the equivalent of an average of 302 inhabitants per bed.[37] The official figures for this period recognized the existence of 813,815 poor families, that is, a group of approximately 3.25 million inhabitants, equivalent to 16.33 per cent of the census.[38] Meanwhile, there were a total of 7,769 municipal doctors, which was equivalent to 419 poor people per practitioner.[39] Some years later, in 1927, municipal charity covered 595,132 families with free domiciliary care – approximately 2.38 million people, equivalent to 10.10 per cent of the population – with a service of 7,555 doctors and 3,458 pharmacists, and 315 poor people corresponding to each doctor.[40] Apart from the domiciliary care, in the 1920s provincial charity provided thirty-five civilian hospitals located in provincial capitals, five combined civilian-military hospitals and twelve auxiliary or district centres, all of them dealing with common illnesses.[41] In the 1930s, the main causes of death in Spain were still infectious and parasitic diseases, diarrhoea and gastritis, influenzas and pneumonias.[42]

Public charity was not an unlimited service, for doctrinal, economic and budgetary reasons. Possible beneficiaries were classified in two general categories: those unable to work (the poor sick, the disabled, the old or children) and those able to work but temporary victims of epidemics, disasters or accidents. Consequently, charitable medical and hospital care was unavailable for the overwhelming majority of the population that was economically dependent on low wages and only had recourse to pecuniary medical benefits. The saving capacity of the majority of working-class homes was very poor, even when all the members contributed to the family budget.[43] With such precarious domestic economies, the onset of sickness meant poverty and social exclusion. Along with the loss of work, the main source of income, sickness was also accompanied by an increase in spending on medical and pharmaceutical care, which made it the main fear in Spanish homes during the nineteenth century and the beginning of the twentieth century.

Private insurance companies were not an alternative for sickness coverage in Spain prior to the Civil War.[44] The majority of companies were small-scale, with a reduced geographical area of operations, with little capital and run by professional doctors and non-professionals from the insurance sector. The backwardness of actuarial techniques and the exiguous demands for capital, reserves and deposits in the sickness branch did not favour either the capitalization of these companies or their concentration.[45] In 1912 there were only thirty-two companies operating in sickness and death insurance, all of them Spanish and the majority concentrated in Madrid and Barcelona. The top five companies together accounted for 68 per cent of premiums. These were: *La Esperanza* (Madrid), *La Verdadera Unión Española, El Instituto Español de Seguros, Patria* (Barcelona) and *La Equitativa de Madrid*. New companies joined the sector in the following decades under a great variety of organizational forms, including mutuals with or without administrative management, sole traders and unlimited companies, and were a cover for miscellaneous activities that went beyond the scope of sickness insurance: funeral services, hospital provisions and other kinds of medical activity. The number of companies rose until it reached seventy-five in 1935. The effect on the market, which was already fragmented, was a reduction in the concentration of premiums. While in 1912 the top five companies concentrated 68 per cent of premiums in this branch, by 1920 this figure was down to 49 per cent, by 1930 it was 33 per cent and after the Civil War, in 1940, it was 41 per cent.[46] Between 1912 and 1940 the number of companies in this branch was very high, but the branch had very little weight in the overall activities of private insurance and its area of operations was very limited. During the whole period from 1912 to 1940 the premiums of the sickness branch did not exceed 6 per cent of the premiums of all the branches comprising private insurance. The weight of this branch further declined with the passing of the years until it was down to a mere 2.85 per cent in 1935. For the most part it consisted of medical *igualatorios* (doctors' associations) that were made up of professionals of the sector including, in some cases, doctors qualified in medical-surgical specialities who were located in the larger cities, principally in Barcelona and Madrid.

Sickness Coverage through Friendly Societies

Collective solidarity was the only possible response to the limitations of charity and the tightness of the family budgets of working-class families in Spain. The formulas of solidarity among workers enabled them to confront the vicious circle of sickness–loss of income–poverty, without falling under the stigma of charity. The first associations were formed as a result of the transformation of the confraternities and brotherhoods of the Old Regime at the beginning of the nineteenth century. Later, other new ones were created that in the majority of cases originated through the autonomous initiative of workers, although we also find some that were sponsored by supporting members. However, the main source of financing for the friendly societies came from their members' fees, while the contributions of patrons, supporting members and employers barely reached, on average, 5.83 per cent of the common reserve fund in 1925.[47] Some entities with greater financial capacity invested part of their social funds in low-risk investments such as buying state or municipal securities.[48] Nevertheless, the majority kept their funds in cash or, at most, deposited them in a savings bank due to the need for immediate liquidity. As already mentioned above, these societies initially had an urban and commercial focus with an important professional, and at times confessional, influence.[49] However, after the law of associations of 1887 – in effect until the Civil War – professional friendly societies and trade unions gained importance.[50] As regards the rural environment, in the late nineteenth century the agricultural friendly societies were also emerging forcefully through mutuals, cooperatives, unions and rural saving institutions, which played a fundamental role in the struggle of agricultural workers to improve their conditions, and in the adaptation of the rural world to the demands of the capitalist market.[51]

The predominance of friendly societies that offered health care coverage is notable (54.36 per cent in 1915 and 51.54 per cent in 1925), followed by death (19 per cent in 1915 and 22.6 per cent in 1925) and disability (12.3 per cent in 1915 and 11.9 per cent in 1925) insurance (Table 5.3). Some reached agreements for health care and pharmaceutical provisions with clinics, hospitals or private sanatoriums, although there were still many that could not even count on the services of their own private doctor. The majority of friendly societies shared common patterns of internal functioning, regardless of whether they were located in urban or rural areas or whether they were of a popular or a professional nature.[52] Their administration was carried out by the members themselves who rotated in the posts of the board of directors. The lack of professionalism in this sense led to a lack of actuarial rigour. One of the keys to their success was the confidence that members had in the society. For this reason it was considered preferable to limit the number of members per society in order to guarantee their individual control and facilitate the inspection services. In general, three basic requisites were demanded in order to become a member: be presented by two or more members of the society, as a guarantee of a select recruitment; pass a medical examination by the society's doctor; and not be over a maximum age of around 40–5 years. Some societies also charged a small entrance fee as a guarantee of the saving capacity of the new member.

Table 4.3: Distribution of insured according to risks covered (percentage).

	1915	1916	1917	1918	1919	1920	1921	1922	1923	1924	1
Sickness (1)	35.25	36.30	36.01	36.76	36.62	36.70	37.11	41.54	36.81	36.53	3
Funeral expenses	7.58	7.03	6.61	6.02	6.03	5.75	5.62	5.04	5.28	5.47	
Maternity (2)	1.12	1.17	1.28	1.47	1.39	1.33	1.23	1.39	1.53	1.57	
Disability	12.30	13.32	12.67	12.65	12.14	12.22	12.50	11.62	12.68	12.54	1
Old age	3.08	2.91	2.84	2.67	2.64	2.49	2.52	2.31	2.65	2.81	
Death	19.02	19.97	20.56	20.98	21.39	21.86	22.63	21.59	23.73	23.50	2
Medical treatment (3)	9.73	8.50	9.84	9.21	9.43	9.19	8.28	7.46	7.77	7.83	
Pharmaceutical treatment (4)	8.25	7.36	6.99	6.54	6.63	6.51	5.98	5.35	5.53	5.71	
Widowhood	2.64	2.19	1.91	1.76	1.72	1.55	1.53	1.37	1.40	1.36	
Orphanhood	0.31	0.23	0.21	0.20	0.19	0.17	0.23	0.20	0.20	0.19	
Other risks	0.53	0.85	0.95	1.61	1.70	2.09	2.20	1.99	2.28	2.35	
No data	0.20	0.16	0.14	0.13	0.14	0.16	0.16	0.13	0.14	0.14	
Total (1+2+3+4)	54.36	53.33	54.12	53.98	54.06	53.72	52.61	55.75	51.65	51.64	5
Total	435,123	565,607	649,823	692,953	743,628	798,744	821,840	943,375	923,536	963,402	1,048,

Source: INP, *La cuestión del seguro de enfermedad ante la X reunión de la Conferencia Internacional del Trabajo, Ginebra, mayo 1927* (Madrid: Sobrinos de Sucesora de M. Minuesa de los Ríos, 1927), p. 101.

Once their application was accepted, members agreed to pay a small monthly contribution, which was either standard or proportional to age, although they did not start to be entitled to their rights until they had completed a qualifying period of approximately three months.[53] The standard contribution was roughly equivalent to 0.5 per cent of the normal monthly wage. In some cases, members had to pay an entrance fee (between six and ten monthly payments) and could pay an extra fee in order to extend the social coverage to their immediate family. In the situations prescribed by internal regulations, society members provided aid and mutual support to affected members with money from the reserve fund. The most common support mechanisms consisted in the granting of a modest cash benefit (generally equivalent to half of the wages) or in covering medical and/or pharmaceutical requirements during a limited period of time of less than three months a year.[54] Travelling and funeral expenses also became another of their main specialities. Situations that were the result of bad behaviour (drunkenness, venereal diseases, fights, etc.) remained outside the scope of mutual coverage, as did catastrophes and epidemics.

By observing the cost structure of the *Montepío de la Caridad*, it can be seen that a large part of the funds were used to pay sickness benefits and medical fees (in 1901: 32.87 per cent and 39.50 per cent respectively) (Table 5.4). However, sickness benefits remained stagnant in the long term, which effectively meant a loss of their purchasing power and a fall in percentage terms compared with medical costs, which came to account for more than half of the total expenditure of the society in the 1930s (in 1935: 15.15 per cent and 61.64 per cent, respectively). The cost of medical fees increased during the Second Republic (1931–6) and especially in the first years after the Civil War, when medical associations approved substantial salary increases.[55] Meanwhile, some medical specialties were incorporated into the insurance coverage during this period, including, among others, surgeons, ophthalmologists, dentists and the services of midwives. On the other hand, despite the fact that it is not perceptible in the analysis of the expenditure of the mutual societies studied, there are qualitative sources that indicate that, during these years, medical advances and the application of new treatments and medicines, such as sulphonamides, increased pharmaceutical costs, upsetting the accounts of the mutual societies.[56] The advances in bacteriology and immunology, thanks to the discoveries of Pasteur and Koch, galvanized pharmacological medicine. In 1928, Sir Alexander Fleming discovered the first antibiotic, penicillin, and the drugs started to come into circulation during the following decade, although they did not come into general use until the Second World War.[57]

Table 4.4. Expenditure of the Montepío de La Caridad (1901–50) (percentage of total).

	Porter	Sickness benefit	Death benefit	Medical fees	House/ premises	Expenditure on medicines	Banks	Other expenses
1901	5.05	42.87	4.21	39.50	5.05	0	0	3.28
1903	6.07	38.20	0	41.65	6.07	0	0	7.99
1911	7.37	43.76	8.60	31.77	5.90	0	0.85	1.72
1915	6.19	22.58	8.26	30.40	4.95	6.15	19.42	2.01
1916	6.53	27.16	4.35	34.37	5.22	10.92	8.82	2.59
1918	4.13	44.34	8.95	27.39	3.30	7.51	0	4.35
1919	5.62	29.91	7.49	41.78	4.49	7.03	0	3.65
1920	4.96	31.92	2.76	49.02	4.02	4.32	0	2.96
1923	4.39	19.38	4.27	58.73	4.16	7.66	0	1.37
1924	4.29	20.00	1.19	64.02	4.64	4.80	0	1.03
1927	4.09	15.90	3.41	63.60	0	3.63	7.59	1.75
1929	4.61	10.75	4.48	63.74	0.58	3.70	10.99	1.12
1930	4.93	13.20	4.79	62.30	0.51	3.74	8.99	1.50
1931	5.45	17.07	2.27	60.85	1.57	4.41	7.47	0.87
1932	5.28	17.85	4.40	58.76	2.03	3.38	7.35	0.91
1934	5.65	19.30	3.92	60.74	4.70	3.46	0	2.20
1935	6.04	15.15	2.51	61.64	1.32	2.67	5.18	5.45
1936	6.33	21.40	5.27	54.22	1.56	3.51	2.34	5.34
1937	7.94	10.44	3.33	60.25	1.93	4.36	5.00	6.70
1938	7.78	11.45	6.49	57.89	2.34	2.66	8.66	2.70
1939	8.30	14.39	2.30	60.06	2.29	5.70	3.46	3.46
1940	8.26	11.00	4.59	59.71	1.86	4.13	2.87	7.55
1941	7.11	14.02	2.87	47.83	7.36	12.91	4.59	3.28
1942	11.26	13.72	4.38	58.87	4.38	3.40	0	3.96

Source: *Archivo del Reino de Mallorca*, lligall 1609/expediente 1100.

The elite of the friefndly societies was represented by the societies founded by the employers who ran large companies, although there were also some exceptions. The high costs of systematized protection limited the viability of these programmes to companies of a certain size and number of workers, which had the capacity to organize and administrate complex programmes of welfare and health care coverage.[58] Smaller companies could not meet these costs so they opted for more paternalistic and interim practices. Industrial welfare practices took root in the country's main industrial zones, such as Asturias, Biscay, Guipúzcoa or Madrid, coinciding with the development of typical sectors of the Second Industrial Revolution (large-scale iron and steel industry, electricity, textiles, paper industry, transport) and with an intense labour movement at the beginning of the twentieth century.[59] This phenomenon also spread to public companies such as tobacco factories or railway companies. In many cases, the management offered programmes of health care coverage with the aim of improving their workers' working and living conditions and thereby reducing strike action.

The functioning of employers' mutuals had certain peculiarities, as the majority were controlled by the companies and were funded by fees deducted from the workers' wages (around 2 per cent of the wage) supplemented by contributions from the company.[60] Generally speaking, the company also reserved for itself the tutelage and patronage of the society, controlled the board of directors, where there was a minority workers' representation, and controlled the system of benefits. In the majority of cases the benefits and provisions were of better quality than in the workers' friendly societies, as they offered specialized medical attention for employees and their families, medicines in approved pharmacies, hospital admissions and surgical operations, and also a cash benefit. In larger companies with a high risk of industrial accidents (such as, for example, in the mining operations of *Rio Tinto Company* in Huelva or *La Unión* in Cartagena) they installed their own hospitals and dispensaries to attend to workers who had suffered an accident and to carry out appropriate medical examinations.[61] All in all, the workers who benefited from these systems were a minority as the average size of companies in Spain before the Civil War was fairly small. At this time, in general, workshops still tended to predominate over factories and traditional methods of workmanship were still very common in the productive process.[62]

Table 4.5: Number of Mutual Insurance Funds (percentage).

	1915	1916	1917	1918	1919	1920	1921	1922	1923	1924	192
West Andalusia	2.75	2.93	2.95	3.06	3.11	3.04	3.28	3.44	3.81	3.89	4.(
East Andalusia	0.08	0.23	0.22	0.21	0.20	0.20	0.32	0.31	0.30	0.29	0.3
Aragón	4.24	4.28	4.17	4.03	3.93	3.96	4.12	3.99	3.87	3.77	3.7
Asturias	1.73	1.65	1.80	1.81	1.83	1.92	1.87	1.78	2.02	2.15	2.4
Castile-La Mancha	0.39	0.45	0.72	0.70	0.68	0.66	0.64	0.61	0.60	0.58	0.5
Castile and León	4.63	4.58	4.67	4.73	4.60	4.69	4.64	4.48	4.46	4.36	4.5
Catalonia	73.4	72.8	71.9	71.8	71.1	70.3	69.9	67.7	66.8	66.2	65
Extremadura	0.55	0.68	0.65	0.63	0.61	0.59	0.58	0.55	0.54	0.52	0.5
Galicia	1.41	1.35	1.29	1.25	1.35	1.32	1.29	1.23	1.25	1.34	1.3
Madrid	0.39	0.53	0.58	0.56	0.54	0.59	0.71	3.26	3.81	4.36	4.8
Murcia-Albacete	0.24	0.23	0.22	0.21	0.27	0.33	0.39	0.37	0.42	0.41	0.4
Navarra	0.24	0.30	0.29	0.28	0.27	0.33	0.39	0.37	0.36	0.35	0.3
Basque Country	4.16	4.28	4.67	4.73	5.15	5.48	5.41	5.41	5.30	5.23	5.(
Santander	1.73	1.65	1.65	1.81	1.96	1.98	1.93	1.84	1.79	1.80	1.8
Valencia	4.08	4.13	4.24	4.24	4.40	4.56	4.57	4.67	4.70	4.76	4.6
Total (N)	1,274	1,332	1,391	1,438	1,477	1,514	1,553	1,628	1,680	1,722	1,77

Note: The data for the Basque Country does not include information about the provinces of Biscay and Álava. Albacete currently pertains to the autonomous region of Castile-La Mancha. Source: IRS (1927), p. 89.

From a territorial point of view, mutual insurance coverage in Spain was very unequal. According to the figures available, the majority of friendly societies (not dependent on any company, neither an employers' mutual nor a commercial insurance company) were concentrated in Catalonia, which was home to 73.39 per cent of these societies and 56.26 per cent of their members in 1915 (Table 5.5).[63] In particular, the province of Barcelona – the most industrial in Spain at this time – set itself up as the dynamic centre of Catalan associationism. In 1896 the Catalan Federation of Mutual Provident Societies was founded, the first of its kind in Spain, which then became the Federation of Friendly Societies of the Province of Barcelona in 1918. The intention was that the *Mancomunidad de Cataluña* (a federation of the four Catalan provincial councils) should intervene directly in promoting, regulating and organizing social welfare in Catalonia. These demands were finally met in the Constitution of 1931 and the Catalan Autonomy Statute, which recognized the exclusive competence of the Catalan government over its mutual institutions. Later, the Catalan Act of 1934 established the legal bases for cooperatives, mutual societies and agricultural trade unions and dedicated a specific chapter to the Federation.[64] Catalan legislation was pioneering in Spain, where the outdated and imprecise law of associations of 1887 continued in force. The only legislative change in Spain as a whole was in 1925, and concerned the creation of a Central Health Office within the Directorate General for Health, organized into territorial committees, where the mutuals and insurance companies of the branch, their members and the doctors and pharmacists all participated.[65]

Table 4.6: Distribution of expenditure in societies in the province of Barcelona (current pesetas).

Sickness benefits			Disability			Administra-
Medicine	Major surgery	Minor surgery	benefits	Death benefits	Other benefits	tion costs
1,322,263.00	86,292.52	154,470.20	105,781.90	213,602.60	18,470.55	337,973.3.0
954,096.50	70,403.6	134,216.30	88,387.49	179,146.90	18,129.05	310,624.80
964,610.15	86,867.25	152,206.75	73,915.01	376,115.45	17,433.35	359,677.30
1,261,673.70	114,715.00	191,349.55	112,000.90	414,141.00	28,967.22	622,093.10
1,517,671.50	96,785.7	156,704.25	101,962.90	302,405.10	26,591.90	379,254.60
927,455.60	81,362.00	124,280.00	97,151.25	186,022.40	32,838.70	420,833.80
825,682.50	96,182.10	130,045.50	106,801.30	150,930.80	38,973.05	581,938.40
868,807.10	124,874.90	151,070.50	117,426.20	185,740.40	54,448.80	494,698.20
1,007,691.50	136,560.65	166,155.90	118,964.60	197,788.25	8,420.00	636,389.00
1,515,834.40	179,142.70	210,557.25	201,704.80	286,978.65	61,865.25	714,005.50
1,534,435.60	214,009.27	185,091.85	199,072.60	270,827.03	72,685.90	695,694.20

Source: See source for Table 4.4, above, p. 101.

Table 4.7: Societies that covered the risk of sickness in the province of Barcelona (current pesetas).

			Number of patients who received sickness benefits			Average cost of a day of sickness		
Societies	Beneficiaries	Resources (fees and interests)	Medicine	Major surgery	Minor surgery	Medicine	Major surgery	Minor surgery
14	664	140,667	2,316,726.04	16,993	818	3,346	3.47	3.15	2.22
15	547	126,898	1,941,983.14	11,642	710	2,867	3.49	3.2	2.26
16	580	129,317	2,363,592.77	13,094	958	3,203	3.50	3.26	2.33
17	726	177,234	3,125,820.49	16,176	1,159	4,191	3.50	3.17	2.30
18	610	144,133	2,380,597.82	22,474	1,062	3,204	3.67	3.21	2.67
19	600	126,735	2,271,860.45	11,905	969	2,270	3.74	3.49	2.23
20	573	132,199	2,506,126.23	10,335	946	2,354	3.86	3.51	2.55
21	564	133,814	2,649,751.13	9,075	954	2,424	4.35	3.89	2.86
22	519	127,477	2,859,686.15	10,327	1,011	2,567	4.51	4.15	2.98
23	653	169,443	3,806,591.61	14,612	1,249	3,136	4.63	4.39	3.00
24	641	166,894	4,010,376.58	14,878	1,565	3,074	4.76	4.71	2.91

Source: See source for Table 4.4, above.

About 600–700 societies can be counted in the province of Barcelona between 1914 and 1925, which provided coverage to an average of 143,000 beneficiaries, a figure that is equivalent to 23 per cent of the population of the city of Barcelona (Tables 5.6 and 5.7).[66] There were as many as 641 friendly societies federated in the province of Barcelona in 1923 that offered medical care, with a total of 166,894 members. More than 60 per cent of the benefits offered by these societies were in the form of medical care and major and minor surgery. The average daily cost of sickness of a member was almost 4 pesetas at a time when the average daily wage of an industrial worker in Spain was only 2.88 pesetas in 1910 and 6.33 pesetas in 1920.[67] These figures give an idea of the important work carried out by these societies. This density of societies in Catalonia was a reflection of its earlier industrial evolution, characteristic of sectors of the first industrialization with small and medium-sized companies, which encouraged the development of friendly societies of a working class and traditional nature. On the contrary, in the other most industrialized region of Spain, the Basque Country, we find a greater number of societies linked to large companies typical of the Second Industrial Revolution, which had developed later and were of a more modern nature. A similar case occurred in Madrid at the beginning of the twentieth century, when a lot of mutuals of companies related to the development of the large electricity groups started to function.

The Decadence of Friendly Societies, Debate on Sickness Insurance and the Franco Dictatorship

During the decades prior to the First World War, different systems of sickness insurance were established in Europe. Before 1914, nine countries had already passed laws of compulsory sickness insurance and another six had established a system of subsidized voluntary pensions.[68] Throughout the interwar period an accelerated development and diffusion of social insurance took place for different reasons. The Treaty of Versailles (1919), the creation of the International Labour Office (1919), the Washington Conference (1921) and the creation of the International Social Security Association in 1927 played an important role in diffusion and gave a new boost to state interventionism in social relations.[69] The impact of the First World War on social demands, the strengthening of the labour movement, the development of democracy and the needs arising from the Great Depression also resulted in an increase in the responsibilities of the state in the more advanced countries. In this way, during the 1920s and 1930s, the majority of pioneer countries were completing their sickness insurances, progressing from subsidised voluntary pensions to insurance of an obligatory nature. Meanwhile, compulsory sickness insurance was spreading inside and outside the European continent. As a result of this process, thirty-eight countries had legislated compulsory sickness insurance before the Second World War.[70]

Unlike the insurance against industrial accidents (1900/33), old age (1909/22), maternity (1923/31) or unemployment (1932), the Spanish government neither legislated, regulated nor financed the risk of sickness before the Civil War (1936–9).[71] Consequently, health care coverage was left in the hands of private initiatives and under a statutory regime allowing total liberty prior to 1936. The state's responsibility was limited to protecting the public against any abuses or fraud committed by the different funds or societies providing private insurance, whether in terms of health care provision or of an economic nature.[72] As we have already seen, at this time the public authorities only took responsibility for financing charitable medical care, earmarked exclusively for those who possessed an official certificate of poverty. In this way, the welfare of a large part of the population depended on their capacity to access private medical services, an alternative that was beyond the means of most people.

This situation is rather paradoxical if we take into account that in the questionnaire prior to the International Conference on Sickness Insurance held in Geneva in 1927, Spain took up a position within the group of fourteen countries that supported the introduction of a compulsory sickness insurance with broad coverage and substantial duration.[73] This support, however, did not result in any political measures being taken. Why? The Spanish government justified its abstentionist policy in the field of health care by implying that the country's social needs in this respect were already satisfied. In particular, the authorities pointed out that thousands of Spanish wage earners had sickness risk covered through a private insurance, either with a friendly society or with a private insurance company. Their argument was that 'only those with insufficient education in the need for providence or with difficulties to pay their contributions do not have this coverage'.[74] But, how many thousands of workers fell into this category?

As seen in the previous section, the close association between health and socio-economic status perpetuated sickness as one of the problems most feared by Spanish workers and one of the most flagrant failings of the state welfare system. Although aware of this situation, the Spanish delegation at the Geneva Conference also showed itself to be against subsidizing friendly societies, for three reasons: this would oblige the societies to accept anybody who applied as a member, which would create problems in ideologically motivated organizations; it would promote the creation of a network of societies that were eligible for subsidies but not very efficient; and it would hamper the constitution of friendly societies in smaller towns, aggravating territorial imbalances. Nevertheless, during the 1920s and 1930s the state did end up granting, upon request, small economic subsidies, funded from the General State Budget, to workers' mutuals offering medical and pharmaceutical care. The subsidies implicitly reveal the official recognition of the work carried out through popular solidarity in a field which concentrated the greatest failings of the state welfare system.[75] However, the small number of societies subsidized and the limited quantity of official aid rule out the idea of a system of health care provision that was privately managed but subsidized by the state.

So what were the causes that led the state to abandon health care coverage? The historiography suggests that the main factors of the state's abandonment could be the complex infrastructure, the high cost of management demanded by the insurance in relation to the state's financial capacity, and the obstacles interposed by the medical profession and private insurance companies.[76] However, the most serious of these obstacles was without doubt the lack of modernization of the tax system which made it difficult for the state to increase its income through direct taxation and, thus, impeded the creation of all the health care infrastructure necessary to apply sickness insurance to the entire population. In this respect, it should be remembered that, from 1845 onwards, when the Mon-Santillán reform tried to transform the *ancien régime* tax system into one more compatible with the liberal system, the Spanish system of public finances underwent various attempts to direct it towards a progressive model that would base the majority of its income on direct taxes. However, these attempts failed, in most cases due to the resistance of the wealthy classes, and the result was a low tax burden, low tax collection and a high public debt.[77] On the other hand, the opposition of the majority of employers, medical associations, mutuals and insurance companies, who felt their private business interests to be at risk, continued. Even workers showed themselves to be unwilling to accept an insurance based on contributions, as they were hoping for greater state coverage without having to pay contributions, as was the case with old age pensions. Nevertheless, in spite of the severe obstacles, we can point out two initiatives that were intended to promote state coverage of the risk of sickness.

First of all, an interesting political debate took place during the first decades of the twentieth century between representatives of the friendly societies and representatives of the state. The topic was, above all, the issue of health care.[78] The National Conference on Sickness, Disability and Maternity Insurance, held in Barcelona in 1922, served as a forum for the non-profit-making entities where they could voice their legal and economic demands.[79] One of their main complaints was in relation to the lack of legislative protection that they had suffered throughout their long history. In contrast to other European countries, where friendly societies benefited from specific legislation, workers' mutuals in Spain continued functioning under the generic Law of Associations of 1887. In order to solve this problem, an ambitious preliminary draft law was presented. It contained thirty articles which pursued two fundamental objectives: to constitute a more solid legal framework for their operations and to guarantee their active participation in the incipient system of state welfare.

As had occurred in other countries, the collaboration between the state and the friendly societies could have served as a guide for the development of sickness insurance in Spain, but no agreement was reached. Both the presentation of the preliminary draft law by the friendly societies' representatives and its reception by the state were riddled with contradictions. On the one hand, the societies showed a desire to collaborate, which required a metamorphosis of the mutual system, but without concealing their rejection of having their activities controlled by the authorities. Although they were aware of the fact that they were risking a good part of their possibilities of survival in the process, they were at no time prepared to lose their own identity and autonomy.[80] In this sense, it is surprising that the request for state financial aid always occupied a secondary position in their demands. They were aware of the fact that accepting money from the state would require allowing the authorities a greater degree of control and intervention, something that was not desirable from their point of view. On the other hand, the state implicitly recognized the important work carried out by the workers' mutuals, but completely ignored their demands through a legislative silence and a lack of information.

The lack of understanding between the state project and the friendly societies, mainly related to the health care coverage of their members, resulted in a missed opportunity in the legislation of sickness risk in Spain. The Spanish government's late intervention in sickness coverage prolonged the survival of the friendly societies, which had been losing market share with the implementation of other state insurances.[81] For example, the approval of maternity insurance in 1929 led to the abandonment of the midwifery service that the mutuals had been offering to women related to their members since the end of the second decade of the twentieth century.[82]

The second attempt to legislate sickness insurance before the Civil War was the work of the socialist Labour Minister, Largo Caballero, who tried to get a project of sickness insurance underway during the first two years of the Republic (1931–3). The bureaucratic process became drawn out as the political make-up of the government changed during the second two-year period of the Republic. Finally, the project was presented at the beginning of 1936, but now included in a wider project intended to bring about the unification of all different types of social insurance. Its main objective was to incorporate Spain into the European trend which advocated an integrated and universal insurance. However, the partial failure of the coup d'état of 18 July 1936 and the subsequent outbreak of the Civil War prevented the passage of this legislation.[83]

While these attempts to approve a state sickness insurance were taking place, the friendly societies survived as a way to cover the risk of sickness among the common people. However, during the Primo de Rivera dictatorship (1923–30) and the Second Republic (1931–6) a series of factors were accumulating that explain the start of the crisis of this model. On the one hand, the previously mentioned increase in state intervention, as in the case of maternity insurance, eliminated some coverage needs. On the other hand, the creation of private insurance companies, created especially by the medical profession, and employers' relief funds, increased the private offer of coverage. The lack of interest of young workers in the friendly societies must also be taken into account. This led to an increase in the average age of members, with the consequent increase in costs and medical fees. In some cases the number of supporting members went down in view of the increase of class conflicts during the Second Republic.[84] The *coup de grâce* for the friendly societies came from the Franco regime and the approval, finally, of a state-run compulsory sickness insurance.

One of the first interventions of the government of the Franco dictatorship was to regulate the heterogeneous world of friendly societies and other kinds of mutual institutions with the intention of excluding all those whose aim was to make a commercial profit. In 1941 the law on *montepíos* and mutual societies was passed, and then in May 1943 the regulations developing the law were passed. These laws considered the following to be welfare institutions: burial societies, mutual societies and *igualatorios* offering sickness insurance (with health care provisions and monetary benefits), maternity insurance, old age insurance, industrial accident and disability insurance, and others that covered capital assets (fire, crops). They were obliged to change their name and include the word 'previsión' ('welfare') in the new name, although what was most important was that they were still not required to have any type of reserves to guarantee their solvency, although they were now obliged to register. After the law of 1941, some 1,200 entities were registered in the Ministry of Labour.[85] This law created an initial filter which led to the disappearance of many friendly societies, especially less active ones that had not requested their registration in view of the imminent passage of a new compulsory sickness insurance law.

The law on compulsory sickness insurance law (*Seguro Obligatorio de Enfermedad*, or SOE) was passed on 14 December 1942, in the early years of the Franco dictatorship. Just like the entire system of social welfare in force in the post-Civil War period, compulsory sickness insurance served the dictatorial regime as a tool for applying its repressive power and for exerting control over the workers.[86] At the same time, this insurance comprised part of the paternalistic social propaganda that the regime tried to exploit as a way of legitimizing its power and eliminating any social or labour tensions and disputes. In order to implement compulsory sickness insurance, the state sought the support of the medical organizations, employers and insurance companies that had opposed its introduction for decades. The Francoist regime managed to neutralize the opposition, above all that of employers, who accepted the insurance in return for other privileges. Employers were compensated with an extremely harsh system of repression of any labour disputes, and also with the possibility of playing a part in administering the insurance. The medical organizations, for their part, were won over by means of the progressive incorporation of their doctors into the staff of the compulsory sickness insurance, although the old clans of health care workers remained outside this process.[87] This legislation covered employees with an annual income of less than 9,000 pesetas and offered health care provisions in the event of sickness and maternity; workers' financial compensation for loss of earnings and an indemnity for funeral costs in the case of death. The family of the insured was also covered.[88] Responsibility for offering these health care services lay with the National Welfare Institute (*Instituto Nacional de Previsión* or INP), but it could reach agreements with other public and private institutions in order to provide these services.[89]

In practice, it was only possible to organize this insurance thanks to these special agreements with private entities. Only the company funds, mutual societies and medical *igualatorios* constituted prior to the Civil War could sign these agreements with the National Welfare Institute. On 2 March 1944 a decree was issued authorizing the agreements between the National Welfare Institute and the collaborating bodies, and then the Ministry of Labour Order of 8 March 1944 announced the regulations for the execution of the decree. However, not many of the friendly societies were able to sign such an agreement with the National Welfare Institute. The great obstacle was the requirement of a guarantee deposit and the need for available liquidity, imposed by the obligation to liquidate the premiums deducted from the workers in the National Sickness Insurance Fund on a quarterly basis. Within the imposed time limits, they had to hand over the difference between the percentage agreed and the premiums collected or the difference between the premiums paid by employers and workers, according to the official rate, and pay for the provisions of the insurance, after the administration costs, which were also fixed by the special agreements, had been deducted.[90]

In practice, the majority of the National Welfare Institute's agreements were reached with employers' industrial accident mutuals, company funds and medical *igualatorios* created by members of the medical profession.[91] Only the larger-scale friendly societies were able to collaborate with the National Welfare Institute. This was the case of the Catalan Federation of Mutual Provident Societies, which had gone through different transformations in order to adapt to the law until, in accordance with the directives of the new Law on Mutual Societies of 1941, it recovered the name of Catalan Federation of Mutual Provident Societies in 1944.[92] In 1945, this entity, heir to the Catalan Federation of Mutual Provident Societies that had been created at the end of the nineteenth century, took 3.1 per cent of the premiums of all the collaborating bodies that were operating in the branch of compulsory sickness insurance.

The new Francoist state preferred to hand over the management of the new insurance to those bodies created by employers or professional doctors, groups that had mainly supported the cause of the Nationalists, rather than facilitate the incorporation of those welfare mutuals that were heir to the nineteenth-century workers' societies. In the years following the implementation of compulsory sickness insurance, as its coverage was gradually extended to the working population, the majority of friendly societies dissolved or became simple recreational societies. The increase in medical fees that had started in the 1930s, became more acute in the 1940s, and along with the implementation of compulsory sickness insurance made the continuation of health care provisions and sickness or death benefits unsustainable.[93]

5 SICKNESS INSURANCE AND WELFARE REFORM IN ENGLAND AND WALES, 1870–1914

Bernard Harris, Martin Gorsky, Aravinda Guntupalli and Andrew Hinde

During the last two decades, historians and social scientists have paid increasing attention to the history of friendly societies and other forms of mutual support. In Britain, authors such as Eric Hopkins, David Neave, Martin Gorsky, Simon Cordery and Daniel Weinbren have examined the role played by friendly societies both as cultural organizations and as sources of welfare support, and Weinbren has also explored the relationship between friendly societies and philanthropy.[1] Nor has interest been confined to purely historical circles. In recent years, commentators on both left and right have attempted to invoke the vibrancy of Britain's mutualist tradition as an alternative to the 'top-down' welfare state.[2]

One of the most important issues raised by these debates has been the relationship between mutualism in general, and the friendly societies in particular, and the growth of state welfare in the early years of the twentieth century. The friendly societies played a central role in the process because of their own responsibility for the provision of both sickness insurance and pension benefits. This chapter begins by looking at the societies' own attempts to estimate welfare needs by examining their efforts to measure the sickness experience of their members. It then goes to review the role played by the societies in the introduction of both old age pensions and national health insurance.

Sickness Experience

During the eighteenth and nineteenth centuries, friendly societies played a key role in protecting the working-class population from the economic risks associated with sickness, old age and death. Although may societies, such as the Antediluvian Order of Buffaloes and the Ancient Order of Foresters, attempted to trace their origins back into the mists of time, the first 'modern' society was established in Bethnal Green in 1687, and the first General Act for the regulation of friendly societies was only passed in 1793.[3] This Act, entitled 'An Act for the Encouragement and Relief of Friendly Societies' (33 Geo. III C. 54) defined

friendly societies as 'societ[ies] of good fellowship' established 'for the purpose
of raising ... by voluntary contributions, a stock or fund for the mutual relief and
maintenance of all every member thereof, in old age, sickness and infirmity, and
for the relief of widows and children of deceased members'.[4]

As Peter Gosden has explained, the earliest friendly societies were small,
local societies, often centred on the local ale-house. However, during the 1830s
and 1840s these gradually began to be superseded by the growth of the 'affiliated orders', such as the Ancient Order of Foresters, the Independent Order of
Oddfellows, Manchester Unity (hereafter the Manchester Unity of Oddfellows),
the Grand United Order of Oddfellows, the Order of Druids, the Loyal Order
of Ancient Shepherds, the National Order of Oddfellows, and the Nottingham
Ancient Imperial Order of Oddfellows. These were national organizations which
themselves comprised large numbers of individual courts, lodges or branches.
There were also a number of other organizations which also came under the general heading of 'friendly societies' during the nineteenth century. These included
local town, village or country societies; particular trade societies; dividing societies; deposit friendly societies; county or patronized societies; collecting societies;
annuity societies; and female friendly societies. The majority of these organizations were democratically-accountable to their members and primarily concerned
with the provision of sickness benefits and funeral grants, or death benefits, but
there were exceptions. The 'county' or patronized societies were founded and
managed by members of the local gentry, and the collecting societies were large,
centralized organizations specializing in the provision of funeral benefits.[5]

It has often proved difficult to provide reliable estimates of the total number of friendly society members. This reflects the deficiencies of registration and
the difficulty of allowing for double-counting. However, it is generally agreed
that the numbers of both organizations and members rose rapidly during the
late-eighteenth and early-nineteenth centuries. In 1801, Frederick Morton Eden
estimated that there were approximately 7200 societies with a total membership
of 648,000; and in 1803 it was estimated that there were 9672 societies with a
total members of 704, 350. In 1818, the Select Committee on the Poor Laws
calculated that the number of members rose from 821,319 in 1813 to 925,429 in
1815. In 1875, the Royal Commission on Friendly Societies estimated that there
were 26,087 separate societies or branches of societies throughout the United
Kingdom and that the number of members was 2,254,881, but it also conceded
that these figures reflected a great deal of under-registration. During the next
forty years, the quality of registration improved and the number of recorded
members increased to more than 7.5 million.[6] The vast majority of members
were working-class men aged eighteen and over.[7]

Although many people may have been drawn to friendly societies for social
and recreational reasons, their primary function was to provide members with a
form of insurance against the risks posed by the loss of income associated with
ill-health. In order to do this efficiently, the societies needed to be able to estimate

the prevalence of these risks. One of the earliest attempts to do so was undertaken by the Highland Friendly Society in 1824, and Charles Ansell conducted a second attempt, based on the experience of English friendly societies, in 1835.[8] Further attempts were made by Francis Neison Sr. in 1845 and Alexander Glen Finlaison in 1853, and the two largest societies, the Ancient Order of Foresters and the Independent Order of Oddfellows, conducted their own enquires at different stages between 1850 and 1886.[9] Their investigations were followed by large-scale investigations by William Sutton and Alfred Watson in 1896 and 1903 respectively.[10]

These investigations are particularly important because they enable us to develop a series of snapshots illustrating the relationship between sickness and age at different times during the course of the nineteenth century and to use these snapshots to show how sickness rates changed during this period. As we can see from Figure 5.1, sickness rates were relatively low between the ages of twenty and fifty, but started to rise quite rapidly after men had passed their fiftieth birthdays. However, the picture for changes over time is more complicated. Although age-specific sickness rates appear to have fallen between 1836–40 and 1846–8, they rose during the 1870s and between 1876–80 and 1893–7. The apparent increase in recorded morbidity provoked a great deal of discussion at the time and has since become the focus of a good deal of historical controversy.[11]

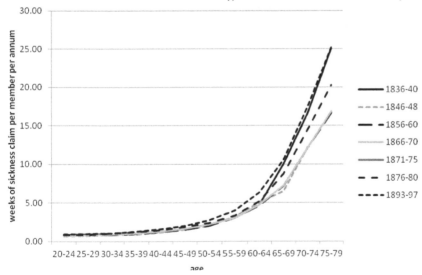

Figure 5.1: Recorded sickness rates among members of British friendly societies, 1836–97.

Notes: Figures for 1836–40 and 1876–80 are based on returns from all registered friendly societies; figures for 1846–8, 1856–60, 1866–70 and 1893–7 are based on returns from the Manchester Unity of Oddfellows; and figures for 1871–5 are based on returns from the Ancient Order of Foresters.

Source: Harris *et al.*, 'Ageing, Sickness and Health', p. 655.

Although some historians have been inclined to interpret the published statistics as evidence of a real increase in sickness experience,[12] many contemporaries were also anxious to explore the extent to which they might be explained statistically. In 1882, the actuary, Francis Neison Jr., suggested that one of the factors which might have been driving sickness rates upward was a difference in secession rates. He argued that individuals who made fewer claims in the early years of membership were more likely to secede than individuals who made a larger number of claims, and that this meant that there was an inherent tendency for friendly societies to 'silt up' with less healthy lives.[13] George Hardy also claimed that 'healthy members' were much more likely to secede than those who had previously submitted sickness claims.[14]

Some writers thought that the statistics might have been distorted in other ways. As Weinbren has pointed out, many early friendly societies were joined by relatively large numbers of 'honorary' members who provided the societies with financial and managerial support but were not expected to make any claims.[15] The proportion of such members declined over time and some observers believed that this was also likely to make reported sickness rates increase. As an anonymous contributor to the *Oddfellows Magazine* commented in 1873: 'one not unlikely cause of the higher rate of sickness ... may be the fact that in former years there was a large percentage of members whose position enable[d] them to forego their claim.[16]

One issue which received quite a lot of attention was the question of whether sickness rates were influenced by changes in the types of area in which people lived. Both Francis Neisons (senior and junior), Alexander Glen Finlaison and Henry Ratcliffe compared the sickness rates of men who lived in rural districts (i.e districts which contained fewer than 5,000 inhabitants) with those of men who lived in towns (containing between 5,000 and 50,000 inhabitants) and cities (containing more than 50,000 inhabitants), but the results were inconclusive. If we add together the results from all these surveys (excluding Finlaison's), we can see very little difference between sickness rates in the three types of area (see Figure 5.2).[17] In 1903, Alfred Watson conducted a similar investigation, based on the experience of members of the Manchester Unity of Oddfellows living in urban and rural districts. Although he found that there was a small advantage in favour of the rural class, his overall conclusion was that 'such tendency is not sufficiently marked to require recognition in the preparation of standard tables'.[18]

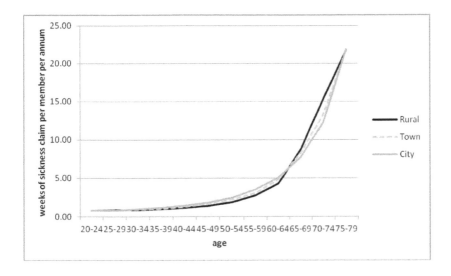

Figure 5.2: Sickness rates in rural areas, towns and cities.
Source: Neison, *Rates of Mortality*, pp. 44–7.

Watson's own view was that sickness rates were much more likely to be influenced by occupational factors[19] but this had two different dimensions. In the first place, as Francis Neison Sr. had pointed out in 1849, 'the sickness of friendly societies ... is incapacity from labour' and, as his son explained in 1873, this meant that a man might be signed off work for one occupation, even though a member with a very similar complaint might have no difficulty in working in another.[20] However, it was also recognized that some occupations, such as coalmining, were inherently more dangerous than others. Nevertheless, when Watson sought to investigate the extent to which changes in friendly society sickness rates might be attributable to occupational changes, the only information he could find showed that the proportion of members who described themselves as coalminers had barely changed. He therefore concluded that even if some of the increase in recorded sickness rates had been associated with an increase in the proportion of members engaged in hazardous occupations, there were no data to support this.[21]

In the absence of definite information about the occupational characteristics of friendly society members, many observers sought to explain changes in sickness rates in more behavioural terms. As Edward Brabrook put it, 'there is also the moral consideration, that a man of firm mind and industrious temperament will continue at work, when a man of flabby and lazy disposition would lie up for the same disorder'.[22] This consideration was echoed by G. H. Ryan during a discussion at the Institute of Actuaries:

> To instance only one point in which the human will was very largely concerned, there was he called 'malingering' on funds. There were also other respects in which the exercise of the individual will entered into and influenced the results presented by a friendly society.[23]

Whilst it might be difficult to deny the importance of what Brabrook called 'personal equations',[24] it was more difficult to explain why their nature or impact might have changed over time. However, some observers thought such an explanation might be found in the growth of 'over' or 'excessive' insurance. In 1834, the first Registrar of Friendly Societies, John Tidd Pratt, told the Royal Commission on the Poor Laws that 'in most cases, the allowances made by the societies are so adjusted as to make it the interest of every member not to receive relief ... so long as he can earn his usual wages'.[25] However, Alfred Watson believed that this constraint had been undermined by the introduction of graduated benefit scales, which meant that individuals who paid higher contributions could claim higher benefits in return. In 1910, he told members of the Institute of Actuaries that there was a clear relationship between the entitlement to higher benefits and the cost of sickness claims.[26]

Watson and his contemporaries also believed that some friendly society members qualified themselves for 'over-insurance' by joining more than one organization. Although it has often been assumed that the vast majority of members only belonged to one society, this was not necessarily true. In 1909, the Permanent Secretary of the Ancient Order of Foresters reported that 'many persons are members of more than one Society, so that there is a duplication in numbers to a considerable extent', and C.W. Morecroft estimated the extent of double-membership at around eight hundred thousand.[27] Watson himself believed that it was 'impossible to make any estimate of duplicate memberships' but P.M. Rea told members of the Royal Statistical Society that 'the majority of those who were insured in a friendly society were insured in two, and sometimes three, and ... this provided a powerful incentive for a man 'to "lay off" until he got strong and vigorous'.[28]

It is difficult to estimate the extent to which 'overinsurance' might have inflated friendly society claim statistics. However, during the late-1890s and early-1900s it was often suggested that the introduction of a statutory workmen's compensation scheme in 1897 had encouraged friendly society members to remain off work for longer. In 1910, John Brown told members of the Ancient Order of Foresters that 'in 43 out of the 44 Courts relieved at the last High Court the cause of insolvency was wholly or partly excessive sickness, mainly through accidents. If the recommendations of the Committee be adopted and sick pay restricted when the member is in receipt of compensation under the Workmen's Compensation Act, a great step will be taken to make our deficiency Courts solvent, and will, to a large extent, prevent future insolvency'.[29] This assessment was echoed by the Official Valuer, Samuel Hudson, during the same meeting. He asked 115 Courts whether 'the operation of the Workmen's Compensation Act tend[s] to increase the duration of sick claims'. 53 Courts replied in the affirmative, 57 in the negative and five were unable to give an opinion. However, when he confined the investigation to those Courts which contained members who followed 'hazardous occupations', a clear majority (47 Courts out of 67) said that the duration of claims had increased. He therefore concluded that 'the evidence is overwhelmingly in support of the contention that the Workmen's Compensation Act has injuriously affected Friendly Societies, our own Courts among [them] ... wherever and whenever the two interests have come into simultaneous operation'.[30]

Some writers believed that a member's propensity to claim sickness benefits was also related to the culture of the societies' themselves. As we have already seen, the majority of societies offered a combination of social and recreational attractions and welfare benefits and these attractions played a central role in helping to develop the sense of trust and mutual obligation on which the viability of the societies depended.[31] However, during the second half of the nineteenth century, the societies' own desire for 'respectability', combined with official disapproval of inappropriate expenditure and the growth of alternative leisure attractions, may have conspired to weaken this. In 1885, the Chief Registrar of Friendly Societies, John Ludlow, told the Select Committee on National Provident Insurance that 'a man's selfishness is to some extent checked by *esprit de corps*, or by the pleasure of seeing his society prosperous and so forth',[32] but others thought that this constraint may have been waning. In 1913, Alfred Watson told a meeting at the Royal Statistical Society that friendly society sickness benefits used to be regarded 'more in the spirit of a gift than a definite insurance. That spirit did not obtain today'.[33]

It has sometimes been argued that members' attitudes to sickness claims may have been influenced by the financial health of the organizations to which they belonged. In 1892, Jacques Bertillon suggested that 'when the societies grant compensation they attach less importance to their regulations than to the state of their till' and claimed that this was 'the sole cause' of the differences between British friendly societies and their French counterparts.[34] G. H. Ryan also thought that 'when a society boasted of being in a condition of great prosperity, the tendency amongst its members was to claim more sick pay than might otherwise be the case'.[35] However, although such factors may have helped to explain some of the differences between societies, it is difficult to see how they might have influenced trends over time, given the societies' own complaints about their financial difficulties.

Although some writers attributed the increase in sickness rates to changes in the behaviour of friendly society members, others focused attention on the societies' ability to police that behaviour. In 1910, the Chief Registrar of Friendly Societies calculated that there were more than 29,000 separate friendly society branches, of which more than 20,000 belonged to 'affiliated orders' such as the Ancient Order of Foresters and the Manchester Unity of Oddfellows.[36] These branches varied considerably in size, and this led to calls for some of the smaller branches to amalgamate in order to reduce their financial vulnerability.[37] However, some observers believed that the development of larger societies also added to their administrative difficulties.[38] In 2003, the historian, Simon Cordery, described how the 'old type of friendly society man' who devoted himself to the management of the societies' affairs was becoming increasingly rare in the years leading up to the First World War, and the historian of the Ancient Order of Foresters, Audrey Fisk, also claimed that the increase in the size of the Foresters' courts meant that they were becoming increasingly unwieldy.[39]

Alfred Watson attempted to place these concerns on a more statistical footing. He argued that 'the efficacy of supervision depends, to a great extent, upon the knowledge of both the circumstances and dispositions of the members which the officers are able to acquire', and that this was likely to decline as the size of the societies increased. In 1900, he examined the cost of sickness claims within different branches of the Manchester Unity of Oddfellows and found that 'the results will be seen to fully agree with expectation'. Although only 41 per cent of branches with fewer than eighty members reported 'excessive' sickness, more than eighty per cent of the branches with over 500 members incurred costs which exceeded those which might have been predicted previously (see Table 5.1).

Table 5.1: Sickness experience among members of the International Order of Oddfellows (Manchester Unity), 1891–5.

			Sickness cost					
		High			Normal		Low	
Number of members in lodge	Total number of lodges in group	% of the whole number of lodges	Number of lodges	% of the number of lodges in the group	Number of lodges	% of the number of lodges in the group	Number of lodges	% of the number lodges the group
<80	823	23.0	337	40.9	255	31.0	231	28.1
80–149	1,059	29.6	543	51.3	314	29.7	202	19.1
150–249	877	24.5	504	57.5	212	24.2	161	18.4
250–349	425	11.9	278	65.4	87	20.5	60	14.1
350–499	279	7.8	206	73.8	47	16.8	26	9.3
≥500	118	3.3	97	82.2	11	9.3	10	8.5
Total	3,581	100.0	1,965	54.9	926	25.9	690	19.3

Source: Watson, 'Methods of Analysing and Presenting the Mortality, Sickness and Secession Experience of Friendly Societies', p. 291.

As this discussion has demonstrated, many contemporary observers believed that age-specific sickness rates were rising and that this was one of the factors which was placing an increasing burden on the societies' finances, but they did not believe that the increase represented an 'objective' deterioration in their members' health status. They preferred to attribute the increase to behavioural changes and to changes in the societies' capacity to police sickness claims. These questions have also played an important part in recent historical debates. Some writers have argued that the increase was 'real', whereas others have attributed it to changes in the cultural definition of sickness and the operation of the labour market,[40] and some have questioned whether it was really as great as contemporary writers and the majority of historians have supposed.[41] However, the main focus of this chapter is on the way in which the perceived increase in sickness rates may have affected attitudes to the introduction of old-age pensions and national health insurance, and these are the issues to which we now turn.

Old-Age Pensions

During the last three decades of the nineteenth century, a series of commentators put forward proposals for the introduction of state-backed pensions. The underlying aim of these proposals was to provide a form of financial support for older people which would protect them from the need to apply for poor relief. However the proposals differed over whether participation should be voluntary or compulsory and, most importantly, whether the provision should be insurance-based or wholly state-financed.

Although the Royal Commission on Friendly Societies briefly considered the possibility of offering deferred annuities to people who had reached a particular age,[42] it is usually argued that the first person to develop a formal proposal for the introduction of a statutory old age pension scheme was Canon W.L. Blackley.[43] He proposed an insurance-based scheme under which all wage-earners would be obliged to contribute an average of £14 per head between the ages of seventeen and twenty-one.[44] The scheme would be administered by central government and it would be used to pay for sickness benefits of eight shillings a week up to the age of seventy, and a pension of four shillings a week from the age of seventy onwards.[45] In the following year, R. P. Hookham advocated a much more radical proposal for a non-contributory scheme which would provide a universal pension graduated according to age. Individuals would receive a pension of six pence per day (3s. 6d. per week) at the age of sixty or sixty-five; nine pence a day (5s. 3d. per week) at the age of seventy; and one shilling a day at the age of eighty.[46]

The distinction between Blackley's insurance-based proposal and Hookham's non-contributory scheme was echoed in the proposals introduced by Charles Booth and Joseph Chamberlain at the beginning of the 1890s. Booth argued that a significant proportion of the population lacked the opportunity to save enough money during their working lives to provide for their own old age and that it was wrong to subject such people to the indignities of the poor law.[47] He therefore recommended the introduction of a non-contributory state pension worth five shillings a week for everyone aged 65 and over. By contrast, Joseph Chamberlain advocated the establishment of a voluntary insurance scheme. He argued that individuals would pay money into the scheme either through the Post Office Savings Bank or through a friendly society, and the value of their contribution would be matched by a contribution from the Treasury. Chamberlain's proposal would have given friendly societies a direct stake in the operation of the scheme, but would also have required them to submit to a much greater degree of state control.[48]

Although Chamberlain's proposal was the only one to involve friendly societies directly, they all affected the societies indirectly. When the proposals were first introduced, the societies were generally quite hostile. They believed that suggestions for the introduction of non-contributory schemes would undermine the importance of thrift and that the establishment of a state-supported contributory scheme would either undermine the work of existing thrift agencies, in the case of Blackley's proposal, or undermine their independence, in the case of the ideas advanced by Joseph Chamberlain. However, during the 1890s they began to revise their earlier attitudes and by the early-1900s they were beginning to come round in favour of some kind of reform. Nevertheless, they continued to be opposed to the introduction of contributory schemes and began to focus more of their own efforts on the support of non-contributory proposals.

There have been a number of attempts to explain the evolution of the societies' attitudes. During the 1960s, Bentley Gilbert argued that the societies' position was shaped by two conflicting sets of issues. On the one hand, they were engaged in a fierce competition with each other for new members, and this prevented them either from raising contribution levels or reducing benefits, even though some combination of the two might have been essential if they were to ward off insolvency. On the other hand, they were also beset by a problem of rising costs associated with the 'rapidly lengthening longevity and proportionate ageing of the existing membership'.[49] However, Gilbert's main aim was to focus on the societies' opposition to the introduction of a contributory pension scheme. He concluded that 'the tradition of Victorian *laissez-faire* was too strong' and that the societies 'preferred insolvency to immorality' and he failed to pay much attention to any evidence of support for alternative forms of pension provision.[50]

Although other historians have shown rather more awareness of the full range of friendly society positions, they have also echoed Gilbert's underlying analysis of the problems the societies faced. According to James Treble, 'the root

causes of the financial troubles of the major friendly societies have been analysed by Professor B. B. Gilbert. Among other things, they failed to understand
the precise relationship between longevity and the pattern of sickness claims.
Reform of their finances was also inhibited by the keen competition ... for new
members, the failure of ... officials to impress upon the rank and file the meaning
of "actuarial soundness", the payment of what was essentially a pension to their
elderly members out of ... sickness funds, and the upward movement of interest
rates during the Boer War'.[51] However, some of the assumptions which underpin
this analysis have also been challenged in recent years. Both John Macnicol and
Nicholas Broten have queried the assumption that the societies were necessarily
beset by insolvency, and Macnicol has also cast doubt on Gilbert's warnings of a
demographic apocalypse.

In his major study of *The politics of retirement in Britain*, Macnicol argued that
Gilbert had underestimated the societies' capacity to adjust to changing financial circumstances and that late-nineteenth century actuaries greatly exaggerated
the extent of their vulnerability. He claimed that 'in 1910, the President of the
Institute of Actuaries, George Francis Hardy, candidly admitted that previous
valuations had given a far too pessimistic view of the societies' financial condition, and commended them on their reformatory moves to greater solvency'.[52]
This assessment has been echoed by Nicholas Broten, both in an LSE Discussion Paper and in his contribution to this volume (see Chapter 6 below). Broten
examined the accounts of eight branches, or Courts, of the Ancient Order of
Foresters and concluded that 'seven of the eight ... were strongly financially
sound'.[53] However, even though it might be wrong to assume that the societies
were necessarily insolvent, it would also be wrong to underestimate the extent of
the challenges they faced.

As we have already seen, the societies possessed a great deal of evidence to
show how sickness rose with age (see for example Figures 5.1 and 5.2 above).
They also had good grounds for believing that sickness rates were rising at each
age, even if some of this increase may have been exaggerated. However, the most
important problem was the increase in the proportion of members at higher
ages. As we can see from Table 5.2, the percentage of members in the Manchester Unity of Oddfellows who were aged fifty or over increased from 4.17 per
cent in 1846/8 to 20.75 per cent in the period 1893/7, and this had a dramatic
effect on overall sickness rates. In 1893/7, the average number of sick weeks per
member per year was 2.344. If the age structure of the Oddfellows' membership
had remained unchanged between 1846/8 and 1893/7, the average sickness rate
would still have increased (from 0.98 sick weeks per member per year to 1.286
sick weeks), but the increase would have been much smaller than that which
actually occurred.[54]

Table 5.2: Age distribution of members of the Manchester Unity of Oddfellows,
1846/8–1893/7.

Age	MUOF 1846–8 N	MUOF 1846–8 % in each group	MUOF 1856–60 N	MUOF 1856–60 % in each group	MUOF 1866–70 N	MUOF 1866–70 % in each group	MUOF 1893–7 N	MUOF 1893–7 % in each group
16–19	–	–	–	–	–	–	101,912	3.40
18–19	5,214	0.84	6,241	0.62	11,756	0.89	–	–
20–24	77,266	12.43	133,429	13.26	191,154	14.47	434,117	14.49
25–29	145,359	23.39	172,867	17.18	274,642	20.79	468,235	15.63
30–34	144,953	23.32	151,744	15.08	231,411	17.52	433,525	14.47
35–39	116,561	18.75	151,342	15.04	162,818	12.32	368,474	12.30
40–44	67,998	10.94	135,200	13.44	115,786	8.76	310,484	10.36
45–49	38,311	6.16	111,682	11.10	102,118	7.73	257,359	8.59
50–54	16,285	2.62	73,530	7.31	86,732	6.57	213,469	7.13
55–59	5,894	0.95	42,659	4.24	70,952	5.37	163,886	5.47
60–64	2,455	0.39	18,677	1.86	41,479	3.14	110,375	3.68
65–69	874	0.14	6,147	0.61	21,693	1.64	63,323	2.11
70–74	284	0.05	1,978	0.20	8,014	0.61	39,302	1.31
75–79	68	0.01	598	0.06	2,010	0.15	21,195	0.71
80–84	35	0.01	140	0.01	421	0.03	7,861	0.26
85–89	4	0.00	25	0.00	51	0.00	1,941	0.06
90–94	–	–	13	0.00	10	0.00	247	0.01
95–99	–	–	–	–	1	0.00	19	0.00
	621,561	100.00	1,006,272	100.00	1,321,048	100.00	2,995,724	100.00

Sources: Neison, *Rates of Mortality*, pp. 46–7; Watson, *Account of an Investigation*, p. 21.

When Bentley Gilbert first addressed these issues, he argued that changes in the societies' age structure were caused by increasing longevity but, as Macnicol has shown, this explanation is misleading.[55] The main reason why the age structure was changing was because the societies were unable to maintain a sufficient supply of new recruits. This created a demographic bulge which was similar to that experienced by the country as a whole during the course of the twentieth century.[56]

Although many friendly societies may have been relatively relaxed about their financial prospects, they were also concerned about the relationship between sickness and age and the extent to which the increase in the proportion of older members might expose them to greater risks in the future. As result, they made strenuous efforts to establish their own superannuation schemes. However, as James Treble showed,[57] take-up of these schemes was extremely low, and this may therefore help to explain why the societies spent so much time worrying about the use of sickness benefit as a form of *de facto* pension for older members.[58]

This account suggests that the societies' attitude to the provision of state pensions was influenced, at least in part, by their perception of their own interests. They remained opposed to contributory pensions because they feared that this would either expose them to the risk of competition or threaten them with subordination, but they became increasingly sympathetic to calls for the introduction of non-contributory pensions because these offered a potential solution to some of their own difficulties.[59] However, as both Treble and Macnicol have demonstrated, the societies' attitudes also reflected their assessment of the broader political context. In his account of the role played by friendly societies in the coming of old age pensions, Treble argued that opposition to pension provision was undermined partly by divisions between the societies themselves, partly by a breakdown in relations between the societies and the Charity Organisation Society over the granting of votes to friendly society members who applied for poor relief, and partly by the emergence of 'unmistakable signs that some politicians were coming to realize that the state had a moral obligation to alleviate cases of hardship amongst the aged'.[60] As the Permanent Secretary of the Ancient Order of Foresters, J. Lister Stead, explained in 1907: 'The majority of the people in the United Kingdom are in favour of some better provision being made than now exists for easing the burden of old age.... There is now an overwhelming demand for legislation to deal with what is admitted to be a pressing social problem. How is the problem best treated?'.[61]

National Health Insurance

The previous sections of this chapter have looked at the ways in which the societies sought to interpret evidence of increasing sickness rates and at the role these organizations played in the introduction of the statutory old age pension scheme. In the final section, we turn to the relationship between friendly societies and the introduction of national health insurance.

One of the earliest attempts to consider how the state might either complement or even replace some of the main functions of a friendly society was made by the Royal Commission on Friendly Societies in 1874. As we have already seen, the Royal Commission briefly considered a proposal to extend the benefits of a government deferred annuity scheme to 'the humbler classes',[62] but it devoted more detailed attention to the case for statutory provision for insurance against either sickness or death. It thought that there were good grounds for introducing some form of state burial insurance[63] but it was less convinced by the merits of statutory health insurance. It identified a number of different grounds for this, including the claim that 'it would be difficult, if not impossible ... to organize any system of government sick insurance which would not carry with it something of the appearance of a relief system' and this would 'tend ... to break down the barrier of honourable pride which now deters many from claiming assistance from the poor rates'.[64]

Statutory health insurance also formed an integral part of Canon Blackley's proposal for national insurance. If Blackley's scheme had been implemented, it would have provided a weekly sickness benefit of eight shillings for those under the age of seventy, and a pension worth four shillings a week for those aged 70 and over.[65] During the mid-1880s, when the Select Committee on National Provident Insurance investigated this proposal, the Oddfellows' Actuary, Reuben Watson, protested that 'friendly societies ... ought not to be interfered with by the establishment of any system which would be injurious to them', but the Committee decided that 'no conclusive evidence was given to show that the establishment of a compulsory society on a national basis could endanger the funds or affect the soundness of any existing voluntary society conducted on a sound principle'.[66] However, the Committee still regarded Blackley's scheme as 'unworkable'. There were various reasons for this, including the fear that a national society would be unable to control malingering; that many people would be unable to afford the contributions; and that individuals who had no need for health insurance benefits would nevertheless be compelled to contribute to the benefits received by others.[67]

Although the Select Committee on National Provident Insurance rejected statutory health insurance, the idea was revived by the Chancellor of the Exchequer, David Lloyd George, in 1908. According to Bentley Gilbert, Lloyd George's original intention was to extend the non-contributory old-age pension scheme to cover widows and orphans and to make provision for the support of incapacitated and chronically-ill workers under the age of seventy. However, after returning from a fact-finding trip to Germany, he began to frame plans for a much more far-reaching compulsory insurance scheme, covering not merely chronic illness and incapacity, but also more 'ordinary' forms of short-term sickness.[68]

One of the original objections to Canon Blackley's proposal was that it would compete with the friendly societies' own schemes, and Lloyd George tried to meet this objection by involving the societies directly in the administration of the scheme, instead of setting it up in opposition to them. In Gilbert's words, 'the Government was proposing to use the friendly societies to fill in the gaps left by existing welfare legislation'.[69] However, whilst this may have helped to assuage some of the societies' fears, it also inflamed others. As the Editor of the *Foresters' Miscellany* put it in 1909: 'It may be a good thing that those who cannot now join a friendly society, because of ill-health, shall be provided for by the state, but what are we to say to the class who can but will not now join, the loafers, wastrels, spendthrifts etc. ... that will all come under the scheme. What a desirable class for our members to mix with'.[70]

While some of the opposition to compulsory health insurance may have been based on snobbery, these were not the only concerns. Many members are likely have shared 'Another PDCR's' view that 'state aid will destroy the independent spirit of dogged perseverance by which the AOF has surmounted its difficulties in the past, and I fear would result in our number, instead of increasing, gradually receding to a vanishing point'.[71] C.W. Morecroft told a meeting of AOF Past Officers in Cambridge that 'the past hundred years may be described as a period of great social uplifting and self-improvement' and that 'the working man ... is [now] more self-reliant and possesses more moral backbone than ever before. And if the state steps in and says "we are now going to help you to do what you have been doing for yourself for so long, and we are going to compel you to accept our aid", do you not think that such a step savours very much of putting back the hands of the clock?'.[72]

As these comments suggest, many friendly society members were convinced that national health insurance was, as R. F. Calder concluded, both unnecessary and undesirable.[73] However, others believed that was in the interests of the friendly societies themselves and society at large. The Secretary of the Eastern Star Court of the AOF, C. W. Narlborough, believed that one of the major problems facing the friendly societies was the cost of supporting members who were ill for very long periods, and that the introduction of a government scheme would enable them to deal with cases of illness or invalidity extending beyond twelve months and thereby help to restore their solvency.[74] Edward Tranter argued that a state scheme would help to protect 'genuine' friendly societies from the threat posed by dividing societies, remove the need for charity and strengthen the values on which friendly societies had been built by making men 'realise their responsibility' and 'help each other'.[75] E. B. Deadman thought that statutory insurance would help to protect friendly society members from the shadow of the poor law. Would it not be far more desirable, he asked, 'for friendly societies, whilst maintaining their present position, to assist in the provision of a state brotherhood, wherein the healthy should be compelled to form a permanent society, rather than to be cajoled by slate clubs organised ... by Church, Dissent and public house, to the detriment of ... true brotherhood?'.[76]

The most forceful supporter of statutory health insurance within friendly society ranks was probably J. Lister Stead. As Treble demonstrated, Lister Stead came to national prominence in the late-1890s as 'a tireless worker ... in the campaign against state pensions'[77] but he subsequently changed his mind on this question and he carried the strength of his conversion through to the debates on national health insurance. In November 1909 he told a Foresters' meeting in Ilkeston that 'I hold no brief for Mr Lloyd George or any other politician, but I feel that in order to have some understanding of the present situation, we must widen our vision; we must not look at the question simply as it affects ourselves;

we must not leave out of consideration those who are outside our ranks; we must not forget to try to understand the motives of those who press changes upon us; and we must not fail to observe the stream which carries them along'.[78]

As these comments suggest, although there was considerable opposition to the introduction of national health insurance within the friendly societies' ranks, this was far from universal. However, support for the proposals was compromised by the existence of other 'players' in the relationship between the societies and the state, namely the medical profession and the private insurance industry. The activities of both these groups had a profound effect on the societies' negotiations with the government and the future shape of the insurance scheme.

Although this chapter has concentrated on the role the societies played in the provision of cash benefits, or financial compensation for loss of earnings, they were also significant providers of health care.[79] During the nineteenth century, doctors had played two important roles in the development of friendly society sickness benefits. In the first place, they helped to establish the truth of a member's claim for benefit by certifying illness. Second, they also provided medical attention in the hope that this would accelerate recovery.[80] However, although the societies provided an important source of medical income, many doctors resented the terms on which this was offered, and they were determined to ensure that the new national health insurance scheme did not become a means of reinforcing their dependence.[81] When Lloyd George drafted his initial proposals, he had intended to make friendly societies responsible for the administration of medical treatment as well as cash benefits, but he was forced to back down in the face of medical hostility. The decision to separate the provision of cash benefits from the administration of medical attendance was an important victory for the medical profession and a significant defeat for the friendly societies.[82]

The second additional player was the private insurance industry. This discussion has focused on the provision of sickness insurance but Lloyd George's original proposals also included plans for the payment of pensions to widows and orphans. Although the friendly societies had also been responsible for the payment of burial insurance, their interests in this area were dwarfed by those of the collecting societies and, most importantly, the private insurance companies. These organizations argued that the provision of widows' and orphans' benefits would undermine their own business because, like funeral benefits, these benefits would be paid on the death of the insured contributor or policy-holder. However, from the friendly societies' point of view, this concern was probably rather less important than the decision to allow insurance companies to register as 'approved societies' under the National Health Insurance scheme. When the scheme was first proposed, Lloyd George had tried to protect the position of the friendly societies by insisting that the status of 'approved society' would be limited to democratically-controlled membership organizations but the insurance companies were neither democratic nor membership-based. However, they were able to make up for this deficiency by being politically very powerful, and this forced Lloyd George to overcome his previous concerns and admit them to the scheme.[83]

A number of commentators have tried to argue that the introduction of national health insurance sounded the death knell for Britain's long tradition of self-help and mutual aid[84] but this is only the part of the story. During the late-nineteenth and early-twentieth centuries, the main threat to mutual organizations came not from the state but from the private welfare industry. This is an important dimension of social welfare history which has not always received the attention it deserves from historians of either mutual aid or the welfare state.[85]

Conclusions

This chapter has examined a number of different aspects of the relationship between friendly societies, sickness experience and the origins of the 'welfare state' in Britain in the late-nineteenth and early-twentieth centuries. The first part of the chapter showed how the societies sought to account for the apparent increase in recorded morbidity between *circa* 1850 and 1914. We then moved on to consider how this experience may have helped to shape their attitudes to the introduction of old age pensions and national health insurance between 1908 and 1911.

Although the societies' attitudes were undoubtedly influenced by their perception of sickness trends, this was not the only factor which helped shape their approach to public welfare provision. Even though some of their concerns were linked to the recorded increase in age-specific morbidity, they were probably more concerned by the increase in the proportion of members at higher ages and by the particular question of increases in sickness duration. However, their views were not only dependent on internal developments. They were also aware of changes in the attitudes of the society around them and therefore their approach to public welfare provision was shaped not only by their immediate interests but also by a pragmatic adaptation to processes of social change.

Acknowledgements

The first part of this chapter is based on B. Harris, M. Gorsky, A. Guntupalli, and P. R. A. Hinde, 'Ageing, sickness and health in England and Wales during the mortality transition', *Social History of Medicine*, 24 (2011), pp. 643-65. We are grateful to the UK Economic and Social Research Council for financial support (RES 062–23–0324).

6 FROM SICKNESS TO DEATH: REVISITING THE FINANCIAL VIABILITY OF THE ENGLISH FRIENDLY SOCIETIES, 1875–1908

Nicholas Broten

This chapter summons new evidence to examine a half-century old claim: that the English friendly societies were mortally ill by the turn of the twentieth century, when the first state pension schemes were introduced. Since Gilbert's 1965 paper, it has been widely held that the insolvency of the friendly societies towards the end of the Victorian period dampened their opposition to state pension schemes and inspired support for such schemes within some societies. In Gilbert's argument, the friendly societies faced two problems as the nineteenth century wore on. First, intense competition between societies for new recruits made increases in required contributions or reduction of benefits infeasible. Second, dramatic increases in life expectancy led to a gradual aging of many society memberships, and with that, greater liabilities. As Gilbert points out, these two problems fed off each other. As societies became more and more burdened by sick payments, they required more new recruits. But in seeking new recruits, they not only faced competition from other societies, but also a 'growing reluctance of men in early life to join societies at all'.[1] Key to this reluctance, Gilbert argues, was a widespread fear among youths that the societies were financially unsound, and thus would be unable to compensate them in their old age.

This argument, though drawing from demographic realities of the period, is puzzling, for it treats the friendly societies as static, inadaptable institutions. In particular, it does not account for the possibility that societies had access to other mechanisms than benefits and contributions to maintain solvency. This seems unlikely to be true. At least some of the Ancient Order of Foresters courts studied in this chapter, for example, had some assets invested in stocks that could have been sold if needed.[2] Another, more important problem with Gilbert's hypothesis is that it is largely based on analysis from nineteenth-century actuaries that misrepresented the day-to-day operations of most lodges. This chapter re-examines the claims of the nineteenth-century actuaries with data from the Ancient Order of Foresters, and in so doing casts new light on Gilbert's argument that insolvency led the societies to support the 1908 Old Age Pensions Act.

The Structure and Style of the Friendly Societies

Among the institutions offering remedy for the challenges of nineteenth-century working-class life, the friendly societies were unique in their promotion of self-help. Neave describes them as the 'largest and most representative working-class organizations' in late nineteenth-century Britain.[3] Gilbert says 'the friendly societies epitomized the Victorian ideals of thrift and respectability, of individual responsibility and self-help'.[4] Indeed, in almost every public utterance, friendly society members referenced their commitment to enabling and demanding personal responsibility. This rhetoric was embedded in their design.

Most societies collected weekly dues totalling between 1 and 2 pounds per year that were then used to provide sickness and death benefits to members who had amassed sufficient contributions.[5] Contributions were usually fixed, though in later years some societies began charging higher fees for older entrants.[6] Membership in a society usually required an application and the written approval of the head of the local lodge, ensuring that high-cost members were unable to join. Societies typically met monthly, at the local public house or in a private lodge, to discuss business, drink beer, enjoy the merriments of socializing, and share news from family and friends.

The friendly societies also enjoyed a mixed reputation with the political establishment. Many societies listed members of parliament and the royal family as honorary, non-contributory, members, though most refrained from declaring outright political allegiances. As Gosden points out, the relationship between the friendly societies and the political elite of Victorian England was discontinuous and constantly evolving.[7] In the early period of friendly society growth between 1815 and 1830, criticism of the societies emphasized the negative effects of mutual combination on village and town life. For example, a London engineer writes:

> As long as bodies of journeymen are allowed to constitute themselves into societies under any denomination of benefit while the present laws of management of such societies exist, your memorialists have no hope of having the evils [of mischievousness and drunkenness] redressed'.[8]

Even in this atmosphere of suspicion, however, the friendly societies had political influence. Because of the regular contributions required to join, membership was censored towards the better off. Gilbert, for example, claims that 'like Victorian England herself, the friendly society movement was rich, influential, and conservative'.[9] Workers in unstable industries or with too little wages to pay the annual contributions would either be expelled for lack of payment – a common practice – or would not join in the first place. In times of difficulty, such workers' only recourse was often the poor law.

The Friendly Societies and the Campaign for Old-Age Pensions

In a 1965 paper, Bentley Gilbert made the case that the friendly societies were insolvent in the late nineteenth century due to the aging of their memberships and the inability to attract new, younger, and healthier recruits.[10] According to Gilbert, the sickness benefits – which acted as a kind of *de facto* pension – societies provided their older members were insufficiently funded by contributions, and exposed lodges to the threat of bankruptcy and dissolution, which further decreased new memberships. Many friendly societies were forced to seek external sources of support. Though staunchly opposed to state intervention, their deteriorating financial condition led many societies to support state pensions at the turn of the century in order to reduce their financial burden. According to Gilbert, this shift in psychology was a necessary, if not sufficient, condition for the passage of pension reforms in Parliament, and was a key force in the passage of the 1908 Old Age Pensions Act. In Gilbert's words: 'So, on the first day of January 1909, old age pensions began in Great Britain with the acquiescence, if not the enthusiasm, of the friendly societies who had been a so important factor in their planning'.[11]

In Gilbert's argument, the friendly societies' primary function in the history of old age pensions was to deflect support away from a contributory pension scheme modelled after the German experience, towards a non-contributory one.[12] The tension between advocates of contributory schemes and those in favour of non-contributory, tax-funded, pensions springs from the origins of the debate. Both sides furiously presented their arguments. A commentary by Charles Booth, noted poverty activist and ardent supporter of non-contributory pensions, for example, clarifies the issue:

> It is impossible to conceive any plan by which contributions can be drawn from the masses of the people alongside of Friendly Society contributions without interfering with the Friendly Societies; nor could the Government enter into a sort of partnership with them, which is not only undesirable but would never be accepted'.[13]

Indeed, plans were discussed that would have joined the friendly societies into an agreement with the government but never gained significant support.[14]

The argument that the friendly societies helped shape the 1908 legislation by their resistance to contributory pensions and later support of non-contributory ones is buttressed by contemporary accounts. The feeling of financial insecurity amongst many societies was acute, although this was not unique to the later nineteenth century. As early as the late eighteenth century, friendly societies were reported to be dissolving due to financial stress.[15]

The Viability of the Friendly Societies: an Empirical Test

The argument that the friendly societies were insolvent is almost exclusively based on the accounts of eighteenth-century actuaries, the majority of which were published in the years between the 1875 Friendly Societies Act and the Old Age Pensions Act of 1908.[16] The methods used by the actuaries were constantly evolving; indeed, the friendly societies were one of the first institutions to use sophisticated actuarial analysis.

Nonetheless, numerous flaws in the methods used by nineteenth-century actuaries have been observed. While the actuarial techniques used to address the insolvency of the friendly societies were well-suited for funded insurance programs, they were ill-suited for the pay-as-you-go schemes that societies actually ran.[17] Societies kept their record books such that each year's sick payments were balanced against contributions in that year; the contributions of new, younger members thus paid for the sickness of the old and decrepit. Actuaries of the period, however, used experience tables, filled with information on expected life expectancy and the probability of sickness, to estimate the *total* liability of a lodge.[18] On the income side of the actuarial tables lay all of the lodge assets in present and in future, adjusted for the interest rate. If predicted benefits were sufficient to meet predicted liabilities, then the lodge was deemed solvent; if predicted contributions were less than predicted liabilities, than the lodge was reported to be insolvent. In the reports of the Chief Registrar of Friendly Societies for the later years of the nineteenth century, more societies reported actuarial deficiencies than surpluses.[19] Since friendly societies were collecting dues each week to pay for sickness benefits, they were much more flexible institutions than these actuarial tables account for.

Before re-examining the solvency of the friendly societies, some understanding of the dynamics of friendly society membership is needed. Emery and Emery's dichotomy of an old man's society versus a young man's society can help explain these dynamics.[20] The old man's society exists to protect elderly men from the infirmities of their age. The sickness benefit is therefore a deferred annuity: it allows men to contribute to a fund in their healthy youth in order to draw from it in their sickly old age. This view characterizes the friendly society as a sort of miniature pension scheme for the Victorian working class. The young man's society exists for entirely different reasons. The young man has no family or life savings, and is seldom sick; his membership in the friendly society is therefore driven by a desire to create a social and financial support structure on which he can lean in times of immediate need.

Data on admissions and membership for the Ancient Order of Foresters offer some credibility to the 'old man' hypothesis: even as admissions fell in the last decade of the century, total membership increased due to rising life expectancies.[21]

Why were fewer men joining societies in the late nineteenth century? Various hypotheses have been proposed: both Gosden and Moffrey suggested that the societies held a much lower appeal in the social hierarchy of late Victorian Britain than in earlier periods as modern technologies replaced the quaint excitement of mutualism and fraternization.[22] Gilbert has suggested that the insolvency of the friendly societies at the time discouraged would-be members from joining.[23] These hypotheses can be addressed in a unified way with a regression model.

Data Sources: Problems and Possible Solutions

Data on the friendly societies can generally be found at the local, district, and national level. The most commonly used data for historical research are the annual records of the Chief Registrar of Friendly Societies, which include the number of members in the society, the value of its assets, and its location. Although Chief Registrar data were compiled from returns mailed in from society lodges around England and Wales, its coverage is highly inconsistent and seems to be biased towards urban areas.[24]

The affiliated orders such as the Foresters and Oddfellows were international, complex, and highly organized institutions by the late nineteenth century, and therefore kept robust records. The Foresters kept annual record books at the district level that documented the financial progress of each court for each year.[25] The accuracy of district classifications has received significant attention: Gosden notes that courts listed under Middlesex, for example, could actually be located in Northampton but registered in the London district.[26] Accordingly, Gosden reclassified the data for his major work. (The extent of this problem, however, is likely small, and this chapter does not correct for the bias involved.) The district records hold information on the number of members in each court, the total worth of their funds, the number of members initiated in each year, the number of members who left in each year, and the total amount of sick claims paid out by each court in the year. The way in which these data are constructed carries a number of advantages. Unlike the data found in the Chief Registrar of Friendly Societies, the Foresters' district data reflect a complete population of Foresters courts and therefore can be used to test the determinants of friendly society membership. District accounts, however, give too little information about the financial operations of the courts to make meaningful insolvency estimates. They provide no information on annual expenditure for operating costs or the composition of assets, sick payments, and income. The annual balance sheets of the local courts are therefore the only source suitable for this sort of analysis.

The annual balance sheets of Foresters' courts have received little or no scholarly attention. The reason for this is undoubtedly logistic: of the roughly three thousand courts that made up the Foresters at the end of the nineteenth century, very few of the annual balance sheets are still available in the Foresters' archives for the late Victorian period. The balance sheets for the eight courts included in this study were the only ones available for the relevant dates, though several more were available for the mid-twentieth century. Table 6.1 shows the names, locations, and available years of the eight courts used.[27] Though the courts are scattered across the country, the scarcity of balance sheets makes national generalization difficult. One problem is survivor bias: the possibility that the balance sheets that still exist were associated with societies with long life spans and relatively few financial problems. There are three reasons, however, why the problem of survivor's bias might be insignificant. First, as noted by Logan, societies failed to keep annual balance sheets for a number of reasons, not all of which were related to financial insecurity. For example, in a small village the secretary of a court might pass away leaving no one with the necessary skills to keep competent records; or the entire court might move locations or merge with another court, thus removing the need for a distinct balance sheet. Though both of these occurrences were likely to be rare, they are illustrative only, and are intended to capture the ephemeral nature of the lifespan of a normally operating court. More importantly, there seems to be no indication that the courts for which balance sheets are available were abnormally successful in terms of life expectancy. Most of the balance sheets cease in the years of World War I, beyond the scope of this study. Finally, it also remains plausible that longevity could be associated with greater insolvency as memberships aged. The problem of survivor bias should be noted but does not undermine the basic results of the chapter.

Table 6.1: Court Balance Sheet Summary Statistics.

Court Name	Court Number	Location	Years (not always consecutive)	Geography
Prince of Wales	3100	Stowmarket	1887–1914	Town
Anchor of Hope	3603	Ipswich	1894–1911	Town
Eleanor Rummyn	3182	London	1879–1910	City
Pettiword	9056	Ipswich	1904–1915	Town
Pride of Reading	4961	Reading	1885–1915	Town
Brounlow	6444	Berkhamstead	1879–1895	Rural
Equity	2992	Cambridge	1878–1911	Town
Perseverence	6089	Bedmond	1880–1912	Rural

Test 1: Society Membership

Two strands of argument have emerged on the demand for friendly society membership. Gosden has attributed the growth of societies in the early nineteenth century to the requirements of the industrial labour market.[28] Other authors have emphasized the role of income growth in driving society membership: as workers became richer, they diverted more of their resources into luxury insurance schemes.[29] Other questions hover around this basic one: Was friendly society membership more concentrated in regions with mining or textiles? Were Protestants more likely to join societies than Catholics? Were societies the domain of the young or the old? Were friendly societies more concentrated where use of the poor law was minimal? A paucity of data at a meaningful level of spatial precision makes investigation of these questions difficult. Some studies, however, have made important progress.

Using data from the poor law returns of 1803 and 1813–15 and various censuses, Gorsky presents correlation statistics between friendly society membership and several other variables. His primary findings are that friendly society growth is strongly correlated with the concentration of the mining and manufacturing sectors and that the timing of friendly society growth coincided strongly with the economic explosions of the industrial revolution.[30] Gorsky's reliance on correlations, however, hinders his argument. Correlations do not control for the interrelatedness of different variables, both observed and unobserved, and thus tend to exaggerate causality. This chapter improves upon this by using regression analysis to examine membership dynamics in the Ancient Order of the Foresters, though it does not include as many variables as does Gorsky, and the fact that the data are limited to the Foresters means that they may not necessarily be representative of the friendly society movement as a whole. As the Foresters' district-wide data are provided at a cross-sectional, county level for a series of years, it represents a sort of panel. With this in mind, the following cross-sectional regression model with time dummies was run:

$$MEMBERS = r_0 + r_1 POP + r_2 OLD + r_3 WAGE + r_4 MED + r_5 BACH + YEAR$$

Where *MEMBERS* is the log of the number of members registered in a Foresters court in each of the forty British counties for the years 1875, 1880, 1885, 1890, 1895, 1900, 1905, and 1910; *POP* is the log of the population of each county in 1871 as reported in the 1871 census and compiled by Mitchell;[31] *OLD* is the proportion of the population in each county over the age of sixty from the 1861 census, and is meant to capture two possible demographic effects. First, it captures the lingering effect of society admissions in the early nineteenth century. Second, since most data suggest that members joined in their early years, an older population might correlate with greater contact between youths and elders, and thus a more favourable view towards society membership amongst the youth;[32] *WAGE* is the agricultural wage in each district for 1867–70 from Hunt, and serves as a proxy for the income effect of insurance demand;[33] *MED* is the number of medical men per 10,000 persons in each county from the 1861 census, and accounts for the possibility that courts were constrained by the medical infrastructure of their locality;[34] *BACH* is the proportion of unmarried men in each county as reported in the 1861 census, and is meant to capture the young man's effect – the possibility that younger men sought out friendly society membership in order to protect against financial and social insecurity; and *YEAR* represents a dummy variable for each of the years, excluding 1875. The yearly dummies pick up any time-sensitive factors that are not absorbed into the other stationary variables.

A defence of the use of data from the 1861 census is required. It is improbable that the age structure of a county in 1861 would approximate its age structure in 1910, from which some of the data are compiled. Data from the 1861 census would therefore be ill-suited for an analysis of the determinants of friendly society *admissions* in 1910. It is important to note that the dependent variable in the above regression is the log of the total membership of the district, and is therefore strongly connected to historical growth in membership. Friendly societies in general, and Foresters in particular, experienced rapid growth in the early 1860s, the effects of which lingered for most of the century.[35] The regression therefore seeks to capture the demographic conditions at the time of significant society growth, the effects of which could still be felt at the early twentieth century.

Table 6.2: Membership Regressions.

Dependent variable: MEMBERS

	Coefficient	T-statistic	P-value
POP	1.103	19.73	0
OLD	9.008	2.15	0.033
WAGE	0.088	3	0.003
MED	0.15	3.77	0
BACH	-0.043	-3.42	0.001
1880	0.313	1.76	0.079
1885	0.369	2.08	0.039
1890	0.54	3.03	0.003
1895	0.601	3.35	0.001
1900	0.591	3.32	0.001
1905	0.596	3.35	0.001
1910	0.528	2.97	0.003

R-squared: 0.61; Adj R-squared: 0.60; N=320

Table 6.2 shows the regression results. All of the variables are found to be statistically significant at the 95 per cent level with the exception of the 1880 yearly dummy. As the dependent variable is the log of total membership, a one-unit change in each of the coefficients can be interpreted as a change of 1 per cent in the membership of the court. Foresters membership was significantly higher in regions with older populations in 1861 and was slightly lower in districts with a higher proportion of bachelors. The agricultural wage, an imperfect proxy for wages in other occupations, has a relatively small effect in increasing Foresters membership. Though weak, this finding lends some credibility to the argument that workers responded to the income effect: as wages increased, insurance against sickness became more affordable. It is, of course, possible that the coefficient on wages is picking up by proxy a sort of industry effect: perhaps industries with higher wages, such as mining or manufacturing had close traditional ties to the friendly societies and also higher agricultural wages due to market competition. This argument is partially buttressed by Gorsky's finding that society membership was greater in mining and manufacturing than agriculture. The positive coefficient on the proportion of medical men suggests a beneficial relationship between the medical community and the Foresters. Unfortunately, whether localities with more doctors allowed more society growth or whether towns with more Foresters courts gave doctors gainful employment cannot be teased from the data.

A few conclusions can be gathered from the results in Table 6.2. Most notably, the Foresters seem to be the domain of the old. The striking coefficient on *OLD*, and the weak but still negative coefficient on *BACH* seems to suggest that the ethos of the Foresters was largely tied up with the older population. Not only were younger members not joining the Foresters as the nineteenth century wore on, but the districts where membership was most abundant were those with older populations. This suggests some correlation between membership across generations in high-recruitment areas, and possibly a positive social attitude towards the Foresters in those areas. It also suggests that the Foresters were more successful in recruiting younger members in districts with a larger elder population, possibly reflecting the fact that in districts with a small population over sixty, youths had the opportunity to join several competing social organizations and had less direct exposure to the rituals and rules of the friendly societies.

Test 2: Insolvency

As mentioned earlier, the nineteenth-century actuarial data on which most of the current analysis of friendly society insolvency is based incorrectly characterizes the friendly societies as funded insurance schemes rather than pay-as-you-go ones. Two concepts from the economics of insurance offer alternatives to these actuarial analyses – the implicit degree of risk loading and the probability of ruin. As suggested in its title, the degree of risk loading measures the extent to which the price of an insurance contract, or in this case a friendly society contribution, covers the cost of expected claims associated with the contract. A financially unsound court would tend to have a negative risk loading value as its price would be too low to cover the complete costs of expected claims, though the value would not necessarily be negative in all years of the court's operation. Conversely, a financially sound court would have mostly positive risk loading values, though in some abnormal years – for example, in the early years of a court's existence – the value might be negative. There is a possibility that the risk loading value could be too large – reflecting an inefficient pricing mechanism – though the threshold between sound and excessive risk loading would be court specific and difficult to quantify.[36]

The intuition behind the probability of ruin is straightforward: it approximates the likelihood that a court's claims will be greater than its income and assets in a given year, forcing the court to close. The probability of ruin calculation requires three pieces of information: the average or expected sick claim in a given year; the court's income in each year; and the structure of the distribution of sick claims around the mean.

The probability of ruin estimates presented here rely on several assumptions about the internal operation of a court. First, they assume that the court had no access to reinsurance or external sources of funding not documented on the court balance sheets. This is likely to be true. Though some of the courts occasionally received supplementary income from the Foresters' district account, this income was recorded in the balance sheets along with other sources of income and thus appears in the calculation of ruin probabilities. It is unlikely that any reinsurance beyond this took place. The estimates of probability of ruin also require an understanding of the composition of lodge assets. Most courts had floating balances that were reasonably large, though the degree of liquidity of these balances likely fluctuated from court to court. For example, one court might have its balance invested in a public house – with very little access to it in a time of emergency – and another in a savings account – readily at hand in times of need. The data used herein, however, do not allow for a consistent examination of the composition of assets across courts.[37]

Some explanation of the aggregate claims distribution used in the calculations is needed. First, data limitations demanded that the claims distribution be modelled collectively – as the claims distribution of the entire court – rather than individually – as the sum of the individual risk profiles of the members of the court.[38] This is justified for two reasons. First, the Foresters did not engage in actuarial pricing such that the price of membership corresponded to the risk profile of the individual. The relationship between an individual price and an individual's claims distribution is therefore of little worth for understanding the court's solvency condition. Second, the courts' funds were pooled aggregately and distributed uniformly upon sickness. The size of sick payments was not a function of the type of claim but its duration; this, again, makes individual claims distributions less informative than the collective distribution of claims.

A second consideration is the shape of the claims distribution. Though Emery and Emery model the aggregate claims of a friendly society as a Compound-Poisson process, the Foresters data do not allow this since the number of claims each year is not always given. This chapter therefore models the claims distribution as a single process, using a Poisson regression model. The close fit between the model and the data, and the very low *P*-values on each coefficient, suggest that the Poisson process is an accurate representation of the claims distribution.[39]

Results: Risk Loading and the Probability of Ruin

Table 6.3 shows the risk loading estimates for five years for each court. Years were chosen to reflect the period before the 1908 Old Age Pensions Act and were based on availability of data.

Table 6.3: Sample Risk Loading Estimates.

Anchor of Hope			Pettiward	
Year	Risk Loading		Year	Risk Loading
1903	-0.056		1904	-0.302
1904	-0.072		1905	-
1905	-0.057		1907	0.168
1906	-0.086		1908	0.138
1907	-0.135		1909	0.158

Equity			Brounlow	
Year	Risk Loading		Year	Risk Loading
1907	0.304		1890	1.05
1908	0.304		1891	1.01
1909	0.307		1892	1.02
1910	0.239		1893	1.29
1911	0.267		1894	1.03

Pride of Reading			Eleanor Rummyn	
Year	Risk Loading		Year	Risk Loading
1902	0.333		1900	0.258
1903	0.321		1901	0.231
1904	0.288		1902	0.252
1905	0.295		1903	0.222
1906	0.241		1904	0.203

Prince of Wales			Perseverence	
Year	Risk Loading		Year	Risk Loading
1888	0.141		1895	0.551
1889	0.183		1896	0.523
1890	0.165		1897	0.488
1891	0.161		1898	0.470
1892	0.202		1899	0.471

With the exception of one court, Anchor of Hope, almost all risk loading measures were positive and relatively large, sometimes greater than one. Court Pettiward showed a negative risk loading measure in its first year but positive values thereafter.

Table 6.4 shows estimates of the probability of ruin for five years for each court. The probability of ruin estimates are given in two formats: based on total income with assets excluded; and based on only member contributions as income. Ruin probabilities were also calculated using total income and assets, and the values were near zero for each court. The column excluding assets but including all other sources of income shows the estimated probability that a court's claims will exceed the income it receives from member contributions, interest, initiation fees, and other sources. The column calculated using just contributions shows the probability that a court's claims in a given year will be greater than member contributions. If a court were unable to translate its assets or income from investments into liquid assets, this column would reflect the actual probability of ruin, though it is likely that most courts had at least some immediate access to their assets.

Table 6.4: Sample Probability of Ruin Estimates.

Anchor of Hope			Pettiward		
Year	Pr (NA)	Pr (C)	Year	Pr (NA)	Pr (C)
1903	0.0001204	0.794	1904	0.00000183455	0.978
1904	0.00	0.862	1905	–	–
1905	0.0000193	0.802	1907	0.00000000002	0.050
1906	0.0000449	0.901	1908	0.00	0.081
1907	0.0001220	0.980	1909	0.00000000124	0.054

Equity			Brounlow		
Year	Pr (NA)	Pr (C)	Year	Pr (NA)	Pr (C)
1907	0.00	0.00000006	1882	0.00	0.000002708
1908	0.00	0.00000008	1883	0.0000000000078	0.000000204
1909	0.00	0.00000009	1884	0.0000000008	0.000000032
1910	0.00	0.00001824	1885	0.00	0.0000000002305
1911	0.00	0.00000301	1886	0.00	0.0000000000002

Pride of Reading			Eleanor Rummyn		
Year	Pr (NA)	Pr (C)	Year	Pr (NA)	Pr (C)
1907	0.00	0.00	1901	0.00	0.00087814
1908	0.00	0.000000003	1902	0.00	0.00246081
1909	0.00	0.00	1903	0.00	0.00112529
1910	0.00	0.00	1904	0.00	0.00337470
1911	0.00	0.00	1905	0.00	0.00671019

Prince of Wales			Perseverance		
Year	Pr (NA)	Pr (C)	Year	Pr (NA)	Pr (C)
1904	0.00	0.000000285	1889	0.0000004069	0.000647936190
1905	0.00	0.000000286	1890	0.0000000004	0.000049515204
1906	0.00	0.000003020	1891	0.0000000025	0.000000261688
1907	0.00	0.000000123	1892	0.00	0.000000032234
1908	0.00	0.000000768	1893	0.00	0.000000004679

Pr(NA) shows the probability of ruin with total income but no assets; Pr(C) shows ruin probabilities calculated with just income from contributions.

In both columns, with the exception of Anchor of Hope, probabilities of ruin are generally very small. With assets included, ruin probabilities are all zero; without assets, the largest ruin probability is 0.000122 for Anchor of Hope in 1907. Pettiward in its first year shows a ruin probability of 0.978 if only member contributions are included in the estimate, but it should be noted that Pettiward was a young court and did not have time to amass a large member base. It is notable that Pettiward's ruin probability decreased significantly with time, to just over 5 per cent within five years of existence. Taken in concert, the risk loading and probability of ruin estimates assert that the Foresters were much less financially insecure than assumed by the nineteenth century actuaries. Only one court, Anchor of Hope, shows signs of financial stress for the period.

Conclusions

Gilbert's hypothesis that the friendly societies in England acquiesced to calls for state pension schemes due to their impaired financial status is appealing for its clear delineation of cause and effect. It is tempting, in accordance with Gilbert's argument, to believe that the relative decline of the friendly societies around the turn of the twentieth century was due to shifting costs in the provision of insurance. While the results of this chapter are limited to a single society, the Ancient Order of Foresters, they still cast some doubt on the basis of Gilbert's argument – that the friendly societies were insolvent.

In our first test, we saw the dynamics that underlie Gilbert's argument at work. Membership in the Foresters was strongly correlated with age, suggesting that recruitment of younger members was more difficult in younger districts. This almost certainly placed financial strain on the Foresters. Our second test, however, showed another trend. Despite declining admissions and aging memberships, only one of our eight courts showed any sign of financial stress, and the others were strongly solvent.

If the friendly societies were solvent, then why did they register support for state pension schemes when they did? One obvious hypothesis is that the results here are wrong. Indeed, they only cover eight of several thousand courts and are by no means a wide sample of the friendly society population. Another, possibly more likely hypothesis is that the societies were unaware that they were solvent – that the panic of the moment led them to act as if they were insolvent when they actually were not. The results presented here, however, seem to suggest otherwise, at least in the case of the eight courts studied. Our estimates are based on data from local balance sheets, and any dramatic gesture to prevent bankruptcy, such as selling off court assets, would have been visible in the data. That no such evidence was found suggests that the seven courts we studied that were soundly solvent *knew* they were solvent. A third possibility is that the societies were hedging – they saw the non-contributory pensions provided by the 1908 Act as more desirable than the possibility of a contributory pension scheme. There are any number of other reasons why society members may have changed their minds on the state insurance question – perhaps some society leaders were encouraged by their wives to support a pension program that better benefited women. Testing these hypotheses is beyond the scope of this chapter and should be the terrain of future research. What we have accomplished here is not to provide an answer to the question of why the welfare state emerged when it did, with mild support from the friendly societies, but to cast new light on one popular hypothesis.

7 AMERICA'S REJECTION OF GOVERNMENT HEALTH INSURANCE IN THE PROGRESSIVE ERA: IMPLICATIONS FOR UNDERSTANDING THE DETERMINANTS AND ACHIEVEMENTS OF PUBLIC INSURANCE OF HEALTH RISKS

J. C. Herbert Emery

Between 1883 and 1920 many European countries introduced government health insurance through social insurance arrangements or state-promoted expansions of existing voluntary mutual-aid arrangements. Progressive reformers in the US interpreted state-provided health insurance as the necessary and inevitable response to the moral and economic inadequacies of voluntary insurance and self-help arrangements for protecting households against the consequences of sickness.[1] Given the developments in Europe and the introduction of Workers' Compensation in many states before World War 1, the reformers believed that government health insurance was the next step in social progress for the US.[2] At the initiative of the American Association for Labour Legislation (AALL) between 1915 and 1920, as many as eighteen US states investigated but rejected compulsory state health insurance (CHI). The AALL reformers and many scholars today consider this outcome to be a policy failure[3], one that is significant for explaining why there has been, and continues to be, so much opposition to the introduction of national health insurance in the US.[4]

If CHI was efficiency enhancing and stood to make some or all wage-workers better off, as the AALL reformers argued, why then were legislators and political 'brokers' unable to evoke the necessary political action for its introduction? Anderson[5] argues that the indifference of Americans towards compulsory health insurance in this early period left organized groups, such as doctors and life insurers with political clout and vested interests in the defeat of CHI, to determine the outcome. Social reformers, such as members of the AALL, interpreted public indifference to CHI as evidence that wage-workers were ignorant of their true needs for economic security, and/or ideologically driven to reject social insurance as 'un-American' despite their dire need for the programmes.

Fox[6] suggests that most scholars who have studied the failure of the United States to enact CHI have accepted the reformers' claims uncritically. Consequently the literature about the alleged failure of this early CHI movement emphasizes 'supply side' explanations for the adoption of government programmes: taking the existence of need or demand for the programme as given, the adoption/non-adoption reflects the capability of government to implement the social insurance.[7] A notable exception is Peter Lindert's work.[8] To explain 'American failure' on the social policy front, Rodgers[9] describes social-policy historians as engaged in a search for 'structures and materials distinctive to the United States'. Guided by the observation that the US appears to be the only western (developed) nation today without national health insurance, this search for exceptional characteristics inevitably settles on explanations that emphasize unique American ideology and/or institutional structures and/or interest group powers.[10] The argument follows that since these exceptional conditions that discourage the adoption of government health insurance are slow to change, the reasons for the rejection of CHI in this early period can also explain the absence of national health insurance today[11].

Rodgers[12] denies the existence of a 'special 'American idea' that is inhibitive to the adoption of social insurance'. While the US did not adopt CHI, Americans did introduce Worker's Compensation before 1920 and public old-age insurance in the 1930s[13]. Lubove[14] observes that worker's compensation programmes in the US demonstrated that social insurance could be adapted to voluntary values and institutions. Moss[15] argues that in the United States, 'the progressive concept of security – widely attacked as socialistic and un-American during the Progressive Era – has developed into one of the bulwarks of American public policy'.[16] If the rejection of CHI by Americans in this early period can be understood in terms of issues specific to CHI or to this early period – rather than to general American conceptions of the role of the state – then the failure of the AALL CHI movement is not part of a path-dependent process. As Moss[17] suggests, changing economic conditions in the United States could lead Americans to reassess American social welfare institutions, including the possible benefits of national health insurance.

The literature has been dismissive of an alternative view of the need for CHI in the US put forward by 'moneyed interests' (as AALL reformers named them) such as business organizations, employers' associations and insurance companies, who opposed the introduction of CHI in the progressive era. These groups argued that CHI was unnecessary due to the superior earning power of American wage-workers relative to their European counterparts. Americans had a greater capacity to save and to purchase insurance coverage through voluntary arrangements. From this perspective, for government action on CHI to have been politically profitable for legislators and political brokers, significant failures in private markets must have existed, therefore making CHI a wealth enhancing, institutional alternative to the market.

Emery[18] shows that the AALL's proposed CHI contract was an expensive duplication of insurance available through voluntary avenues. Emery further shows that – contrary to the claims and evidence of the AALL reformers – American wage-workers could insure against sickness without CHI. Further, the capacity to self-insure or to purchase insurance coverage increased over the life cycle, and for wage-workers under age forty, it increased between the late nineteenth century and 1920. Emery demonstrates that the differences in savings rates across US states are informative for explaining why some US states pursued commissions, investigations and, in some cases, legislation toward the introduction of CHI while others showed no interest in the arrangement.

If these observations are informative for explaining the political failure of the CHI movement in the United States, it follows that wage-workers in nations that have introduced CHI should have greater measurable needs or demand for government health insurance than American wage earners. Following Emery's approach to measuring household savings capacities with data for 1888–90 for five European nations[19], I present evidence that in Germany and Belgium, which introduced government health insurance and subsidies for health insurance early, households did not have the same capacity to self-insure as the UK, France, Switzerland and the US, which saw much later development of government action on health insurance. This work suggests the importance of insurance capacities of individuals and labour market contexts for understanding the rise of public insurance for health risks.

The Historical Background for Compulsory State Health Insurance in the US

During the nineteenth and early-twentieth centuries, lost income due to illness was one of the greatest risks to the standard of living for a wage earner's household in North America and Europe.[20] Consequently before 1920, sickness/health insurance was for income stabilization, which was thought to be useful for the prevention of poverty.[21] Prior to the introduction of state health insurance programmes in Europe, similar 'patchworks of protection'[22] – issuing from mutual-aid organizations, trade unions, commercial insurers, discretionary charity and self-reliance through thrift – were available to workers on both sides of the Atlantic.[23] Reformers and many scholars concluded that the obvious shortcomings of voluntary arrangements were the impetus for government involvement in social insurance arrangements.[24]

Proponents of state social insurance and most scholarly examinations of voluntary methods of self-help in Europe, England and North America conclude that the patchwork system of voluntary income protection was 'woefully inadequate'[25] if not a 'dismal failure for meeting the economic and medical needs of a populace'[26]. Lubove[27] cites Rubinow's assessment that voluntary mutual aid had been 'tried and found wanting'. Rodgers[28] describes the voluntary mutual assistance arrangements in the North Atlantic economy as 'both a fixture of everyday life and inadequate to it, far-flung and full of holes'. Critics of voluntary insurance arrangements allege that self-help organizations like the friendly societies were plagued by financial problems associated with aging memberships,[29] and could never have been relied on to cover the poorest classes of workingmen most in need of protection.[30]

Between 1883 and 1914 several nations in Europe used the administrative machinery of friendly societies and other mutual-aid organizations as the vehicle for introducing and delivering compulsory (government) sickness/health insurance.[31] Compulsory health insurance arrangements implemented by government (and as proposed in the US) closely resembled the contracts of the voluntary mutual-aid organizations.[32] Important differences between the voluntary arrangements and compulsory (government) arrangements were the sources of finance, the extent of coverage in the population, and the coverage of medical services costs. Government health-insurance coverage included prime aged workers under an income ceiling and typically excluded the self-employed, agricultural workers, and often, dependents of workers.

In contrast to the developments in Europe, governments in the US showed little activity on the health/sickness insurance field prior to World War 1, even though the voluntary sickness insurance arrangements of friendly societies declined from at least the 1890s, despite growing memberships in the organizations up to the 1920s.[33] The origin of the compulsory (government) health insurance (CHI) movement in the United States was the formation of the American Association for Labor Legislation (AALL) in 1906, which by 1913 had 3,300 members consisting largely of academics, academic physicians, intellectuals and social reformers.[34] The AALL interpreted the lack of CHI in the US as evidence that the nation was a social laggard in a natural and inevitable evolution from deficient voluntary arrangements.[35] Fisher[36] argues that while 'the most enlightened and progressive nations of the world have, one after another, adopted compulsory health insurance', the US could be grouped with European countries without government health insurance: Italy, Spain, Portugal, Greece, Bulgaria, Albania, Montenegro and Turkey.[37]

The first steps towards CHI came with an AALL committee report in 1912 that recommended some form of insurance to offset income losses associated with accident and illness. By 1914 the AALL had drafted model legislation for a public health insurance system that could be used by states interested in introducing legislation. Between 1915 and 1920, as many as eighteen US states investigated Compulsory Health Insurance.[38] Anderson[39] argues that the AALL movement peaked in 1918. According to Paul Starr[40], a movement for health insurance did not exist in the 1920s. With the dire conditions of the 1930s, the interest in government health insurance was re-invigorated, but unlike the earlier era, the discussions of health insurance shifted away from insuring income loss and towards the coverage of physician services and hospitalization.

Given that AALL reformers expected gains for industrial wage-workers from CHI to be large enough to mobilize workers' interests and thus aid in the passage of CHI, they were surprised by the indifference of the general public to their cause.[41] Given their belief in the shortcomings of voluntary arrangements, including the capacity of households to save, AALL reformers asserted that wage-workers needed social insurance. With the AALL proposal that employers and states pay 60 per cent of the cost of insurance, AALL reformers argued that workers would pay a fraction of the cost of a generous level of health and sickness insurance coverage. CHI would extend insurance coverage to the lowest paid and most vulnerable of the wage-earning classes.[42] The AALL reformers interpreted the greater extent of coverage in the compulsory systems as a success of such arrangements over the voluntary insurance systems.[43]

Opponents of CHI proposed higher wages, voluntary thrift, voluntary insurance and public health initiatives as workable alternatives to state insurance. In the view of the National Civic Federation, an alliance of American employers and conservative labour leaders:

> American workers were too well-off to require such a system (like the British insurance system) ... British workers were so low paid that the Insurance Act is a boon to them [but] prosperous American workers would reject similar assistance from the state ... the economic condition of the average American workman enables him to provide for medical attendance and pecuniary support during sickness in his own way and at his own cost.[44]

Labour market opportunities, earnings and the ability to accumulate wealth differed between American workers and European workers. Americans on average were wealthier than their European counterparts. Haines and Goodman[45] find that there were higher rates of home ownership in the US, and higher levels of wealth. There was a more egalitarian distribution of wealth in the US than in the UK.[46] American workers benefited from a labour market that produced higher income levels, higher income growth rates and lower risk of unemployment. Costa[47] argues that the costs of sickness before 1930 could be handled by 'thrifty' middle and upper income households, who relied on savings, while lower income households could rely on charity, friends and neighbours.

A major challenge for the reformers pushing for health insurance for Americans, suggests Hoffman[48] was that they had to 'defend the very idea that the United States had grave industrial problems comparable to Europe's. The reformers interpreted the economic insecurity of wage-workers as an inherent feature of industrial development, and social insurance as an obvious solution for the wage-worker's situation[49]. Rubinow claimed that American workers lived with the risk of more accidents, more sickness, more premature old age and invalidity, and more unemployment than wage-workers in most European countries. While the wages of Americans were higher than those of European workers, the reformers believed they were still inadequate for American households to accumulate and protect themselves against economic hardship from events like sickness, unemployment, old age and invalidity.[50]

Reformers argued that transitory economic boom conditions, particularly in the 1920s, caused Americans to lose 'sight of their true need for social insurance', resulting in a setback for the movement towards social insurance and social legislation in the United States.[51] Douglas[52] also notes this possibility with respect to savings for old age:

> The consensus of public opinion was that American citizens could in the main provide for their own old age by individual savings ... the upward surge of the stock market, was a powerful force holding back all protective legislation while the rise in real wages lulled the majority of the working class into a condition of more or less acquiescent satisfaction.

Rubinow[53] claims that the American wage-earning family did not have the necessary surplus in their budget to save for the 'rainy day' or to buy the insurance that they needed.[54] The AALL's view of the American family's inability to save in order to address income risks was not an evaluation of the actual saving experiences of households. Rather Rubinow[55] judges the high level of American wages in relation to the American cost of living and the 'American Standard of life'. Indeed he compares American wages against what the American standard of living 'ought to be' – not how the majority of the working class lived, but the standard that existed for some wage-workers and to which all workingmen could aspire. Accumulation, savings or extra income could not provide legitimate protection if they were not the product of one earner per household and if the other standards of decency in consumption were not met.[56] According to Rubinow[57] a large majority of wage-workers had insufficient income to maintain a 'normal' standard of living and to have a surplus, hence 'saving for all possible future emergencies must necessarily mean a very substantial reduction of a standard already sub-normal'. Over time scholars came to interpret this notion of a minimum standard of decency in consumption as an insufficiency of income to meet subsistence needs.[58]

To maintain a proper standard of living, Rubinow assesses that 'families having from $900 to $1,000 a year are able, in general, to get food enough to keep body and soul together, and clothing and shelter enough to meet the most urgent demands of decency'.[59] He estimates that 90 per cent of males living east of the Rockies and north of the Mason-Dixon line earned less than $800 a year and that 95 per cent of female workers earned less than two-thirds of the amount necessary for 'physical efficiency and decent existence'. According to the reformers, conditions of working Americans got worse, not better, after World War 1. Where the general statistical pattern was believed to have shown dramatic increases in wages between 1866 and 1900, Rubinow[60] presents indices showing that real weekly earnings were not rising between 1890 and 1907 because of falling hours of work and rising food costs. Epstein concludes that:

> in the last decade only very few of our workers have earned enough to maintain for themselves and their families a decent American standard of living ... They have rarely been able to meet fully the day-by-day expenses of decent living, let alone laying aside any savings against rainy days'.[61]

In the minds of the reformers, a growing American economy was not going to solve the problems of the working class and eliminate the need for social insurance.

Modern-Scholarly and Contemporary Appraisals of the AALL CHI Movement

Scholarly interpretations of the failure of the AALL health insurance movement side with the AALL view of the superiority of compulsory government arrangements over voluntary arrangements. The conclusion follows that the lack of CHI in the United States represents a policy failure, since wage-workers would have been better off with CHI than with voluntary arrangements for meeting the costs of illness. To explain this policy failure, scholars have looked to distinctive features of American society, such as ideology, political institutions and interest groups. As these features of society are slow to change, the interpretation follows that the reasons for rejecting CHI are informative for understanding why the US remains the only advanced industrial nation without national health insurance. This class of explanations for the failure of the AALL CHI movement has failed to produce a satisfactory explanation, and the reason likely rests with AALL views on the needs of American wage-workers, views that have directed the scholarly investigations.

Rubinow[62] blames the failure of the AALL health insurance movement on the failure of reformers to educate labour 'to appreciation of its own interests'[63] and thus enable it to overcome its ideological biases against social insurance.[64] Labourers mistakenly believed that health insurance was 'un-American', fearing it would subvert individual initiative and self-reliance. After World War 1 they also accepted opponents' arguments that health insurance was too 'socialist' and too 'Prussian'.[65] According to Numbers[66], anti-Prussian sentiment was an important reason that the AALL followed the British approach of calling their proposed arrangement 'health insurance', rather than using the German term for the arrangement, 'sickness insurance', even though the AALL had modelled their proposed CHI legislation on the German rather than the British system.

These American ideological biases were not as exceptional as the literature suggests. Rodgers[67] notes that the American debates over social insurance were similar to the 'polarized rhetorical contests in Germany in the 1880s and in Britain after 1908'. Gilbert[68] argues that the Victorian ethics of self-reliance and *laissez-faire* were important impediments to the introduction of old-age pensions and health insurance in England in the last quarter of the nineteenth century, but that they were overcome by World War 1. Rodgers[69] notes the irony that Bismarck had introduced social insurance as an 'antisocialist' project, but that in the United States in the AALL campaign for compulsory health insurance, it was a reframed as a 'socialist' demand.

Moss[70] argues that CHI threatened special interests more than other forms of labour legislation.[71] Fraternal insurers opposed CHI since the model legislation excluded them as possible insurance carriers, and commercial-life insurers feared that funeral benefits in CHI would undermine the demand for their industrial insurance.[72] Scholars have identified doctors, organized through the American Medical Association, as providing the strongest opposition to state sponsored health insurance before 1920, even though physicians could anticipate enriched incomes if the state assumed responsibility for paying for physician services.[73] While many labour leaders expressed support for compulsory health insurance, Samuel Gompers, President of the American Federation of Labor, opposed compulsory insurance based on his belief that higher wages would solve workers' problems arising from illness.[74] Sombart[75] argues that the exceptional social mobility of American workers diminished their interest in socialism generally. Since American wage-workers could expect large gains in their material well-being because the benefits of growth were shared between labour and capital, they had less reason to look to the State to improve their well-being.[76]

Once again, these claims about interest group responses to the proposed CHI legislation for US states were not unique to the US. Rodgers[77] argues that mixed and ambivalent attitudes towards compulsory social insurance on the part of organized labour were not unique to the United States. Before 1914, labour organizations were not a significant force in the adoption of social insurance or involved in the design of the schemes. Labour organizations throughout the North Atlantic economy resisted the levies on wage-workers that social insurance required.

In the policy-failure interpretation of the absence of government health insurance in the US, scholars argue that political power is too decentralized in the US to facilitate introduction of government health insurance and other large-scale social programmes.[78] Starr[79] observes that the US had universal male suffrage early in its history, whereas CHI was introduced first in authoritarian and paternalistic regimes and only later in liberal democratic societies. Beland and Hacker[80] note that the United States has never been as centralized as European nation states, in part because its constitutional structure divides political power so as to discourage the construction of authoritative majorities and powerful bureaucracies. In this context, constitutional limits have prevented the federal government from introducing national health insurance and constrained state government actions.[81] Moss[82] argues that the threat of a 'competitive disadvantage' for states that introduced CHI compared to states that did not was a critical impediment for the CHI movement. A puzzle remains, however, as to why these institutions would be barriers to the development of compulsory health insurance, but not to public pension legislation in 1935, nor to workers' compensation laws before World War 1.

As Lubove[83] argues, Worker's Compensation demonstrated the ability of interest groups to adapt their private ends to a collective welfare programne, whereas the failed campaign for CHI reflected the mobilization of resources by these same interests to thwart a form of social insurance from which they anticipated no material advantages. For employers, CHI would have introduced a liability rather than shifting an existing liability as under Worker's Compensation.[84] AALL reformers expected social insurance, as exemplified by CHI, to redirect market forces so that employers would profit by preventing the leading sources of poverty, industrial accidents, disease and unemployment[85] By internalizing the external costs of industrial society, social insurance was akin to a Pigouvian tax whereby the employer's liability for workman's compensation and unemployment benefits was an incentive to provide a safer, healthier workplace and regularize employment.[86] The expected outcome of social-insurance-induced incentives for prevention would be a society with reduced incidences of disease, accident and idleness and with gains for employers, workers, their families and communities that paid poor relief.[87] The failure of the AALL CHI movement suggests that interested parties were not convinced by the line of argument that social insurance would reduce their costs through the prevention of disease and illness.[88]

Was CHI Likely to have been Welfare Enhancing for Americans?

Was it true that American wage-workers' incomes were insufficient for households to save, or to allow households to purchase sickness/health insurance through voluntary arrangements, as the AALL reformers alleged? Emery's comparison of the AALL proposed CHI contract with the voluntary IOOF sickness insurance contract[89] shows that CHI – with its higher cost insurance – was intended to benefit lower wage-workers who chose not to purchase lower-cost voluntary sickness insurance. Rodgers[90] describes how some proponents of compulsory health insurance in the United States viewed social insurance, like CHI, as nothing more than a complicated scheme for compulsory savings. The main purpose of CHI would have been to compel wage-workers to purchase higher levels of insurance coverage. Whether compulsory savings benefitted households would depend on whether or not they were otherwise unable to meet the expected costs of sickness.

Emery[91] uses income and expenditure data from the US Dept of Labor survey, 'Cost of Living of Industrial Workers in the United States and Europe, 1888–1890'[92], and from the US Dept of Labor, Bureau of Labor Statistics survey, 'Cost of Living in the United States, 1917–1919'[93]. As compulsory health insurance would primarily have covered male household heads, Emery considers the size of the household surplus (total income minus total expenditures) relative to the husband's income to measure a savings rate that would be comparable to the percentage of earnings that would have been deducted for CHI coverage.[94] He focuses on median values of savings rates since the distribution of household surpluses is skewed in favor of high incomes resulting in high mean values for incomes and savings.

Emery[95] compares the median savings rates for US households by age-group of the household head in 1888–90 and 1917–19 to the expected income loss due to sickness. The median savings rates for 1888–90 for males under age forty were low, at below 2.5 per cent, while for males over age forty, savings rates increased to over 5 per cent and reached almost 10 per cent for households with heads aged in their fifties. Despite the low savings rate for males under age forty, the expected percentage loss of income from sickness was less than 1 per cent of income; and as the size of the expected loss increased with age, so did the savings capacity of American households. This increase in savings capacity over the life cycle would have weakened demand for CHI, since younger wage-workers would rationally expect that even if surpluses were small, they would rise in the future. As Emery and Emery[96] argue, the demand for sickness insurance in North America was a transitory demand that disappeared over the life cycle as the capacity to self-insure through savings and additional workers in the family developed.

Based on J.C.H. Emery's estimates of savings rates, a CHI premium of 4 per cent would have removed any income surplus for most households with heads under age forty. This level of premium would in all likelihood have resulted in a reduced standard of living for insured households due to the high cost of the insurance. As Costa[97] suggests, CHI was an expensive substitute for what workers already had. CHI would have locked Americans into saving for a single purpose for the length of their working lives. The commitment of so much of household income to the insurance of a single risk was not necessarily desirable. Unlike CHI, the household's savings could be used for covering any losses of income due to illness, or unemployment.[98]

Did the capacity of American wage-workers to save and meet sickness-related costs deteriorate after 1888–90 as the reformers claimed? Emery[99] finds that estimates of household savings rates in 1917–19 for males under age forty had increased substantially. Even by the standards of the reformers, the condition of wage-workers' households had improved, as these higher savings rates were accomplished with less reliance on income from working children.[100] As Weaver[101] has argued for Old Age Insurance, the need for CHI was falling between 1889 and 1920. The same forces of economic growth behind those developments were also at work with compulsory health insurance.

While households may have had annual surpluses large enough to meet the expected costs of sickness, CHI could have improved their ability to meet infrequent but large sickness costs.[102] In this case, the annual savings rate is less informative than information on a household's wealth. A reserve equal to 33 per cent of annual income was equivalent to the maximum cash benefits that CHI – as proposed by AALL – would have provided. Rubinow[103] assesses that the numbers of savings and other time-deposit accounts suggest that over 40 per cent of the population had accumulated savings, and that the average account size was $500. Rubinow argues that Epstein's 'careful statistical work'[104] shows that – as the bulk of the value of aggregate savings in the US was not that of 'workingmen' but of the 'middle class'– a better estimate of the average-size account for the workingman who did save was under $200. With annual incomes of $1200 reported by Epstein[105] for the late 1920s, these estimates of aggregate savings would represent a reserve equal to 14–33 per cent of average income. It is possible that CHI's coverage for 'catastrophic costs' would have represented an improvement over what workers had through voluntary arrangements, but it is also important to recognize that savings deposits are only one possible savings vehicle. Without knowing how much other wealth was accumulated by workingmen in the form of equity in the home, consumer durables like furniture and so forth, one can only guess that the reformers' case was pessimistic.

Were American Savings Rates Exceptional?

Emery[106] concludes that, for many American households, CHI would not have provided anything over what they had available from voluntary arrangements for meeting the sickness risk. Emery also shows that variations in savings rates across US states are informative for explaining why some US states pursued commissions, investigations, and in some cases, legislation, toward the introduction of CHI while others showed no interest in the arrangement. If these observations are informative for explaining the political failure of the CHI movement in the United States, then it should be the case that wage-workers in nations that introduced CHI did not have the same capacities in their budgets as their American counterparts to save and/or purchase voluntary insurance to address the income risks of illness.

Following Emery's construction of household surpluses[107], Table 7.1 presents the median values for household (total) income, the husband's income and the household surplus for the US and five European countries from the 1888–90 cost-of-living data described in the previous section. Unfortunately, for Germany, France, Belgium and Switzerland, the sample sizes are relatively small which are limitations for making statistical inferences.

Table 7.1. Median Incomes, Surpluses, Sickness and Death Expenditures and Savings Rates for US and European Households, 1888–90.

	Obser-vations	Total Income ($)	Husband's income ($)	Husband's Income/ Total Income	Household Surplus ($)	Sickness and Death Expenses ($)	Surplus/ Total Income	Surplus/ Husband's income	Sickn and D Expens Husba incon
Germany	142	272	225	0.83	-0.23	3.75	-0.001	-0.001	0.
Belgium	104	339	211	0.62	-0.3	1.93	-0.001	-0.001	0.
France	319	345	241	0.7	11.73	0.68	0.034	0.049	0.
Great Britain	1001	462	370	0.8	16.31	2.43	0.035	0.044	0.
Switzerland	52	340	181	0.53	9.15	7.72	0.027	0.051	0.
United States	5608	572	448	0.78	9.68	12	0.017	0.022	0.

Notes: The surplus measure is total household income less total expenditures reported. The surplus is divided by the husband's income to calculate the savings rate. The median savings rate was determined and reported in this Table. Observations with missing values for income or expenditures have been dropped from the set of observations used to calculate median values. All incomes and expenditures are reported in the 1888–90 survey as US dollars. Values denominated in national currencies were converted to US dollars using exchange rates between the currency and US dollars.

As opponents of CHI argued, American incomes were higher than incomes in Europe; and as proponents of CHI argued, the higher incomes were not generating unusually high surpluses for American families compared to lower- earning Europeans. Table 7.1 shows that, for American households in 1888–90, the median value of this measure of the savings rate was 2.2 per cent; so at least half of the households in the sample were able to set aside enough current income to meet the full wage loss associated with the expected spell of sickness or to purchase a voluntary contract.[108] In contrast Germany, where CHI was introduced in 1883, had a median savings rate of 0 per cent, as did Belgium, where subsidies to extend voluntary coverage were used after 1894. It is possible that premiums paid for health insurance in Germany since 1883 eliminated any surplus that households might have had in the absence of CHI. France, Great Britain and Switzerland – nations which did not move towards state insurance until after 1900 – all had median savings rates twice as high as that for the US. It is important to recognize that American households were generating budget surpluses even after incurring expenses related to sickness. American households had higher expenditures reported in the survey category 'sickness and death'. The median expenditure in this category for the US was $12 where European households expended less than $5. If we consider these expenditures as those that would be covered under CHI, then the median size of household surplus and expenditures on sickness and death suggests that American households represented almost 5 per cent of the husband's income in 1888–90.

Table 7.2 presents median savings rates by five-year age groups for the US, Great Britain and Germany in 1889–90. Switzerland, France and Belgium are also included but along with Germany, there are small numbers of observations for these countries in the 1888–90 data for the age groups. Where the median savings rates for the US and Great Britain are positive for all age groups and rising above 5 per cent after age forty, the median savings rates for Germany are, in most cases, negative for ages below fifty-five. Thus in Germany, not only were savings rates low overall, but wage earners would have had little expectation that this situation would improve over the life cycle. There are two possible interpretations of this finding. First, without life-cycle savings and wealth accumulation, German wage earners would not have had the same self-insurance capacity for sickness risk as their counterparts in the US and UK, a circumstance that would have maintained their need for insurance contracts over their lifetimes. Aging populations would have resulted in growing demand for insurance in Germany. Alternatively, the absence of savings in German households could be caused by compulsory insurance costs eliminating any surplus in the budget. The consequent impairment of life-cycle savings that is demonstrated in Table 7.2 suggests the costs of public coverage of one risk could create the need for subsequent public insurance of other needs such as pensions.

Table 7.2. Median Savings Rates for US and European Households by 5-Year Age Group, 1888–90.

	United States		Great Britain		Germany		France		Switzerland		Belgium
	Savings rate	N	Savings rate	N	Savings rate	N	Savings rate	N	Savings rate	N	Savings rate
20–24	0.7%	277	0.0%	37	27.6%	4	4.8%	3	49.5%	1	9.5%
25–29	2.1%	742	1.9%	101	0.1%	25	8.8%	51	-7.0%	2	-7.4%
30–34	1.2%	1001	1.9%	184	0.0%	27	1.3%	44	-16.6%	9	-1.5%
35–39	1.3%	953	2.4%	206	-5.2%	24	0.8%	54	7.9%	2	0.6%
40–44	2.8%	785	6.5%	157	1.3%	18	9.4%	41	9.1%	7	-15.2%
45–49	6.2%	619	9.7%	105	-0.9%	21	4.6%	35	14.4%	16	-1.9%
50–54	5.7%	417	16.7%	110	-2.8%	7	26.9%	27	7.5%	2	4.9%
55–59	7.5%	249	11.3%	37	11.7%	4	25.0%	17	-22.3%	4	9.4%
60+	4.6%	220	6.3%	35	-1.5%	10	13.6%	17	-24.0%	2	28.6%

Notes: N is the number of observations for the age group in a given country. See notes for Table 7.1, above for explanation of the calculation of the median savings rates.

The savings estimates in Tables 7.1 and 7.2 for France, Switzerland and the UK suggest that the timing of these nations adopting government health insurance arrangements could be a product of diminishing savings capacities of households in their economies after 1890. According to Gilbert,[109] friendly society opposition and a lack of working-class enthusiasm prevented the introduction of a contributory pension plan in England in 1890, but a non-contributory pension plan was implemented eighteen years later, as friendly society opposition weakened with growing financial difficulties due to ageing memberships. Gilbert[110] also indicates that by 1905, pension legislation was perceived as a good way to buy votes.

Conclusions

Murray[111] finds that the network of voluntary insurance arrangements served American wage earners well before 1930 and this must explain the lack of demand for government health insurance in this early period. Consistent with Murray's view, the discussion presented in this chapter suggests that CHI was rejected in the United States before 1930 because not enough American workers expected to benefit from it to generate the necessary political support. In this early period, the costs of sickness were frequent, but manageable for most wage earners through voluntary insurance contracts and self-insurance. This conclusion suggests some new interpretations for the normative assessment of voluntary insurance as unconditionally deficient for meeting income security needs and compulsory government insurance as unconditionally superior to voluntary schemes.

In contrast to CHI, voluntary insurance coverage for sickness may not have been an end in itself for risk mitigation, but instead a means by which household self-reliance developed over the life cycle.[112] Voluntary insurance arrangements for sickness risks were contingent claims – forms of precautionary savings for which self-insurance through savings or accumulated wealth was a substitute. Over the life cycle, the demand for precautionary savings for health insurance will be altered by two influences of aging. First, the increasing risk of sickness that accompanies aging will increase the demand for insurance. Second, the accumulation of wealth/reserves for life-cycle savings motives will develop an individual's capacity for self-insurance as a by-product as he ages and accumulates wealth for consumption in retirement. Whether or not the demand for third-party insurance (from private or public sources) increases with age depends upon which of these two influences dominates.[113]

Rodgers[114] describes how some proponents of compulsory health insurance in the United States viewed such a programme as nothing more than a complicated scheme for compulsory savings. As a contingent claim contract, CHI would have locked households into saving for a single purpose for the breadwinner's working life. In contrast to a lower-cost, lower-benefit voluntary contract that could be discontinued, the compulsory purchase of a generous insurance contract could have undermined the capacity of households to accumulate wealth over the life cycle, resulting in diminished consumption later in life. Lee[115] demonstrates that precautionary savings declined in importance for American households over the twentieth century as life-cycle savings motives became more important, along with the rise of modern retirement patterns. Lee argues that the accumulation of wealth by American households provided insurance through an annuitization of income; whereas government insurance in England and much of Europe built on, or at least resembled, the existing network of voluntary private insurance arrangements. This suggests that the rise of compulsory state social insurance in Britain and other parts of Europe represents a response to an increase in demand for precautionary savings in aging populations and an expansion and entrenchment of voluntary precautionary savings arrangements as exemplified by mutual-aid organizations.

Health insurance in this earlier era was for income stabilization, which was thought to be useful for the prevention of poverty. The costs of sickness and poor health include lost income; direct medical costs of hospitals, physician care and medicine; and for society, lost productivity. Up to 1920, lost income was the important risk for workers, and voluntary insurance was effective for managing this risk. Medical costs were rising after 1920, and the significant cost by the 1940s was due to technical changes in medical treatment, the organization of care around hospitals and the growing strength of medical associations in North America.[116] Armstrong[117] reports that in 1915, for government health insurance arrangements, the proportion of health insurance benefits paid in cash versus 'in kind' ranged from 42–98 per cent. By the late 1920s, these proportions ranged from 16–56 per cent. With this shift in the nature of the costs associated with sickness, health insurance contracts changed to address direct medical costs that carried the risk of catastrophic loss (enormous costs). Later health insurance movements in the United States and the centralization of health care administration in countries with health insurance addressed direct medical costs rather than income loss.[118] And, as Murray[119] describes, commercial insurance with different actuarial technologies grew after the 1930s in the US, while voluntary insurance arrangements went into decline. The advantages of smaller, local insurance arrangements for efficiently insuring small, regular wage losses may have been disadvantages for the efficient insurance of irregular, large losses, which needed greater pooling of risk in the population and more centralization in insurance administration.

Acknowledgements

This work was funded by SSHRC Research Grant 410–2005–0529.

8 MEDICAL ASSISTANCE PROVIDED BY *LA CONCILIACIÓN*, A PAMPLONA MUTUAL ASSISTANCE ASSOCIATION (1902–84)

Pilar León-Sanz

Obligatory insurance was introduced in Spain in the 1940s. Until that time, a high percentage of workers and their families entrusted healthcare to the Mutual Assistance Societies, Mutual Insurance Associations and other private institutions. For this reason, analysis of the assistance offered by these organizations during ill health is of interest.

Mutual benefit societies were voluntary associations whose members participated in management and administration. Profits belonged to the members as a whole and were distributed following statutes or regulations. In general, these organizations were classified following the ideological inspiration of their sponsors and their social composition.[1] In the first third of the twentieth century there were numerous mutual benefit societies in Spain, which gave social and heath care to much of the population.

The interest in the study of mutualism and its evolution with reference to the introduction of Obligatory Heath Insurance and the National Health has been underlined.[2] Particularly in Spain, the meagre budget provided for the *Instituto Nacional de Previsión* (INP) from its creation (1908) was the reason for reliance on the Mutual Benefit Societies and other private associations to organize precautionary measures for workers and their families.[3]

The evolution of the system and identity of a Mutual Benefit Society: the 'Sociedad Protectora de Obreros *La Conciliación*' from its beginning in 1902 until 1984, reflects the medical-social reforms carried out in the country during this period, and provides us with an opportune viewing point for understanding the complexity of the introduction of the Social Security system. It also permits us to see how healthcare was provided for a great part of the society.

The chapter analyses, on the one hand, the *Conciliación* until the Spanish Civil War. During this decades, this Society was the most important Mutual Assistance Association in Pamplona, the capital of a region in northern Spain. Until 1936, the structure's changes were connected to the world of labour more than the regulations on Public Health or labour safety; the organization gave medical-assistance cover for the common illnesses of the workers and their families, and this was of a subsidiary nature. Political structures changed the Association's membership to one exclusively for workers.

During the years prior to the 1936–9 Civil War, a new healthcare system was being formulated, with the help of the organized workers' movement and that of a group of healthcare professionals who were prepared to bring medical care 'to the furthest and most modest villages of the motherland', as was stated at the First National Health Congress in 1934. But, in fact, the introduction of the Obligatory Health Insurance had to wait until the 1940s.

The last part of the chapter deals with the changes in the Mutual Assistance Association *La Conciliación* from the end of the Spanish Civil War until the disappearance of the association in 1984. The outbreak of the Spanish Civil War, in 1936, made a difference, as, from then on, the organization underwent major changes, both in the number of members and in its structure. In spite of the changes, *La Conciliación* maintained a strong sense of its own particular identity throughout the years.

What makes the case of the *La Conciliación* so interesting is the high number of members and the length of time the organization lasted (1902–84). Up to 1936, there were always over 1,000 worker members, that is to say, close to one third of the working population of the city.[4] However, the call-up during the war resulted in a drop of 200 members during the second half of 1936 and in 1937. The reduction of members continued until its disappearance.

The beginning of the Sociedad Protectora de Obreros *La Conciliación*

The 'Sociedad Protectora de Obreros *La Conciliación*' was founded in Pamplona in 1902, as a mixed society, made up by worker, employer and protector members with labour, healthcare and economic objectives.[5] The 'Sociedad de Obreros *La Conciliación*' was the result of the social action of the Roman Catholic Church, based on Pope Leon XIII's Encyclical on social justice, *Rerum novarum* (1891).[6]

La Conciliación was formed by workers' associations from every trade, together with employer associations and the protector members. There were workers' guilds for bricklayers, carpenters, locksmiths, weavers, stonemasons, cobblers, unskilled labourers, farmers, tailors, shop-assistants, bakers, typographers, painters, chocolate makers and miscellaneous. Gradually, the guilds with fewer members merged and were joined by new ones, for example from the chemical industry, in 1928. Both the workers and the employers had to live within 10 km of the city.[7]

The main services offered by the Society were: labour mediation, assistance for the worker members and their families through economic subsidy, medical attendance, pharmaceutical service (beginning in 1910), the Chronic Fund (beginning in 1914) and the midwifery service (beginning in 1914); post-mortem aid (beginning in 1918); it also had a Savings Bank and a cooperative (between 1912 and 1922). It organized educational and recreational activities in addition. *La Conciliación* was part of the medical healthcare network in the city. From this Society established relations with other local and national organizations.

This study is based on the documents from the Society archive: all the Books of Minutes from 1902 to 1984, as well as the regulations, accounts, correspondence, etc.

Changes in *La Conciliación* Structure (1902–36): the Worker Members' Demands and the Political Requirements

At the start, *La Conciliación* was governed by the so-called Mixed Board with eighteen members, six from each group (workers, employers and protectors). And although the most important activity of the organization was healthcare for the worker members and their families, the first demands for change were due to the social-labour character of *La Conciliación*. So, from 1911 on, the members demanded greater involvement in the Mixed Board. These demands and industrial disputes increased simultaneously. In Pamplona, as in the rest of Spain, industrial disputes increased from 1911 to a high point in 1920, which was the year with most disputes in the history of Spain until 1936.

In 1917, the insistent claims of the worker members led to the first modification of the structure of the Mixed Board, as they were not happy with the same six-person representation for each member group. The protests produced new regulations and abolished the representation of the employers. This came into effect in January 1920. *La Conciliación* continued with its industrial arbitration now between the workers' guilds –who demanded better wages and working hours – and the Association of Employers. Strangely enough, it was at times like these that most agreements were reached and not when the employer members were 'conciliated'.

The directors of the workers' guilds went on demanding that 'the presidents of every Guild should have a say' on the Mixed Board.[8] And after several attempts and much bargaining, in 1922, they found another, not yet definitive, solution: all the Guild Masters could attend the meetings of the Mixed Board, although only half of them had voting rights.[9]

Between 1922 and 1926, the legislation of the times intended to strengthen local governments and, simultaneously, the new labour regulations, as the continuation of the ancient guilds, supported the trade corporations and established the creation of workers Associations.[10] Therefore, in March 1925, the Minutes record the necessity of new regulations for the Society, so that the members could stand for the posts of councillors foreseen in the Municipal Statute. The approval process of the new regulation again made the tensions between the worker members and the protector members blatantly obvious.[11] The misunderstanding was cleared up over the following months.[12] But distrust again appeared when a worker member proposed that both worker and protector members should be allowed to take office as President of the Society.[13]

During the first few days of August 1925, exceptional meetings were called for the approval of three regulations: one for the *Asociación Protectora de Obreros La Conciliación* (Workers Protection Association), another for the professional societies which would replace the ancient guilds and a third for the worker Mutual Benefit fund of *La Conciliación*, which corresponded to the former Aid Fund. All three were later ratified by the Bishop of the diocese[14] and the Civil Governor of the province in early 1926. The result of this change was that *La Conciliación* underwent a threefold transformation: 'La Asociación Protectora de Obreros de Pamplona *La Conciliación*' became 'Sociedades Obreras de *La Conciliación*'; the guilds became the 'Professional Societies' for each trade, and the 'Reglamento de la Caja de Socorros' was, from 1926, the 'Reglamento de la Mutualidad Obrera de la Asociación de Sociedades Obreras de *La Conciliación*'. The Mixed Board also received a new title, and was now called the Superior Management Board of *La Conciliación*. The apparent continuity of the Society can be seen in the fact that the Management Board was composed of protector members and workers.

The 1926 Regulations were an indispensable step towards the changes which occurred later. Also significant is that it was the worker members who were responsible for the new regime. And it is worth mentioning that less dependence on the Church was proposed for the Society.

The 1928 Regulations: the Split in the Mutual Benefit Society

More in-depth and general was the reorganization based on the Royal Decree approved by the National Corporative Organization (26 November 1926 and 12 May 1928), which recognized the legal persona of the employers', workers' or mixed associations, but established that labour activity had to be guided by elementary cells of the Corporative Organization: local Joint Committees, which were established by internal ballot within the associations of a corporation.[15] The law foresaw the constitution of local joint committees, corporation councils and a delegate commission of councils, in order to regulate labour relations in the different professions and trades, and to resolve conflicts between workers and employers. The workers' societies linked to *La Conciliación* were refused the right to register on the Census that permitted the election of the committee members, because, as the president explained, the powers-that-be believed that 'in their societies there was not only a direct relationship, but also a certain dependency on the Mutual Benefit Society'.[16] *La Conciliación* was forced, in record time, in early 1928, to approve a Regulation which transformed it into a Mutual Insurance Society, and the professional Societies which belonged to it became independent, except for the unique aims of mutual benefit.

The Statutes increased the rights of the worker members and completely excluded 'the intervention of the employer element' in labour arbitration, which meant the disappearance of one of the founding features of the organization.[17] Therefore, the President of the Society claimed that what remained was 'enough to call it a continuation, the fundamental idea and the basis of its existence, its Catholic character inspired in the doctrine of the Church, in a word, the denominational nature of the Association'.[18] The changes did not affect either the internal regime of the mutual benefit society or the professional societies.

The reforms were successful, as in the minutes of January 1930 there appears the certificate from the Ministry stating that those Societies that had applied were included in the electoral census.[19] In January 1930, shortly after Primo de Rivera's resignation, the social conflicts began anew, which demonstrated the double-edged effect of the joint committees: the supposed labour arbitration function could not avoid political demands.

Squaring the Circle: the 1933 Reform

On 14 April 1932, one year after proclamation of the Republic, with the Socialist Francisco Largo Caballero as Minister for Work and Social Security,[20] a law was passed regulating 'all Associations set up or that may be set up by employers or workers for the defence of the interests of the respective classes in certain professions, industries and branches of these'.[21] In its second provision the law stated that professional associations 'will have to be composed exclusively' by employers or by workers. This regulation was followed by two ministerial Orders which established 31 October 1933 as the deadline for the registration of the reformed statutes of the Professional Associations of Employers and Workers at the corresponding provincial Labour Delegation.[22] This law was in response to a political project that invalidated the possible existence of mixed societies such as *La Conciliación*; therefore it had to modify its characteristics in order to continue existing.

On 9 October 1932, a Commission was set up to study the future character of *La Conciliación*. During the course of this reform, it came to light that the Society could no longer be denominational and also the return of the above-mentioned tension between protectors and workers.[23] For example, in January

1932, the worker member Teófilo Martínez proposed a motion of no confidence on the protector members, as they did not attend the Society General Board Meeting.[24] This issue was still dragging on the following year, when the President of *La Conciliación*, Luis Ortega, justified his absence from the previous year's meeting because he was attending the inauguration of the new *Casa de la Misericordia*. And when, in the assembly, another member proposed a correction in the Minutes, the president asked for it to remain unchanged 'as it will thus show how they had been treated'.[25]

In July 1933, one month before the deadline given by the Government, an exceptional Board meeting with a great number of members present approved a new, fundamental alteration of the regulations which changed *La Conciliación* into a workers' society now called '*La Conciliación* Association of Workers' Societies'. The meeting was not trouble-free. The President, Don Andrés José Aldaba, had to insist that the reason for the change was 'the need to adjust the norms that had governed this Society to the demands of social legislation'. *La Conciliación* was defined now 'as a merely workers' society, which kept its foundational spirit intact'.[26] The professional associations and unions together with the centre for professional worker unions would remain at the *La Conciliación* social premises, 'provided their statutes maintained the Christian spirit which they have upheld from their beginning and that they follow the norms of Catholic morality'.[27]

The new Association of Workers' Societies was be managed by a board of directors composed of 12 members elected from among the presidents of the workers' unions and the professional workers' societies'.[28] The objectives of the association were expressed in Article 4: 'The fundamental aim of this association will be to promote the moral and economic well-being of the working class within the principles of Christian equity and justice. The issues of its responsibility and study will thus be the religious and moral instruction of the worker, his social training, promotion of savings banks, aid, assistance, medical and pharmaceutical services, post-mortem aid and everything to do with his development'.

To a certain extent, the protector members remained because, as Article 6 states, 'having settled the social assets and liabilities, the general board will surrender the remaining property together with the social building, to the patronage group which will now be designated for this end'. In this way, a patronage group was created made up of 'the president, secretary, treasurer and bookkeeper from the last directive board, plus four of the previous protectors, the first of whom should be the ex-presidents and then those who have held positions on the board of directors, in order of seniority'.

From what is described, we can understand the complications brought about by the new Regulations: no longer does *La Conciliación* depend on the Church, but declares that Catholic ideals inspire it; no longer does it have protector members, but they go on assisting the Society through patronage; the healthcare assistance and objectives remain, but the labour mediation, educational and recreational ends disappear. The minutes continue to reflect the day-to-day running of the organization.

Characteristics for Assistance in Ill-Health (1902–36)

At one of the first meetings of the Society, its governing body (the Mixed Board) set up the Aid Fund Commission which was entrusted with 'organising assistance both during unemployment and illness, and in the latter case, economic subsidy and medical care'.[29]

One month later, it was agreed that 'from January 5th and at the expense of the General Fund of the Society, the sum of 1.50 pesetas was to be paid to those ill members who fulfil the conditions laid down in the Regulations'.[30] The workers' representatives proposed that the subsidy should be higher for those who were not assisted by the medical service of *La Conciliación*, but the Board maintained the same sum for everyone.[31] Subsequently, the minutes of the meetings of the Mixed Board included the list of names of the workers who received subsidies, specifying the number of days for which the aid was approved. We can see this example from the minutes of the meeting held on 18 January 1903: 'The following assistances are agreed: Santiago Sarrias for 7 days sick leave; Silverio Usoz for the same reason and the same number of days'.[32]

A constant issue at the Board Meetings was the revision of the concession of paid sick leave. Next we see the conditions laid down in the Regulations, how the allowances were controlled and, from an economic perspective, the difference made by this sick leave aid given by *La Conciliación* until 1936.

Beneficiaries

As we have commented, the worker members and their families were the only beneficiaries of medical assistance. And only the worker members received economic subsidies, as laid down in Article 6 of the Regulations, passed in 1905: 'The worker members who fall ill and their families are entitled to assistance. The ill family members of the worker member are entitled only to free medical and pharmaceutical care, when this is in order. If the ill person is a worker member, he shall also be entitled to financial benefit, which, currently, is fixed at the one peseta fifty cents per day'.

To receive this aid, one had to have been a member of *La Conciliación* for at least three months and not owe more than three monthly subscriptions.[33] The monetary subsidy was paid from the fourth day of sick leave and the maximum period of payment was six months. If the illness continued, the member was entitled to aid from the Fund for chronic patients, which was financed by the worker members and the protectors.

As was common practice for institutions of this type, in order to become a member, workers had to present a medical certificate guaranteeing good health, noting specifically the absence of chronic illnesses. Later, they also accepted candidates who were excluded from cover of the illnesses they had before joining. Thus, in 1912, a member was admitted who suffered from a disease of the eyelids, on the condition of not receiving assistance from *La Conciliación* for this ailment nor its consequences. As time passed, more ailments were excluded, such as [inguinal] hernias, chronic conjunctivitis, suppuration of the ears ... In 1918, the Board asked the Society physician Ramón Sanz, if an epileptic patient could be accepted, and if so, in what conditions. And in January 1919, a worker member was accepted but excluded from the sick leave benefits caused by heart disease and its consequences; the modification was that his family would also be excluded from post-mortem aid if heart disease were the cause of death.

From the start, 'rheumatism without fever' and 'mental insanity, at any level' were excluded from financial benefit, but 'any illness with no link to the condition suffered by those who have said illnesses' was attended.[34] In the case of rheumatism without fever, at the meeting on 7 December 1902, it was agreed 'to authorise the Aid Fund Commission to adopt the pertinent solution in each case', but in practice, no exceptions were authorised.[35]

Nor was sick leave benefit given to mental patients, but the Board was more tolerant of these patients, and other benefits were found for them. For example, when a member committed suicide, the Board made a donation to the family to the value of the post-mortem subsidy. And, in 1928, the Board agreed to continue the Society membership of Ricardo Iso, from the Mixed Services Society, who 'has been unfortunate enough to have been admitted to the Asylum due to dementia, despite his owing thirteen payments'. The Board agreed that those members who were admitted to the *Casa de Misericordia* should be treated in the same manner; they would only pay 15 cents per week and in the future their family would be entitled to the post-mortem subsidy.

The maximum age limit for members was a constant source of debate between the worker members. In October 1904, a maximum age-limit of fifty was accepted for admission of worker members on their demand. Some worker members wanted members over 45 years old to receive medical care only, and not financial assistance, but this was not accepted.

In 1915, to reduce costs, the guilds suggested that 40 should be the limit for admission with the right to aid and medical care, with 3 and 6-months limitations and double medical certification. They returned to the initial idea that those who were between forty-five and fifty should only receive medical care, but again it was rejected.[36] Two years later, in 1917, they decided that the admission of members between 40 and 50 would entail double subscriptions.[37]

However, a minimum age limit had not been mentioned until, in 1918, a youth of 14 applied for membership. After a careful debate, his membership was accepted because the then valid Labour Law allowed people of that age to be employed.[38] The practice was that the average age at which members were admitted was between 35 and 40.

Procedure for Granting Aid

When a worker member fell ill, he had to visit the Association Secretary and present a sick note drawn up by the physician within four days.[39] If there was delay in presenting a sick note, an investigation was carried out to discover if the member or the physician was responsible, because if the delay was not justified, the economic aid corresponding to the four days before the presentation of the sick note was refused.[40] Delay in presentation of sick notes at the headquarters of the Society was the most frequent reason for refusal or reduction of sick leave benefit.[41]

In order to facilitate the control of sick leave, the procedures were gradually changed. Originally, the sick note had to be signed by a physician belonging to *La Conciliación*. But in 1914, coinciding with an increase in sick leave, the Mixed Guild requested that the members be permitted to visit physicians who did not belong to *La Conciliación*, that the members would pay the corresponding fees, but that the Society would admit both the prescriptions and sick notes drawn up by these physicians.[42]

In 1916, the physicians were urged to draw up the sick notes at the *La Conciliación* headquarters.[43] At the meeting held on 26 May 1928, the reforms introduced to facilitate the procedure were reported, using a 'new filing system instead of the old-fashioned register system'.[44] And in 1935 it was decided that sick notes for illness or accident would only be admitted on week-days between 7:30 and 21:00 hours, and the corresponding membership card had to be presented.[45]

Over the years, the physicians refused to assist or sign sick notes for those worker members who were treated by folk healers, which meant that, according to the Society Regulations, they could not receive monetary benefit. But the Mixed Board systematically gave donations equal to what they would have been entitled to.[46]

Cases of leaving the City or Absence of the Ill Members

As stated in Article 9 of the Regulations, 'any ill member who leaves the area shall lose his right to aid, unless he has to do so under doctor's orders, in which case, before travel, he must give the Mixed Board a certificate signed by the *La Conciliación* physician who attends him'. The member's family also lost their right to assistance when the member left the city. There were very few infringements of the rule on not leaving the city.[47]

This medical authorization was demanded even when the travel was for treatment. In the minutes, every week, there is approval of travel to the countryside or to hydrotherapy centres, authorized by physicians. The worker members also applied for authorization for surgical treatment in other towns such as Bilbao (Hospital de Basurto), Santander (Hospital de Valdecilla), Valladolid, Saragossa, San Sebastian or Madrid.[48]

While absent, the members had to send a sick note at weekly intervals, unless, in exceptional circumstances, the Board stated otherwise. The reason for this exception was usually the cost to the patient of obtaining a sick note.

There was also the possibility that the worker might fall ill when outside Pamplona. In such cases it was decided that the patient should present a sick note witnessed by the parish priest of the place where he was. Every eight days, the parish priest would send a note to the Board detailing the course of the illness.[49]

Other Reasons for Loss of Aid

The worker members and their families had no right to assistance if they were unwell 'because of their bad behaviour, or because of injuries received in fights they had caused or accepted, or because of wars or public riots, when the interested party had taken part in same'.[50] Thus at the meeting held on 13 September 1926, the Mixed Board refused to assist the member Donato Huarte, who had received a gunshot wound. However, a year later, once the law courts had cleared things up, the Board decided to pay him the assistance due during his sick leave.

According to the third paragraph of Article 16, 'workers on sick leave would lose their right to assistance if during their illness or convalescence they visited establishments dealing in food, drink or coffee, etc., or did not return home before 10 pm in spring or summer, and 7 pm in autumn and winter, if their physician has permitted their leaving their homes'. This was the cause of most accusations by the Society inspector.

And, logically, the Regulations stated that those who 'by pretending to be ill misused assistance, and those who used any means to extend assistance' would no longer receive aid and would be expelled from the Society.[51]

Worker Members and Benefit Control

Surveillance to avoid abuse of assistance benefit was entrusted from early on to the workers' guilds, the Society physicians and an inspector employed for this task. They were all requested to ensure that the Regulations were fulfilled strictly. When the number of workers on sick leave rose, the Board asked everyone involved to 'exercise extreme care' and to increase their vigilance.[52] Every year, the workers' guilds designated an official visitor entrusted with visiting the ill members and carrying out a follow-up of the physician's care.[53] An example of this is the agreement of the Mixed Board to withdraw benefits from Julio Hualde because of the accusation made by another member, 'of [the patient] having been in a drinking establishment and having has a fight with another individual'.[54]

The physicians also contributed to the control of aid. Thus, in 1917, when a member requested changing to a different physician and retaining his benefits because he was not getting better with the treatment prescribed by the Society physician, Agustín Lazcano, the Board agreed without difficulty, but warned him that the *La Conciliación* physicians had to be watchful of everyone.[55] Again and again the physicians were reminded about being punctual with the writing of sick notes and discharges, which was a means of getting the physicians' collaboration in the control of sick leave.

There are cases when the Board suggests the physicians be vigilant of a member who was suspected of misusing the benefit system.[56] And the physicians' collaboration in this task is documented. For example, in January 1918, the physician Ramón Sanz reported that he had found a member of sick leave absent from his home, on the 14th, 15th and 16th; thus the Board cut his benefits.[57] The physicians went so far as to use extraordinary measures to ensure the conditions for the granting of benefit were fulfilled. This is the case of the physician who did not find the ill member José Amorena in his home at 6 am on a certain day, and reported to the Board, which agreed 'to stop benefits until it had more information on the matter'.[58] And again, Joaquín Soria, a physician who worked for the Society, sent the Board a letter in July 1918 suggesting measures to avoid the misuse by the members from Villava. The Board speedily passed these suggestions and demanded more watchfulness from the Society inspector.[59]

The Board put pressure on the physicians and applied the Regulations strictly.[60] But the Board itself was restricted by the regulations, so, in November 1917, when Joaquín Soria reported a member who was full of vigour and energy, the Board admitted that there was nothing they could do until the physician discharged him. This insistence on the role of the physicians in controlling sick leave continued: in March 1935, acting on a proposal by the then President of *La Conciliación*, Sr. Udobro, it was again agreed that: 'as soon as they are well, the patients must return to the doctor, in order to avoid abuse of assistance benefit'.[61]

The Society Inspector

The efforts made by the 'visitors' and the physicians to contain expenses and control the members were soon considered inadequate, so, in December 1906, an inspector, Sr. Casimiro Arrastia, was contracted and worked for the Society until 1935. His duties were: 'To visit ill members during their sick leave on a discreet but regular basis. To watch over convalescents, and report if they broke the rules in any way'. An example of his work can be found in the minutes of the meeting held on 26 February 1923: 'A formal complaint by the Inspector of the Society against the ill member Vicente Cilveti from the Carpenters' Guild was read out, as he had left this capital city without giving previous notice to the office, thus breaking Article 9 of the Benefit Regulations'.[62]

Most of the inspector's accusations referred to members working while receiving benefit. We also find complaints referring to the timetables for being absent from home, drinking, gambling, etc. The minutes of 29 January 1923 report the accusation against the member Antonio Pérez Seviné from the miscellaneous guild, as he was on sick leave because of strained ligaments in his right foot, an injury caused in a football game. But taking into account the Society Regulations, and the fact that there was no article on the withdrawal of benefits for such a reason, the Mixed Board decided to pay all the time due until he was discharged.[63]

In addition, the Mixed Board agreed that the Inspector should see that the *La Conciliación* patients were receiving proper medical attention. There are frequent notes such as: The inspector is requested to be doubly careful and to inform the Board if he found any shortcomings in the physicians' treatment [of the ill members],[64] etc. In turn, the inspector/visitor was supervised by the Guild Boards who reported at weekly intervals at the meetings of the Mixed Board.[65]

The Board of the Society believed the inspector's labour to be so necessary as, in January 1934, to employ a provisional 'visitor' because Sr. Arrastia has been unwell for a time and there was no-one to inspect the patients.[66] In the same year, the Board took the decision to give the 'visitor' a sheet with the patient's name to simplify the follow-up of sick leave.[67]

The penalty for disregarding the conditions in the Regulations was usually suspension of the full or partial benefit payment. If it was repeated, the expulsion of the member was proposed. In July 1935, an inspector's complaint led to a member losing six days' benefit.[68] Later, faced with two complaints, one member was refused benefit and another was expelled from *La Conciliación*, as there were three formal complaints against him.[69]

The explanations given by the members or the physicians were always heard when faced with a complaint by the inspector. For example, on 24 June 1935, when the accused member sent a letter to the association explaining the circumstances, it was agreed that the complaint should be ignored.[70] In other cases, the loss of benefit or the expulsion from the Society was upheld.

Towards the end of the period we have studied, a new control system was introduced: on 21 December 1936, the Board approved the employment of two new medical inspectors (Sres. Manuel Galán and Joaquín Ariz), who came from the *Mutualidad Obrera Profesional*, with which institution *La Conciliación* merged shortly afterwards. They would also carry out the checkups on admission or change in category within the Mutual Society.[71]

Data on Benefits Offered

Figure 8.1 shows the annual cost in pesetas of sick leave benefit over the years. In the analysis of the economic subsidy for illness granted by *La Conciliación* we will ignore the years 1902 and 1903, when the *La Conciliación* activities began, as the quantities are minimal and cannot be compared with the remaining years (1902: 2,887.5 Pts.; 1903: 2,004 Pts.). We will also ignore the year 1918 because the influenza pandemic that affected Pamplona between September and November that year meant an increase in the number of sick leaves and subsidies (24,085.05 Pts.) which would bias the analysis of the remaining years.

Taking the above into account, the mean cost of annual sick leave benefit was 15,788 Pts. per annum. There were four years (1904, 1907, 1906 and 1915) when the annual cost was over 20,000 Pts. per annum, and fourteen years when it was below average. The average number of sick leaves per annum covered by economic benefit was 1,675. That is, the mean length of sick leave was six days.

If we compare the economic subsidy for sick leave with the number of members, it fluctuates between 19.57 Pts/member per annum in 1907 and 9.97 Pts/member per annum, in 1923.

The figure shows that the annual variations in subsidies affected the control of the illness rate. A rise in this rate brought about a reaction resulting in a drop in the rate the following year. For example, in 1915, when there was a rise in the morbidity rate, the Board of the Society heightened sick leave control. For the good of the Society, the physicians were repeatedly asked to be extremely careful in the management of sick notes and discharges.[72] And in 1916 it was agreed that the sick notes and discharges granted by physicians not belonging to *La Conciliación* should be controlled.[73] In the same year, the Board went a step further and asked the physicians to make home visits to the convalescents and not to wait for them to attend surgery to ask to be discharged. Shortly afterwards, this was stated more specifically when the physicians were told to visit the patients every three days in order to be extra careful. The second time a patient is not found at home, he was to be declared discharged.[74] The result of this was that the years 1916 and 1917 had the lowest illness rate (compared to the number of members).

Furthermore, we see a drop in the illness rate from the beginning until the 1920s, when the tendency is reversed until 1936. We believe that one of the reasons for this to be the aging of the worker members of *La Conciliación*.

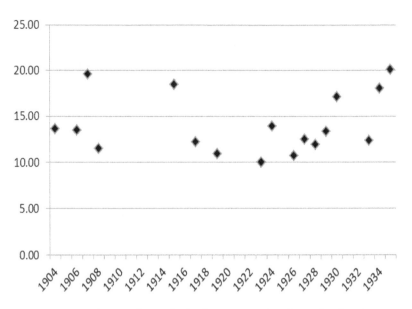

Figure 8.1: Evolution of annual subsidies compared with membership figures (1904–35).
Sources: Minute books *La Conciliación* Archive (1904–36).

Seasonal Character

As it was common in similar institutions, the evolution of the sick leave rate in *La Conciliación* shows a seasonal rhythm. As could be expected, the number of sick leaves increased in the first and last trimesters of the year. In the second decade (1910–19), the lowest number of paid sick leaves was 12 (April 1912) and the highest 78 (March 1915), with the exception of the year of the influenza pandemic (1918).

Sick Leave Costs

The amount paid in benefit remained 1.50 Pts. per day from 1902 until May 1928. At the annual general meeting held on 26 May of that year, an increase of 25 cents per day was approved.[75] Three years later, the extraordinary Board Meeting, held on 8 March 1931, they again increased the benefit by 25 cents per day because they halved the labour accident subsidy. This change was influenced by the fact that legislation on obligatory insurance covering labour accidents was passed in Spain (1932). From the outset, *La Conciliación* had defended the subsidiary nature of its assistance, so this new legislation facilitated the reduction in economic benefit in such cases.[76]

Throughout the years analysed, the cost of sick leave benefit was the most important item of expenditure for *La Conciliación*: approximately 60 per cent in the first ten years, which later dropped to 45 per cent. At the same time, we see that from 1923 on, the tendency changed and the cost of sick leave gradually increased when compared with the total expenditure of the Society, as can be seen from Figure 8.2.

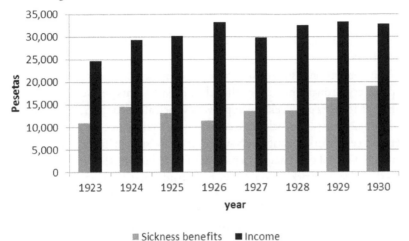

Figure 8.2: Total income and cost of sick leave (1923–30).
Sources: Minute books *La Conciliación* Archive (1902–36).

In the first eight years, the workers' dues did not cover the cost of the subsidies for sick leave, which was paid in part by the subscriptions from employers and protector members and from other donations. From the second decade on, sick leave cost between 42.6 and 64 per cent of the workers' subscriptions. We can also note that, from 1922 on, sick leave required a higher percentage of the income from the workers' dues.

Despite this, the minutes of the extraordinary General Meeting held on 12 December 1934 show anxiety about the Society's shortfall in the previous years.

According to the Board, the reasons for this situation were: firstly, that the members' dues had not been raised; in addition, after thirty-two years' activity the members were older, so more was spent on spent on post-mortem aid and attending to illness. They also had to add the cost of insurance against unavoidable unemployment which began in the early 1930s and the drop in the number of protector members.

They admitted that the negative economic situation the Society was experiencing was not an isolated incident, but was part of a general crisis because of

which other organizations and mutual societies had had to reduce their allowances for labour accidents and the amount of post-mortem aid. This was the case
of the Pamplona branch of the *Instituto Obrero de Seguros Sociales de Barcelona*
which, in December 1932, had been restructured as the *Mutualidad Obrera
Profesional* due to their poor financial results.[77] In *La Conciliación*, in order to
resolve the problem, the Board proposed maintaining the assistance and controlling the spending on physicians, as they believed this to be the most costly item
and that which caused the loss. The Board had calculated that if the medical
service were eliminated from the accounts, there would have been a surplus of
3,514.10 Pts.

This contention justified the proposed increase of 25 cents per week in the
medical service dues which, until then, had been 10 cents per week. Finally, a rise
in dues of 15 cents per week was approved, which allowed the Society to survive.

For many years, the sick leave subsidy was equivalent to 34 per cent of the
average weekly worker's wage in Navarre, as can be seen in Table 8.1.[78] Therefore,
although it was of great help to a patient's family budget, the benefit was far less
than the wage the worker would have been paid when working.

On this point, we must take into account that, sometimes, the workers
belonged to more than one organization and could be paid more than one
subsidy. In fact, the Pamplona organizations exchanged data to avoid the hypo-
thetical case of a worker receiving more in benefit than he would in wages. And
one mutual association, the *Mutualidad Obrera Profesional* went so far as to propose preventing double membership in order to avoid double benefits.[79]

A comparison with the rise in the mean wage contextualizes the 25 cents per
week increase in subsidies which occurred in both 1928 and 1931. Even so, we find
a continuous drop in buying power for those members who are ill, as the subsidy of
2 Pts per day was equivalent to 21.5 per cent of the weekly wage in 1930.

Table 8.1: Spanish wages (1914–30).

	Mean wage rate per hour				Average weekly wage			
	1914	1920	1925	1930	1914	1920	1925	1930
Navarra	0.44	0.78	0.91	1.16	26.32	38.10	43.10	55.93
Spain	0.43	0.80	0.93	0.92	24.90	39.06	44.76	44.34

Source: Ministry of Labour, *Estadística de salarios y jornadas de trabajo referida al periodo
1914–30.*

Changes in the Configuration of Welfare Systems: *La Conciliación* (1940–84)

The Civil War (1936–9) was the cause of an important crisis all over the country which clearly affected this type of organizations. After the conflict, the military government imposed a political regime to which the Mutual Assistance Associations had to adapt. In the case of *La Conciliación*, it meant that its objectives had to be redefined to fit in with the regulation of Mutual Benefit Associations and *Montepíos*, an institution similar to other Mutual Aid Society. The continuity of *La Conciliación* in the 1940s was conditioned by its reluctance to collaborate with the new Franco regime's project for obligatory health insurance. As we shall see, the development of the law on National Health (1963) sparked off a crisis in the organization which continued to pay out healthcare subsidies until the 80s, when it disappeared.

The Refusal of La Conciliación to participate in the National Health Service

The social healthcare policies of the early Franco regime were connected to those created during the Second Republic, even though the political regimes that shaped them were very different. An example of this is that the organization responsible for carrying them out, the *Instituto Nacional de Previsión,* National Institute for Social Security (INP), was directed, to a certain extent, by the same individuals as in the previous era; this continuity was unchanged by the war. For this reason, at the end of the war the project for the creation of the Spanish National Health Service, which was about to be made law before the military coup on 18 July 1936, was retrieved.

Curiously, one of the obstacles to setting this insurance project in motion after the war years (1936–9) was the rivalry between two of the groups belonging to the new political regime. On the one hand, there were the 'social' Catholics, among whom were some of the technicians and politicians who had set up the former INP. On the other, the Falangists, followers of José Antonio Primo de Rivera, founder of the Falange, the Spanish fascist party. From the start the Falangists raised the flag of social politics, in agreement with their idea of establishing a National-Socialist state. Although both groups had the similar aims, these frankly conflictive circumstances meant that, in spite of the echoes of international innovation on the issue of Social Security which were heard in Spain, and of the advanced projects for the unification of social insurance, the healthcare system that was finally endorsed in 1942, proposed by the Falangist José Antonio Girón, Minister of Labour between 1941 and 1957, turned out to be complex and fragmentary.[80]

In a small provincial capital, this situation was to have clear repercussions on *La Conciliación*. In its Minutes there are recurrent references to the projected new 'Law on Obligatory Health Insurance'.[81] However, its managers and directors were reluctant to collaborate with the system, and decided not to join the newly-created Social Security as a collaborative agency. In a letter dated 2 August 1944, containing the Regulations and working experience of *La Conciliación*, the directors explained: 'Our attitude to the new State Law on Obligatory Healthcare Insurance is somewhat passive, as we wait to see how the many uncertainties will be cleared up. We really have no interest in this collaboration as it is regulated'.[82] This decision, little by little, led to the disappearance of *La Conciliación*, which was unable to compete with either the Social Security or with the collaborating labour mutual societies, nor with the private insurance companies which were new at the time.

The lack of financial resources also affected the development of the Spanish Social Security system. After the Civil War, the economic levels reached in 1929 – which, worldwide, were the high point of the first half of the twentieth century – were not again reached in Spain until around 1945.[83] The Obligatory Healthcare Insurance suffered from a lack of infrastructure, and for this reason the Government Decree of 2 March 1944 permitted agreements with private organizations, basically with the Labour Accident Mutual Societies, which had clinics and dispensaries offering medical attention. *La Conciliación* was different, in that it offered general medical care in the doctors' consulting rooms and medical homecare.

The Reconstitution of La Conciliación (1941)

After the Civil War, those insurance organizations linked to political or trade union movements were disbanded.[84] The effect of this on *La Conciliación* was that, in 1938, during the War, the Workers' Societies belonging to it disappeared gradually. In January 1938 it was the Pamplona Bank Employee Workers' Union; the Professional Employee Workers' Society and the Professional Painter Workers' Society. In June 1938, it was the turn of the Professional Society of Labourers and Assistants at Public Entertainment and Similar. And finally, in August 1938, the remaining 26 (the Workers' Societies of stonemasons, carpenters, unskilled labourers, cobblers, ...). *La Conciliación* thereby lost its foremost original aim: involvement in the world of labour and mediation in professional conflicts. Up till then, this had been the most important feature in the evolution of the Society, which, over the years, had adapted to socio-labour rather than to healthcare legislation, although its medical-social assistance activity was also of importance.

The regulation of Mutual Assistance Societies was dealt with in the Law of 6 December 1941 which, together with the 1943 Regulations on application (Decree of 23 May), controlled the working of the Mutual Assistance Associations and Montepíos for Social Security. This law was similar to the 1934 Catalonian Law on Mutual Assistance Associations, passed by the Parliament of Catalonia during the Second Republic, so this meant a certain continuity with the past.[85]

The Law created the section on Montepíos and Mutual Assistance Associations (Art. 1) at the Ministry of Labour which was in charge of: approval, operation, promotion and surveillance of these organizations (Art. 2); it also took charge of the registers of the montepíos and Mutual Assistance Associations (Art. 3). Its intention was to control the associations whose 'objectives were to deliver benefits to their associates, on pensions, illness, death and unemployment, or on improvements in existing or future social insurance policies, old age pensions, family and maternity allowances'. The regulations referred to those organizations in which the members had equal rights and obligations; they were non-profit making; worked in the area of social and charitable care; and were funded by contributions from the members or sponsors. In Spain, this legal format remained unchanged until 1984.

La Conciliación quickly asked to be registered, as we can see that on 11 December 1942 its new Regulations were approved by the Ministry of Labour, register number 432. In its application for approval, it states that it is an organization which 'was established legally 38 years ago and was already registered; the recent creation in the Ministry of Labour of the section for Montepíos and Mutual Assistance Associations affects the general Management of this division directly'.

These new Regulations affected *La Conciliación,* as they did the other Mutual Assistance Associations, both in the mission of the organization and in the way it worked.

Firstly, the approval of the 'Professional Worker Mutual Assistance Association *La Conciliación*' meant a re-definition of the institution. In the minutes of the General Board Meeting on 22 October 1941 it was explained that the new regulations meant 'the disappearance from the Regulations of several Articles – which are unnecessary nowadays and referred to the Professional Workers Unions'. Specifically, 'everything which in the previous version referred to the possible signing of contracts with employers has been replaced by the obligations arising from the Law on Labour Accidents (Art. 3, nn. 2 and 18 section f)'. In addition, 'everything referring to accident insurance'. *La Conciliación* proposed to give medical service and economic subsidies for illness which would complement what was covered by Social Security, if the worker belonged to *La Conciliación*, and to grant it to those who were not covered. It also maintained the *postmortem* subsidy. 'Our aspiration, if we are allowed, is to reinsure the margin between the 50 per cent paid by the State and the maximum stated in the Law, 90 per cent of the wages or salaries'.[86]

Secondly, greater interventionism by the authorities is documented. Control of the Mutual Assistance Associations and Montepíos affected the economic issues and regime of the organizations. At the start, there was even double dependence on the departments of Health and Labour. The board members of *La Conciliación* complained that 'the medical service was imposed and controlled by the *Obra del 18 de julio*', an institution dependent on the Ministry of Labour.[87] The *Obra* Sindical, the official union, wanted *La Conciliación* to stop giving medical care and to restructure the Mutual Assistance Association. Later, when the Obligatory Healthcare Insurance was approved, the Board of *La Conciliación* had to insist that this service should continue.

There was only one political party, one Central trade union and one Law on Trade Union Unity, all of which allowed the Navarrese Provincial Delegation of the Central National Union to place a representative in the areas of *La Conciliación*. The person appointed had to attend 'the sessions and assemblies that the board of this organization should hold with the task of ensuring the scrupulous observance of the statutes of same organization and with the power of a suspensive veto'. The Navarrese Provincial Delegation of the Union also demanded 'copies of all sessions held' from January 1940.[88]

The explanation of the reasons for the Law on Mutual Assistance Associations and Montepíos (1941) showed a certain distrust of the Mutual Associations when it stated that 'frequently, as there is not a suitable balance between the good wishes and the technical skill in calculation and in interpretation or for administrative reasons, moral frauds occur which discredit the institutions of social security and bring irreparable loss to the insured members who entrusted their future to the administration of the organization'.

The Government was not far wrong in demanding economic precautions in the mutual associations. In the case of *La Conciliación*, in order to clear the deficit of the Illness Fund, the subsidy for illness was reduced by 1 peseta per week, leaving it at 7 pesetas per week.[89] After a year the accounts were back in order, so they raised the subsidy again.[90]

During these years the cost of the medical service also rose. Indeed, in January 1941, 'a letter from the Official College of Physicians of Navarre was read out', which required an 'increase of the agreed fee from 12 to 25 pesetas per year'. The increase in payment for the physicians was passed without any difficulty as, in spite of the increase, it was considered 'advantageous, because the fee for family medical care in the city was 60 pesetas'. Moreover, a supplement of three pesetas was levied on the members who lived on the outskirts of the city to cover transport costs for the physicians.[91]

In April 1944, *La Conciliación* had 1,060 members and a medical staff of five physicians.[92] That is, the membership figures were similar to those at the beginning of the Civil War.

Approval of Obligatory Healthcare Insurance: New Regulations in 1945 and 1949

In Spain, when Social Security was begun, Mutual Assistance Associations and montepíos participated in the designing this insurance: at least they gave their opinions, and a gradual transfer of the members of this association to the state healthcare system was even considered. They also hoped to take part in the administration of this insurance.

At *La Conciliación*, while the project for the Law on Obligatory Health Insurance was being developed, a committee was set up to revise the Regulations of the association. This was urgent because until the amendments were approved, there could be no changes in the categories of the Mutual members, nor could new members be accepted.[93] After a laborious process and several general assemblies of members, on 25 January 1945 an 'Extraordinary Board Meeting for changes in the Regulations due to the Law on Obligatory Health Insurance' was called.[94] The changes meant that the members would not receive the benefits of the Mutual Association for six months (instead of three), except in the case of medical service which was given, as before, 'from the first day of the month following acceptance into the association'. The Society membership fees, categories and subsidies were also modified (Art. 13). The categories were divided into the following groups: from twenty to twenty-five years of age; from twenty-five to thirty; from thirty to thirty-five; and from thirty-five to forty. The special category for retired members or those who were not covered by Social Security was retained.[95]

Those insured in the special category would receive a daily subsidy of 3.50 pesetas when ill, to a maximum ninety days per year, for one or more illnesses. The death benefit they were entitled to would be 100 pesetas in one payment.

By law (Art. 67) it was established that the social funds were 'obliged to acquire mortgage bonds which had been recognized by the Dirección General de Seguros (General Board of Insurance)' or 'State, provincial or municipal bonds'. These low-yield investments eventually seriously damaged these institutions.[96]

The President insisted on the advantages of belonging to *La Conciliación* by means of an 'explanatory table of the sums which would be paid to the insurer and to the Mutual Association and the sums which would be received'. There was even a proposal 'of establishing the obligation of belonging to this Mutual Association only'. And freedom to subscribe to the medical service was suggested. But both issues continued pending.

The fact of remaining outside Social Security led them to justify their mutual status again and again. So, on 5 July 1944, *La Conciliación* sent an official note to the Official College of Physicians of Navarre defending the physicians who worked for the association. The note 'commented on their *astonishment* because the Society's physicians were not recognized for Health Insurance as it was a private organization covering health insurance dating from before 1936'. And when in the same month the Navarrese INP sent *La Conciliación* 'the norms for the appointment of the General Medical and charity practitioner for the area', the official note was filed with the comment: 'Not applicable to this Mutual Association'.[97]

In Spain in 1946, a movement to bring the mutual associations together was begun, as was planned in the Law of 6 December 1941. *La Conciliación* thus became part of the 'Northern Mutual Federation' which grouped the mutual associations and montepíos of Vizcaya, Guipuzcoa, Alava, Navarre and Santander. The Federation was to represent and transmit the questions of the mutual associations and montepíos to the Ministry of Labour.[98]

The Regulations of *La Conciliación* were updated in June 1949. The change reduced the categories to two, plus the special category. The sums corresponding to fees and subsidies were also updated. This was passed unanimously by those who attended the Extraordinary Board Meeting on 17 June 1949.[99]

However, it took years for these regulations to receive the approval of the authorities, which negative affected to *La Conciliación*. An item in the Acts for August 1955 states: 'The document from the Dirección General de Previsión Montepíos y Mutualidades indicating the rectification of some omissions of statuary obligations was read out'. It dealt with 'modification of articles of the Regulations by indication of the Dirección General de Previsión Montepíos y Mutualidades.[100] Despite all this, the everyday activities of the organization carried on, which can be seen in that the Board Meetings approved the changes in dues, the financial reports and those of the activities of the society, etc.

Consequences of the Law on Social Security (1963) for La Conciliación

Almost 25 years after the beginning of the military regime, one of the social measures carried out was the expansion and reform of the Social Security system, paying particular attention to industrial workers. In 1963, a law was passed which, among other things, modified the management of the Social Security System. Little by little, with differences depending on the industrialization of the various areas, there was an increase in the number of people covered by Obligatory Healthcare Insurance.

In 1957, 31.66 per cent of the Navarrese population was covered, a percentage slightly below the national average (31.92), but well below the figures for the neighbouring provinces of Vizcaya (81.20 per cent) and Guipuzcoa (62.82 per cent). This was due to the mainly agricultural character of Navarre. Towards the end of the 50s, the Pamplona City Council approved an aid plan for newly-created industries. And in 1964, the *Diputación* de Navarra, the regional government, organized an ambitious 'Programme for Industrial Promotion', which, in the following ten years, gave support to 307 new companies which created 28,000 jobs all over Navarre. Pamplona, and Navarre as a whole, went from being a region with many emigrants to having positive population growth. Pamplona, which had had a population of 61,188 in 1940 and 97,880 in 1960, had 147,168 inhabitants in 1970.[101]

Precisely, during the sixties was when the crisis in *La Conciliación* became blatantly obvious. The growing coverage of the society by Social Security, the administrative obstacles in the approval of its Statutes which hindered the promotion of new members, the ageing of its associates ... this was all against *La Conciliación*. To such an extent that, in 1960, they did not manage to present a financial report in which the administration costs were less than 25 per cent of the budget, as was demanded in Art. 22 of the regulations of montepíos and Mutualities.

The Dirección General insisted on a settlement, and *La Conciliación* replied that it had 'insurmountable problems' due to the 'low numbers in the Mutual Association, which has fallen year by year since the introduction of the State obligatory insurance, [which] means that the current number of associates is 545'. That is to say, the organization had lost 50 per cent of its members in the previous 15 years. The expenditure proposed by the Society was in fact well-regulated, but only 17,094 pesetas/year were collected in dues. However, the Ministry was adamant and sent a new official note in November 1961, insisting that, 'the administration costs cannot exceed 25 per cent in the accounts report'.[102] The crisis was becoming dramatic and at the Annual Board Meeting in January 1965, the first proposal for the liquidation of the society was registered: 'Don Román Pomares Rubio used his turn to speak to make several disparaging comments on the Mutual Association and to ask for its liquidation'.[103]

The Board did not ignore this and ordered a study of the viability of *La Conciliación*. The result was a long 'Confidential Report', dated January 1967, and was unsigned, although thanks to an annotation that appears in the Minutes two years later, we know that it was prepared by the lawyer Sr. Ezponda, who was mutual actuary. Ezponda's analysis emphasized the ageing of the members and the need to carry out a 'complete reorganization' of the Association which would include creating new categories and attracting young members: 'A Society without young people is a society that will soon die'. Moreover, a good advertising campaign was needed, because *La Conciliación* was 'unknown to most people at present'. They needed to advertise in the press and on the radio, by means of fliers and among members' families and to contract an agent who would receive a guaranteed salary and commission for each member recruited.

The 'membership recruitment plan' was to be based on the following points: 1st Modernization of the Regulations; 2nd A change of name; the word 'worker' had to disappear as, according to the author of the report, it closed the doors to the whole middle class (office workers, technicians, professionals, etc.) who are the lifeline of Spanish mutual associations; 3rd Not to accept even one member who had a physician, as 'this is disastrous for the physician and at any time they can abandon us and create a problem in *La Conciliación*'. Ezponda suggested that having one single physician was enough, 'he would earn more and the patients might be better looked after'.

The analysis included a proposal for up-dated dues. He also suggested an increase in compensation and *postmortem* benefits: 'We also believe the payments are very poor. The fact that they receive nothing after six months, and for a year unless they have another illness, does not happen in other societies'. With these figures, Ezponda presented a viability study – which we will not include here as it goes beyond the aims of this chapter – based on a group of 100 members.[104]

The weighty report was presented at the Annual General Meeting in 1967 and the consequences were immediate: a large number of members who were in arrears in their dues resigned and a Commission for Reform of the Regulations was set up, made up, as was traditional in *La Conciliación,* by the President, Vice-president and other ex-presidents, together with the lawyer Ezponda, the author of the famed 'Confidential Report'.[105]

This commission worked very swiftly, as in November of the same year we find the project for the Regulations which was passed by the Extraordinary Board Meeting in January 1968.[106] However, the approval of the Ministry for Labour took two years, although the objections it presented were not particularly relevant.[107] Thus it is not at all remarkable that in January 1969, the minute reflects the positive acceptances of the new Regulations: 'The Board was pleasantly surprised and gave a warm, spontaneous round of applause when the President presented the new regulations which had been approved by the Ministry of Labour, due to the steps he had taken personally, for which we are sincerely grateful and state for the record in the Minutes'.[108]

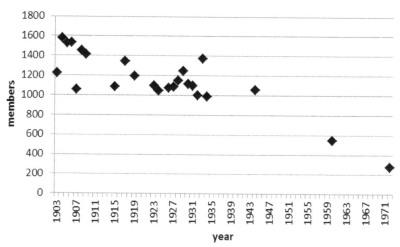

Figure 8.3: Evolution of *La Conciliación* member numbers 1903–72.
Sources: Minute books *La Conciliación* Archive (1903–72).

Liquidation of the Mutual Assistance Association

Since the spring of 1968 there was another cause for anxiety for the governors of the Society: the difficult economic situation of the Association.[109] Several commissions were organized: one to 'Study Sale of Building',[110] another, with the help of the business agent Sr. Díaz, who was 'very competent in sales, construction and rentals', revised how to 'channel the economic future of the Mutual Association'. And in June 1972, they entrusted their investment portfolio to a company 'Crececinco'.[111] They also studied the means to make more profit from the rental of the premises in the *La Conciliación* building.[112]

In December 1971, the approval of the new categories was again proposed to the Ministry – an issue, which, again, meant a two-year delay. This time the Ministry had mislaid the documentation.[113]

They also studied the possibility of setting themselves up as an insurance collective, but the Ministry warned that this change in approach would endanger their continuity.[114] The problem was that there were fewer and fewer members. In 1972 there were only 276 left, and *La Conciliación* called on the 'Agencia Atesoi', an image-making agency, to develop a promotional campaign for the Mutual Association.[115] *La Conciliación* also asked advice of SURNE, an insurance mutual association in Bilbao which still exists. SURNE's reply was very pessimistic. They did not see that an organization with only 253 members could be viable as they had 18,000 members.[116]

Under these circumstances *La Conciliación* had to refuse 50 people who wished to join as a group, but would not undergo the obligatory medical check-up for admittance. And shortly afterwards, in 1972, 33 members cancelled their membership, because the ironworks company they worked for had gone into liquidation.[117]

The situation got worse during the 1974 fiscal year, with a shortfall in the accounts. The year began with 90,101.85 pesetas, in November it was 1,853.21, but in December, there was a shortfall of 10,696.89 pesetas.

In mid-November 1974, having commented on the many meetings held with the lawyer Don Francisco J. Muro, the board called a general meeting to be held in January 1975, to be considered both 'ordinary and extraordinary', in order to ask 'the assembly to dissolve the current Mutual Association and create a society with exactly the same title and rights, to appoint the board of liquidators and when this were done, to approve an extraordinary board meeting to be held in February to endorse the Minutes of the previous one and the dispatch of a copy of the Act of Dissolution to the Ministry in order to begin the procedure which we imagine will take a long time'.[118] The good news was the sale of the *La Conciliación* building, which was a relief, financially.[119]

The board of liquidators appointed at the extraordinary general meeting held on 25 January 1975 reported in June on the steps taken and the proposed distribution of the assets of the Mutual Association. The commission, in agreement with Article 58 of the Association Regulations, proposed the assets should be divided into three equal shares of 101,878.24 pesetas. The first 101,878.24 pesetas were shared among ten of the 133 retired members with over ten years' seniority. The second share was given to another ten members with children or grandchildren who were studying (there were 202 members in the draw, that is, all but 23). And 101,878.24 pesetas were given to the neediest old folks' home in Pamplona. As was traditional, the home managed by the Little Sisters of the Poor was chosen. The Minutes state that twenty members benefited from these sums.[120] After the liquidation of the Society, a 'management commission' was set up and prepared the documents needed to change *La Conciliación* into a Limited Company.[121]

The requirements for the legalization of the Statutes were notarized and on the 22 April 1977 the new Limited Company was registered by the Diputación Foral de Navarra (provincial government). The final annotation in the Minutes Book of the Mutual Assistance Association *La Conciliación* is dated 21 June 1977: 'We are advised that the statutes of the new Society have been rejected by the Land Registry. These are minor details of no great importance. They have been sent to Rubio Notary's Office to be corrected and re-sent to the Registry. And as there are no more points to be dealt with, the meeting is declared closed and the pertinent document is certified by me as secretary'.[122]

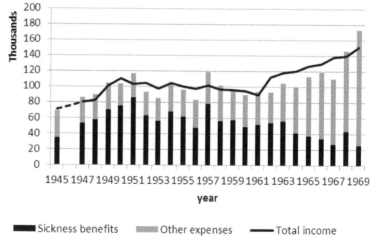

Figure 8.4: Incomes and expenses of *La Conciliación* (1945–69).
Sources: Minute books *La Conciliación* Archive (1945–72).

Decline of the Institution: La Conciliación, Ltd (1978–84)

The Society was created with 173 shares which corresponded to the same number of associates. It provided a social fund of over 4 million (4,551.182,67) pesetas. The Board set the value of each share at 6,000 pesetas for the year 1978. Thus, 27 associates who so wished and 8 families of associates who had passed away in 1976, each received 6,000 pesetas.[123] The following year, 1979, the value of each share was set at 8,000 pesetas, and this was the value maintained until the dissolution of the Society in 1984. In addition, the associates continued to pay their monthly dues.[124]

On 28 January 1978, with Don Joaquín Ibiricu Senosiain as president, Don Martín Laso Lasa as secretary and the attendance of four advisors (Messrs. Turrillas, Echarte, Bescos and Argos), the first ordinary meeting of the General Board of *La Conciliación de Pamplona S. A.* was held. These meetings were held annually. The Meetings also gave information on their economic status and the report on activities which were being reduced. In 1979, the medical service was cancelled, as at the time there was 'only one member on the list'.[125] Two years later, in January 1981, the home visits that were still made to ill members were suspended.[126]

And finally, in January 1983, 'the assembly, by majority vote, agrees that, in the future and as of this year 1983, no illness subsidies will be paid'. If anyone should need it, he could always apply 'to the system established by the society for that economic assistance that the managing board should decide'.[127] Thus finished the most important work carried out by *La Conciliación* for 80 years. In addition, few of new *La Conciliación* objectives were achieved. Its 'Aid to Members' was granted once (5,000 pesetas to a needy member in 1978); only one 'study grant' was offered, in 1978, for 'members and their children', in which 42,738 pesetas were awarded; 'Assistance for holidays' was enjoyed by two people in 1979; and in 1982 they managed to organize a collective outing. Also, an annual gift was given to each member.[128]

At the General Board Meetings an account was kept of the unremitting drop in membership. Most cancellations were caused by death, as over half the 160 members remaining in 1978 were over sixty-five years old. Each year, the Minutes commented 'light-heartedly' on the average age of the members. In 1979, it was sixty-two years and three months.

During this period, the main problem for the organization was controlling the 173 shares issued. With this in mind, in January 1979, a Project was developed on the transfer of actions by live members and another on the sale of shares to the family of members. If the strict conditions established were not fulfilled, the shares returned to the Society.[129].

There was no annual general meeting in 1984. The only record is the payment of some bills. The Society was dissolved because it did not fulfil the regulations for limited companies established in 1984.[130]

Conclusions

The case of *La Conciliación* is a good example for the study of social security and the social-healthcare assistance systems in the twentieth century. The position of *La Conciliación* coincides, generally speaking, with the studies that are being carried out on similar organization in other areas in Spain.

The study exemplifies the route followed by the Mutual Assistance Associations and other mutual benefit societies which looked after the healthcare of a high percentage of workers and their families until the establishment of obligatory health insurance in Spain in the 1940s and then when it was consolidated as the main assistance system in Spanish society.

The conditions in which the 'Sociedad Católica Protectora de Obreros *La Conciliación*' granted sick leave subsidy between 1902 and 1936 are similar to those laid down in other contemporaneous Societies and Mutual Assistance Associations.[131] But we must emphasize its importance, because of its total capacity and the economic assistance it granted over the years.

We have seen that between 1902 and 1936, *La Conciliación* evolved from a mixed Mutual Aid Society into a Workers' Association and, finally, into a Mutual Insurance Association. The changes happened gradually and reflect the growing role of the worker members. We will find growing class-consciousness that became apparent in the attempts to separate the employees firstly from the employers, and later from the protector members. This fact, which was contrary to the mixed character of the institution, created conflicts.

The modifications show the relationship of the organization with the world of labour and the need to adapt to social-labour legislation, such as the approval of obligatory retirement insurance (1919), cover for redundancy or the law on the Corporative Organization of Labour' (1926) and later the law on Professional Associations (1932). *La Conciliación* ceased to be a mixed association, became a Mutuality, integrated with a score of assorted worker associations and lost its denominational character (1932).

The evolution of the Society was affected to a far lesser extent by the new regulations on public health or labour safety and hygiene, and by the legislation on labour accidents. This is because the organization gave medical-assistance cover for the common illnesses of the workers and their families, and this was of a subsidiary nature.[132] In spite of everything, *La Conciliación* was part of the framework for medical assistance in the city.[133]

The repercussions of the different political options are noteworthy in the evolution of the Society. Both the Dictatorship (1923–30) and the governments of the Second Republic (1931–9) tended to make labour relations more horizontal or equitable. The greater radicalism of the republican governments was seen in the elimination of the protector members from the management areas of *La Conciliación*.

After the Spanish Civil War (1936–9), *La Conciliación* and the Mutual Associations in general, who were the heirs to the older Mutual Benefit Societies, were deprived of one of their main objectives, as was their participation in labour matters. Trade unionism was only permitted in the so-called *Obra sindical*, under the control of the Ministry of Labour. This research has also shown that the State interventionism conditioned the development of this entity.

The Mutual Assistance Association, such as *La Conciliación*, continued giving medical attention and paying different subsidies, which made sense during the 1940s and 1950s because of the deficient coverage offered by the Obligatory Healthcare Insurance. But from then on, the slow but sure introduction of social security and the development of labour mutual associations and of insurance companies meant that there was no role left to play for organizations that did not offer sufficient economic or healthcare advantages.

As we have described and is clear in the case *La Conciliación*, one of the causes of the decline of these mutual associations was the ageing of its members and the increased expenditure in medical fees and subsidies and compensation due to illness and demise of the members. The long lifespan of the organization has allowed us to see how it was affected by the high inflation and the economic crisis which began in the 1970s in the Western world.

Many organizations went into bankruptcy. This did not occur to *La Conciliación* due to, on the one hand, its meticulous management; on the other, due to the low cost of the medical attention it offered. This Mutual Association only covered the visits to the general practitioner and home visits, so it was not affected by the increasing expenses brought about by medical technologization. But these characteristics also made it less competitive. Although it was financially viable until the end, the project went into self-liquidation, as it was limited to one city and a certain kind of membership which shared the ideals of the institution. This complicated the admission of new younger members with no links to the original project of *La Conciliación*.

La Conciliación languished over twenty years. It could not evolve and change for the needs of private insurance and Labour Mutual Associations. Nor was *La Conciliación* capable of changing into a recreational society, as others did, because, in our opinion, it waited too long and was not completely convinced. *La Conciliación* probably lasted until 1984 because it adapted to the regulations as they appeared, until it became a limited company, in 1977. This last change allowed it to survive, as it was not affected by the laws passed in the early-1980s, with new requirements and economic reserves for mutual associations, in order to guarantee their solvency. The redesigning of Mutual Associationism in Spain was carried out when the Law for the Ordering of Private Insurance was passed in 1984, at which time *La Conciliación* no longer existed.

Analysis of the changes in the statutes of *La Conciliación* and its supportive activities has permitted us to understand the identity of the association, its characteristics and its historical reality, which are reflected in its operative reality. Simultaneously we can see the continuity of the original project.

As Professor Olabarri states, the mutual benefit and mutual aid societies were not only of great importance in the material maintenance of the workers, but also in the formation of not just one 'worker culture', but, in fact, several.[134] They underline the difference and, at the same time, the relationships between social history and the history of social politics.

The study of the life of *La Conciliación* allows us to contemplate the lengthy course of Spain's policy on healthcare and to examine the complex relations between political regimes and the social policy on healthcare.

9 IN IT FOR THE MONEY? INSURERS, SICKNESS FUNDS AND THE DOMINANCE OF NOT-FOR-PROFIT HEALTH INSURANCE IN THE NETHERLANDS

R. A. A. Vonk

The introduction of the *Zorgverzekeringswet* (Health Insurance Act) on 1 January 2006 ushered in a new era of health insurance in the Netherlands. The old dual system of social and private health insurance was replaced by a social health insurance scheme under private law. With the reform the official ban on profit-making in health care was lifted. Opponents of this market-oriented change feared that by allowing profit, long-held principles as social solidarity, equal access to health care and ultimately the quality of care itself would be subverted.[1]

Not surprisingly, they depicted the reform as a victory for the commercial health insurance industry and their neo-liberal political supporters. However, if we take a look at the health insurance carriers that were active in the Netherlands around the time of the reform, virtually all of them were not-for-profit entities. This suggests that, contrary to popular belief, even the alleged stronghold of commercial insurers, the private health insurance industry, was heavily influenced by not-for-profit thinking. But how did this come to be that way?

This chapter will attend that question. I will examine in what way the not-for-profit health insurance ideology, personified in sickness funds and their (social) health insurance scheme, has influenced for-profit health insurers in the Netherlands during the twentieth century. I will conclude that both the government and sickness funds, though not always intentionally and not always in a coordinated manner, have tried to either neutralize or incorporate for-profit insurers in the broader system of health care financing. While on the other hand commercial health insurers internalized most of the not-for-profit insurance principles.

The Genesis of Private Health Insurance, 1910–30

At the start of the twentieth century sickness funds were the only providers of health insurance in the Netherlands. During the first half of the nineteenth century commercial sickness funds were predominant, but by 1900 they had virtually disappeared. Physicians had successfully rooted out commercial tendencies in the world of sickness funds.

Sickness funds insured around 18 per cent of the Dutch population. Their insurance scheme was based on service benefits, usually limited to basic medical and pharmaceutical care. To this end, sickness funds concluded contracts with physicians and pharmacists. As reimbursement for their services these care providers received a capitation fee: a fixed payment per year for each enrolled person in their practice.[2]

Sickness funds restricted their insurance scheme in several ways. First of all, they applied an income threshold for enrolment. Secondly, sickness funds only insured people living in a certain 'service area', usually a city and the surrounding rural region. Finally, high-risk groups such as the chronically ill, disabled, pregnant and elderly could not join the insurance scheme. However, if money allowed, most sickness funds tried to be lenient when it came to accepting high-risk individuals.[3]

During the nineteenth century the thinly spread system of sickness fund insurances seemed to be sufficient. The demand for access to health care was limited, as was the need for health insurance. During the first half of the twentieth century this changed significantly. At the end of the *Belle Époque* scientific medicine was advancing rapidly, especially in the eyes of contemporaries. Slowly but surely, new treatments became available, involving novelties such as electricity, X-rays, radioactive radium and synthetic chemicals. The locus of medical treatment shifted from the kitchen sink in the patient's house to the rapidly modernizing hospital.[4]

At the same time, economic developments were pushing the demand for health insurance. Years of rapid economic growth in the 1920s were followed by a profound economic recession in the 1930s. While the demand for professional health care started to grow, the financial means to pay for it were shrinking. As a result, the membership base of sickness funds grew from 18 to 45 per cent during the interwar years. The increasing demand for insurance wasn't restricted to the lower income groups. Even the well-to-do were looking for ways to insure themselves against the rapidly rising costs of health care.[5]

Much to the chagrin of the *Nederlandsche Maatschappij ter bevordering der Geneeskunst* (NMG), the Dutch Medical Association, a small number of sickness funds tried to expand their market to the wealthier middle classes. Some sickness funds raised the income limit to allow the middle classes to join the insurance scheme. For most physicians the private fee-for-service-practice was predominantly made up of middle-class families. Expanding the sickness fund scheme and its system of capitation-fees to the middle classes would therefore seriously reduce the physician's income.[6]

In 1912 the NMG issued a Binding Resolution in order to safeguard their private practice and profitable patients. This resolution obliged physicians to restrict their contracts to those sickness funds which met the requirements of the NMG. The most important requirement in this case was the employment of specified income-thresholds. Since around 95 per cent of all Dutch physicians were members of the NMG this resolution successfully divided the health insurance market into two segments: one consisting of sickness funds providing health insurance to lower-income groups and one segment consisting of out-of-pocket payment.[7]

A few entrepreneurs, seeing a potentially significant market, established both not-for-profit (mutual) and commercial (stock) private health insurance companies. These companies mimicked sickness funds in several ways. They were specialized mono-line insurers, meaning that health insurance was their core business. Their insurance scheme provided coverage for a comprehensive package of benefits, such as treatment by a general practitioner, prescription drugs, hospitalization and specialist treatment. Contrary to sickness funds, private health insurers mostly worked on a national level, selling their products via a widely spread network of agents. Furthermore, they did not conclude contracts with physicians. Policyholders were treated as private patients and got reimbursed afterwards. Instead of an insurance covering the full costs of medical care, policyholders were free to determine the extent of insurance coverage by choosing among different levels of cash reimbursement. There was no need to intrude in the 'sacred relationship' between patient and physician. [8]

There was no actuarial basis for indemnity-based health insurance, which was still a rather new branch of the insurance industry. Though they were aware of the threats of adverse selection and moral hazard, most insurers didn't have sufficient information about the applicants to even think about premium-differentiation. Furthermore, they could not shift financial risks to the physician like sickness funds did.

In order to keep their insurance plans financially sound, insurers more or less followed the example set by sickness funds, though they were not (and could not be) as lenient. Applications of possible high risk individuals were systematically denied and portfolios were regularly checked for policies with high claim rates. Nonrenewal and interim termination of insurance contracts were common practice, both among commercial and not-for-profit carriers. Not surprisingly, the reputation of the private health insurance industry among the public, physicians in particular, suffered greatly from these perceived malpractices. It seemed that profit was more important than providing access to health care.[9]

A New Attitude, 1930–40

By the end of the 1920s private health insurance was still a minor branch of the insurance industry. And a struggling one at that: between 1910 and 1930 seventeen out of twenty-nine private health insurance companies had gone bankrupt.[10] Health insurers were selling the wrong product. There was little demand for comprehensive health insurance among the middle classes. While the economic crisis of the 30s did have an adverse effect on the development of wages and income, most middle-class families could still afford to go to a family doctor or to buy prescription drugs. Hospitalization and surgery, on the other hand, were swiftly becoming costly and possibly ruinous calamities.

In the rural areas of the Netherlands the growing demand for hospital insurance plans was met by local, not-for-profit hospital insurance funds. In the urbanized parts, the more esteemed, larger and financially strong multiple-line insurance companies gained a strong foothold. For them the limited hospital insurance plans – covering the costs of hospitalization and specialist treatment – had several advantages. These products were less vulnerable to adverse selection and moral-hazard and considerably cheaper – and thus easier to sell – than the comprehensive health insurance plans offered by the mono-line insurers.[11]

The large multiple-line insurance companies brought a different attitude towards health insurance to the market. Other than the mono-line insurers, whose existence was based on this product, they considered health insurance to be a 'friendly' insurance product. If the policyholder was satisfied with his health insurance, it could be used as a 'bridge' to sell more profitable products such as fire or liability insurances. Making a profit on health insurance wasn't the main goal. Losses, of course within reasonable limits, were acceptable and could be compensated by the profits made in other branches. Furthermore the large insurance companies had an important advantage over the smaller mono-line insurers: they were considered to be more trustworthy.[12]

This strategy seemed to pay off. In 1940 roughly 9 per cent of the population (around 800,000 people) had bought a private hospital insurance plan, while only 1 per cent had bought comprehensive health insurance. If we take the local hospital insurance funds into account, the success of hospital plans becomes even more apparent. In the same year they insured 24.5 per cent of the population.[13] Profits, on the other hand, were indeed low. In 1938 the market-leader in hospital insurance plans, with a portfolio of 250,000 policyholders and a turnover of 1 million guilders, paid out a total of 2,800 guilders in dividends.[14]

Despite their growth, private health insurers were still marginal players in the field of health care by 1940; as was the case in other countries. Both in Germany and the United States private health insurance covered roughly 10 per cent of the population. In some aspects the Dutch private health insurance industry stands out. First of all, there was a large number of companies that offered private health insurance: roughly ninety. That's roughly 4.5 times the number of health insurance companies that were active in Germany in the same period. Secondly, for most of these companies health insurance wasn't their core business.[15]

Despite the fact that the private health insurance industry had grown considerably during the 1930s, the civil servants of the Ministry of Social Affairs didn't pay much attention to private health insurers. It was, after all, still a minor and highly fragmented branch of the insurance industry. They were more interested in creating a legal framework for sickness fund insurance. Private health insurance was linked to profit-seeking, malpractice and swindling and everyone agreed that these things were to be banned in the future system of health insurance.[16]

Though not-for-profit health insurance was judged to be morally superior to commercial health insurance, especially by the NMG, both sickness funds and private health insurance companies coexisted relatively peacefully. The NMG didn't like commercial health insurance, but it was more a nuisance than a threat. Nobody doubted that the government would introduce social health insurance sooner or later. But given the political climate, most insurers expected that it would at least take another twenty years. By then they would be so entrenched in the system, they couldn't be ignored.[17] But social health insurance came much sooner than many had anticipated and when it came it changed things forever.

The Introduction of Social Health Insurance, 1940–5

In November 1941 the German occupying authorities issued the Sickness Funds Decree, based on socio-political and economical motives. This decree created both a compulsory social health insurance scheme for wage workers and their dependants and a voluntary social health insurance scheme for non-wage-earners. Both schemes were limited by an income-threshold and were carried out by officially recognized sickness funds. The funds were obliged to accept all eligible applicants. The benefits of the compulsory scheme, followed in 1947 by the voluntary scheme, were extended to cover a broad spectrum of medical care, including hospitalization and specialist treatment. Everyone with an income above the income-threshold had to buy private health insurance or pay for their medical expenses themselves.[18]

The premium of compulsory social health insurance was income dependent. Both employee and employer paid half of the premium. The revenues were collected in a General Fund, from which the sickness funds were retrospectively reimbursed. This was not the case with the voluntary scheme. The government had set the rules: open enrolment, no age-limits and community-rated premiums. Yet, sickness funds were the primary risk-bearers. They were responsible for setting the premiums and that the deficits on the voluntary insurance were not reimbursed. Voluntary social health insurance was to be completely financed by premium revenues. Furthermore, it was not entirely separated from private health insurance. Those eligible for the voluntary social health insurance could opt for private health insurance.[19]

The introduction of social health insurance in the Netherlands had major repercussions for the private health insurance industry. In the decades before 1941 the often local income-threshold separating sickness fund insurance schemes and private health insurance plans rarely exceeded the amount of 2,500 guilders per year. The Sickness Fund Decree however, imposed a national income-threshold of 3,000 guilders. As a result most private health insurance companies lost up to 70 per cent of their health insurance portfolio, without any kind of compensation. It could have been worse, though. The local hospital insurance funds were virtually annihilated. During the course of five years their combined membership base dropped from 2.4 million to 400,000 people.[20]

The decree also marked the beginning of government supervision on health insurance. Social health insurance would be supervised by the Ministry of Social Affairs. There were plans to place the private health insurance industry under supervision as well, as was the case in Germany itself. After all, supervision would guarantee 'a fair and effective insurance plan'. Something they thought was sorely lacking.[21] This plan was mothballed in 1943. The war had taken a turn for the worse and the German authorities had other problems to worry about. Supervision, at least for private health insurance, boiled down to strict monitoring of the premium-setting by the Directorate-General of Price-Control.

After the dust of the Sickness Fund Decree had settled, the first conflicts arose. Sickness funds, reduced to the status of mere administrative bodies, looked for a way to regain some degree of autonomy. The Sickness Fund Decree did not specifically forbid sickness funds to create their own supplementary insurance schemes. Within a couple of years virtually every sickness fund made use of this loophole in the Decree.[22]

Being cheap and easy to market the supplementary scheme was an instant success. In 1943 the sickness funds in Amsterdam claimed to have insured 85 per cent of the total compulsory and voluntarily insured under their combined supplementary schemes. In their enthusiasm to market this new insurance scheme sickness funds claimed that private insurance schemes were automatically nullified when members joined the sickness fund's own scheme, urging members to stop paying premiums for this 'obsolete' product.[23]

Naturally, insurers thought otherwise. They were of the opinion that it was against the law for sickness funds to enter the field of private health insurance. For the first, but certainly not for the last time, the civil servants of Price-Control and Social Affairs decided to look the other way. As long as sickness funds could keep supplementary insurance financially sound without compromising social health insurance – which was virtually impossible – they could do as they pleased.[24] Keeping the supplementary insurance schemes viable while at the same time offering a broad package of benefits wasn't easy. Most sickness funds used the reserves they had built up in the years before social health insurance, which had more or less removed the need for reserves, to keep the supplementary schemes afloat.[25]

Private health insurers couldn't compete on either premium-setting or coverage, nor did they employ the same lenient selection criteria. Price-Control urged insurers to remove the interim-termination-clause and get rid of risk-selection. These suggestions were courteously but firmly cast aside.[26] The private health insurance industry was still oblivious to the fact the social and political climate was changing.

Social Justice versus Profit-Making, 1945–50

During its wartime exile in London the Dutch government had designed plans for a new system of social security in the Netherlands. Heavily inspired by the spirit of the Atlantic Charter and the English Beveridge Report, a special government committee chaired by Aart van Rhijn advocated the institution of a system of social security, controlled by the national government. After the war, these plans, which had given virtually no consideration to existing institutions or power-relations, proved to be politically unfeasible.[27]

As a result, the Sickness Fund Decree remained in force despite its tainted origin. Its most obvious Nazi feature, the concentration of power in the hands of a single individual, was replaced by a *Ziekenfondsraad,* or Sickness Fund Council. This council, consisting of representatives of sickness funds, the NMG, trade unions, employers and the Ministry of Social Affairs, would supervise compulsory and voluntary social health insurance and manage the resources of General Fund. More importantly, it was the main advisory body for the government on the subject of health care and health insurance.[28]

The private health insurance industry regained much of its old freedom after the war. The policy of price-monitoring was stopped in 1947. Price-Control once again advised the health insurance industry to loosen up some of their underwriting standards to show they acknowledged their social responsibility. Despite the failure of Van Rhijn's system, the idea of state-guaranteed social security based on solidarity, social justice and equal access to health care had gained considerable support, not in the least in the halls of the Ministry of Social Affairs. [29]

This advice was again largely ignored. Private health insurers remained steadfast in their old and proven ways. By the start of the 1950s, non-renewal and the interim termination of insurance contracts were still normal. Likewise, the elderly, chronically ill and other high-risk individuals were for the most part still unable to buy private health insurance. However, contrary to the 1930s this was no longer tolerated. The private health insurance industry became the target of severe criticism in the media and the political arena. The denial, termination and non-renewal of insurance weren't seen as ways to guarantee the continuity of the company. Instead these policies were explained as results of the policy profit-maximization. This was deemed to be incompatible with the social responsibility that health insurers had: to secure access to health care. Besides their social responsibility, it was not considered to be very civil to make profits when the country itself was still recovering from the consequences of five years of occupation.[30]

On the whole, commercial health insurers were extremely slow to respond to this critique. Though a small group of health insurers tried to meet the demand for a more fair and accessible health insurance product, the majority of health insurance carriers didn't change a thing. In their view, insuring was all about separating high and low risks: even in something as socially loaded as health insurance.[31]

The slow response of commercial insurers, combined with the drive of sickness funds to regain their autonomy, compelled sickness funds to break the boundaries of social health insurance. As soon as 1947 regional conglomerates of sickness funds had established special foundations that would act as not-for-profit private health insurance companies. These foundations were soon called *bovenbouwers* (superstructures).[32]

The *bovenbouwers* were created with the idea that economies of scale would enable sickness funds to introduce principles of social health insurance in private health insurance, such as non-selection and the inclusion of pre-existing conditions. Furthermore, the link between *bovenbouwer* and sickness funds considerably lowered the costs of administration and acquisition and secured a steady flow of potential policyholders from the social health insurance schemes. As a result their health insurance policies could cover a broad package of benefits for a relatively low premium.[33] The *bovenbouwers* were immensely successful. In the course of a decade their market share in private health insurance increased from 8 to 40 per cent, while the market share of commercial health insurers dropped from 57 to 35 per cent.[34]

There was just one problem: *bovenbouwers* were illegal. The regulations clearly stated sickness funds were not allowed to offer health insurance to people with an income above the income-threshold.[35] In order to bypass this restriction sickness funds made sure there was strict legal seperation between sickness funds and their *bovenbouwers*, but this division was virtually non-existent in the daily routine. The board of directors of the *bovenbouwer* consisted of the directors and administrators of the associated sickness funds. Furthermore the *bovenbouwer* held office in the same building as the sickness funds and used its administrative and agency services for a symbolic fee.[36]

Commercial health insurers complained bitterly about this newest intrusion of sickness funds in their domain. They had every right to feel threatened. Despite fact that *bovenbouwers* were in clear violation of the intended separation of social and private health insurance, the Sickness Fund Council in which sickness funds happened to have a strong position was satisfied with the legal separation of *bovenbouwers* and sickness funds. This was a pivotal ruling, since it officially established the right of sickness funds to provide private health insurance. This ruling becomes all the more remarkable if we take into account that in Germany, the *Heimat* of Dutch social health insurance, the separation was strictly enforced. For the council the annihilation of the 'antisocial pursuit of profit' in health insurance was considered to be more important than keeping the separation intact.[37]

Commercial Insurers try to Adapt, 1950–60

After this decision most commercial health insurers realized it was now or never. The council had opened the door for sickness funds to enter and possibly conquer the market for private health insurers. Neither the government, nor the physicians, unions and employers seemed to mind that prospect.[38]

Forced by increasing political and social pressure and the loss of market share many commercial health insurance companies tried to adapt to the new situation. They gradually introduced more beneficial health insurance policies. Waiting periods and the interim-termination-clauses slowly disappeared and newborn children were accepted without risk-selection. A few rather bold insurance companies even introduced so-called 'cost-price-policies'. With a direct reference to social health insurance, these policies guaranteed the reimbursement of the actual costs of treatment instead of the predetermined maximum amounts, making underinsurance a thing of the past.[39]

It was clear though, that more had to be done in order to successfully compete with the *bovenbouwers*. Collaboration between commercial health insurers became the new trend. In 1957 around thirty-nine commercial health insurers formed a cartel. They collectively replaced their old health insurance policies with a new uniform ANPZ-policy. This policy combined all of the above-mentioned changes and novelties. Most importantly, the ANPZ-policy was based on the 'cost-price' principle, which was soon adopted by virtually every commercial health insurer in the Netherlands.[40] At the same time the ANPZ-cartel established a pool for substandard risks. If the applicant had been insured under social health insurance for a full year prior to his application, the risk-pool would enable him or her to buy private health insurance. The terms were comparable to those of the ANPZ-policy, though the premium was set considerably higher.[41]

With the ANPZ-policy and the risk-pool commercial health insurers hoped to counter the continuing decline of their market share and simultaneously convince the government not to expand social health insurance. Though the coverage of the ANPZ-policy wasn't as broad as the insurance policies offered by most *bovenbouwers*, commercial health insurers were adamant that they were as generous as they possibly could be. Still, risk-selection wasn't entirely abandoned. Though many insurers had become somewhat apologetic about it, it was still deemed to be an indispensable instrument. The bankruptcy of the largest private health insurer at the time, the *bovenbouwer* AZR, in 1960 due to excessively low premiums and non-selective underwriting only strengthened the commercial health insurers in this belief.[42]

Nevertheless, by giving in to the social demands – albeit slowly – commercial health insurers gradually lost their pariah-like status. *Bovenbouwers* became aware that they had a lot of things in common with commercial insurers. Both agreed that the health insurance of middle and high income groups had to be kept out of the reach of the government, at all costs. By establishing *bovenbouwers*, sickness funds had committed themselves firmly to the dual system of social and private-health insurances, but there was more.[43]

The Interdependency of Social and Private Insurance

With the earlier mentioned bankruptcy of AZR the rapid expansion of the *bovenbouw*-insurance ground to a halt. During the 1960s both the *bovenbouw* and the commercial health insurers controlled roughly 40 per cent of the market, leaving the remaining 20 per cent in the hands of the struggling local hospital insurance funds and mutual categorical insurers. All in all, there were approximately 180 health insurance companies while the potential market consisted of roughly 3 million people (around 25 per cent of the total population). Nevertheless, due to the rapid expansion of the health care sector and the increasing demand for health insurance, virtually all health insurers were able to expand their business. The share of private health insurance in the total health care expenditure increased from 3.2 per cent to 12.8 per cent between 1953 and 1968.[44]

Contrary to the 1950s – a period in which the eradication of profit in health care seems to have been a driving force behind the attitude of both the government and sickness funds towards private health insurance – the 1960s can be seen as the period in which commercial insurers were gradually incorporated into the system of health care financing. Profit was still frowned upon, but it wasn't the abomination it was before.

Apart from the fact that the commercial insurers had proved that they were able to adapt and fit into a system in which profit wasn't the main objective, there was another reason for this change of heart. Social health insurance had become increasingly dependent on the existence of a private health insurance industry. Family doctors and specialists agreed with the relatively low fees paid under social health insurance, because they could charge their private patients more.[45] By the end of the 1960s this system of 'hidden' cross-subsidization between social and private health insurance had become essential to the system. In aggregate, the costs of care provided by GPs or specialists per private patient (roughly 30 per cent of the total population) were 50 per cent higher than for patients covered under social health insurance. Yet, the number of visits to the family doctor and specialist per private patient was considerably lower.[46]

As long as the Dutch economy was booming and money seemed to be abundant, as was the case in the 1950s and 1960s, this system of indirect solidarity between high and low income groups seemed justified in the eyes of physicians, government officials and sickness funds. Even private health insurers were not entirely opposed to it. It was 'not exactly the most healthy situation', according to one of them, but they didn't complain much either. At least they were an integral part of the system now and they were starting to get recognition.[47]

The first step in embedding private health insurance in the broader system of health care financing, was the inclusion of commercial and other private health insurers in the *Centraal Orgaan Ziekenhuistarieven* (COZ, Central Institute for Hospital Charges). In 1962 hospital charges, which were still set by the bureau of Price-Control, were officially liberalized. Yet, the COZ was established to give hospitals, sickness funds and private health insurers a platform to collectively set the prices.[48]

In order to effectively participate in the COZ the four branch-organizations of health insurers (commercial, mutual, *bovenbouw* and hospital insurance funds) joined forces in a new umbrella organization, with the rather prosaic name *Kontaktcommissie Landelijke Organisaties voor Ziektekostenverzekering* (KLOZ, Contact Committee for National Organizations of Private Health Insurers). In the KLOZ-meetings ideological antagonists like commercial and not-for-profit insurers tried to establish a cohesive view on private health insurance. As a result it brought former opponents closer together. In their capacity as managers of the *bovenbouwers* leading individuals from the world of social health insurance were discussing common problems and issues with the managers of for-profit health insurance companies. Though there was still little trust, polarization was slowly replaced by appeasement and cooperation.[49]

Incorporating Commercial Insurers in a Broader System

Via the KLOZ the private health insurance industry became an acceptable party in the health care debate. The Catholic Minister of Social Affairs, Gerard Veldkamp, even invited them to hearings concerning his restructuring plans. Compared to the 1950s, this mildly benevolent attitude towards private health insurers from the ranks of the government was quite a change; not without reasons, though.

Veldkamp needed all the support he could get. Not only was he faced with a voluntary social health insurance scheme that hurried towards insolvency, but also with profound changes in the nature of health care demand. The share of long-term care was increasing. Yet, the Poor Law and other municipal social provisions which up until then had financed care for the elderly, mentally ill and disabled, were not designed to cope with either the increasing demand nor the higher costs of increasing professionalization. Veldkamp wanted to solve both problems by one stroke: a set of two interdependent national health insurance schemes.[50]

The national insurance scheme for long-term care, called AWZ, would be the basis. It would replace the Poor Law as the main source of funding for nursing home care, long-term psychiatric care and care for the mentally and physically disabled. The AWZ-scheme was widely supported, even among the ranks of commercial health insurers who traditionally abhorred national insurance schemes.[51]

In addition, Veldkamp wanted to create a restricted compulsory health insurance scheme, called BVV. This scheme would provide health insurance to wage-earners and non wage-earners alike. However, there would still be an income threshold. By combining wage workers and non-wage workers the premiums charged to non wage-earners could be considerably lowered, just as many political parties and the association of small and medium-sized companies had demanded. Furthermore, social and private health insurance would be completely separated, because the former 'grey area' of the voluntary social health insurance scheme would cease to exist.[52]

By leaving the segment for private health insurance undisturbed, Veldkamp acknowledged the importance of the indirect flow of money between social and private health insurance. It's not surprising that the commercial health insurance industry was mildly positive about the BVV-plan. For them it really didn't change a thing. Indeed, the market for private health insurance products would increase since the income-threshold the new scheme would be lower than the current one.

The opposition against the BVV was mainly fuelled by physicians and employers. Physicians saw it as a first step towards fulfilling their darkest nightmares: the complete nationalization of the health care sector. Employers dreaded the increase in social premiums they had to pay and weren't enthusiastic about the fact they had to subsidize the health insurance of people who weren't in their employment, like the elderly or the self-employed. Their combined effort forced Veldkamp to withdrawn the BVV-bill in 1966.[53]

After the failure of the BVV, Veldkamp aimed at the inclusion of hospitalization and specialist treatment in the AWZ. By including these benefits, the financial pressure on both the compulsory and voluntary social health insurance schemes could be considerably relieved as well. This, however, caused a massive uproar among sickness funds and private health insurers. They rightly considered the insurance of hospital care and specialist treatment as the backbone of their industry.[54]

Veldkamp's new plans threatened both commercial health insurers and *bovenbouwers* alike. In order to thwart Veldkamp's amended AWZ-plan, the managers of the *bovenbouw*-insurers practically badgered their commercial colleagues into solving the 'problem' of risk-selection. After all, the existence of risk-selection was the main reason why Veldkamp got political support in the first place.

Since *bovenbouwers* could sustain their policy of non-selective acceptance because of their comparatively large health insurance portfolios, they suggested that the commercial insurers could create something similar. They were of the opinion that by establishing a national insurance pool for sub-standard risks even commercial insurers could abandon risk-selection. It would at least show they were aware that health insurance was all about providing access to health care instead of making a profit. This suggestion was accompanied by a thinly veiled threat that *bovenbouwers* were ready and willing to take over the entire private health insurance industry.[55]

The appeal to social solidarity, combined with a little bit of coercion, pushed commercial health insurers to do something they feared to do. At the same time they realized that nobody would be willing to defend their interests if they didn't find a way to discard risk-selection. For most commercial insurers, health insurance had become too important to lose.[56] In 1968, private health insurance had a premium turnover of more than 4.8 billion guilders. This corresponded with a share of roughly 31 per cent in the total turnover of the non-life insurance industry.[57]

After long and rather heated debates in the KLOZ and a lot of talking within the branch-organization of commercial health insurers, a national risk-pool was established in 1967. The *Nederlandse Onderling herverzekeringsinstituut Ziektekosten* (NOZ, Dutch Mutual Reinsurance Institute for Health Insurance) enabled health insurers to offer health insurance to formerly uninsurable substandard risks. The premiums were only moderately higher than the average premiums.[58]

The NOZ was presented as the 'ultimate solution' for the problem of risk-selection. Because virtually every private health insurer joined the risk-pool, the private health insurance industry was able to insure almost everyone who wanted to. The founding of the NOZ-risk pool led to a drop in the proportion of uninsured individuals from 18 per cent in 1954 to 2.5 per cent in 1968.[59]

Mainly due to this initiative Veldkamp lost most of his support. Hospitalization and specialist treatment were taken out of the benefits package of the once-again amended AWZ-bill. The bill, rechristened to AWBZ, passed parliament in 1968 under Veldkamp's successor, Bouke Roolvink. Private health insurers finally got their long sought appreciation: they were officially recognized as carriers of the new scheme alongside sickness funds.[60]

This official recognition crowned a long process of incorporating commercial health insurance in the system of health care financing. Between them, the sickness funds and the national government had moulded commercial health insurance into a prevailing not-for-profit framework. Commercial insurers were in a tight spot, but they carefully guarded this fragile equilibrium. They preferred a quiet market. But it couldn't last forever. Just how fragile the system was became clear during the 1970s.

An Inevitable Rebellion, 1970–80

At the end of the 1960s the steady economic growth which had lasted for nearly twenty years was beginning to stall. The turmoil on the international monetary market caused by the collapse of the system of Bretton-Woods severely crippled the Dutch economy. The oil crisis of 1973 more or less finished the deal. The time of economic growth was replaced by years of rampant inflation. The government decided to intervene, by re-establishing a general price-control policy which would remain in force until 1987.[61]

This undermined the delicate equilibrium in the private health insurance market. The difference between the expected costs of low-risk and high-risk policyholders was quickly growing out of proportion. The existing system of undifferentiated, community-rated premiums made those companies with a large amount of high risks (mostly elderly) in their portfolio increasingly less attractive to low-risk individuals. Especially the larger commercial health insurers were suffering from rapidly aging portfolios. They were now paying the price for their effort to safeguard an important part of their business. Much was sacrificed in order to catch up with the *bovenbouw*-insurers, get recognition from the government and to pacify the private health insurance industry. With the introduction of 'cost-price'-policies commercial health insurers had agreed with open-ended financing, leaving little room for them to put a cap on expenditure when the costs became too high. Furthermore, they had more or less welcomed adverse selection with open arms by agreeing to refrain from risk-selection.[62]

The price-control policy severely limited the room for private health insurers to differentiate their premiums. Even so, it's doubtful if commercial insurers really wanted to. After all, they had the least room to offer premium discounts to low-risk groups. Contrary to the *bovenbouwers*, who had the advantage of a more or less continuous supply of relatively young former sickness fund enrolees, and the rather small portfolios of mutual not-for-profit health insurers, the commercial insurers had comparatively old and large portfolios. They would need large sums of money to cross-subsidize the loss-making policies of high-risk individuals. This made premium differentiation a dangerous strategy.[63] Besides, there was a widely supported reluctance of risk-rating among commercial health insurers. It would give the government all the ammunition it needed if they wanted to nationalize private health insurance.[64]

The introduction of deductibles was the only sensible way for commercial health insurers to avoid a deadly premium spiral. At the start of the 1970s the generation of the post-war baby-boom was coming of age so the supply of low-risk individuals would be abundant. This plan backfired completely. It wasn't the commercial health insurance industry which profited the most from health insurance policies with high deductibles. A few small mutual not-for-profit mutual insurers stole a march on commercial insurers. Because of their small and young portfolios, they could match any premium-discount the commercial insurers had to offer and still be more generous. Contrary to commercial insurers who still used agents to sell insurance products, the mutual health insurers had discovered the benefits of direct-mailing. They started an aggressive campaign to attract new subscribers.

This new attitude didn't go well with the not-for-profit character of these mutual insurers. In fact they kept it quite vague whether or not they changed into for-profit companies. Now they had the best of both worlds. Not surprisingly, the market share of the mutual health insurers increased, mostly at the expense of the commercial health insurers.

High deductible policies were soon copied by most other health insurers, with the notable exception of most *bovenbouwers*. The sickness funds, still in tight control of the *bovenbouw*-insurers, strongly opposed the introduction of deductibles and age-adjusted premiums in their *bovenbouw*-insurance scheme. Nevertheless, by the end of the 1970s almost every health insurer offered a policy with high deductibles.[65]

The introduction of deductibles in private health insurance proved to be disastrous for the voluntary social health insurance scheme. Lured away by cheaper health insurance policies, many twenty-two to twenty-nine year olds bought private health insurance. This led to a relative increase of elderly in the voluntary scheme which subsequently lead to rapidly rising premiums.[66]

During the 1960s the private health insurance industry was more or less integrated within the system of social insurance. But now it seemed that the private health insurance industry was rapidly spinning out of control. This was enough reason for the social-democrats in the Den Uyl-government (1973–7) to reconsider the introduction of national health insurance. Both the political and social consensus was still very much in favour of this idea.[67] Even the branch-organization for commercial health insurers seemed to have set aside its traditional aversion to national insurances. In 1971 they presented their own ideas about national health insurance.[68]

According to the commercial health insurance industry national health insurance under private law carried out by competing carriers was the best way to curb the newly risen problems of premium-differentiation and the concealed risk-selection. The emphasis the report placed on a self regulated market-equilibrium complemented by social health insurance principles can be seen as result of the decade of interaction between *bovenbouwers* and their social health insurance principles and liberal free-market thinking of commercial insurers within the ranks of the KLOZ.[69]

Nevertheless, at the end of the 1970s the 'the era of collectivism' seemed to be over. The social-democratic plan for an extensive reconstruction of the health care system was withdrawn in 1975 after Ministry of Finance made clear that there was simply not enough money available to fund it. At the same time sickness funds were losing control over the *bovenbouw*-insurers, as a new generation of managers started to replace long-held principles of social solidarity with commercial entrepreneurship. Even *bovenbouwers* started to offer policies with high deductibles.[70]

No Nonsense: the End of Private Health Insurance, 1980–90

At the start of the 1980s the economic crisis had worsened into a more long term recession and the political climate had changed significantly. The centre-left government of the 1970s was succeeded by a centre-right coalition. The Lubbers government (1982–6), strongly advocating a no-nonsense approach, announced that drastic measures had to be taken. As part of a comprehensive plan of budget cuts, the investments in health care and social health insurance schemes had to be cut down with 3 billion guilders. This task was given to a former *bovenbouw*-chairman, Joop van der Reijden, who became state-secretary for Health.

Like most of his predecessors, Van der Reijden was faced by the huge financial difficulties of the voluntary social health insurance scheme. But by 1982 failure was imminent. Extensive skimming by mutual, and to lesser degree commercial health insurers, had brought it to its knees. At the same time the escalating risk-segmentation and premium-differentiation had made financial access to health care for the privately insured elderly and other high-risk groups increasingly difficult.[71]

In order to keep the government or at least national health insurance at bay, the organization of sickness funds and the KLOZ agreed to create a system of voluntary cross-subsidization. The private health insurance industry would sponsor the voluntary social health insurance scheme with 180 million guilders per year. Though this somewhat relieved the pressure on the voluntary scheme, it was clear this wasn't enough. In a sudden revival of the old 'special relationship', sickness funds and *bovenbouwers* proposed to solve this problem together. They were of the opinion that a merger of *bovenbouwers* and sickness funds could save voluntary social health insurance. Van der Reijden was not enthusiastic about this suggestion. He wanted to separate private and social health insurance altogether, while at the same time institutionalizing the already existing flow of money between the private and the social health insurance.

The love affair did however further antagonize relations in the KLOZ. Van der Reijden had made it clear that if the private health insurance industry backed his plans for the reorganization of health insurance system, they could count on a transfer of roughly 700,000 new applicants to the private health insurance industry. The commercial health insurers forced the *bovenbouwers* to take sides: either with them or with the sickness funds. *Bovenbouwers* choose the latter as they were well aware they would absorb the vast majority the former voluntarily insured anyway due to their association with the sickness funds.

On 25 March 1986 the *Wet op de Toegang tot de Ziektekostenverzekering* (WTZ, Act on the Access to Health Insurance) passed parliament. Both the voluntary social health insurance schemes and the social health insurance scheme for the elderly were dissolved. The membership bases of both schemes (roughly 2.5 million people) were transferred to either the compulsory health-insurance scheme or the private health insurance industry.[72]

The WTZ made sure that everyone with private health insurance would remain privately insured, even after reaching the age of sixty-five and even when his or her retirement income would drop below the income-threshold. The same held for those insured under the compulsory social health insurance. Hereby social and private health insurance were successfully separated, for the first time in history.[73]

In order to facilitate these changes, government regulation of the private health insurance sector was needed. After all, the government realized that – given what had happened in the 70s – most commercial and mutual health insurers were not going to accept elderly and other high-risk groups just because they were asked to. Therefore the government introduced a *Standaard pakket polis* (SPP, Standard Insurance Policy) which offered a standardized package of benefits and predetermined premiums. Furthermore health insurers were obliged to accept all applicants.[74]

With the SPP policy the government introduced a social health insurance policy within the private health insurance market, the first step in socializing the private health insurance industry. At the same time the flow of money between private and social health insurance was institutionalized. The *Wet Medefinancier-*

ing Oververtegenwoordiging Oudere Ziekenfondsverzekerden (MOOZ, Act on the Co-funding Over-representation Elderly Sickness Fund Insured) created a system of mandatory cross-subsidization between compulsory social health insurance and private health insurance. Policyholders insured under private health insurance were paying additional solidarity-fees, on top their normal premium. This money was used to co-finance the care for the elderly insured under social health insurance and the SPP-policyholders within private health insurance.[75]

The Best of Both Worlds? 1990–2006

The WTZ, or 'minor system reform', was meant as a temporary measure. It was to be replaced by a more extensive reorganization of the health insurance sector. In order to plan this extensive reorganization a special committee was appointed, led by ex-Phillips CEO Wisse Dekker. In their report, soon known under the acronym 'Dekker', the committee proposed the introduction of national health insurance combined with regulated competition.

The new system would remove the distinction between the various health insurance schemes (social health insurance, AWBZ, private health insurance, civil servant schemes, etc.) One scheme, a 'basic insurance', would provide coverage for the entire population. This scheme would be carried out by competing insurers. The committee hoped that competition would drive down prices and lead to greater efficiency.[76]

Not surprisingly, the Dekker-plan provoked mixed reactions. The government was forced to postpone a direct implementation of the Dekker-plan, though the idea of managed competition within the framework of national health insurance wasn't abandoned. Dekker would be introduced in phases. By the end of 1992 the new system of health insurance should be fully realized.

Within the world of health insurance, most sickness funds and virtually every *bovenbouwers* was fervently in favour of the idea. Commercial health insurers on the other hand, were not at all enthusiastic. If Dekker came into being, there would be no-one to stop the merger of sickness funds and *bovenbouwers*. How could the relatively small commercial health insurers possibly compete with organizations that insured millions? For commercial health insurers it was fundamental that the social and private health insurance would remain separated.

But they didn't. On New Year's Eve 1991 Hans Simons, the state-secretary of Health, allowed a small mutual health insurance company to establish its own sickness fund. By allowing this, Simons, probably without fully realizing it, single-handedly lifted the iron curtain between social and private health insurance. In the years that followed, virtually every *bovenbouwer* merged with one or more sickness funds, while former sickness funds branched out into private health insurance.[77]

Since the boundary between social and private health insurance had effectively ceased to exist, there was no need to keep both branch-organizations
intact. In 1995 the VNZ, the branch-organization of sickness funds and the
KLOZ merged into *Zorgverzekeraars Nederland* (Health Insurers Netherlands).
The darkest dreams of commercial health insurers had become reality. While
bvoenbouwers and sickness fund grew, commercial insurers started to sell their
health insurance portfolios. By 2006, when managed competition was finally
introduced, there were only a handful of commercial insurers left in the private
health insurance industry. The new not-for-profit juggernauts that came out of
the merger process controlled roughly 95 per cent of the industry.[78]

Conclusions

The influence of sickness funds and their not-for-profit approach to health insurance on the development of commercial health insurance in the Netherlands has
been immense. Though not-for-profit health insurers were active in the private
health insurance industry, commercial insurers controlled most of the market.
Still, between 1910 and 1930 commercial health insurers more or less mimicked
sickness funds in every way. This isn't surprising since sickness funds had a long
track record in health insurance, while indemnity-based health insurance plans
were relatively new.

However, the indemnity-based insurance plans gave commercial insurers a
significant disadvantage. They couldn't shift the brunt of financial risks to physicians like sickness funds did through the system of capitation fees. Health
insurance proved to be too risky a business. The failure-rate in the private health
insurance industry was immense and the way in which commercial insurers
tried to counter the effects of moral hazard and adverse selection ruined their
reputation. This didn't change when multiple-line insurance companies entered
the market with specialized products: limited hospital insurance plans. Commercial health insurance was something both physicians and the government
disapproved of. Yet, by the end of the 1930s private health insurance was still too
minor a branch for the government to get worried about.

This attitude of benevolent indifference changed after the introduction
of social health insurance in 1941. While the Sickness Fund Decree severely
weakened the private health insurance industry, it also more or less officially recognized it as a part of the health insurance system. This forced the government,
physicians and, most importantly, sickness funds to rethink their strategy after
the end of the war. This resulted in a process of contestation, adaptation and
assimilation of commercial health insurance its pursuit of profit.

In this development of contestation and assimilation one defining moment
stands out: the decision of both the Sickness Fund Council, representing the

majority of stakeholders in the health care sector and the Ministry of Social Affairs to allow sickness funds to penetrate and conquer the private health insurance market. In the years directly after the end the German occupation making profit in healthcare, and thus indirectly the right of commercial health insurers to exist, was widely questioned in the Netherlands. The spirit of social justice and the drive towards universal coverage stimulated the penetration of private health insurance by sickness funds.

The success of the *bovenbouwers* forced commercial health insurers to adapt. By extending benefits and adopting a more social approach to health insurance, commercial insurers gradually shifted towards a not-for-profit attitude. This wasn't a complete break with the past because multiple-line insurers never intended to maximize their profits on health insurance products. By the end of the 1950s the intention to annihilate the commercial health insurance industry was replaced by the policy of incorporation. It was clear that social and private health insurance had become interdependent. Together they formed a system of unintended income-solidarity. Private patients paid more for specialist treatment which enabled specialist to lower the fees for patients insured under social health insurance.

For the government this meant there was something to gain by the official incorporation of private health insurance and its commercial components. When commercial insurers dropped risk-selection in 1968, the dream of universal coverage was reached without the need to create a system of national health insurance.

However, during the 1970s it became clear that the balance that was needed to sustain this was brittle. When the costs of health care exploded, the carefully wrought equilibrium in the private health insurance industry came crashing down. Heavily burdened by ageing health insurance portfolios and lacking the possibility to cap expenditure, commercial health insurers were forced to fall back on drastic 'anti-social' instruments, such as premium-differentiation and deductibles. By the mid-1980s the government was forced to intervene. It was clear that, even though commercial health insurers were fundamentally opposed to the idea of social solidarity and equal access to health care, it just could not be achieved on a voluntary basis. A more enduring, accessible system of health insurances could only be achieved by government regulation. With the introduction of the WTZ-scheme, private health insurance was effectively socialized and the already existent cross-subsidization between high and low income groups was formalized by a system of solidarity fees.

For commercial health insurance the WTZ-reform was the beginning of the end. The government had taken control and wasn't going to give it up. Even though the 1980s did bring the promise of managed competition, it was always in combination with the threat of national insurance. The decision of Simons to lift the iron curtain between social and private health insurance in 1991 more or less signed the death warrant for commercial health insurers. Their portfolios were not large enough to compete with on equal terms with the expanding *bovenbouwers* and sickness funds. From the start of the 1990s commercial insurers gradually sold their health insurance portfolios. By the time profit-making was officially allowed, it had – at least in the health insurance industry – become virtually extinct.

Acknowledgments

I wish to thank Bernard Harris, Herb Emery, Danièle Rigter, Karel-Peter Companje and Anna Dlabačová for their comments.

10 BELGIAN MUTUAL HEALTH INSURANCE AND THE NATION STATE

D. Rigter

For a variety of reasons governments over time have tried to make sure that as many people as possible protect themselves against risks. Some of these risks are considered to be more damaging to society than others and are deemed to be in need of governmental regulation. Risks involving sickness and old age are among them. The way in which Belgian citizens took care of those risks and the reaction of their government in the form of regulations and laws, is the subject of this chapter.

Modern Belgian health insurance, which is part of the social security system, has experienced problems as a result of rising medical costs, greater demand for medical care and the steadily increasing number of elderly people. In this respect the Belgian situation is similar to that of most of other developed countries. Total health care costs in Belgium rose from 8.6 per cent of GDP in 1998 to 10.9 per cent in 2009 and the rise in costs seems to be accelerating.[1] The growth and ageing of the population were expected to be responsible for an increase in health costs of 0.9 per cent per year.[2] The percentage of people over the age of sixty-five was projected to rise from 15.1 per cent in 1990 to 20 per cent by the year 2020. In 2008 the percentage had risen already to seventeen and was expected to rise to thirty in 2060.[3] These numbers are among the highest in OECD countries. In the last year of their life many patients cost their health insurers more than in all previous years combined. Continuity, affordability and accessibility are key elements in the discussions concerning reform of the system.

The Belgium health insurance system has, like Germany and the Netherlands for instance, its own specific characteristics. During the age of nationalism in the nineteenth and twentieth century, similar and comparable problems were dealt with somewhat differently in each nation state. The countries however were keeping a keen eye on developments elsewhere. Most of the Belgian health insurance funds (for a large part mutual societies) have a long history. After the introduction of the compulsory health insurance in 1945 the mutual societies were given an important role in its implementation.

In what way do the historical roots of the Belgian system play a part in the rising costs and in the way this problem is dealt with? How did the formation of the Belgian state and the challenge this still poses influence the health insurance system and the way its problems have been handled?

In general, a strong 'monolithic' central government has been shown historically to be an essential prerequisite for the introduction of compulsory health insurance. This probably has to do with overcoming the resistance against the high costs involved and the presence of existing organizations that are well grounded in society. The waning power of Belgium's federal government, especially in the last decades, has undoubtedly influenced the modernization of the health insurance system and the tackling of rising costs. The developments in Belgium are an interesting case study for the way in which the European convergence in health care may work out. European rules that stipulate the free exchange of peoples and goods frustrate cost cutting measures taken on a national level so that eventually managing costs only seems possible with a strong European consensus and a strong European executive. On every executive level, from mutualities to the European parliament, democratic values must be in effect to be able to ensure popular support.

This article deals with the following: the origins of mutual health insurance in Belgium, the incorporation of mutual schemes within the state scheme, the challenges now facing this scheme and the way in which the unique characteristics of the scheme are shaping its responses to these challenges. It also deals with the question how these characteristics may pose a unique set of problems for Belgium in comparison with other European countries, even though the basic challenges of an ageing population and rising health care costs are common to all of them.

National Supervision of Local Initiatives

Mutual aid provided by relief funds with sometimes compulsory membership was well known in most cities and towns in the Netherlands. From the last quarter of the eighteenth century the enlightened absolutist Habsburg, French and Orange rulers tried to implement a national policy to relieve poverty. They all met with the particularism of the cities and of existing organizations like the church, guilds and brotherhoods.[4] In 1812 the French Minister of Internal Affairs instructed the prefects of the Dutch districts to hold an inquiry which resulted in the questionnaire 'Caisses de secours et de prévoyance'.[5] The report gave insight into a number of mutual organizations in the Netherlands. The French Le Chapelier Law, which in Belgium was in force from 1795 until 1866, forbade professional associations and promoted free trade and labour. It was no longer allowed to impose compulsory membership of organizations.[6] Despite the ban on organization, local authorities permitted and even promoted collective solidarity. After 1815 the effects of the law were in some ways alleviated. It was recognized that private funds relieved the burden of the municipal poor relief. The end of the guild system meant that the general funds, where occupation wasn't a factor, became an alternative.[7]

From 1815–30 the former Austrian Low Countries were part of the Dutch Kingdom. A royal decree of 1820 settled the consequences of the French ban on guilds. It also contained a summons on municipalities to stimulate the founding of voluntary insurance funds, thereby undermining the ban on associations. Mutual aid funds that had been part of the guilds had to be put into separate entities and could no longer exclude non-guild members. The local governments had to maintain oversight but their permission was no longer required.[8] The Council of State [Raad van State] deemed it self-evident that one of the requirements was that the boards of these insurers should be chosen by the insured.[9] The fact that membership wasn't allowed to be compulsory had its effect on the solidity of the funds. It made local and occupational funds more vulnerable. Their membership was ageing.[10]

The national government was not always able to enforce its rules. It is for instance noticeable that in Ghent autonomous industrial funds, craft-trade funds and the factory societies until 1850 largely retained their exclusive character 'and did not admit members from other professions'. In the rest of the Netherlands the number of occupationally-based mutual societies declined.[11]

From 1822, a committee installed by King William's son researched poverty in the Netherlands. It could not reach an agreement on the question whether national rules for relief organizations were necessary. The southern members were in favour, but the northerners were afraid that national interference would be detrimental to private and local initiatives and would lead to more government spending.[12]

Sickness and funeral funds were excluded from the royal decree of 1820. At the end of the 1820s, animosity arose between the departments of Poor Relief and that of National Industry of the Ministry of the Interior about who was responsible for these funds and for the widows-and-orphans funds. Eventually these last funds fell under the rules of the department of National Industry because the poor had no access to them. Such funds were increasing in number and didn't just operate locally.[13]

Sickness and funeral funds were kept track of in the reports of the department of Poor Relief.[14] At this department the southern civil servant E.J. Prévinaire made a study of them. He was of the opinion that all sorts of funds and societies, including those for widows and orphans, needed extra supervision from the government. In his view the internal rules and regulations of these organizations needed to be renewed to prevent malpractices and insolvencies. It was the government's duty to protect its citizens against malfunctioning organizations because they were unable to see through these practices. He was against profit-making by the funds. The regulations that the Department of National Industry was proposing for the widows-and-orphans funds were also to be applied to the sickness and funeral funds. The Ministry of Finance however, opposed this plan because it would hamper the founding of new funds. Prévinaire also suggested a national pension plan because of the non-viability of the existing pension funds.[15]

In 1824 welfare funds got certain privileges and in 1827 a decree subjected them to strict supervision by local authorities. The Chapelier Law no longer applied to these funds.[16] In 1830 life insurances were put under government supervision. Pension funds and sickness and funeral funds were exempt from this rule.[17]

In 1830 Belgium became an independent state and a parliamentary monarchy with ministerial responsibility. The constitution of 1831 was among the most liberal in Europe. One of its articles provided freedom of association.[18] The country was also the first after England to industrialize. The separation of the southern Netherlands from the north led to a further divergence of the social policies of both countries. The Belgian government was more activist but the country lacked national organizations such as the 'Maatschappij tot Nut van 't Algemeen' which played a role in the establishment of mutual aid funds in the Netherlands.[19]

To Protect the Worker is to Protect Society

Belgium's liberal government began to show an interest in the mutual societies, not in the least due to the widespread famine of the 1940s and the resulting social and political fallout. An inquiry into the conditions of the working classes and into child labour was published during 1846–8.[20] Self-help was an important element in the liberal ideology and the belief that private organizations could alleviate the burden imposed on local authorities by poor relief still prevailed. Besides: 'Each providential worker would be one more defender for society'.[21]

From the beginning of the nineteenth century, the government initiated and supported relief funds in the Belgian mining industry. Its workers had a compulsory insurance. This paved the way for a more activist role of the state.[22] In 1848 the minister of the Interior, Ch. Rogier, gave his provincial governors instructions to promote mutual relief funds. In 1849 the government installed a provincial register for the mutual societies and a committee was instructed to design a state pension fund where citizens could insure themselves on a voluntary basis. This committee also made plans to regulate and stimulate mutual societies.[23] In that same year two million francs were allocated to help them.[24] Sickness funds were best left in the hands of private parties but had to be stimulated by local authorities. Rogier saw the state as the best agent for insuring pensions.[25]

The need to do something for its poor citizens, the insight that the position of the workers had to be improved and the need to deal with the problems with the existing mutual societies prompted the government to establish a *Lijfrente-kas* [General Annuity Fund] and stimulate the work of mutual societies.

In 1849 M.A. Visschers wrote a report for the minister of the Interior on the 'sociétés de secours mutuels', the mutual societies, which gave insight into their historical roots.[26] Details on the Belgian mutual societies were also part of the commentary by a committee on the proposal for a law of 31 January 1850 and the report of the House of Representatives of 1851.[27]

There were governmental mutual societies, employer societies, guild and brotherhood societies, local general mutual societies (neutral, catholic and socialist) and commercial insurers.[28] For ten years the government had sought to promote in all ranks of society, the idea of 'waarborgfondsen' and mutual societies, whose practices remedied so much suffering.[29]

The provincial authorities had collected data on 199 mutual societies with a total membership of 68,297.[30] The government admitted that it was difficult to get a clear picture but concluded that there was much work to be done, especially compared to France, Germany and particularly England.[31]

As an employer, the government had its own mutual aid funds, the first of which had been introduced by the Dutch. By Royal Orders of 31 December 1842 and June 22, 1848, the government established provident funds (waarborgfondsen) for primary teachers in cities and rural communities.[32]

Most other organizations had a mixed character. They were controlled by the authorities but were otherwise independent.[33]

The government granted patronage and assistance to associations modelled on examples from Germany, which were very successful in many cities and rural communities. They were expanding steadily, thereby showing that mutual associations could include more than one objective.[34]

The government then proposed a law concerning the private mutual societies. In the commentary on this proposal from a Committee of the House of Representatives there was an explanation why it was important for the government to set rules.[35] There were two main reasons it felt that it had to intervene. Firstly to compensate for the negative consequences of the freedom of labour and secondly to protect its citizens against recurrent problems with some mutual insurers. They were sometimes poorly managed, wrong calculations were made, the boards were not always independent, sometimes acting mainly in their own self-interest and not giving insight into their administration. It was important that members had knowledge of how the funds functioned and would be able to be part of the boards. But to what extent should the public authority intervene in the creation and management of these companies? The intervention itself might present disadvantages. However, it was necessary to prevent abuses, and also to set rules in the interest of development of these associations.[36]

To resolve the issue and then specify the mode of intervention that best suited the government's purpose and the Belgian system of law, the situation in other countries was reviewed: France, Germany, Sweden, the Netherlands, Switzerland, Italy, and most notably the friendly societies of Great Britain. The United Kingdom had the best laws with clear rules and more transparency, more mutual societies with more members and larger accrued capital than Belgium.[37] In Holland, such friendly societies, based on a principle similar to those in England, were also numerous. The funds were very old and mostly for widows. The government controlled them and therewith protected the members.[38] The pension funds of France and Germany didn't fulfil the needs of the workers.[39]

The committee, with A. Quetelet as vice-president, was of the opinion that the government should do more than control and supervise. It should do something positive, besides the national Pension Fund. Intervention by the government should not thwart the private organizations, but as a sponsor it could set boundaries. The law should stipulate requirements for recognition of the societies. This recognition would mean the societies would be guaranteed by the state thereby gaining some privileges. It also was clear that the founding and membership of these societies should be voluntary.[40]

A recognized society could subscribe to the pharmacy of a welfare organization. It could also arrange a number of beds with a hospital. Adequate payment of physicians was necessary to ensure that workers received proper care.[41] These medical costs remained the most considerable part of the mutuality system and were an important reason for the employers to oppose a compulsory insurance law. The Mutuality Law of 1851 showed that every direct government initiative regarding health and disability insurance was deemed superfluous.[42]

In the royal decree of 1852 the rules were set by which the Belgian mutual societies were allowed to go to court without cost, one of the perks promised in the law of 1851. The recognized charitable societies had held this privilege since the law of 1824.[43] The mutual societies were under no circumstances allowed to insure pensions. The state only wanted to back funds that insured temporary risks. The fact that most of these funds were governed by the working class meant that the insured had to be protected against faulty calculations. The young had to be safeguarded against false promises. 'Notwithstanding the fairness of the boards of these mutual societies, the experience in England and France has shown how difficult it is to provide regular assistance to the old and infirm. We have to take note of these societies because they are constituted of people who have not yet reached their ripe old age'.[44]

It wasn't reasonable to demand of young members that they should support elderly whom they hardly knew.[45] To issue pensions would make the mutual societies unpopular with young people and it would pose a big risk for the funds. It isn't fair to ask young people to join a mutual society which has already incurred large debts, whereas earlier generations didn't. Such an act of sacrifice can't be expected. It is also very important to make sure that societies who have accepted heavy burdens with regard to old age and long term illness do not at the same time accept women.[46] The societies had to promote the use of the governmental *Lijfrentekas* or they could make their own deal with this national Pension Fund, de Algemeene Pensioenkas.[47]

No organization could insure pensions better and cheaper than the public Pension Fund.[48] The committee of the House of Representatives stated that it would be crazy and dangerous if the mutual societies tried to compete with the National Pension Fund.[49]

The law of 1851 did not offer the mutualities systematic financial support. The government wished to prevent the mutual societies from acting as militant social interest groups and forbade them to insure unemployment for fear that these benefits would be used as strikers pay. Some mutualities, however, did act as general social interest organizations. They can in some ways be seen as fore-runners of modern trade unions.[50]

Good Intentions but not Enough Result

The Mutuality Law prescribed the installation of a commission for the mutual societies. This commission published reports on the mutual societies in which it remarked that the law failed to deliver the desired results.[51] The number of recognized societies was small and the number of people insured hardly seemed to grow. The prevention of malpractices was insufficient.

The chairman of the committee for the mutual societies, M.A. Visschers, attributed the refusal of most mutual societies to file for recognition to the fact that they didn't want to give up their pension funds.[52] Both in France and the United Kingdom the national government backed savings societies and pension funds.

Napoleon III was in his social policies an example for the German Chancellor Bismarck. In 1850 he had founded a National Pension Fund and he gave subsidies to mutual organizations. They had to be acknowledged and their boards had to accept control by an impartial chairman.[53]

The fact that the Belgian government hadn't installed a national savings society, a Nationale Spaerkas, hindered the success of their mutual societies.[54] In England the backing of the savings banks by the government was the foundation of the pension and mutual society system. In France the people had confidence in the state savings funds or those savings funds that were guaranteed by the government. In Belgium there was mistrust of governmental institutions and this was not without reason. Only a law concerning the savings banks would remedy this. Then both private persons and organizations could place their capital without risk.[55] In 1865 the National Pension Fund became part of the National Savings Fund (ASLK).[56]

In general the requirements for recognition of mutual societies were too strict. Some societies had no interest in official recognition because it entailed the requirement to allow the insured to have a place on the board.[57] In Ghent for instance, only two out of the twenty-nine mutual funds that were established between 1850 and 1876 were given recognition. Many workers' funds could not be recognized because they were part of a larger organization. This is why after the repeal of the ban on associations in 1866, which meant that labour organizations could operate freely, more relief funds escaped governmental control.[58]

In 1863 a federation of neutral mutualities was set up. At the same time socialist and catholic mutual societies became more popular. By the end of the 1980s 10 to 12 per cent of the Belgian workers were participating in a mutuality, either in recognized or 'unofficial' societies. As a result of the electoral reform of 1883, board members of recognized mutualities received municipal and provincial voting rights.[59] At the Catholic Congresses at Liège compulsory social insurance was promoted. However, the catholic government shied away from this due to pressure exerted by the employers and in 1894 passed another voluntary Mutuality Law instead.[60]

The law of 1894 mitigated some of the requirements for official recognition and brought more generous subsidies, by the national as well as the provincial and local authorities. Coupled with a general increase in wealth and with more effective workers' organizations this meant that a larger number of workers got insured. In 1890 54,347 people were members of a recognized society; ten years later this number had risen to 185,201. In 1910 there were half a million members. Mutual societies were required to put their money in savings banks and/or to acquire government bonds. Initially they were not allowed to run their own pharmacies but this rule was amended a few years later.[61]

It was suggested that the mutual societies should be allowed to set their own pensions, without recourse to the general pension fund. The government was unwilling to accept this innovation because it believed that companies should limit their role to that of intermediary.[62] The idea was that pensions were still best guaranteed by the state.[63] The law of 1894 did allow the forming of regional and national federations.[64] In general, the government tried to protect its citizens with this law while allowing social organizations some semblance of independence.

In 1898 a new law rendered subsidies by municipal and provincial governments to non-recognized organizations illegal. The decision on recognition was put in the hands of the national government. Subsidies were also given to federations of mutualities.[65] The feeling among socialists and liberals was that the government favoured the catholic mutualities.[66] In 1913 there were around four thousand mutualities.[67] About the same time in the Netherlands some 2,500 sickness funds were counted and 620 health insurance funds. In some organizations both functions were combined. The growth of the Belgian mutualities was also stimulated by the Pension Law of October 1900.[68]

To ensure their survival, the mutualities had to impose restrictions. This meant that not everyone was accepted and that a medical examination was required. Women and children were often not admitted.[69] In 1900 barely 6 per cent of the membership was female. The poor were excluded because they could not pay the premiums.[70] It became clear that the mutualities would have to increase in scale and pool their resources in order to be able to cover the growing costs, of health care, long-term illness and disability, A process of professionalization and federalization on regional and national level ensued.[71] As a result not only the established relationship between party, union and mutuality lessened but also the influence of and bond with the members. In its place came the abstract solidarity of the welfare state.[72]

Compulsory Insurance is the Way Forward

In countries like Great-Britain and France the effectiveness of the voluntary insurance system was being questioned. In 1917, F. J. W. Drion, a Dutch liberal member of parliament, testified that he had been strongly in favour of the Belgian system. He had personally visited the country and studied its system of mutual care, in high hopes of finding a shining example to help solve the Dutch social problems. After his visit he had to acknowledge that the facts had bitterly disappointed him.[73]

Just before the First World War the catholic Belgian government proposed a compulsory Old Age, Sickness and Disability Insurance Act which was inspired by the British National Insurance Act of 1911. It provided insurance for workers in industry, business and agriculture with an annual income of less than 2,400 francs. Workers, employers and the state would contribute to pay for the costs but the employees would pay most.[74] It was also suggested that part of the money for the funding of the welfare organizations was to be put in the social security funds because it was expected that there would be a decline in the need for welfare.[75]

The insured would have a free choice of insurance against sickness and disability and the government would install regional organizations for those who did not want to be a member of a mutual society. The mutual societies could still decide which members they wanted to exclude. The national pension fund would be the sole insurer of old age pensions. Both socialist and liberal members of parliament came with their own proposals. The socialists aimed at more centralization and wanted only one mutual society per region. The liberal proposal aimed at greater financial stability and put the governmental institutions at the forefront. This proposal also suggested that there would be only one medical service for both members of government institutions and of mutual societies. This would ensure better and more affordable health care. The proposal also explicitly mentioned women as those that had to be insured.[76] Some employers were wary of the costs they expected as a result of an insurance to which they would be forced to contribute. The government stuck to its own proposal but the war prevented it becoming law.

During the German occupation of Belgium the country was split into two administrative entities, Wallonia and Flanders. In Flanders work was done on a compulsory social insurance law based on the pre-war plans. In April 1918 a compulsory sickness law was published but eventually not implemented. After the war there were a number of reasons to forget about this episode.[77]

Following the war the socialists were able to take part in the government. The catholic proposal for a compulsory social insurance law from 1914 was amended but the socialist Minister of Labour found fault with it. He asked a committee of doctors, mutualities, politicians and technicians to make a thorough study. He asked the committee to make a seperate proposal for a compulsory pension law which was approved by parliament in the middle of the 1920s.[78]

The number of people enrolled in a socialist mutuality became larger than that of their catholic counterparts. In 1919 the socialist insurance funds had 283,484 members whereas the number of people that had joined the National Alliance of Christian Mutualities had dropped from 188,690 in 1913 to 113,367 in 1919. In total there were 4,127 mutual societies. This number declined in the years that followed. In 1930 there were 3,390 left although unlike the German government, the Belgian authorities did little to try to achieve greater efficiency by scaling up the organizations. 'Perhaps the matter was too politically delicate for such radical measures. The big national alliances had a powerful foothold within the political parties and even in the government for vigorously defending their interests.'[79]

At the end of the 1920s, the five national mutualist alliances that still exist today had formed: the Neutral Association of Health Insurance Funds (LNZ), the National Alliance of Socialist Mutualities (NVSM), the National Alliance of Christian Mutualities (LCM), the Alliance of Liberal Health-Insurance Funds (LLM) and the National Alliance of Occupation-Related Mutualities (since 1990 LBBOZ). Of the 1.1 million members of mutualities in 1930, 44 per cent were members of socialist organizations, 32 per cent belonged to Christian ones, 13 per cent to neutral mutualities, 5 per cent to liberal ones and 6 per cent to occupationally-based organizations. The influence of the socialist members on the administration of their mutualities was larger than in the Christian ones. In the latter influence of the workers was greater in the Flemish than in the Walloon organizations, which were more paternalistic. In some areas the labour movement started funds in factories, bars, music halls and brotherhoods.[80] In comparison with Germany the number of employers that founded their own insurance fund was small. The number of workers without any mutual insurance was estimated at around 1 million.[81]

All three major political parties were convinced a compulsory social insurance system was necessary. Among them, however, there were great differences about the way in which the system had to be organized and who had to pay for the costs. This hindered its implementation. During the economic crisis of the 1930s compulsory social security was no longer a viable idea. In the meantime the mutual societies played a crucial role in the development of Belgian health care, which became their core business. Because of competition and their local and regional autonomy the level of care offered by the societies differed greatly. The authorities also had a part in this through the subsidizing of the mutualities. In 1938 the national government paid almost 32 per cent of the costs of the mutual societies. In return the authorities upped their demands, particularly concerning the minimum number of members each society ought to have. This led to a further centralization, although local organizations fought tooth and nail for their autonomy.[82]

The mutualities tried to get the medical profession to come to an agreement on a local or regional level about tariffs. This was not always successful. In 1920 the government installed a commission which succeeded in making a deal on pharmaceutical costs but failed to do the same for doctors' rates. The mutualities eventually made their own deal with the physicians which made it possible to get a grip on expenses.[83]

National Consensus on Social Security

Like most western nations after the Second World War Belgium became a welfare state. In 1944, a national government comprised of all the major parties succeeded in realizing a compulsory social insurance system to lessen (the fear of) misery as a result of accident or sickness for as much working men and women as possible.[84] Both employers and employees paid the premium which was a percentage of the workers' wages. These monies were deposited at the National Social Security Office which then allocated payment to the National Fund for Insurance against Sickness and Disability (Rijksfonds voor Verzekering tegen Ziekte en Invaliditeit, RVZI). The government would contribute 16 per cent of the necessary means. Workers could insure themselves at a regional branch of the RVZI or with a mutuality of one of the five national mutual organizations. These reimbursed medical expenses on the basis of their own rates, regardless of the real costs, although they tried to get as close to them as possible. The law stipulated the sort of services that could be reimbursed but not the tariffs the care providers could ask. This stimulated health care providers to raise their fees 'leading to an upward spiral that pushed up the expenditure of the health-insurance funds'.[85] People could voluntarily insure themselves for care not included in the compulsory insurance. These insurances were also available for Belgians not covered by the compulsory system, mainly civil servants and the self-employed. The government continued to subsidize these insurances.

The board of the RVZI was made up of an equal representation of national employers and workers organizations. The government was represented by a civil servant who could only advise. It was the RVZI instead of the local mutualities which had to negotiate a deal on tariffs with the care providers.[86] Physicians were of the opinion that government intervention would be detrimental to the quality of care. What they feared most was a state medical system 'in which they would have to work as civil servants or waged employees'.[87]

The new social security laws did little to solve two big problems: the financial difficulties of the sickness and disability insurance and the politicized system of the state subsidies which in turn favoured the catholic, socialist or liberal mutualities. An attempt to tackle the first problem met such fierce resistance from the doctors that the government retracted its proposal.

The centralization of the social security system made it vulnerable to centrifugal forces within Belgium. In connection to the sickness insurance they became apparent in the 1950s when a conflict arose between the Walloon Christian Federation and the National Christian Alliance which torpedoed another governmental attempt to solve the financial problems. Between 1945 and 1963 the government had to cover a deficit of more than 3.5 billion francs.

In 1960, a parliamentary working group consisting of members of the three major parties tried to produce a general framework to reform the system. Based on fundamental principles of social security, practical experience and the specific character of Belgian politics, this group's report became the basis for the so-called Leburton Act of 1963, which is considered to be a milestone in Belgian social security history. This law entailed the separation of sickness and disability insurance and made possible a truly national health care insurance in the sense that more and more civilians were covered. Health care providers were made part of the executive. For the first time they were involved in the legislative process. The system remained a hybrid combination in which the mutualities played a key role, although for people who didn't want to insure themselves with them there was an Auxiliary Fund. Monitoring and supervision was done by the state, the National Institute for Health and Disability Insurance (RIZIV) which replaced the RVZI and the Institute of Medical Control.[88]

To tackle the problem of the deficit, the care providers had to keep their rates in check. This government requirement provoked the anger of the doctors and led to the first national strike in the health sector. In 1964 a compromise was reached, after which agreements between the government and the physicians were made without much fuss. Despite this, the deficit continued to grow and the government subsidy rose from 35 per cent of the health insurance income in 1966 to 40 per cent in 1975. The 'Petit Report' that was commissioned by the government in 1975 led to much debate but had a slow and not very structural effect. The government was responsible for nearly 44 per cent of the compulsory health insurance budget in 1981 but still the deficit rose. Another official committee concluded that this was caused by the tariffs, by the ageing population, by the economic circumstances and by the spiralling costs of hospitals, clinics, laboratories, pharmacies, medicine and the incomes of care providers. The health care sector was restructured, but the deficit was only brought down at the end of the 1980s as a result of the booming economy. In the first part of the 1990s health care costs accounted for something like 7.5 per cent of GDP. In 1994 legislation curbed the growth of costs to 1.5 per cent per year. Co-payments have been a part of the system for a long time and that means that patients take care of a number of costs on top of their premiums.[89] OMNIO and MAB systems are there to reduce patient co-payments and to maintain a certain level of accessibility.[90]

Age-Old Problems Remain Unresolved

Whereas mutualities were accustomed to blaming financial troubles on the care providers, doctors pointed at inefficiencies and wrong-doings of the mutualities. Within the mutual societies disagreements also came to a head. The socialist mutualities had 29 per cent of the insured but received 36 per cent of the government subsidies. This led to protests from the other mutualities.

In order to get a grip on developments, the government decided to replace the nearly century old Mutuality Law. As a result of the law of 1990 local mutualities were forbidden. The national associations became the main providers of compulsory health care insurance. The room for manoeuvre for private insurers had become very small as almost everyone was covered by the compulsory insurance. Stipulations for control and regulation of the mutualities became more strict. The Christian mutualities which were part of the LCM held around 45 per cent of the market. Only the National Union of Professional and Independent Health-Insurance (LBBOZ) was able to increase its market share from more than 10 to nearly 15 per cent. As a consequence of the law of 1990 the mutualities became for the most part colleagues instead of competitors.[91]

Only in the realm of the voluntary and supplementary insurance was fierce competition still possible. In the fight for new members the mutualities more and more became providers of welfare in various forms like holidays for the chronically ill and disabled, holiday camps for the young and care in their own institutions at home and abroad. Certain additional benefits were forbidden by the government in 2001. The revenues of the voluntary and supplementary insurance were increasingly used to provide for the newest medical procedures. The competition on a regional level caused strife between the language groups. For instance: within the LCM there was a difference of opinion between the Flemish and Walloon funds about hospital insurance. 'While the Walloon funds extend cover to everyone in the interest of solidarity, and consequently introduced a sharp increase of premiums for voluntary insurance, the Flemish funds exclude members over the age of 60 in order to avoid having to increase these premiums'.[92]

The Belgium health insurance system has often been typified as hybrid.[93] It offers broad coverage and is based on universal, compulsory insurance financed by social premiums and taxes. It has a highly regulated, centralized organizational structure with a prominent role for the government. The few hundred remaining mutualities and other independent insurance companies have a limited position in this system. They are third-party payers, acting as intermediaries between patients and care providers and are directly responsible for paying the costs of health care. The health insurance funds tend to operate as a cartel and use their social and political network to influence governmental policy. On the other hand, Belgium has a liberal provider market with a large degree of freedom for both patients and care providers. The latter are mostly paid on a per-treatment basis. High value is placed, especially in the French-speaking part, on technical and specialized medicine. As a consequence there are more diagnostic examinations in the south of the country, with prescriptions for stronger medicines and more frequent use of antibiotics. In the Flemish part there is more emphasis on the general practitioner, curative medicine and preventive care. This means that health care is more expensive in the south, which has led to a 'considerable transfer of funds' from the north to the south.[94]

Over the years health care costs have become an increasing part of the total social security revenues and taxes. Total health care expenses rose from 8.6 per cent of GDP in 1998 to 10.2 per cent in 2008.[95] Government expenditure increased by 33 per cent and the amounts paid by families by a staggering 65 per cent. The yearly increase in costs lay between 6.3 and 7.5 per cent, which is much higher than the 3.7 per cent rise in the period between 1980 and 2004 and higher than the predicted norm of 4.5 per cent. The government had to raise its growth norm from 1.5 to 2.5 and even to 4.5 per cent, which is still the limit today. Since 2006, the increase of expenses remained below 4.5 per cent but this is a struggle to maintain. As a result of ageing and non-demographical factors like scientific, technological and industrial progress and higher labour costs the health-service expenditure is predicted to rise from 9.7 per cent of GDP in 2004 to 12.8 per cent in 2030. Coupled with the estimated rise in pension costs and the consequences of the economic crisis (that since the end of 2008 affected

Belgium like the rest of the world), measures are needed to keep governmental budgets in check.

However no one seems to dare to grapple the highly complex system with its historical roots 'involving numerous delicate and subtle balances between the various interest groups (national health insurance funds, doctors, paramedics, political parties, employers, employees, hospitals, patients and the government)'.[96] The annual budget which determines who pays and who receives what, is made by a great many consultative bodies. The practice of automatically following their proposals was questioned by the government. The health insurance funds have a quasi-monopoly which is anchored in legislation and they are deeply embedded in the political structure. Competition with private companies is limited to supplementary insurance. European legislation was used by the commercial insurers to fight this monopoly and the Belgian government was instructed to adjust its health insurance funds legislation. The government countered with the argument that the activities of the mutualities were based 'on social welfare, mutual help and solidarity and not on making profit' and that unlike the commercial insurers they excluded no one.[97]

According to the government the social security system does not fall under the European insurance guidelines. The supplementary services of the mutualities should not be seen as economic activities but as services for the common good which aren't subjected to any European guidelines. 'The health-insurance funds are waiting in fear and trembling to see how the European Commission will evaluate this argument'.[98]

The mutual funds not only compete with commercial insurers but are also engaged in a 'fierce competitive battle' among themselves.[99] The results are only minor. The market share of the Christian mutualities is shrinking slightly but they remain the market leader. The socialists are gaining ground slowly. Nearly three-quarters of employee claimants are members of these two funds and they are still closely linked with certain political parties. Since the beginning of the 1970s the national political parties are split along the language divide. The national organizations of mutualities remained intact but when one looks at some of their websites one can see that the regions have their own distinct characteristics. The Flemish argument is that language and cultural differences matter in the receiving and giving of health care. The fact that many patients from abroad choose, for a number of reasons, to be treated in Belgian care institutions, seems to belie this argument.[100] Studies have shown that not culture but both the availability of care and the level of freedom of doctors are instrumental in the different levels of use of care.[101]

Regionalism and a Bigger Role for Europe

The north–south community discussions have had an effect on the developments in the Belgian social security system. As difficulties in containing the rising costs became more apparent they also became part of the demand of the north to split the system and stop transference of monies from the north to the south. The French speaking parts of Belgium pointed to the threat to national solidarity. Although the constitutional revision of 1980 transferred the responsibility for health care to the regions, anything relating to social security remained in the hands of the federal government. When measures to limit costs were taken by a Flemish minister they provoked negative reactions from the French speaking public and vice versa. In 2005 Minister Demotte was able to carry out some reforms. Hospitals were getting lump sum finance and treatment by general practitioners was given preference. This led to apparent results as the transfer of money from Flanders to Wallonia and Brussels dropped by 150 million euros a year.[102]

In 2001 the Flemish government introduced a compulsory health care insurance for non-medical care like convalescent and nursing homes. Unlike the existing health care insurance not only the national associations of mutualities are managing the funds but private insurers are also allowed to be involved. In addition to this there is the governmental Flemish Health Care Fund.[103]

A number of Dutch and French speaking social security specialists advocated that the regions should take responsibility for certain parts of the social security program. The regions would have to take care of their own finance. With an objective distribution formula of the still centralized accumulated funds the interregional solidarity could remain intact, 'each region would be free to emphasize whatever areas of health care it chose, and greater financial responsibility would stimulate the more efficient use of available funds'.[104]

According to a recent study, nearly 75 per cent of the Flemish general practitioners are in favour of a total devolvement of health care to the regions. The same number of French speaking general practitioners don't want any transference at all.[105] The liberal mutualities fear that a regionalizaton would be detrimental to the quality of health care and are opposed to the waning of solidarity between the regions.[106] Those in favour of regional health care point to cultural differences and to the regional health care systems of Spain, the United Kingdom and Canada.[107]

The difficulties associated with the formation of a new government in 2010 have put the reform of the pension and health care system on hold. Some form of defederalization is being discussed among politicians but it's a very sensitive subject. Especially the Walloon parties and the Social-Democrats in Flanders are wary of lessening the inherent solidarity of the federal social security system. In recent reports on the Belgian health insurance system the emphasis is laid on structural reform to face challenges whilst saving the strong elements, including some role for the mutualities.[108]

Since the beginning of the nineteenth century state and mutual insurers have been involved in providing care for the Belgian people. Continuity, affordability and accessibility have been constant matters of concern. During the nineteenth century ideology played an ever growing role in the mutualities. They centralized and were more and more subjected to control and governance by the state. In the twentieth century, especially after the Second World War, people became more affluent and gained welfare. The Belgian state became an active member of the European Union and also federalized. Just as during the nineteenth and twentieth century, the challenge of the cost of an aging population for the whole system needs to be taken head on.

The future of the national health insurance system of Belgium seems unclear. The political and economic crises of recent years have thwarted attempts to solve societal and incremental problems, thereby adding to the uncertainty of the future of the health insurance system. In his Christmas speech of 2009, King Albert pointed out that Belgium is a potential role-model for Europe in showing the way in which cultural differences can be overcome.[109] For the time being there is no sign of this happening. Whether through regionalization or greater European unity, national borders sometimes seem a thing of the past. The doggedness of the effects of historical roots underlines the importance of historical research.

Acknowledgements

Special thanks to K. P. Companje, T. van Doorn, R. Schouten, R. Spierings and R. Vonk.

NOTES

Introduction

1. P. Blond, *Red Tory: How Left and Right Have Broken Britain and How We Can Fix It* (London: Faber, 2010), p. 282.
2. M. Glasman, 'Labour as a Radical Tradition', in M. Glasman, J. Rutherford, M. Stears and S. White (eds), *The Labour Tradition and the Politics of Paradox: the Oxford London Seminars 2010–11* (2011), p. 29.
3. See http://www.southampton.ac.uk/morbidity/conference/index.html for further details.
4. M. van der Linden, 'Introduction', in M. van der Linden (ed.), *Social Security Mutualism; The Comparative History of Mutual Benefit Societies* (Bern: Peter Lang, 1996), pp. 11–38, at p. 13.
5. See e.g. M. Gorsky, 'The Growth and Distribution of English Friendly Societies in the Early Nineteenth Century', *Economic History Review*, 51 (1998), pp. 489–511; S. Cordery, *British Friendly Societies, 1750–1914* (Basingstoke: Palgrave Macmillan, 2003); D. Weinbren, 'Beneath the All-seeing Eye: Fraternal Order and Friendly Societies' Banners in Nineteenth- and Twentieth-Century Britain', *Cultural and Social History*, 3 (2006), pp. 167–91.
6. B. Gilbert, 'The Decay of Nineteenth Century Provident Institutions and the Coming of Old Age Pensions in Great Britain', *Economic History Review*, 17 (1965), pp. 551–63; B. Gilbert, *The Evolution of National Insurance in Great Britain: the Origins of the Welfare State* (London: Michael Joseph, 1966); E. P. Hennock, *The Origin of the Welfare State in England and Germany, 1850–1914: Social Policies Compared* (Cambridge: Cambridge University Press, 2007).
7. E.g. S. Yeo, 'Working Class Association, Private Capital, Welfare and the State in the Late-Nineteenth and Twentieth Centuries', in N. Parry, M. Rustin and C. Satyamurti (eds), *Social Work, Welfare and the State* (London: Edward Arnold, 1979), pp. 48–71; D. Green and L. G. Cromwell, *Mutual Aid or Welfare State: Australia's Friendly Societies* (Sydney: George Allen and Unwin, 1984); D. Green, *Working Class Patients and the Medical Establishment: Self-help in Britain from the Mid-Nineteenth Century to 1948* (Aldershot: Gower/Maurice Temple Smith, 1985); D. Beito, *From Mutual Aid to the Welfare State: Fraternal Societies and Social Services, 1890–1967* (Chapel Hill: University of North Carolina Press, 2000).
8. This issue is also discussed in Chapter 6 below.

9. L. Tomassini, 'Mutual Benefit Societies in Italy, 1861–1922', in van der Linden, *Social Security Mutualism*, pp. 225–71.

10. It is interesting to compare this remark with the comments made by Santiago Castillo in his contribution to the van der Linden volume: 'In Spain, no general work is devoted specifically to mutual benefit societies. Until recently, such associations appeared solely in related references or marginal comments. Only in recent years have they begun to attract attention'. See S. Castillo, 'Mutual Benefit Societies in Spain in the Nineteenth and Twentieth Centuries', in van der Linden, *Social Security Mutualism*, pp. 273–86, at p. 273.

11. In Chapter 8, Pilar León-Sanz looks at the particular history of the *Sociedad protectora de obreros La Conciliación*, which provided medical assistance to workers in Pamplona from 1902 to 1984. Leon's account suggests that *La Conciliación* did not surrender all its medical functions immediately but she does explain that the society's decision to remain outside the state scheme did lead to its eventual disappearance.

12. Gilbert, 'The Decay of Nineteenth-century Provident Institutions'; see also Gilbert, *The Evolution of National Insurance*, pp. 165–80.

13. G. Emery and J. C. H. Emery, *A Young Man's Benefit: The Independent Order of Odd Fellows and Sickness Insurance in the United States and Canada 1860–1929* (Montreal: McGill-Queen's University Press, 1999).

14. See e.g. J. Murray, *Origins of American Health Insurance: A History of Industrial Sickness Funds* (New Haven: Yale University Press, 2007).

15. L. Jacobs and T. Skocpol, *Health Care Reform and American Politics: What Everyone Needs to Know* (New York: Oxford University Press, 2010).

16. J. C. H. Emery, 'La Prévoyance volontaire aux États-Unis et la montée de l'assurance maladie publique et obligatoire avant 1920', *Revue Européenne d'Histoire Sociale*, 16 (2005), pp. 8–19 ; J. C. H. Emery, '"Un-American" or Unnecessary? America's Rejection of Compulsory Government Health Insurance in the Progressive Era', *Explorations in Economic History*, 47:1 (2010), pp. 68–81.

1 Benson, 'Coalminers, Accidents and Insurance in Late Nineteenth-century England'

1. M. van der Linden, 'Introduction', in M. van der Linden (ed.), *Social Security Mutualism: The Comparative History of Mutual Benefit Societies* (Bern: Peter Lang, 1996). The thirty-four-page index to J. E. Williams's magisterial *The Derbyshire Miners: A Study in Industrial and Social History* (London: Allen and Unwin, 1962) contains just six references to friendly societies and six to permanent relief funds; the thirteen page index to Carolyn Baylies's *The History of the Yorkshire Miners 1881–1981* (London: Routledge, 1993) contains only two references to friendly societies.

2. For example, J. Benson, 'English Coal-Miners' Trade-Union Accident Funds, 1850–1900', *Economic History Review*, 28 (1975); J. Benson, 'The Thrift of English Coal-Miners, 1860–95', *Economic History Review*, 31 (1978).

3. R. Church, *The History of the British Coal Industry, Volume 3, 1830–1913: Victorian Pre-Eminence* (Oxford: Clarendon Press, 1986), p. 598; J. Benson, *British Coalminers in the Nineteenth Century: A Social History* (London: Longman, 1989), p. 196.

4. C. G. Hanson, 'Craft Unions, Welfare Benefits, and the Case for Trade Union Law Reform, 1867–75', *Economic History Review*, 28 (1975), p. 245; D. R. Green, *The Welfare State: For Rich or for Poor?* (London: Institute of Economic Affairs, 1982), p. 38. Also A. Seldon, *Wither the Welfare State* (London: Institute of Economic Affairs, 1981), pp. 24–5.

5. For the view that 'industrial occupations with their greater risks of ill health and injury ... supplied compelling reasons for joining a friendly society', see E. Hopkins, *Working-class Self-help in Nineteenth-Century England* (London: UCL Press, 1995), p. 10. Also G. Crossick, *An Artisan Elite in Victorian Society: Kentish London 1840–80* (London: Croom Helm, 1978), p. 174.

6. M. Gorsky, 'The Growth and Distribution of English Friendly Societies in the Early-Nineteenth Century', *Economic History Review*, 51 (1998), pp. 506–7.

7. Gorsky, 'Friendly Societies', p. 507. Also Church, *Coal Industry*, p. 598.

8. The miners' permanent relief funds have received a good deal of criticism: R. Challinor, *The Lancashire and Cheshire Miners* (Newcastle-upon-Tyne: Frank Graham, 1972), p. 163; M. Lieven, *Senghennydd, The Universal Pit Village 1890–1930* (Llandysul: Gomer, 1994, pp. 189–90.

9. R. Harrison 'Introduction', in R. Harrison (ed.), *Independent Collier:The Coal Miner as Archetypal Proletarian Reconsidered* (Hassocks: Harvester, 1978), p. 14. See also J. Laslett, 'Why Some Do and Some Don't: Some Determinants of Radicalism among British and American Coalminers 1872–1924', *Bulletin of the Society for the Study of Labour History*, 28 (1974).

10. A. Campbell, 'Honourable Men and Degraded Slaves: A Comparative Study of Trade Unionism in two Lanarkshire Mining Communities, *c.* 1830–1874', in Harrison (ed.), *Independent Collier*.

11. Pat Spaven, 'Main Gates of Protest: Contrasts in Rank and File Activity among the South Yorkshire Miners, 1858–1894', in Harrison (ed.), *Independent Collier*.

12. M. J. Daunton: 'Down the Pit: Work in the Great Northern and South Wales Coalfields, 1870–1914', *Economic History Review*, 34 (1981).

13. J. Benson (ed.), *The Miners of Staffordshire, 1840–1914* (Keele: University of Keele, 1993).

14. S. Berger, A. Croll and N. Laporte (eds), *Towards a Comparative History of Coalfield Societies* (Aldershot: Ashgate, 2005).

15. R. Church and Q. Outram, *Strikes and Solidarity: Coalfield Conflict in Britain 1889–1966* (Cambridge: Cambridge University Press, 1998), p. xvii. See also R. Fagge, *Power, Culture and Conflict in the Coalfields: West Virginia and South Wales, 1900–1922* (Manchester: Manchester University Press, 1996); L. S. James, *The Politics of Identity and Civil Society in Britain and Germany: Miners in the Ruhr and South Wales 1890–1926* (Manchester: Manchester University Press, 2008).

16. Benson, *British Coalminers*, pp. 9–12.

17. J. Benson, 'Introduction', in Benson (ed.), *Miners of Staffordshire*, p. 5.

18. Benson, *British Coalminers*, p. 216; E. Billington, 'North Staffordshire', in Benson (ed.), *Miners of Staffordshire*, pp. 13–15; R. Seifert, 'The Importance of Being Permanent: A Study of the North Staffordshire Miners' Federation from 1869 to 1874', *Midland History*, 31 (2006), p. 69.

19. Central Association for Dealing with Distress Caused by Mining Accidents, *1890 Report*, p. 10. See P. H. J. H. Gosden, *The Friendly Societies in England 1815–1875* (Manchester:

Manchester University Press, 1961), pp. 86–7; P. H. J. H. Gosden, *Self-Help: Voluntary Associations in Nineteenth-Century Britain* (London: Batsford, 1973), pp. 110–11.

20. There were also three much smaller funds: the Midland Counties Miners' Permanent Relief Society (1879), the Midland District Miners' Fatal Accident Relief Society (1883) and the Thorncliffe and Rockliffe Permanent Relief Society (1889). See G. L. Campbell, *Miners' Insurance Funds: Their Origin and Extent* (London: Waterlow, 1880; G. L. Campbell, *Miners' Thrift and Employers' Liability: A Remarkable Experience* (Wigan: Strowger and Son, 1891).

21. *Provident*, March 1881; Campbell, *Miners' Insurance Funds*, pp. 12–13.

22. Campbell, *Miners' Insurance Funds*, p. 12.

23. The ordinary members were always in the majority. *Rules of the West Riding of Yorkshire Miners' Permanent Relief Fund Friendly Society*, 1882, no. 6; Lancashire and Cheshire Miners' Permanent Relief Society, *1st Annual Report*, p. 3; Northumberland and Durham Miners' Permanent Relief Fund, *8th Annual Report*, p. 3.

24. J. Benson, 'Coalminers, Coalowners and Collaboration: The Miners' Permanent Relief Fund Movement in England, 1860–1895', *Labour History Review*, 68 (2003), p. 184.

25. *Staffordshire Sentinel*, 7 April 1885. Also 7 April 1888, 27 April 1889, 12 April 1890.

26. Church, *Coal Industry*, pp. 582–99.

27. B. R. Mitchell, *Economic Development of the British Coal Industry 1800–1914* (Cambridge: Cambridge University Press, 1984), pp. 112–13; Church, *Coal Industry*, pp. 583–4.

28. Seifert, 'Importance of Being Permanent', p. 76.

29. It is possible, of course, that those most at risk were most likely to enrol. See North Staffordshire Coal and Ironstone Workers' Permanent Relief Society, *30th Annual Report*, p. 11.

30. J. Evison, 'Conditions of Labour in Yorkshire Coalmines, 1870–1914' (BA dissertation, University of Birmingham, 1963), p. 12.

31. J. J. Atkinson, *Reports of H.M. Inspectors of Mines*, 1864, p. 30. Also J. Gerrard, *Reports of H.M. Inspectors of Mines*, 1896, pp. 10–11; A. H. Stokes, *Reports of H.M. Inspectors of Mines*, 1897, p. 17.

32. J. Benson, 'Non-Fatal Coalmining Accidents', *Bulletin of the Society for the Study of Labour History*, 32 (1976).

33. J. W. F. Rowe, *Wages in Practice and Theory* (London: Routledge & Kegan Paul, 1928); Benson, *British Coalminers*, pp. 57–62, 64–74; J. Benson, 'Coalmining', in C. J. Wrigley (ed.), *A History of British Industrial Relations 1875–1914* (Brighton: Harvester Press, 1982), pp. 190–1.

34. Mitchell, *Coal Industry*, pp. 192–3; Church, *Coal Industry*, p. 556. From the late 1880s, Staffordshire wages were negotiated within the so-called federated area, whereas Northumberland and Durham wages were not. J. H. Porter, 'Wage Bargaining under Conciliation Agreements, 1860–1914', *Economic History Review*, 23 (1970).

35. Benson, *British Coalminers*, p. 64.

36. H. S. Jevons, *The British Coal Trade* (London: Kegan Paul Trench Trubner & Co., 1915; reprinted Newton Abbot: David & Charles, 1969), p. 63; Benson, *British Coalminers*, p. 76.

37. Benson, *British Coalminers*, p. 76.

38. But see J. Benson, 'Working-Class Consumption, Saving and Investment in England and Wales, 1851–1911', *Journal of Design History*, 9 (1996).

39. For example, J. Benson, 'Poor Law Guardians, Coalminers, and Friendly Societies in Northern England, 1860–1894: Statutory Provision, Local Autonomy, and Individual Responsibility', *Northern History*, xliv (2007).

40. Central Association for Dealing with Distress Caused by Mining Accidents, *1894 Report*, p. 29.

41. J. Benson, 'The Compensation of English Coal-Miners and their Dependants for Industrial Accidents, 1860–1897' (PhD thesis, University of Leeds, 1974), pp. 137–42.

42. J. Benson, 'Colliery Disaster Funds, 1860–1897', *International Review of Social History*, xix(1974).

43. Benson, 'Compensation', pp. 199–200.

44. *Staffordshire Sentinel*, 12 April 1890.

45. However, the trustees of the Talke fund, unlike those of the Hartley fund, continued to use the interest from their surplus to make grants to those bereaved in the coalfield, *Staffordshire Sentinel*, 12 April 1890.

46. J. Benson and R. Sykes, 'Trade-Unionism and the Use of the Law: English Coalminers' Unions and Legal Redress for Industrial Accidents, 1860–1897', *Historical Studies in Industrial Relations*, 3 (1997).

47. Church and Outram, *Strikes*, pp. 39–40.

48. 43 and 44 Vict. c. 42.

49. *Miner and Workman's Avocate*, 4 March, 8 April 1865.

50. *Durham County Advertiser*, 21 January 1870.

51. Northumberland County Record Office, Northumberland Miners' Mutual Confident Association, minutes, 18 June 1881.

52. Durham County Record Office, Durham Miners' Association, minutes, 9 April, 4 June 1881, 24 June 1882.

53. Cf. C. Frank, 'Let But One of Them Come Before Me, and I'll Commit Him: Trade Unions,Magistrates and the Law in Mid-Nineteenth-Century Staffordshire', *Journal of British Studies*, 44 (2005).

54. Derbyshire Miners' Association, *Minutes*, 3 September 1881 (by courtesy of the late J. E. Williams).

55. Northumberland Miners' Mutual Confident Association, minutes, 6 September 1881.

56. National Union of Mineworkers (North Western Area), Bolton, Lancashire and Cheshire Miners' Federation, minutes, 18 May, 31 August, 8 November, 1 December 1886.

57. Presenting earlier versions of this chapter at Southampton and Wolverhampton helped me to clarify my thoughts on this central point.

58. Church, *Coal Industry*, p. 629. Also R. Moore, *Pit-Men, Preachers and Politics: The Effects of Methodism in a Durham Mining Community* (Cambridge: Cambridge University Press, 1974), p. 77.

59. Cited Benson, *British Coalminers*, p. 213.

60. Billington, 'Mining Settlements', p. 50.

61. Benson, 'Thrift', p. 415.

62. *Royal Commission appointed to inquire into Friendly and Benefit Building Societies, 3rd Report*, 1873, q. 27191, A. Blyth.

63. For example, *Labour Tribune*, 27 June 1891; *Royal Commission on the Poor Laws and Relief of Distress*, Appendix vol. v, p. 289.

64. Durham County Record Office, D/Lo F 698 (1), Seaham Relief Fund, minutes, 29 November 1880; D/Lo F 702, letter 'On behalf of the friends of the lost ones' to the Committee, n.d.

65. *Durham Chronicle*, 19 February 1887.

66. *Royal Commission Friendly Societies, 3rd Report*, 1873, qq. 27148–60.

67. Benson, 'Trade-Union Accident Funds'.

68. For example, *Durham County Advertiser*, 30 September 1870, 18 August 1871; *Labour Press*, 9 May 1874; Benson, 'Compensation', table XIII.

69. Benson, 'Compensation', table XIII.

70. Q. Outram, '"The Stupidest Men in England?" The Industrial Relations Strategy of the Coalowners between the Lockouts, 1923–1924', *Historical Studies in Industrial Relations*, 4 (1997), p. 65. Also M. Dintenfass, 'Industrial Identities and Civic Imperatives: The Life Tales of British Coal Masters and the Problem of Economic Decline', *Business and Economic History*, 25 (1996).

71. J. A. Jaffe, *The Struggle for Market Power: Industrial Relations in the British Coal Industry, 1800–1840* (Cambridge: Cambridge University Press, 1991), pp. 87–92. See also J. A. Jaffe, *Striking a Bargain: Work and Industrial Relations in England, 1815–1865* (Manchester: Manchester University Press, 2000).

72. Church, *Coal Industry*, p. 664.

73. M. Daunton, 'Down the Pit: Work in the Great Northern and South Wales Coalfields, 1870–1914', *Economic History Review*, 34 (1981), pp. 596–7. Also W. R. Garside, *The Durham Miners 1919–1960* (London: Allen and Unwin, 1971), p. 21.

74. Benson, 'Coalmining', p. 196. Also H. Beynon and T. Austrin, *Masters and Servants: Class and Patronage in the Making of a Labour Organisation* (London: Rivers Oram Press, 1994).

75. J. Benson, 'Myopia, Intransigence and Indifference? The British Coal-Owners, 1850–1914', in A. Westermann and E. Westermann (eds), *Streik im Revier: Unruhe, Protest und Ausstand vom 8. bis 20. Jahrundert* (St Kathainen: Scripta Mercaturae Verlag, 2007).

76. *Wigan Observer*, 24 April 1874.

77. *Durham County Advertiser*, 28 April 1882.

78. Northumberland County Record Office, Steam Collieries Defence Association, minutes, 1880–7, pp. 77b-c, *Report of The Secretary on Charities*.

79. *Newcastle Daily Chronicle*, 4 August 1880.

80. Northumberland County Record Office, NCB/C/175, ? Cooper to M. W. Brown, 5 January 1898; Durham Miners' Association, *Monthly Report*, 1 January 1881 *Select Committee on the Employers' Liability Act*, 1886, q. 1452, W. H. Patterson.

81. Northumberland County Record Office, United Coal Trade Association, minutes, 1867–1880, *Cost of Colliery Accidents from September 30, 1879, to September 30, 1880*; Durham County Record Office, Durham Coal Owners' Association, Statistical Return, No. 382.

82. J. Benson, 'Coalowners, Coalminers and Compulsion: Pit Clubs in England, 1860–80', *Business History*, 44 (2002). There were some pit clubs in Northumberland and Durham: see, for example, Northumberland County Record Office, N.C.B./C/176, W. Pattison to R. Guthrie, n.d. [late 1897 or early 1898].

83. Benson, 'Coalowners', pp. 49–51.

84. Campbell, *Miners' Insurance Funds*, p. 6. Also *Colliery Guardian*, 30 June 1866.

85. Benson, 'Coalowners', pp. 53–4.

86. *Wolverhampton Chronicle*, 8 September 1869, 20 January 1875; *Select Committee on Acts forthe Regulation and Inspection of Mines*, 1866, q. 5390, W. Millward.

87. S. Webb, *The Story of the Durham Miners (1662–1921)* (London: Labour Publishing Company, 1921), p. 77; E. Welbourne, *The Miners' Unions of Northumberland and Durham* (Cambridge: Cambridge University Press, 1923), pp. 210–11; J. Wilson, *A History of the Durham Miners' Association, 1870–1914* (Durham: Veitch, 1907), pp. 122–3.

88. Steam Collieries Defence Association, minutes, 1880–7, p. 32, 23 October 1880; North of England United Coal Trade Association, minutes, 1880–97, pp. 11–13, 24 November 1880.

89. *Provident*, March 1881; United Coal Trade Association, minutes, 1880–97, pp. 20–2, 8 December 1880.

90. United Coal Trade Association, minutes, 1880–97, *Twentieth Annual Report and Balance Sheet*, 1887.

91. Wilson, *Durham Miners*, p. 42. Also Northumberland and Durham Miners' Permanent Relief Fund, *7th Annual Report*, p. 9.

92. Steam Collieries Defence Association, minutes, 1880–7, 5 January 1884. Honorary members could subscribe, it was seen above, by making an annual subscription equivalent to between ten and twenty per cent of their employees' contributions.

93. *Provident*, 15 June 1882; Steam Collieries Defence Association, minutes, 1880–7, 5 January 1884. The ordinary members, it will be recalled, were always the majority in managing the society.

94. Northumberland and Durham Miners' Permanent Relief Fund, *21st Annual Report*, p. 18. See D. Weinbren, 'The Good Samaritan, Friendly Societies and the Gift Economy', *SocialHistory*, 31 (2006).

95. Northumberland and Durham Miners' Permanent Relief Fund, *21st Annual Report*, p. 14.

96. *Colliery Guardian*, 1 August 1863; Royal Commission on Friendly Societies, *3rd Report*, q. 27089, A. Blyth.

97. *Barnsley Chronicle*, 25 January 1879.

98. Northumberland and Durham Miners' Permanent Relief Fund, *19th Annual Report*, p. 10.

99. Northumberland and Durham Miners' Permanent Relief Fund, *21st Annual Report*, p. 13.

100. Northumberland and Durham Miners' Permanent Relief Fund, *10th Annual Report*, p. 9.

101. Northumberland and Durham Miners' Permanent Relief Fund, *11th Annual Report*, p. 9; *13 Annual Report*, p. 10.

102. Northumberland and Durham Miners' Permanent Relief Fund, *10th Annual Report*, p. 17.

103. *Staffordshire Knot*, 27 April 1886.

104. *Provident*, March 1881; *Colliery Guardian*, 22 April 1881; *Staffordshire Sentinel*, 19 July 1882.

105. Central Association for Dealing with Distress caused by Mining Accidents, *1882 Report*, p. 11.

106. *Provident*, April 1881; *North Staffordshire Daily Mail*, 23 August 1881.

107. *Provident*, April 1881; *Staffordshire Sentinel*, 11 April 1882, 7 April 1888; *Staffordshire Knot*, 27 April 1886; Campbell, *Miner's Thrift*, pp. 13–14.

108. *Provident*, 3 March 1883.

109. Lancashire and Miners' Federation, *Minutes*, 13 April 1886.

110. Seifert, 'Importance of Being Permanent', p. 68.

111. *Staffordshire Knot*, 27 April 1886; Dintenfass, 'Industrial Identities'.

112. Crossick, *Artisan Elite*, p. 174.

113. Gorsky, 'English Friendly Societies', pp. 506–7.

114. Church, *Coal Industry*, p. 598; Gorsky, 'English Friendly Societies, p. 507.
115. Gorsky, 'English Friendly Societies', p. 507.

2 Guinnane, Jopp and Streb 'The Costs and Benefits of Size in a Mutual Insurance System: The German Miners' Knappschaften, 1854–1923'

1. The term 'Knappschaft' cannot be translated into English directly; it originates in the medieval German term for miner, 'Knappe'.
2. M. Wagner-Braun, *Zur Bedeutung berufsständischer Krankenkassen innerhalb der privaten Krankenversicherung in Deutschland bis zum Zweiten Weltkrieg – Die Selbsthilfeeinrichtungen der katholischen Geistlichen* (Stuttgart: F. Steiner, 2002), pp. 32–3. The *Deutsche Rentenversicherung Knappschaft-Bahn-See*, the result of the 2005 merger of the occupational schemes for the mining, railroad and shipping sectors, is the second important pillar of German statutory old-age insurance (*Deutsche Rentenversicherung Bund*) today, having been opened recently to all occupations; see C. Bartels, *et al.*, 'Vergangenheit und Zukunft sozialer Sicherungssysteme am Beispiel der Bundesknappschaft und ihrer Nachfolger. Ein Forschungsprojekt der Leibniz-Gemeinschaft', *Jahrbuch für Wirtschaftsgeschichte/Economic History Yearbook*, 2 (2009), pp. 195–217.
3. K. Tenfelde, 'Die Knappschaftsversicherung und die Wurzeln der Sozialversicherung in Deutschland', in Bundesknappschaft (ed.), *150 Jahre Preußisches Knappschaftsgesetz* (Bochum, 2004), pp. 16–37.
4. 'KV' stands for '*Knappschaftsverein*'; it is used interchangeably with '*Knappschaft*' in this chapter.
5. U. Lauf, 'Bruderschaft und Büchsengeld: eine Untersuchung zu den mittelalterlichen Wurzeln unserer Sozialversicherung', *Wege zur Sozialversicherung* (2003), pp. 176–88; Wagner-Braun, *Zur Bedeutung berufsständischer Krankenkassen*, pp. 28–32.
6. W. Bülow, *Das Knappschaftswesen im Ruhrkohlenbezirk bis zum allgemeinen preußischen Berggesetz vom 24. Juni 1865* (Leipzig, 1905), pp. 1–34; P. Simons, *Das deutsche Knappschaftswesen* (Mainz, 1895), p. 3.
7. W. Fischer, 'Das wirtschafts- und sozialpolitische Ordnungsbild der preußischen Bergrechtsreform 1851–1865', *Zeitschrift für Bergrecht*, 102 (1961), pp. 181–9.
8. Friedrich Wilhelm IV, *Das neue Knappschaftsgesetz* (Charlottenburg, 1854); O. Steinbrink, *Gesetz vom 19. Juni betreffend die Abänderung des Siebenten Titels im Allgemeinen Berggesetze für die preußischen Staaten vom 24. Juni 1865 – nebst Kommentar* (Berlin, 1908); H. Karwehl, *Die Entwicklung und Reform des deutschen Knappschaftswesens* (Jena, 1907), p. 20; O. Steinbrink, *Gesetz vom 19. Juni betreffend die Abänderung des Siebenten Titels im Allgemeinen Berggesetze für die preußischen Staaten vom 24. Juni 1865 – nebst Kommentar* (Berlin, 1908). Saxony did not adopt Prussian mining law; see U. Elsholz, *Die Entwicklung des sächsischen Knappschaftswesens* (Dresden, 1910).
9. Steinbrink, *Gesetz vom 19. Juni*, pp. 152–6; T. A. Jopp, 'Ein risikoreiches Geschäft? Internes und externes Wachstum als risikopolitische Instrumente im preußischen Knappschaftswesen, 1854–1923', in C. Bartels (ed.), *Berufliches Risiko und soziale Sicherheit. Beiträge zur Tagung „Vergangenheit und Zukunft sozialer Sicherungssysteme am Beispiel der Bundesknappschaft und ihrer Nachfolger' im Deutschen Bergbau-Museum Bochum, 8. und 9. Oktober 2009* (Bochum, 2010), pp. 189–224, pp. 190–1.
10. T. W. Guinnane and J. Streb, 'Moral Hazard in a Mutual Health-insurance System: German *Knappschaften*, 1867–1914', *Journal of Economic History*, 71 (2011), pp. 70–104.
11. Guinnane and Streb, 'Moral Hazard', pp. 73–5. For a more detailed overview, see L. Bluma, S. Schulz and J. Streb, 'Prinzipal-Agenten-Probleme in der knappschaftlichen

Krankenversicherung: Die Bekämpfung des "Simulantentums" durch Anreize und Kontrolle', *Vierteljahrschrift für Sozial- und Wirtschaftgeschichte*, 97 (2010), pp. 310–34.

12. J. Hiltrop, 'Über die Reorganisation der Knappschaftsvereine, mit Hinblick auf die Bildung von Versicherungsgenossenschaften für Arbeiter anderer Gewerbe', *Zeitschrift des königlich-preußischen statistischen Bureaus*, 9 (1869), pp. 216–41, esp. pp. 223–5. („Von der grössten Wichtigkeit für die Nützlichkeit und Leistungsfähigkeit eines Knappschaftsvereins ist aber sein Umfang. Je mehr Mitglieder ein Verein zählt, [...], in um so höherem Grade werden, [...], die Vereine stabiler in ihren Leistungen und den dazu erforderlichen Anforderungen".)

13. Karwehl, *Die Entwicklung und Reform*, p. 71. ('Ein Krebsschaden ist es, an dem das deutsche Knappschaftswesen offensichtlich krankt: die Zersplitterung in viele kleine Vereine').

14. Hiltrop, 'Über die Reorganisation der Knappschaftsvereine', p. 225. ('Das Grundübel ist vielmehr die irrationale Verschmelzung der Kranken- und Pensionskasse, der zu grosse Bezirk einer jetzigen Knappschaftskasse als Krankenkasse und der zu kleine für ihre Functionen als Pensionskasse').

15. Karwehl, *Die Entwicklung und Reform*, pp. 61–2. ('Alle diese Tatsachen zwingen die Knappschaftsvereine, das Krankenunterstützungswesen vom Pensionswesen zu trennen. Eine bloß rechnungsmäßige Trennung genügt dabei nicht; eine organisatorische tut vielmehr ebenso not; denn die Krankenkassen erfordern kleinere Bezirke, damit eine individuelle Kontrolle der Mitglieder untereinander möglich wird, die wirksamer und billiger ist als die verwaltungsmäßige ärztliche, und damit die Ursachen eines vielleicht zu hohen Ausgabeetats leichter erkannt und abgestellt werden. [...]. – Die Pensionskassen hingegen erfordern weitere Bezirke mit größeren Mitgliederzahlen, damit das Gesetz der großen Zahlen zur Geltung kommt, [...]. [...]. Also nur bei einer großen Bestandsmasse lassen sich Regelmäßigkeiten im Invalidewerden und im Absterben der Bergleute erkennen und für die Sicherstellung der bei diesen Ereignissen fällig werdenden Leistungen der Pensionskasse versicherungstechnisch verwerten').

16. R. Carnall (ed.), 'Statistik der Knappschaftsvereine des preussischen Staates', *Zeitschrift für das Berg-, Hütten- und Salinenwesen in dem preussischen Staate*, 1–5 (1854–1858); Ministerium für Handel, Gewerbe und öffentliche Arbeiten (ed.), 'Statistik der Knappschaftsvereine des preussischen Staates', *Zeitschrift für das Berg-, Hütten- und Salinenwesen in dem preussischen Staate*, 7–26 (1859–78); Ministerium für öffentliche Arbeiten (ed.), 'Statistik der Knappschaftsvereine des preussischen Staates', *Zeitschrift für das Berg-, Hütten- und Salinenwesen in dem preussischen Staate*, 27–37 (1879–89); Ministerium für Handel und Gewerbe (ed.), 'Statistik der Knappschaftsvereine des preussischen Staates', *Zeitschrift für das Berg-, Hütten- und Salinenwesen in dem preussischen Staate*, 38–70 (1890–1922)'; Oberbergamt München, *Statistik der Knappschaftsvereine im bayerischen Staate* (München: Oberbergamt München, 1884–1920).

17. R. Carnall, 'Statistik der Knappschaftsvereine', 1855, p. 86–91.

18. For accident insurance and invalidity insurance the years of observation are 1886 and 1897 respectively.

19. Calculated using data from D. Khoudour-Castéras, 'Welfare State and Labour Mobility: The Impact of Bismarck's Social Legislation on German Emigration before World War I', *Journal of Economic History*, 68 (2008), pp. 211–43, at pp. 234–6.

20. Simons, *Das deutsche Knappschaftswesen*, pp. 14–25; A. Köhne, *Die deutschen Knappschaftsvereine, ihre Einrichtung und ihre Bedeutung* (Hannover, 1915), pp. 92–9.

21. R. Eisen, 'Market Size and Concentration: Insurance and the European Internal Market 1992', *The Geneva Papers on Risk and Insurance*, 16 (1991), pp. 263–81.

22. See M. H. Geyer, 'Invalidität und Existenzsicherung im Bergbau 1770 bis 1870', in G. Göckenjan (ed.), *Recht auf ein gesichertes Alter?: Studien zur Geschichte der Alterssicherung in der Frühzeit der Sozialpolitik* (Augsburg: Maro Verlag, 1990), pp. 181–202, for an overview of the KVs' invalidity insurance.

23. Calculated using data from Khoudour-Castéras, 'Welfare State and Labour Mobility', p. 236.

24. E. Menzel, *Bergbau-Medizin einst und jetzt* (Berlin: E. Schmidt, 1989), p. 186.

25. Guinnane and Streb, 'Moral Hazard', pp. 85–6.

26. Guinnane, for example, has tested for German nineteenth century rural credit cooperatives the claim that their small size relative to other banks and their ability to draw on local knowledge enabled them to overcome information asymmetries better than larger organizations; see T. W. Guinnane, 'Cooperatives as Information Machines: German Rural Credit Cooperatives, 1883–1914', *Journal of Economic History*, 61 (2001), pp. 366–89.

27. P. Albrecht, 'Gesetze der großen Zahlen und Ausgleich im Kollektiv – Bemerkungen zu Grundlagen der Versicherungsproduktion', *Zeitschrift für die gesamte Versicherungswissenschaft*, 71 (1982), pp. 501–38; P. Zweifel and R. Eisen, *Versicherungsökonomie* (Heidelberg: Springer Verlag, 2003), pp. 240–3.

28. J. C. Herbert Emery, 'Risky Business? Non-Actuarial Pricing Practices and the Financial Viability of Fraternal Sickness Insurers', *Explorations in Economic History*, 33 (1996), pp. 195–226; G. Emery and J. C. Herbert Emery, *A Young Man's Benefit – The Independent Order of Odd Fellows and Sickness Insurance in the United States and Canada, 1860–1929* (Montreal and London: McGill-Queen's Univeristy Press, 1999); N. Broten, 'From Sickness to Death: The Financial Viability of the English Friendly Societies and Coming of the Old Age Pensions Act, 1875–1908', *Department of Economic History Working Paper* 135/10 (2010), London School of Economics.

29. T. A. Jopp, 'Financial Viability, Exposure to Actuarial Risk and Fund Size: Empirical Evidence from 19 and early 20 Century Knappschaft Insurers', *Working Paper* (2010).

30. See L. Bluma, 'Der Hakenwurm an der Ruhr. Umwelt, Körper und soziale Netzwerke im Bergbau des Kaiserreichs ', *Der Anschnitt*, 61 (2009), pp. 314–29.

3 Tedeschi, 'A New Welfare System: The Friendly Societies in the Eastern Lombardy From 1860 to 1914'

1. The Kingdom of Italy (whose king was a member of the Savoia dinasty) came into existence in 1861, but the Eastern Lombardy was incorporated in the Savoia's Kingdom (called Kingdom of Sardinia) in the summer of 1859 (that is after the end of the Second Italian War of Independence): this means that the administration of the SMS existing in the Eastern Lombard was, for the first time, entirely subjected to the Savoia's laws during the year 1860. Finally, the Savoia's Kingdom was the 'pre-unitary' Italian country with the highest number of SMS: in fact before the birth of the Kingdom of Italy they were 232 SMS in the area. This represented 70 per cent of the total number of Italian SMS. There were only 28 SMS in Lombardy in the same period. There is more information on this in the following notes.

2. The censuses considered here were taken by the Italian government in 1862, 1873, 1878, 1885, 1895, 1897, 1904, 1912 and, only for the Catholic SMS, 1911. See: Maic, *Statistica del Regno d'Italia. Società di Mutuo Soccorso. Anno 1862* (Turin: Tip. Letteraria,

1864); *Statistica delle Società di Mutuo Soccorso. Anno 1873* (Rome, Regia Tipografia, 1875); *Statistica delle Società di Mutuo Soccorso. Anno 1878* (Rome: Stamperia Reale, 1880); *Statistica delle Società di Mutuo Soccorso e delle istituzioni cooperative annesse* (Rome: Tip. Metastasio, 1888); Maic, *Elenco delle Società di Mutuo Soccorso. Anno 1895* (Rome: Casa Editrice Italiana, 1898); Maic, *Elenco delle Società di Mutuo Soccorso giuridicamente riconosciute al 31 dicembre 1897* (Rome: Tip. Bertero, 1900); *Le Società di Mutuo Soccorso in Italia al 31 dicembre 1904 (Studio statistico)* (Rome: Tip. Bertero, 1906); *Società di Mutuo Soccorso giuridicamente riconosciute. Leggi, regolamenti, decreti, circolari, giurisprudenza. Elenco delle società esistenti al 31 dicembre 1912* (Rome: Tip. Bertero, 1913); Maic, *Le organizzazioni operaie cattoliche in Italia* (Rome: Officina Poligrafica Italiana, 1911). Other important data concerning the SMS which was strictly linked to the catholic movement are available in: Unione economico-sociale pei cattolici italiani, *Statistica generale delle Istituzioni Cattoliche d'Italia. Regione Lombardo-Veneta (1910–11)* (Bergamo: Tip. S. Alessando, 1912); N. Rezzara, *Il movimento cattolico nella Diocesi di Bergamo. Appunti e statistiche* (Bergamo: Tip. S. Alessando, 1897). Please note that it is impossible to quote in this chapter the sources and references about all 192 analyzed statutes and organizational regulations of the SMS existing in the Eastern Lombardy, as well as all the local studies concerning some particular SMS, and further articles concerning the SMS which were published in the local newspapers (mainly the catholic ones) from the mid-nineteenth century to the start of the World War 1.

3. There were 880,000 inhabitants of the Eastern Lombardy in 1881. They had increased to more than 1,000,000 at the start of the new century and 1,120,000 in 1911. In 1891 there were 37,300 workers in the textile industry (80 per cent were women), while there were 10,500 workers in mines and in the iron and steel and chemical sectors (only 5 per cent were women). From 1891 to 1903 the number of people working in all industrial sectors (that is including paper mills, cement factories, electricity companies, printing houses, tanneries, carpenters etc.) increased from 58,700 to 74,300 and to 116,000 by 1911. The population of Brescia grew from 62,900 in 1881 to 73,000 in 1901 to 87,200 in 1911; in the same period the population of Bergamo grew from 44,300 to 52,500 to 64,400. Concerning the industrial development of the Eastern Lombardy and the demographic growth of the most important industrial areas see S. Zaninelli, V. Zamagni (eds.), *Storia economica e sociale di Bergamo. Fra ottocento e novecento*, vol. 1, *Tradizione e modernizzazione*, and vol. 2, *Il decollo industriale* (Bergamo: Fondazione per la storia economica e sociale di Bergamo, 1996); F. Facchini, *Alle origini di Brescia industriale: insediamenti produttivi e composizione di classe dall'unita al 1911* (Brescia: Micheletti, 1980).

4. Concerning the evolution of the public and private institutions aiming to satisfy the welfare needs of Lombard people between the birth of the Italian Kingdom and World War 1 see A. Colombo (ed.), *Far bene e fare il bene. Interpretazioni e materiali per una storia del welfare lombardo* (Milan: Guerini, 2010).

5. Most of the best works concerning the Italian SMS limited their analyses to the social and political aspects. Some interesting studies consider the SMS as the first example of new organizations grouping workers and peasants in the kingdom of Italy after the suppressions of the guilds. They mainly explain the links between the guilds and the SMS. Other interesting works clearly describe the relations of the Italian SMS with the cooperatives, the trade unions and the socialist and Catholic movements: they show the evolution of the SMS and sometimes their internal organization, but they rarely examine data concerning the welfare aspects and/or the assets of the SMS and/or the benefits that they granted. For the best

studies of the Italian SMS see the contributions which were published in P. Massa and A. Moioli (eds.), *Dalla corporazione al mutuo soccorso. Organizzazione e tutela del lavoro tra XVI e XX secolo* (Milan: Angeli, 2004), pp. 443–745 and its wide bibliography and in particular L. Gheza Fabbri, *Solidarismo in Italia fra XIX e XX secolo. Le società di mutuo soccorso e le casse rurali* (Turin: Giappichelli, 1996); L. Tomassini, 'Il mutualismo nell'Italia liberale (1861–1922)', in *Le società di mutuo soccorso italiane e i loro archivi*, (Rome: Pubblicazioni degli Archivi di Stato, 1999), pp. 15–53); M. L. Betri and A. Gigli Marchetti (eds), *Salute e classi sociali in Italia dall'Unità al fascismo* (Milan: Angeli, 1982); E. Bartocci, *Le politiche sociali nell'Italia liberale (1861–1919)* (Rome: Donzelli, 1999). For contributes in English language see R. Allio, 'Welfare and Social Security in Piedmont: Trade Guilds Compared with Mutual Aid Societies', in A. Guenzi, P. Massa and F. Piola Caselli (eds.), *Guilds, Market and Work Regulations in Italy, 16th–19th Centuries* (Aldershot: Ashgate Press, 1998), pp. 436–46; L. Trezzi, 'The Survival of the Corporation within the Friendly Societies for Artisan and Workers in Milan during the First Half of the Nineteenth Century', in Guenzi, Massa and Caselli (eds.), *Guilds, Market and Work Regualtions*, pp. 447–64; L. Tomassini, 'Mutual Benefits Societies in Italy (1861–1922)', in M. van der Linden (ed.), *Social Security Mutualism. The Comparative History of Mutual Benefit Societies* (Bern: Peter Lang, 1996), pp. 225–71; M. S. Quine, *Italy's Social Revolution: Charity and Welfare from Liberalism to Fascism* (Basingstoke: Palgrave, 2002). Concerning the Italian industrialization during the analyzed period see V. Zamagni, *The Economic History of Italy (1861–1990). Recovery after Decline* (Oxford: Clarendon, 2003), pp. 47–206.

6.   Please note that Figure 3.1 makes it clear that some years before the 1880s showed a great increase in the number of SMS. In 1862 the number of SMS doubled and in the period 1875–7 there was an 80 per cent increase. These preceded the years or were the years in which the Italian state recorded a census. However, these figures do not necessarily reveal when new SMS came into existence. In cases where the census did not give evidence of the date of foundation, the first news of the new SMS is taken as the date of foundation. Finally, it is important to note that the upsurge of SMS first registered in 1910 simply depended on the year of the publication of the official data concerning the catholic SMS: they showed many 'unknown' small SMS whose dates of foundation were not indicated and which are not mentioned in other sources (and so the year of the publication of data substituted the unknown date of foundation).

7.   Please note that the identified SMS represented the SMS which were registered in at least one census: so this figure is not the same as the number of registered SMS in the eight official census counts. Besides that, the census registered 15 SMS in 1862, 28 in 1873 and 60 in 1878: after the 1880s there were 87 registered SMS in 1885, 203 in 1895 and 180 in 1904. The census of 1897 and the census of 1912 (they respectively registered 32 and 63 SMS) were not useful in charting the number of the SMS, and they only showed some aspects of their organization.

8.   All the sources of data concerning the SMS existing in the Eastern Lombardy are indicated in note 2. See also A. Fappani, 'Dalle società operaie alle unioni cattoliche del lavoro', *Bollettino dell'Archivio per la Storia del Movimento Sociale Cattolico in Italia*, 1 (1966), pp. 83–105; A. Fappani, 'Le società operaie cattoliche nel Bresciano', *Bollettino dell'Archivio per la Storia del Movimento Sociale Cattolico in Italia*, 4 (1969–70), pp. 29–80; L. Trezzi, 'Società di mutuo soccorso in Lombardia tra Ottocento e Novecento. Alcuni risultati di una ricerca sulle province di Bergamo, Brescia, Como e Milano', in S. Zaninelli and M. Taccolini (eds.), *Il lavoro come fattore produttivo e come risorsa nella storia economica italiana* (Milan: Vita e Pensiero, 2002), pp. 653–67. Concerning the

Catholic and socialist newspapers giving information about the SMS in the Eastern Lombardy see 'Il Campanile', 'il Campanone', 'Il Santuario di Treviglio', 'L'Eco di Bergamo', 'La Voce del Popolo', 'Il Cittadino di Brescia' (for the Catholic SMS), 'Il Popolo', 'Il Pensiero', 'Brescia Nuova' (for the socialist SMS).

9. The SMS grouping silk workers of the Filanda d'Almé had 612 members in 1878. The members of the SMS grouping cotton workers of the Cotonificio Hefti in Roé increased from 238 in 1895 to 400 in 1904.

10. It is interesting to observe that the SMS grouping veterans survived after the death of their first members because they included veterans of successive wars. As most of 'mille' (that is the voluntary soldiers, the 'red shirts', who followed Giuseppe Garibaldi in his conquest of the South Italy) arrived from the Eastern Lombardy, they created their SMS in Bergamo: also in this case the SMS survived after the death of the last 'red shirt' because it included the veterans of following Italian wars.

11. Please note that it was also possible that a small trade union was born in an SMS provoking a definitive breach among the members: this could happen in the villages when some members of an 'independent' SMS decided to create a catholic or socialist trade union and in the same instance they also founded a new SMS related to a political movement. Concerning the existing links between the Italian SMS and the associations grouping workers and peasants (such as the trade unions and cooperatives) see: L. Trezzi, *Sindacalismo e cooperazione dalla fine dell'ottocento all'avvento del fascismo* (Milan: Angeli, 1982); L. Tomassini, 'L'associazionismo operaio: aspetti e problemi della diffusione del mutualismo nell'Italia liberale', in S. Musso (ed.), *Tra fabbrica e società: mondi operai nell'Italia del Novecento* (Milan: Feltrinelli, 1999), pp. 3–41.

12. Please note that in the 'independent' SMS there were no Catholic SMS: in their statutes Catholic SMS usually declared their links with the ecclesiastical institutions and so they could not be really considered as 'independent'.

13. The electoral law of 1882 allowed Italian males to vote if they were able to read and write and if they had 19,80 Italian lire or if they had their elementary school licence (that is they had passed the first two years at elementary school). Illiterate people could vote only after the law of 1912: it gave the vote to all Italian males who were 21 years old and were able to read and write or who had done their compulsory military service; Italians males who were illiterate or not able to become a soldier could vote when were 30 years old. These limits were eliminated after World War I: universal male suffrage arrived in 1919.

14. Please note that the first Italian law concerning the female worker was promulgated on June 1902. It limited female work to 12 hours a day and it did not allow women to work during the night.

15. It is evident that in a farm the workload was normally reduced during the cold season or periods of rain, while for metal or chemical workers there were no breaks and they could work seven days a week (the compulsory day of rest was only introduced in Italy in 1907).

16. The first law regulating the exploitation of child labour was promulgated at the end of 1873, but it only prohibited the employment of children in pedlar trades and activities. In 1886 a new law did not allow children under 9 years of age to work in factories and also prohibited boys under 15 years taking dangerous, low-paid work. Only in the first decade of twentieth century did new laws prohibit children under 12 years from working and limited boys under 15 years to 11 hours work a day.

17. The quantitative data of 1862 concerned 15 SMS, that of 1873 and 1878 concerned 27 SMS, that of 1885 concerned 92 SMS, that of 1895 and 1897 concerned 282 SMS, while that of 1904, along with the catholic statistics, concerned 270 SMS. It is important to note that SMS were not the same for all the analysed censuses.

18. Please note that data concerning the more frequent diseases of SMS members existed for the end of 1870s only and so it did not include the diseases linked to the industrialization of the Eastern Lombardy which started later: see Maic, *Statistica della morbosita , ossia frequenza e durata delle malattie presso i soci delle societa di mutuo soccorso* (Rome: Tip. Cenniniana, 1879). The other census on the SMS in fact gave little data about the numbers of subsides granted by the SMS to ill members: in 1862 there were 775 subsides and this had increased to 1,205 in 1873 (the data also included 21 subsides for temporarily jobless members), 1,567 in 1885 and finally 2,888 in the census of 1904 and 1910. The share of SMS which communicated data about their subsides increased from 45 per cent in 1862 (9 of 20 SMS) to 59 per cent in 1873 (26 of 44) but decreased to 11.3 per cent in 1885 (26 of 229) and less than 9 per cent in 1910 (43 of 481). In the period from 1895 to 1897 only one SMS declared the number of its subsides, which was 171, that is more than the average existing in the other periods. This obviously complicated the evaluation of the data.

19. Please note that in the plane of the Eastern Lombardy there were many cases of pellagra even if the income of rural workers was not as low as elsewhere. The pellagra increased because of an ipo-vitaminic diet based on the massive use of maize (polenta): this means that in the villages of the Alpine valleys, where incomes were normally lower than in the plane, pellagra was paradoxically less diffused because people consumed less maize and more milk and dairy products and other cereals. There exists a wide bibliography concerning the pellagra in Italy which is obviously impossible to quote in full in this article, however see: G. Coppola, 'La pellagra in Lombardia dal settecento alla prima metà dell'ottocento', in M. Romani (ed.), *Le campagne lombarde fra Sette e Ottocento. Alcuni temi di ricerca* (Milan: Vita e Pensiero, 1976), pp. 141–78; A. De Bernardi, *Il mal della rosa. Denutrizione e pellagra nelle campagne tra '800 e '900* (Milan: Angeli, 1984); M. Livi-Bacci, 'Fertility, Nutrition, and Pellagra: Italy during the Vital Revolution', *Journal of Interdisciplinary History*, 16:3 (1986), pp. 431–54.

20. Insurance for workplace accidents become compulsory in the agricultural sector only after World War 1. See A. Fontana, 'L'estensione al settore agricolo dell'assicurazione obbligatoria contro gli infortuni sul lavoro', in *Rivista di Diritto Agrario*, 3 (1996), pp. 306–26; A. Cherubini and A. Coluccia, 'La previdenza sociale nell'epoca giolittiana. II. L'infortunio sul lavoro nell'agricoltura', *La Previdenza*, 2 (1984), pp. 351–82.

21. Please note that the Ministero per il Lavoro e la Previdenza (that is the Department for Work and Welfare) was divided from the Ministero per l'Industria e il Commercio (that is the Department for Industry and Trade) by the law of 3 of June 1920: see D. Marucco, 'Alle origini del Ministero del Lavoro e della Previdenza sociale in Italia', *Le carte e la storia*, 1 (2008), pp. 179–90. Until World War 1 all problems concerning the security and health of workers in the workplace were the responsibility of the Ispettorato del lavoro (that is the Labour Inspectorate) which had few financial resources to implement efficient controls: see A. Cardinale, *Salute operaia. Le origini delle istituzioni per la protezione dei lavoratori in Italia (1896–1914)* (Sesto San Giovanni: Archivio del lavoro, 2005), pp. 97–113.

22. Concerning the slow and progressive process of creation of the Italian welfare state and the influence of the associations grouping workers and peasants see D. Marucco, *Mutual-*

ismo e sistema politico. Il caso italiano (1862–1904) (Milan: Angeli, 1981); D. Marucco, *Lavoro e Previdenza dall'unità al fascismo: il Consiglio della Previdenza dal 1869 al 1923* (Milan: Angeli, 1984); R. Romano, 'Sistema di fabbrica, sviluppo industriale e infortuni sul lavoro', in E Della Peruta (ed.), *Storia d'Italia. Annali*, vol. 7. *Malattia e medicina* (Turin: Einaudi, 1984), pp. 1019–55; T. L. Rizzo, *La legislazione sociale nella nuova Italia (1876–1900)* (Naples: ESI, 1988); F. Amoretti, 'Le politiche sociali in età giolittiana', *Stato e Mercato*, 27 (1989), pp. 409–43; A. Cherubini and A. Coluccia, *La previdenza sociale nell'epoca giolittiana* (Rome: INPS, 1986); A. Cherubini, *Beneficenza e solidarietà. Assistenza pubblica e mutualismo operaio (1860–1900)* (Milan: Angeli, 1991); A. Cherubini, *Dalla libertà all'obbligo: la previdenza sociale fra Giolitti e Mussolini* (Milan: Angeli, 1998). For a comparative analysis concerning many European cases also see F. Girotti, *Welfare State. Storia, modelli e critica* (Rome: Carocci, 2005).

4 Vila Rodríguez and Pons Pons, 'Economic Growth and Demand for Health Coverage in Spain: The Role of Friendly Societies (1870–1942)'

1. A. Rumeu de Armas, *Historia de la Previsión Social en España* (Barcelona: Ediciones El Albir SA, 1981).
2. M. Van der Linden (ed.), *Social Security Mutualism. The Comparative History of Mutual Benefit Societies* (Bern: Peter Lang, 1996).
3. For the case of England, see B. Harris, *The Origins of the British Welfare State: Social Welfare in England and Wales, 1800–1945*, (New York: Palgrave Macmillan, 2004); B. Harris, 'The Development of Social Policy in England and Wales, 1800–1945', in H. Bochel, C. Bochel, R. Page and R. Sykes (eds.), *Social Policy: Themes, Issues and Debates* (Basingstoke: Palgrave Macmillan, 2009), pp. 89–109; B. Harris, M. Gorsky, A. Guntupalli and A. Hinde, 'Age, Sickness and Longevity in the Late Nineteenth and Early Twentieth Centuries: Evidence from the Hampshire Friendly Society', *Social Science History*, 30:4 (2006), pp. 571–600; M. Dreyfus, 'Mutual Benefit Societies in France: A Complex Endeavour', in Van der Linden (ed.), *Social Security Mutualism*, pp. 209–24, outlines the evolution of French mutualism, and for the case of the United States, see the following: D. T. Beito, *From Mutual Aid to the Welfare State. Fraternal Societies and Social Services, 1890–1967* (North Carolina: The University of North Carolina Press, 2000) and J. E. Murray, *Origins of American Health Insurance. A History of Industrial Sickness Funds* (New Haven, CT and London: Yale University Press, 2007).
4. For the situation in this respect in the late 1980s, see J. Cuesta Bustillo, 'Las sociedades de socorros mutuos en la España de los años veinte. Un silencio en el Reformismo Social', in *El Reformismo social en España: La Comisión de Reformas Sociales, Actas de los IV Coloquios de Historia* (Jaén: Publicaciones del Monte de Piedad y Caja de Ahorros de Córdoba, 1987), pp. 301–30, esp. p. 301, note 2.
5. S. Castillo (ed.), *Solidaridad desde abajo. Trabajadores y Socorros Mutuos en la España Contemporánea* (Madrid: Unión General de Trabajadores y Confederación Nacional de Entidades de Previsión, 1994); S. Castillo and J. M. Ortiz de Orruño (coord.) *Estado, protesta y movimientos sociales* (Guipúzcoa: Universidad del País Vasco, 1997); E. Maza Zorrilla (coord.), *Asociacionismo en la España contemporánea. Vertientes y análisis interdisciplinar* (Valladolid: Universidad de Valladolid, 2003); S. Castillo and R. Ruzafa (coord.), *La previsión social en la Historia* (Madrid: Siglo XXI, 2009). For a recent

piece of work on the role of the friendly societies in social coverage in which Spain is incorporated into an international context and which includes a synthesis of contributions from social history, economic history and the history of medicine, see M. Vilar Rodríguez, 'La cobertura social a través de las sociedades de socorro mutuo, 1839–1935. ¿Una alternativa al Estado para afrontar los fallos de mercado?', in J. Pons Pons and J. Silvestre Rodríguez (eds.), *Los orígenes del Estado del Bienestar en España, 1900–1945: los seguros de accidentes, vejez, desempleo y enfermedad*, (Zaragoza: Prensas Universitarias de Zaragoza, 2010), pp. 85–122.

6.   E. Maza Zorrilla (coord.), *Sociabilidad en la España Contemporánea: historiografía y problemas metodológicos* (Valladolid: Universidad de Valladolid, Instituto de Historia Simancas, 2002); E. Maza Zorrilla, 'Sociabilidad formal en Palencia: 1887–1923', in M. Valentina Calleja González (coord.), *Actas del III Congreso de Historia de Palencia: 30, 31 de marzo y 1 de abril de 1995*, vol. 3 (Palencia: Edad Moderna y Edad Contemporánea, 1995), pp. 425–44; J. L. Guereña, 'El Espacio mutualista en la sociabilidad popular de la Restauración (1875–1900). El ejemplo asturiano', in Castillo (ed.), *Solidaridad desde abajo*, pp. 205–24.

7.   For more on these nuances about welfare mutualism, see F. Montero García and M. Esteban de Vega, 'Aproximación tipológica al mutualismo popular y obrero en España: El mutualismo asistencial', in S. Castillo (coord.), *La historia social en España. Actualidad y Perspectivas* (Madrid: Siglo XXI, 1991), pp. 457–70.

8.   Montero y Esteban de la Vega, 'Aproximación tipológica al mutualismo', p. 462.

9.   For an analysis of Catholic mutualism, see A. García Checa, 'Ideología y práctica del mutualismo católico femenino en Cataluña, 1900–1930', in Castillo (ed.), *Solidaridad desde abajo*, pp. 125–34; P. Carasa Soto, 'El mutualismo de los sindicatos agrícolas y de las cajas rurales durante el prime tercio del siglo XX', in Castillo (ed.), *Solidaridad desde abajo*, pp. 447–68.

10. This formula was applied in other European countries such as Germany, England or Belgium. For its application in Spain, see S. González Gómez, 'La cotización sindical a base múltiple: puerta de integración del mutualismo obrero en el primer sindicalismo socialista madrileño', in Castillo (ed.), *Solidaridad desde abajo*, pp. 437–46.

11. S. Castillo, 'La sociedades de Socorros Mutuos en la España Contemporánea', in Castillo (ed.), *Solidaridad desde abajo*, pp. 1–30. The idea put forward here is that economic individualism was against the formation of 'resistance societies' or trade unions, and therefore supported the prohibition of the so-called 'resistance societies' (p. 5).

12. Vilar Rodríguez, 'La cobertura social a través de los socorros mutuos obreros', p. 98.

13. For more on this regulation, see F. López Castellano, 'Una sociedad 'de cambio y no de beneficencia'. El Asociacionismo en la España Liberal (1808–1936)', *Ciriec – España. Revista de Economía Pública, Social y cooperativa*, 44 (2003), pp. 199–228; P. Solà i Gussinyer, 'El Mutualismo y su función social: sinopsis histórica', *Ciriec – España. Revista de Economía Pública, Social y cooperativa*, 44 (2003), pp. 175–98.

14. Castillo, 'La sociedades de Socorros Mutuos en la España Contemporánea', pp. 2–3; Montero and Esteban, 'Aproximación tipológica al mutualismo popular y obrero en España' includes Henri Hatzfeld's definition in which it also touches upon the idea that the aim is to insure members.

15. Montero and Esteban, 'Aproximación tipológica al mutualismo popular y obrero en España', pp. 457–70.

16. J. Silvestre Rodríguez and J. Pons Pons, 'El seguro de accidentes del trabajo, 1900–1935. El alcance de las indemnizaciones, la asistencia sanitaria y la prevención', in Pons Pons and Silvestre Rodríguez (eds.), *Los orígenes del Estado de bienestar en España 1900–1945. los seguros de accidentes, vejez, desempleo y enfermedad* (Zaragoza: Prensas Universitarias de Zaragoza, 2010), pp. 123–50.

17. Information of this kind can be found in the following work on rural Catalonia: García Checa, 'Ideología y práctica del mutualismo católico femenino en Cataluña, 1900–1930', pp. 125–34; and on the work on Asturian societies included in the following work: J. Rodríguez González, 'Las sociedades de socorros mutuos en Asturias, 1859–1900' in Castillo (ed.), *Solidaridad desde abajo*, pp. 189–204; J. Siles González, 'Corporativismo femenino durante las tres primeras décadas del siglo XX. El primer colegio profesional femenino. El caso de las matronas de Alicante', in Castillo and Ortiz de Orruño (Coord.) *Estado, protesta y movimientos sociales*, pp. 411–22; A. P. Martínez Soto and M. A. Pérez Perceval, 'Asistencia sanitaria en la minería de Cartagena-La Unión (1850–1914), *Revista de Historia de la Economía y de la Empresa* IV (2010), pp. 93–194; J. Pons Pons, *El sector seguros en Baleares. Empresas y empresarios en el siglo XIX y XX* (Palma de Mallorca: El Tall, 1998), mainly ch. 4, pp. 81–101. P. Pérez Castroviejo, 'La asistencia sanitaria de los trabajadores: beneficencia, mutualismo y previsión en Vizcaya, 1876–1936', *Revista de la Historia de la Economía y de la Empresa*, 4 (2010), pp. 127–52. P. León-Sanz, 'La concertación de la asistencia en la enfermedad en la Sociedad de Obreros *La Conciliación* (1902–1919)', *Navarra: memoria e imagen : actas del VI Congreso de Historia de Navarra*, (Pamplona: Ed. Eunate, 2006), pp. 97–108, P. León, 'Los relatos de los enfermos de los enfermos: análisis de las quejas de los socios en una Sociedad de Socorros Mutuos (1902–1919)', in T. Ortiz Gómez, G. Olagüe de Ros, E. Rodríguez Ocaña, A. Menéndez Navarro, E. Gil García, A. Luna Maldonado, M. T. Sevilla Olmedo and A. J. Gómez Núñez (coord.), *La experiencia de enfermar en perspectiva histórica: XIV Congreso de la Sociedad Española de Historia de la Medicina* (Granada: Universidad de Granada, 2008), pp. 51–4.

18. For how this idea underlies the situation in the late 1980s, see Cuesta Bustillo, 'Las sociedades de socorros mutuos en la España de los años veinte', p. 302.

19. The first stage would include from the Old Regime to the revolutionary period known as the 'Sexenio revolucionario' (1868–74) and the second from the Restoration to the Second Republic. Castillo, 'La sociedades de Socorros Mutuos en la España Contemporánea', pp. 8–19.

20. For the criticism of this source for the case of Catalonia, see P. Sola y Gussinyer, 'El mutualismo contemporáneo en una sociedad industrial. Anotaciones sobre el caso catalán', in Castillo (ed.), *Solidaridad desde abajo*, pp. 71–86, p. 85.

21. These were followed by Madrid with 4,509, Tarragona with 3,974, Alicante with 3,444. and Guipúzcoa with 3,232. The average in Spain was 1,889. F. Montero and M. E. Martínez Quintero, *Orígenes y antecedentes de la Previsión Social* (Madrid: Ministerio de Trabajo y Seguridad Social, 1988), p. 89.

22. In the case of Majorca, the first stage can be established until 1880, during which the societies developed in the capital (Palma de Mallorca). After this date the model spreads

outside this area, that is, in the rural areas, first to the wine-producing municipalities and then to the industrial shoe-making areas. Pons Pons, *El sector seguros en Baleares*, p. 87.

23. R. Campos Marín, *Curar y gobernar. Medicina y liberalismo en la España del siglo XIX* (Madrid: Nivola, 2003); E. López Keller, 'Hacia la quiebra de la mentalidad liberal; las resistencias al cambio', in (various authors), *Historia de la acción social pública en España. Beneficencia y Previsión* (Madrid: Ministerio de Trabajo y Seguridad Social, 1990), pp. 137–60; E. Maza Zorrilla, *Pobreza y beneficencia en la España contemporánea (1808–1936)* (Barcelona: Ariel, 1999).

24. Just as the statistics of this first section show.

25. The friendly societies promoted by older companies located themselves in the Biscay province in iron and steel and railway companies. R. Ruzaga Ortega, 'Tradiciones, imposición patronal y autoorganización: mutualismo obrero en Vizcaya en el siglo XIX', in Castillo and Ortiz de Orruño (Coord.), *Estado, protesta y movimientos sociales*, pp. 371–84 and Pérez Castroviejo, 'La asistencia sanitaria de los trabajadores', pp. 127–52. In the first decade of the twentieth century, friendly societies were detected in Guipúzcoa in a tobacco factory and in a metal construction factory. A. Martínez Marín, 'Las sociedades de socorros mutuos en Guipúzcoa 1880–1936', in Castillo (ed.), *Solidaridad desde abajo*, pp. 155–76. For initiatives that were also developed this decade in the Galician industrial sector, see M. Vilar Rodríguez, 'La cobertura social al margen del Estado: asociacionismo obrero y socorros mutuos en Galicia (s. 1939–1935)', *Revista de Historia de la Economía y de la Empresa*, 4 (2010), pp. 179–206. The friendly societies in Madrid's electricity companies and in the railway companies date from the second decade of the twentieth century. For the former, see A. M. Aubanell Jubany, 'La elite de la clase trabajadora. Las condiciones laborales de los trabajadores de las eléctricas madrileñas en el periodo de entreguerras', *Scripta Nova. Electronic Review*, 119:7 (2002). For the railway companies, see T. Martínez Vara, 'Salarios y Programas de Bienestar Industrial en la empresa ferroviaria MZA (1915–1935)', *Investigaciones de Historia Económica*, 4 (2006), pp. 101–38.

26. On 11 August 1914, the workers of the Port Works Authority of the ports of Almería, Barcelona and Seville had *montepíos* of this type. *Gazeta de Madrid*, 223, p. 350.

27. F. Comín Comín, *Historia de la Hacienda Pública II. España (1808–1995)* (Barcelona: Crítica, 1996), p. 266.

28. Article 18 of the Law of 20 June 1849. *Gazeta de Madrid*, número 5398, 24 de junio de 1849. For more on these aspects, see M. Vilar Rodríguez, '¿Entre la limosna y el bienestar? Origen, desarrollo y consecuencias de las políticas sociales en Galicia (1890–1935)', *Cuadernos de Historia Contemporánea*, 29 (2007), pp. 173–97.

29. M. Esteban de Vega, 'La asistencia liberal española: beneficencia pública y previsión particular', *Historia Social*, 13 (1992), pp. 123–8.

30. A. Marin de la Barcena, *Apuntes para el estudio y la organización en España de las instituciones de beneficencia y previsión* (Madrid: Rivadeneyra, 1909), p. LXV ff. In general, the town and city councils were going through a very precarious situation during the Restoration, which in the case of charity was made worse by the legal straitjacket which prevented more than 10 per cent of the total Budget being earmarked for such causes. For more on this, see Esteban de Vega, 'La asistencia liberal española', pp. 123–8.

31. V. Pérez Moreda, *Las crisis de mortalidad en la España interior (siglos XVI-XIX)* (Madrid: Siglo XXI, 1980); J. Nadal, 'España durante la Primera Revolución Tecnológica', in J. Nadal, A. Carreras and P. Martín Aceña, *España 200 años de tecnología* (Madrid: Ministerio de Industria y energía, 1988), pp. 29–200.

32. E. Rodríguez Ocaña, 'Medicina y acción social en la España del primer tercio del siglo XX', in various authors, *De la beneficencia al bienestar social. Cuatro siglos de acción social,* (Madrid: Siglo XXI, 1988), pp. 227–65.

33. M. Martín Salazar, *El ministerio de Sanidad y del Trabajo* (Madrid: Imprenta. Suc. E. Teodoro, 1921).

34. The towns are defined as population centres that do not exceed 5,000 inhabitants. D. S. Reher, 'Ciudades, procesos de urbanización y sistemas urbanos en la Península Ibérica, 1550–1991', in M. Guàrdia, F. J. Monclús and J. L. Oyón (dir.), *Atlas histórico de ciudades europeas. Península Ibérica* (Barcelona: Salvat, 1994), pp. 1–29.

35. See INP, *La cuestión del seguro de enfermedad ante la X reunión de la Conferencia Internacional del Trabajo,* Ginebra, mayo 1927, (Madrid: Sobrinos de Sucesora de M. Minuesa de los Ríos, 1927), p. 22. Although the *igualas* have been considered as a typically rural phenomenon by Spanish historiography, there is also evidence of their functioning in some urban municipalities of the industrial zone of Biscay province. See Pérez Castroviejo, 'La asistencia sanitaria de los trabajadores', p. 146.

36. E. Rodríguez Ocaña, 'La asistencia médica colectiva en España hasta 1936', in, various authors, *Historia de la Acción Social pública en España* (Madrid: Ministerio de Trabajo y Seguridad Social, 1990), pp. 321–60, p. 336.

37. Ministerio de la Gobernación, *Apuntes para el estudio y la organización en España de las instituciones de beneficencia y previsión.* Memoria de la Dirección General de Administración (Madrid: Establec. Tip. Sucesores de Rivadeneyra, impresores de la Casa Real, 1909), pp. CI-CII and LXIV and *Anuario Estadístico de España,* (1912). The population data correspond to the census of 1910. See R. Nicolau, 'Población, salud y actividad', in A. Carreras and X. Tafunell. (coord.), *Estadísticas históricas de España,* Vol. 1 (Bilbao: Fundación BBVA, 2005), pp. 79–154.

38. Ministerio de la Gobernación, *Apuntes para el estudio,* pp. CI-CII and LXIV.

39. E. Maza Zorrilla, 'El mutualismo en España, 1900–1941. Ajustes e interferencias', in Castillo and Ruzafa (coord.), *La previsión social en la historia,* pp. 333–68, p. 336.

40. INP, *La cuestión del seguro de enfermedad,* p. 22. For the calculations the census of 1930 has been used. See Nicolau, 'Población, salud y actividad'.

41. Rodríguez Ocaña, 'La asistencia médica colectiva en España hasta 1936'.

42. Nicolau, 'Población, salud y actividad', p. 133.

43. D. S. Reher and E. Camps, 'Las economías familiares dentro de un contexto histórico comparado', in REIS, 55/91 (1991), pp. 65–91 and E. Camps, 'Trabajo infantil y estrategias familiares durante los primeros estadios de la industrialización catalana (1850–1925). Esbozos a partir del estudio de un caso', *Cuadernos de Historia Contemporánea,* 24 (2002), pp. 263–79.

44. For this part, see J. Pons and M. Vilar, 'Friendly Societies, Comercial Insurance and the State in Sickness Risk Coverage: The Case of Spain (1880–1944)', *International Review of Social History,* 56 (1) (2011), pp. 71–101.

45. In Spain, the study of actuarial sciences was not introduced in business schools until 1915. J. Pons Pons, 'Multinational Enterprise and Institutional Regulation in the Life-Insurance Market in Spain, 1880–1935', *Business History Review* 82 (2008), pp. 87–114.

46. Sources: *Boletín Oficial de Seguros* (1913 and 1921); *Revista de Previsión* (1931); *Boletín Oficial de Seguros y Ahorro* (1941).

47. INP, *La cuestión del seguro de enfermedad,* p. 102.

48. INP, *La cuestión del seguro de enfermedad,* p. 140 and M. Vilar Rodríguez, '¿Entre la limosna y el bienestar? Origen, desarrollo y consecuencias de las políticas sociales en

Galicia (1890–1935)', *Cuadernos de Historia Contemporánea*, 29 (2007), pp. 173–97. Conclusion obtained from the information about A Coruña and Barcelona.

49. For the mutual societies under the tutelage of the Church, see, for example J. Andrés-Gallego, *Pensamiento y acción social de la Iglesia en España* (Madrid: Espasa-Calpe, 1984); F. Montero García, 'La crítica católica de la economía clásica y el primer catolicismo social (sobre el impacto de la Rerum Novarum y la aportación de los católicos españoles al reformismo social)', in E. Fuentes Quintana (dir.), *Economía y economistas españoles. Las críticas a la economía clásica*, Vol 5 (Barcelona: Galaxia Gutenberg and Círculo de Lectores, 2001). pp. 451–93.

50. In its first article, the Law of Associations recognised the right of the free exercise of association for religious, political, scientific, artistic, charitable or recreational ends, or any other that did not pursue profit and gain as its sole and exclusive end. The friendly societies were included here explicitly, as were welfare societies and production, credit and consumer cooperatives. In the legal text, the basic steps relating to their foundation, internal organization and dissolution were set out. The regulations to be followed in economic questions (accounts, registration, balances...) are also established, as are the mechanisms of official inspection, where the civil governors assumed great responsibility. Vilar Rodríguez, 'La cobertura social a través de las sociedades de socorro mutuo, 1839–1935', pp. 85–122.

51. The majority of these associations reached their peak after the Law of Agricultural Trade Unions of 1906. Among the possible ends of these associations, this law included that of being 'institutions of cooperation, of mutuality, of insurance, of retirement pensions for invalids and the old, applied to agriculture and livestock farming'. See A. P. Martínez Soto, 'Los orígenes del cooperativismo de crédito agrario en España, 1890–1934', *CIREC* (2003), pp. 57–104.

52. Common patterns of internal functioning obtained from Vilar Rodríguez, 'La cobertura social a través de las sociedades de socorro mutuo, 1839–1935', pp. 85–122.

53. The percentages are calculated from data provided in: R. Arnabat Mata, 'Las sociedades de socorros mutuos en Catalunya rural, 1879–1939', in Castillo (eds), *Solidaridad desde abajo.*, pp. 87–106 and for Galicia, see Vilar Rodríguez, 'La cobertura social al margen del Estado', pp. 179–208.

54. Given their economic limitations, the mutuals 'socorrían' más que 'preveían' ('aided' rather than 'prevented') and the distance between both terms was marked by the lack of funds. Quote taken from J. Nadal, J. and C. Sudrià, *Historia de la Caja de Pensiones. La Caixa dentro del sistema financiero catalán* (Barcelona: Caixa - Edicions 62, 1983), pp. 60–1.

55. P. Fullana and A. Marimón, *Història del 'montepío' de Previsió de l'Arraval de Santa Catalina. Centenari 1894–1994* (Palma de Mallorca: 1994) affirm that the society's most serious problem occurred in 1940, when the practitioners demanded substantial increases in their fees, approved by the medical association. This resulted in a 30 per cent increase in the *montepío's* expenses.

56. M. Vilar Rodríguez and E. Lindoso Tato, 'El sector balneario gallego desde una perspectiva histórica (1780–1935)', *Transportes, Servicios y Telecomunicaciones*, 19 (2010), pp. 138–65.

57. A. Menéndez-Navarro and E. Rodríguez-Ocaña, 'From "Accident Medicine" to "Factory Medicine": Spanish Occupational Medicine in the Twentieth Century', in A. Grieco, D. Fano, T. Carter, and S. Iavicoli (eds.), *Origins of Occupational Health Associations in the World* (Amsterdam: Elsevier, 2003), 207–16.

58. A. M. Aubanell Jubany, 'La gestió laboral de l'empresa elèctrica madrilenya en el primer terç del segle XX', *Recerques: Història, economia i cultura*, 37 (1998), pp. 137–64.
59. Nevertheless, it seems that this phenomenon started up at the end of the nineteenth century in areas such as Biscay province, where employers' *montepíos* were created in the iron and steel and transport industries in the 1880s. See Pérez Castroviejo, 'La asistencia sanitaria de los trabajadores', p. 137.
60. For more on this matter, see Aubanell, 'La elite de la clase trabajadora'; Martínez Vara, 'Salarios y Programas de Bienestar Industrial'; Vilar Rodríguez, 'La cobertura social al margen del Estado'; Martínez Marín, 'Las sociedades de socorros mutuos', p. 137 ff.
61. A. Menéndez Navarro and E. Rodríguez Ocaña, 'Aproximación al estudio de los recursos asistenciales sanitarios en los establecimientos minero-metalúrgicos españoles a comienzos del siglo XX', in R. Huertas and R. Campos (coord.), *Medicina social y clase obrera en España (siglos XIX y XX)*, (Madrid: Fundación de Investigaciones Marxistas, 1992), pp. 263–93.
62. A. Soto Carmona, *El trabajo industrial en la España contemporánea, 1874–1936* (Madrid: Anthropos, 1989), p. 67.
63. INP, *La cuestión del seguro de enfermedad*, p. 99.
64. For more on these aspects, see Sola i Gussinyer, 'El mutualismo contemporáneo en una sociedad industrial', pp. 71–86 and http://www.mutualitats.com. In 1935 the federation spread to the whole of Catalonia and became known as the Federation of Friendly Societies of Catalonia. These laws were repealed after Franco's victory in the Civil War.
65. Rodríguez Ocaña, 'La asistencia médica colectiva en España, hasta 1936', p. 332.
66. Percentage calculated on the basis of the average of the population census of the city of Barcelona for 1900 (533,000) and for 1920 (710,000). Figures come from the INE (National Statistics Institute).
67. Figures for salaries obtained from: M. Vilar Rodríguez, 'La ruptura postbélica a través del comportamiento de los salarios industriales: nueva evidencia cuantitativa (1908–1963)', *Revista de Historia Industrial*, 25 (2004), pp. 81–126.
68. A. Herranz, 'La difusión internacional de los seguros sociales antes de 1945', in Pons and Silvestre (eds.), *Los orígenes del Estado de bienestar en España 1900–1945*, pp. 51–83. The countries with compulsory insurance were Germany (1883), Austria (1888), Hungary (1891), Luxembourg (1901), Norway (1909), United Kingdom (1911), Rumania (1912), Russia (1912) and Holland (1913); while subsidised voluntary pension schemes operated in Italy (1886), Denmark (1892), Belgium (1894), France (1898), Iceland (1911) and Switzerland (1911).
69. C. Usui, 'Welfare State development in a World System Context: Event History Analysis of First Social Insurance Legislation among 60 countries, 1880–1960', in T. Janoski and A. M. Hicks (eds.), *The Comparative Political Economy of the Welfare State* (Cambridge: Cambridge UP, 1994), pp. 254–77 and M. Lengwiler, 'Competing Globalizations: Controversies between Private and Social Insurance at International Organizations, 1900–60', in R. Pearson (ed.), *The Development of International Insurance* (London: Pickering & Chatto, 2010), pp. 167–86.
70. Herranz, 'La difusión internacional de los seguros sociales antes de 1945'.
71. The first year refers to the approval of the voluntary system and the second refers to its transformation into a compulsory insurance.
72. There were three state inspection mechanisms: the Civil Governments, the *Comisaría General de Seguros* (general insurance office) and the *Comisaría Sanitaria Central* (central health office). INP, *La cuestión del seguro de enfermedad*, p. 80 and p. 98.

73. Ibid., p. 47.
74. Ibid., p. 22.
75. In the 1880s the state had already published public tenders in order to subsidise the friendly societies with budget funds. During this preliminary stage, the subventions awarded amounted to 200,000 pesetas a year, a much higher figure than those awarded at the beginning of the twentieth century. See F. Montero García, *Los Seguros sociales en la España del siglo XX. Orígenes y antecedentes de la previsión social*, p. 84.
76. M. E. Martínez Quinteiro, 'El nacimiento de los seguros sociales en el contexto del reformismo y la respuesta del movimiento obrero', *Studia Historica*, 4 (1984), pp. 61–83 (p. 78); J. Cuesta Bustillo, *Los seguros sociales en la España del siglo XX. Hacia los seguros sociales obligatorios. La crisis de la Restauración* (Madrid: Ministerio de Trabajo y Seguridad Social, 1988), p. 440; Rodríguez-Ocaña, 'La asistencia médica colectiva en España hasta 1936', p. 321; M. I. Porras Gallo, 'Un foro de debate sobre el seguro de enfermedad: Las Conferencias del Ateneo de Madrid de 1934', *Asclepio*, Vol. 51, 1 (1999), pp. 159–83 (p. 164).
77. F. Comín Comín, 'El Estado y la economía en la España del siglo XX', in J. Velarde, J. L. García Delgado, A. Pedreño (dir), *El Estado en la economía española. VIII Jornadas de Alicante sobre Economía* Española (Madrid: Civitas, 1994), pp. 39- 65.
78. For more on this debate, see Vilar Rodríguez, 'La cobertura social a través de las sociedades de socorro mutuo', pp. 85–122.
79. *Conferencia Nacional de Seguros de Enfermedad, Invalidez y Maternidad* (1922) (National Conference on Sickness, Disability and Maternity Insurance). For interesting reflections on this document, see, J. Cuesta Bustillo, 'Las Sociedades de Socorros Mutuos en el primer tercio del siglo XX: Sociedad sin Estado: una relación fallida', in Castillo (ed.), *Solidaridad desde abajo*, pp. 409–22. The representatives of the Federation of Friendly Societies of the Province of Barcelona assumed a prominent role at this forum.
80. *Conferencia Nacional de Seguros de Enfermedad, Invalidez y Maternidad* (1922), p. 18. The representatives of the friendly societies maintained that the vigilance of their members obviated the need for professional inspection.
81. This factor is considered to be decisive in the following work: A. Rivera Blanco, "Desarrollo y crisis del modelo de sociedad de socorros (Vitoria, 1849–1938), in Castillo (ed.), *Solidaridad desde abajo*, pp. 142–3.
82. This was the case, for example, of the Montepío de la Caridad, a society founded in Palma de Mallorca in 1857 and which operated until 1951. In 1918 it had incorporated the service of two midwives, a service that was continued until 1930. From 1931 onwards this service disappeared from the society's list of expenses.
83. For sickness insurance and its debate in the Second Republic, see Porras Gallo, 'Un foro de debate sobre el seguro de enfermedad'.
84. Rivera Blanco, 'Desarrollo y crisis del modelo de Sociedad de Socorros'.
85. L. M. Avalos Muñoz and J. Sanz Valdés, 'Las Mutualidades de Previsión social: Antecedentes, situación Actual y perspectivas', in Castillo (ed.), *Solidaridad desde abajo*, pp. 543–5.
86. C. Molinero, *La captación de las masas. Política social y propaganda en el régimen franquista* (Madrid: Cátedra, 2005); P. González Murillo, 'La política social del franquismo: el Seguro Obligatorio de Enfermedad', *Revista de historia contemporánea*, 57 (2005), pp. 62–76; J. Pons and M. Vilar, 'Labour repression and social justice in Franco's Spain': the political objectives of compulsory sickness insurance (1942–1957)', *Labor History*. Rodríguez Ocaña, 'La asistencia médica colectiva en España hasta 1936', p. 351 explains

the existence of different positions among doctors during decades. The champions of compulsory sickness insurance included hygienists and social doctors and others of a socialist vocation during the Second Republic, and also technicians of the INP (National Welfare Institute) such as Severino Aznar, but in general nearly all of the professional medical organisations and doctors' representatives opposed this insurance.

87. J. Serrallonga i Urquidi, 'El cuento de la regularización sanitaria y asistencial en el régimen franquista. Una primera etapa convulsa, 1936–1944', *Historia Social*, 59 (2007), pp. 77–98 analyses the intrigues and the objectives of the old clans of health care workers who sided with Franco and the Nationalists with the intention of undoing the health care legislation of the Republic. These groups dominated the leadership of the Directorate General for Health although, nevertheless, the implementation of the compulsory sickness insurance was the responsibility of the Ministry of Labour.

88. The beneficiaries were affiliated workers with annual wages under 9,000 pesetas and their immediate family (ancestors, descendants and siblings under the age of 18). Civil servants and domestic servants were excluded. These provisions included complete medical assistance in both general medicine and specialist services, but in practice, however, only general medicine and pharmacy were covered in the first years. P. Benjumea Pino, 'Sanidad y desempleo', in, various authors, *Historia de la acción social pública en España. Beneficencia y Previsión* (Madrid: Ministerio de Trabajo y Seguridad Social, 1990), p. 451.

89. Benjumea Pino, 'Sanidad y desempleo'.

90. J. Pons, 'El seguro obligatorio de enfermedad y la gestión de las entidades colaboradoras (1942–1963)', *Revista de la Historia de la Economía y de la Empresa*, 4 (2010), pp. 227–50.

91. J. Pons, 'La gestión patronal del seguro obligatorio de accidentes de trabajo durante el franquismo (1940–1975)', *Revista de Historia Industrial*, 45 (2011), pp. 109–43.

92. In October 1935, after the Law of Catalan Mutual Societies had been passed it was called the 'Catalan Federation of Mutual Provident Societies'. In July 1939 it came to be known as the '*Institución Sindical de Mutualidades*', and then later, in 1943, the 'Federation of Mutual Provident Societies of the Province of Catalonia' until a new change took place in 1944 when it recovered its old name. Avalos Muñoz y Sanz Valdés, 'Las Mutualidades de Previsión social', p. 521.

93. By way of example, we could mention the case of *La protección*, a friendly society created in Majorca in 1857 that was finally dissolved in 1951. Pons, *El sector seguros en Baleares*, p. 97. On the same island, in 1950, el Montepío L'Arraval de Santa Catalina abandoned the system of having its own doctors, although it maintained pecuniary aid. Fullana and Marimón, *Història del 'montepío' de Previsió de l'Arraval*, p. 66.

5 Harris, Gorsky, Guntupalli and Hinde, 'Sickness Insurance and Welfare Reform in England and Wales, 1870–1914'

1. E. Hopkins, *Working-class Self-help in Nineteenth-century England* (London: UCL Press, 1995); D. Neave, 'Friendly Societies in Great Britain', in M. van der Linden, (ed.), *Social Security Mutualism: The Comparative History of Mutual Benefit Societies* (Bern: Peter Lang, 1996), pp. 41–64; M. Gorsky, 'The Growth and Distribution of English Friendly Societies in the Early Nineteenth Century', *Economic History Review*, 51 (1998), pp. 489–511; M. Gorsky, 'Mutual Aid and Civil Society: Friendly Societies in Nineteenth-

century Bristol', *Urban History*, 25 (1998), pp. 302–22; S. Cordery, *British Friendly Societies, 1750–1914* (Basingstoke: Palgrave Macmillan, 2003); D. Weinbren, 'Beneath the All-seeing Eye: Fraternal Order and Friendly Societies' Banners in Nineteenth- and Twentieth-century Britain', *Cultural and Social History*, 3 (2006), pp. 167–91; D. Weinbren, 'Supporting Self-help: Charity, Mutuality and Reciprocity in Nineteenth-century Britain', in B. Harris and P. Bridgen (eds), *Charity and Mutual Aid in Europe and North America Since 1800* (New York: Routledge, 2007), pp. 67–88.

2.   P. Blond, *Red Tory: How Left and Right Have Broken Britain and How We Can Fix It* (London: Faber, 2010); M. Glasman, 'Labour as a Radical Tradition', in M. Glasman, J. Rutherford, M. Stears and S. White (eds), *The Labour Tradition and the Politics of Paradox: the Oxford London Seminars 2010–11* (2011). URL: http://www.scribd.com/doc/55941677/Labour-Tradition-and-the-Politics-of-Paradox.

3.   P. Gosden, *The Friendly Societies in England, 1815–75* (Manchester: Manchester University Press, 1961), pp. 1–5; Hopkins, *Working-class Self-help*, p. 29.

4.   Quoted in W. Beveridge, *Voluntary Action: A Report on Methods of Social Advance* (London: George Allen and Unwin, 1948), p. 21.

5.   Gosden, *The Friendly Societies in England*, pp. 1–93; Hopkins, *Working-class Self-help*, pp. 9–70; Neave, 'Friendly Societies in Great Britain'.

6.   Gosden, *The Friendly Societies in England*, pp. 4–5, 13–16; Neave, 'Friendly Societies in Great Britain', pp. 46–52; B. Harris, *The Origins of the British Welfare State: Social Welfare in England and Wales 1800–1945* (Basingstoke: Palgrave Macmillan, 2004), pp. 82–3.

7.   For statistics on the ages of friendly society members, see Table 5.2 below.

8.   Highland Friendly Society, *Report on Friendly or Benefit Societies, Exhibiting the Law of Sickness as Deduced From Returns By Friendly Societies in Different Parts of Scotland, Drawn Up By a Committee of the Highland Society of Scotland* (Edinburgh: Highland Society of Scotland, 1824); C. Ansell, *A Treatise on Friendly Societies* (London: Baldwin and Cradock, 1835).

9.   F. Neison, *Contribution to Vital Statistics, Being a Development of the Rate of Mortality and Laws of Sickness ... From Data Procured By Friendly Societies ... With an Inquiry Into the Influence of Locality on Health* (London: H. Cunningham, 1845); PP 1852–3 955 c, 295, *Report and Tables by Actuary of National Debt Office on Friendly Societies and Mortality Among Members of Friendly Societies to December 1850*; PP 1854 506 lxiii, 501, *Report and Tables by Actuary of National Debt Office on Friendly Societies and Mortality Among Members of Friendly Societies to December 1850*; H. Ratcliffe, *Observations on the Rate of Mortality Existing Among Friendly Societies* (Manchester: Independent Order of Oddfellows, 1850); H. Ratcliffe, *Observations on the Rate of Mortality Existing Among Friendly Societies* (Colchester: Edward Benham Printer, 1862); H. Ratcliffe, *Independent Order of Oddfellows, Manchester Unity Friendly Society, Supplementary Report July 1, 1872*; F. Neison, *The Rates of Mortality and Sickness According to the Five Years 1871–5 of the Ancient Order of Foresters Friendly Society* (London: Harrison and Sons, 1882); H. Ratcliffe, *Report on the Additional Statistics Deduced from the Original Records of the Sickness Experience of the Order, with Special Reference to the New Tables of Contribution and Benefit* (Leeds: McCorquodale, 1886). For a detailed discussion of these studies, see G. F. Hardy, 'Friendly Societies', *Journal of the Institute of Actuaries*, 27 (1888), pp. 245–348, at pp. 281–92.

10.   PP 1896 303 lxxix, 1, *Special Report on Sickness and Mortality in Registered Friendly Societies, by Actuary to Friendly Societies Central Office*; A. Watson, 'The Methods of Analysing and Presenting the Mortality, Sickness and Secession Experience of Friendly Societies, with Examples drawn from the Experience of the Manchester Unity of Oddfellows',

Journal of the Institute of Actuaries, 35 (1900), pp. 268–332; A. Watson, *An Account of an Investigation of the Sickness and Mortality Experience of the IOOF Manchester Unity During the Five Years 1893–7* (Manchester: Independent Order of Oddfellows, 1903).

11. For an introduction to this debate, see B. Harris, 'Morbidity and Mortality during the Health Transition: A Comment on James C. Riley, "Why Sickness and Death Rates do not Move Parallel to One Another Over Time"', *Social History of Medicine*, 12 (1999), pp. 125–31.

12. See e.g. J. Riley, *Sick, Not Dead: The Health of British Workingmen During the Mortality Decline* (Baltimore, MD: Johns Hopkins University Press, 1997).

13. F. Neison, *The Rates of Mortality and Sickness According to the Five Years 1871–5 of the Ancient Order of Foresters Friendly Society* (London: Harrison and Sons, 1882), p. 81.

14. Hardy, 'Friendly Societies', p. 313.

15. Weinbren, 'Supporting Self-help', p. 77.

16. Anonymous, 'The Valuations, Experience and Future of the Unity', *Oddfellows' Magazine* (1873), pp. 100–3, at p. 102.

17. Finlaison's study was not directly comparable with the others because he excluded cases of 'chronic infirmity, demanding little or no medical attention' from his definition of sickness (see Harris *et al.*, 'Ageing, Sickness and Health', p. 654).

18. Watson, *An Account*, pp. 57–8.

19. Hardy, 'Friendly Societies', p. 293; A. Watson, 'Some Points of Interest in the Operations of Friendly Societies, Railway Benefit Societies and Collecting Societies', *Journal of the Institute of Actuaries*, 44 (1910), pp. 168–261, at p. 203.

20. PP 1849 458 xiv, 1, *Select Committee on Friendly Societies Bill. Report, Proceedings, Minutes of Evidence, Index*, p. 16; PP 1873 C. 842 xxii, 291, Royal Commission to inquire into friendly and benefit building societies, *Third Report, Minutes of Evidence, Appendix, Index*, p. 222.

21. Watson, *An Account*, pp. 17–22.

22. E. Brabrook, *Provident Societies and Industrial Welfare* (London: Blackie and Son, 1898), p. 84.

23. Watson, 'Methods', p. 323.

24. E. C. Snow, 'Some Statistical Problems Suggested by the Sickness and Mortality Data of Certain of the Large Friendly Societies', *Journal of the Royal Statistical Society*, 76 (1913), pp. 445–517, at p. 511.

25. PP 1834 (44) xxvii, 1, *Report from His Majesty's Commissioners for Inquiring into the Administration and Practical Operation of the Poor Laws*, p. 130.

26. A. Watson, 'Some Points of Interest in the Operations of Friendly Societies, Railway Benefit Societies and Collecting Societies', *Journal of the Institute of Actuaries*, 44 (1910), pp. 168–261, at pp. 216–7.

27. J. L. Stead, 'Friendly Societies and State Insurance', *Foresters' Miscellany*, 21 (1910), pp. 8–12, at p. 10; C. W. Morecroft, 'Compulsory National Sickness Insurance: is it Desirable?', *Foresters' Miscellany*, 21 (1910), pp. 173–8, at p. 176.

28. Watson, 'Some Points of Interest', p. 169; Snow, 'Some Statistical Problems', p. 514.

29. Anonymous, 'Birmingham High Court – Bro. John Brown's Speech', *Foresters' Miscellany*, 21 (1910), pp. 308–11, at p. 311.

30. S. Hudson, 'Appendix: Workmen's Compensation Act', *Foresters' Miscellany*, 21 (1910), pp. 417–8.

31. Gorsky, 'Mutual Aid and Civil Society', p. 321.

32. PP 1884–5 270 x, 41, Select Committee on National Provident Insurance, *Report, Proceedings, Minutes of Evidence, Appendix, Index*, Q. 1456.

33. Snow, 'Some Statistical Problems', p. 513.

34. J. Bertillon, 'Morbidity and Mortality According to Occupation', *Journal of the Royal Statistical Society*, 55 (1892), pp. 559–600.
35. Watson, 'Methods', p. 324.
36. Harris, *Origins of the British Welfare State*, p. 82.
37. Anonymous, 'The Ancient Order of Foresters: Now and After', *Foresters' Miscellany*, 20 (1909), pp. 545–7, at p. 547; Watson, 'Some Points of Interest', p. 177.
38. Watson, 'Some Points of Interest', p. 252.
39. Cordery, *British Friendly Societies*, p. 137; A. Fisk, *Mutual Self-help in Southern England 1850–1912* (Southampton: Foresters' Heritage Trust, 2006), p. 137.
40. Riley, *Sick, Not Dead*; S. R. Johansson, 'The Health Transition: the Cultural Inflation of Morbidity During the Decline of Mortality', *Health Transition Review*, 1 (1991), pp. 39–65; S. R. Johansson, 'Measuring the Cultural Inflation of Morbidity During the Decline in Mortality', *Health Transition Review*, 2 (1992), pp. 77–87; J. Macnicol, *The Politics of Retirement in Britain 1878–1948* (Cambridge: Cambridge University Press, 1998), pp. 125–31. According to Thomas Strachan, 'those who knew anything of the subject would agree that the amount of pressure upon the management of the society, by which benefits were given to men who were what they called sick, when they were really out of work, was so great as to affect the so-called law of sickness, and instead of striving after some theoretical law, they should rather widen their information, and see how much money had to be paid under the special circumstances of each case for what were called sickness benefits' (Hardy, 'Friendly Societies', p. 345).
41. C. Edwards, M. Gorsky, B. Harris and P. R. A. Hinde, 'Sickness, Insurance and Health: Assessing Trends in Morbidity Through Friendly Society Records', *Annales de Démographie Historique*, 1 (2003), pp. 131–67; Harris *et al.*, 'Ageing, Sickness and Health'.
42. PP 1874 C. 961 xxxiii, 1, *Fourth Report of the Commissioners Appointed to Inquire into Friendly and Benefit Building Societies. Part I. Report of the Commissioners, with Appendix*, para. 849.
43. D. Collins, 'The Introduction of Old Age Pensions in Great Britain', *Historical Journal*, 8 (1965), pp. 246–59; J. Treble, 'The Attitudes of Friendly Societies Towards the Movement in Great Britain for State Pensions, 1878–1908', *International Review of Social History*, 15 (1970), 266–99.
44. Blackley also argued that, once the scheme had been established, it would quickly accumulate a surplus which would enable the premium to be reduced, and he subsequently told the Select Committee on National Provident Insurance that it would be possible for the scheme to operate if contributions were fixed at £10 per head rather than £14. See W. Blackley, 'National Insurance: A Cheap, Practical and Popular Means of Abolishing Poor Rates', *Nineteenth Century*, 4 (1878), pp. 834–57, at p. 852; PP 1887 (257) xi, 1, *Report from the Select Committee on National Provident Insurance, Together with the Proceedings of the Committee, Minutes of Evidence and Appendix*, p. iii.
45. Blackley, 'National Insurance', pp. 840, 851.
46. R. P. Hookham, *The Question of the Day: Outlines of a Scheme for Dealing with Pauperism* (1879; Oxford, reprinted 1891), p. 5.
47. C. Booth, 'Enumeration and Classification of Paupers, and State Pensions for the Aged', *Journal of the Royal Statistical Society*, 54 (1891), pp. 600–43, at pp. 629–41.
48. PP 1895 C. 7684 xiv, 1, *Report of the Royal Commission on the Aged Poor*, paras. 310–42; see also PP 1895 C. 7684-I xiv, 123, *Minutes of Evidence Taken Before the Royal Commission on the Aged Poor, Days 1–26*, QQ. 12,170353; 12,566–767.
49. B. Gilbert, 'The Decay of Nineteenth Century Provident Institutions and the Coming of Old Age Pensions in Great Britain', *Economic History Review*, 17 (1965), pp. 551–63, at p. 553.

50. B. Gilbert, *The Evolution of National Insurance in Great Britain: the Origins of the Welfare State* (London: Michael Joseph, 1966), pp. 179–80; see also P. Thane, *Old Age in English History: Past Experiences, Present Issues* (Oxford: Oxford University Press, 2000), p. 199.

51. Treble, 'The Attitudes of Friendly Societies', pp. 278–9.

52. Macnicol, *Politics of Retirement*, pp. 119–24. This is perhaps a slightly over-optimistic reading of Hardy's actual comments. He said that 'it was satisfactory to find that the societies were gradually reaching a better financial position than formerly.... That no doubt was due to two causes: first, because the worst societies gradually dropped out and became dissolved, or special efforts were made to put them in a sound position; and, secondly, because no doubt the valuations made, by taking no account in the majority of cases of lapse, somewhat underestimated the actual financial strength of the societies' (Watson, 'Some Points of Interest', p. 258). However, other contemporary assessments were also positive. Edward Brabrook conceded that 'some of the societies made truly heroic efforts to achieve solvency, and it is one of the strong points of friendly societies that in almost every case such efforts are successful' (E. Brabrook, 'The Strengths and Weaknesses of a Friendly Society', *Foresters' Miscellany*, 20 (1909), 3–7, at p. 5). H. W. Manly thought that 'it was very encouraging ... to see the progressive financial improvement of friendly societies generally. Most of those who had to do with friendly society valuations had noticed that the general tendency was for the societies to improve with regard to their financial position, and he quite agreed with Mr Watson's remarks as to the increasing respect that was being paid to the views of the actuary on the subject' (Watson, 'Some Points of Interest', p. 253).

53. N. Broten, 'From Sickness to Death: the Financial Viability of the English Friendly Societies and Coming of the Old Age Pensions Act, 1875–1908', *LSE Working Papers*, no. 135/10 (2010).

54. Neison, *Rates of Mortality and Sickness*, pp. 46–7; Watson, *An Account*, p. 21.

55. Gilbert, 'The Decay of Nineteenth-century Provident Institutions', pp. 553–4; Gilbert, *The Evolution of National Insurance*, p. 171; Macnicol, *The Politics of Retirement*, pp. 125–6.

56. D. Coleman, 'Population and Family', in A. Halsey and J. Webb, eds., *Twentieth-century British Social Trends* (Basingstoke: Macmillan, 2000), pp. 27–93, at pp. 71–5.

57. Treble, 'The Attitudes of Friendly Societies', p. 278.

58. See e.g. Anonymous, 'What the Executive Council say: Extracts from their Addresses', *Foresters' Miscellany*, 12 (1897), pp. 235–6, at p. 236; Anonymous, 'Provision for Old Age', *Foresters' Miscellany*, 14 (1901), pp. 521–4, at p. 522; C. W. Narlborough, 'A Proposed Tax on Thrift', *Foresters' Miscellany*, 21 (1910), pp. 200–2.

59. Watson, 'Some Points of Interest', p. 259.

60. Treble, 'The Attitudes of Friendly Societies', p. 286; Macnicol, *The Politics of Retirement*, pp. 131–6.

61. Anonymous, 'Old Age Pensions: Friendly Society Attitude', *Foresters' Miscellany*, 18 (1907), pp. 605–7.

62. PP 1874 C. 961 xxxiii, 1, *Fourth Report of the Commissioners Appointed to Inquire into Friendly and Benefit Building Societies. Part I. Report of the Commissioners, with Appendix*, para. 849.

63. Ibid., paras. 850–2; para. 925, recommendation 43.

64. Ibid., para. 848.

65. Blackley, 'National Insurance', p. 840.

66. PP 1887 (257) xi, 1, *Report from the Select Committee on National Provident Insurance, together with the Proceedings of the Committee, Minutes of Evidence and Appendix*, p. vi.

67. Ibid., pp. iv–v.

68. Gilbert, *The Evolution of National Insurance*, pp. 289–92.
69. Ibid., pp. 296–7.
70. Anonymous, 'Compulsory State Insurance: Shall we be Disillusioned?', *Foresters' Miscellany*, 20 (1909), pp 251–2, at p. 251.
71. Another PDCR, 'To the Editor of the "Miscellany"', *Foresters' Miscellany*, 20 (1909), 274–5. The acronym stands for 'Past District Chief Ranger' (see http://www.epsoman-dewellhistoryexplorer.org.uk/Foresters.html).
72. C. W. Morecroft, 'Compulsory National Sickness Insurance: is it Desirable?', *Foresters' Miscellany*, 21 (1910), pp. 173–8, at pp. 177–8.
73. R. F. Calder, 'Is State Insurance Desirable?', *Foresters' Miscellany*, 21 (1910), pp. 205–7, at p. 207.
74. C. W. Narlborough, 'Infirmity', *Foresters' Miscellany*, 20 (1909), pp. 481–3, at p. 483; see also C. W. Narlborough, 'A Proposed Tax on Thrift'; W. Thomas, 'State Insurance', *Foresters' Miscellany*, 21 (1910), p. 236.
75. E. Tranter, 'Is State Insurance Desirable? Yes', *Foresters' Miscellany*, 21 (1910), pp. 137–8.
76. E. B. Deadman, 'Is State Insurance Desirable? Yes', *Foresters' Miscellany*, 21 (1910), pp. 108–10.
77. Treble, 'The Attitudes of Friendly Societies', p. 295.
78. J. L. Stead, 'Friendly Societies and State Insurance', *Foresters' Miscellany*, 21 (1910), pp. 8–12, at p. 9.
79. Riley, *Sick, Not Dead*, pp. 27–123.
80. M. Gorsky, 'Friendly Society Health Insurance in Nineteenth-century England', in M. Gorsky and S. Sheard (eds), *Financing Medicine: The British Experience Since 1750* (Abingdon: Routledge, 2006), pp. 147–64.
81. A. Digby, *The Evolution of British General Practice 1850–1948* (Oxford: Clarendon Press, 1999), pp. 307–11. See also A. Morrice, '"Strong Combination": The Edwardian BMA and Contract Practice', in Gorsky and Sheard (eds), *Financing Medicine*, pp. 165–81.
82. Gilbert, *The Evolution of National Insurance*, pp. 362–71.
83. Ibid., pp. 318–83.
84. S. Yeo, 'Working Class Association, Private Capital, Welfare and the State in the Late-nineteenth and Twentieth Centuries', in N. Parry, M. Rustin and C. Satyamurti (eds), *Social Work, Welfare and the State* (London: Edward Arnold, 1979), pp. 48–71; D. Green, *Working Class Patients and the Medical Establishment: Self-help in Britain from the Mid-nineteenth Century to 1948* (Aldershot: Gower/Maurice Temple Smith, 1985).
85. See also T. Alborn, 'Senses of Belonging: The Politics of Working-class Insurance in Britain, 1880–1914', *Journal of Modern History*, 73 (2001), pp. 561–602; B. Harris, 'The "Big Society" and the Development of the Welfare State' (unpublished paper presented to the Annual Conference of the Social Science History Association, November 2011).

6 Broten, 'From Sickness to Death: Revisiting the Financial Viability of the English Friendly Societies, 1875–1908'

1. B. Gilbert, 'The Decay of Nineteenth-century Provident Institutions and the Coming of Old Age Pensions in Great Britain', *Economic History Review*, 17 (1965), 551–63.
2. The court, 'Perseverance', for example, held ten shares at ten pounds apiece and ten shares at ten pounds, one schilling, apiece in the company, Water Works, in addition to savings of 64 pounds in a savings bank

3. D. Neave, 'The Friendly Societies in Great Britain', in M. van der Linden (ed.), *Social Security Mutualism: The Comparative History of Mutual Benefit Societies* (Bern: Peter Lang, 1996), p. 41.
4. Gilbert, 'Provident Institutions', p. 551
5. Ibid.
6. P. Gosden, *The Friendly Societies in England, 1815–75* (Manchester: Manchester University Press), 1961.
7. Ibid.
8. Ibid., pp. 156
9. Gilbert, 'Provident Institutions', pp. 552–3.
10. Ibid., p. 553.
11. Ibid., pp. 563
12. Ibid., pp. 561
13. Quoted in ibid., pp. 561
14. Gosden, *Friendly Societies*.
15. Ibid.
16. See F. Neison, *The Rates of Mortality and Sickness According to the Experience for the Five Years, 1871–5, of the Ancient Order of Foresters' Friendly Society* (London: Harrison and Sons, 1882); R. Moffrey, *The Rise and Progress of the Manchester Unity of the Independent Order of Oddfellows, 1810–1904* (Manchester: John Heywood Printers), 1905.
17. G. Emery and J. C. H. Emery, *A Young Man's Benefit: The Independent Order of Oddfellows and Sickness Insurance in the United States and Canada, 1860–1929* (Montreal and London: McGill-Queen's University Press), 1999, pp. 64–85.
18. Ibid.
19. Report of the Chief Registrar
20. Emery and Emery, *A Young Man's Benefit*, pp. 103
21. N. Broten, 'From Sickness to Death: the Financial Viability of the English Friendly Societies and the Coming of the Old Age Pensions Act, 1875–1908', *LSE Working Papers*, no. 135/10, (2010), p. 13.
22. Moffrey, *History*; Gosden, *Friendly Societies*.
23. Gilbert, 'Provident Institutions', p. 554.
24. See Broten, 'Sickness to Death', p. 15 for estimates of response rates per district based on the Chief Registrar data set.
25. A note on terminology: most affiliated orders referred to their local branches as lodges, while the Foresters referred to them as courts.
26. Gosden, *Friendly Societies*.
27. It should be noted that the available years refers to the availability of some, but not all information; classification of courts as rural, town, or city, was made by Logan in accordance with the Foresters' rules.
28. Gosden, *Friendly Societies*.
29. M. Gorsky, 'The Growth and Distribution of English Friendly Societies in the Early Nineteenth Century', *Economic History Review*, 51 (1998), pp. 489–511. See also John Benson's chapter in this volume.
30. Gorsky, 'Growth', p. 509.
31. B. Mitchell, *British Historical Statistics* (Cambridge: Cambridge University Press), 1988.
32. See B. Harris, *et al.*, 'Long-term Changes in Sickness and Health: Further Evidence from the Hampshire Friendly Society' *Economic History Review*, in press, p. 4, for data on the age at which members of the Hampshire Friendly Society joined.

33. E. Hunt, 'Industrialization and Regional Inequality: Wages in Britain, 1760–1914', *Journal of Economic History*, 6 (1986), 935–66.
34. Another possibility, that the existence of a society provided medical practitioners with work and thus a way of life, should be noted.
35. Gosden, *Friendly Societies*.
36. John Murray brought this to my attention.
37. This would be a problem for our analysis if our probability of ruin estimates were near the margin of ruin. However, as the results show, seven of the eight courts we studied were strongly solvent by this measure.
38. See R. E. Beard *et al., Risk Theory: The Stochastic Basis of Insurance*, (London: Chapman and Hall, 1977); J. C. H. Emery, 'Risky Business? Non-actuarial Pricing Practices and the Financial Viability of Fraternal Sickness Insurers', *Explorations in Economic History*, 33 (1996), pp. 195–226.
39. For a more complete explanation of this model, see Broten, 'From Sickness to Death', p. 28.

7 Emery, 'America's Rejection of Government Health Insurance in the Progressive Era: Implications for Understanding the Determinants and Achievements of Public Insurance of Health Risks'

1. A. Peebles, 'The State and Medicine', *Canadian Journal of Economics and Political Studies*, 2 (1936), pp. 464–80; B. B. Gilbert, *The Evolution of National Health Insurance in Great Britain: The Origins of the Welfare State* (London: Michael Joseph, 1966); R. Lubove, *The Struggle for Social Security 1900–1935* (Cambridge, MA: Harvard University Press, 1968); D. T. Rodgers, *Atlantic Crossings: Social Politics in a Progressive Age* (Cambridge, MA: Belknap Press of Harvard University Press, 1998); S. Horrell and D. Oxley, 'Work and Prudence: Household Responses to Income Variation in Nineteenth Century Britain', *European Review of Economic History*, 4:1 (2000), pp. 27–58; B. Hoffman, *The Wages of Sickness: The Politics of Health Insurance in Progressive America* (Chapel Hill, NC: University of North Carolina Press, 2001); J. Kaufman, *For the Common Good? American Civic Life and the Golden Age of Fraternity* (New York: Oxford University Press, 2002); J. Quadagno, *One Nation Uninsured: Why the U.S. Has No Health Insurance* (New York: Oxford University Press, 2005).
2. I. M. Rubinow, 'Public and Private Interests in Social Insurance', *American Labor Legislation Review*, 21 (1931), pp. 181–91; D. A. Moss, *Socializing Security: Progressive-Era Economists and the Origins of American Social Policy* (Cambridge, MA: Harvard University Press, 1996).
3. Lubove, *The Struggle for Social Security*, pp. 2–3; D. M. Fox, 'The Decline of Historicism: The Case of Compulsory Health Insurance in the United States', *Bulletin of the History of Medicine* 57 (1983), p. 599; Quadagno, *One Nation Uninsured*.
4. Hoffman, *The Wages of Sickness*; Quadagno, *One Nation Uninsured*; L. Jacobs and T. Skocpol, *Health Care Reform and American Politics: What Everyone Needs to Know* (New York: Oxford University Press, 2010).
5. O. W. Anderson, *The Uneasy Equilibrium: Private and Public Financing of Health Services in the United States, 1875–1965* (New Haven: College & University Press, 1968), p. 87.
6. D. M. Fox, 'The Decline of Historicism', pp. 596–610.
7. The need for state-provided health insurance was taken for granted by proponents of compulsory health insurance before 1920. See O. W. Anderson, 'Health Insurance in

the United States 1910–20', *Journal of the History of Medicine*, 5 (Autumn 1950), p. 366; I. M. Rubinow in *Social Insurance* (New York: Henry Holt and Company, 1913), states that the need for social insurance in the US was self-evident.

8. P. H. Lindert, 'The Rise of Social Spending, 1880–1930', *Explorations in Economic History*, 31:1 (1994), pp. 1–37; P. H. Lindert, 'What Limits Social Spending', *Explorations in Economic History*, 33 (1996), pp. 1–34; P. H. Lindert, *Growing Public: Social Spending and Economic Growth since the Eighteenth Century* (New York: Cambridge University Press, 2004), vol. 1.

9. D. T. Rodgers, *Atlantic Crossings*, p. 255.

10. D. Beland and J. S. Hacker, 'Ideas, Private Institutions and American Welfare State "Exceptionalism": The Case of Health and Old-Age Insurance, 1915–65', *International Journal of Social Welfare*, 13 (2004), pp. 42–54.

11. For example, P. H. Lindert, in 'The Rise of Social Spending, 1880–1930', p. 28, suggests that the peculiar distaste that Americans have for government aid is durable; J. Quadagno in *One Nation Uninsured*, argues that powerful interests (doctors and insurance companies) have always prevented Congress from passing national health insurance legislation.

12. Rodgers, *Atlantic Crossings*.

13. D. Beland and J. S. Hacker, 'Ideas, Private Institutions and American Welfare State "Exceptionalism" : The Case of Health and Old-Age Insurance, 1915–1965', *International Journal of Social Welfare*, 13 (2004), pp. 42–54.

14. Lubove, *The Struggle for Social Security 1900–1935*, p. 24.

15. Moss, *Socializing Security*, p. 176.

16. D. A. Moss, *When All Else Fails: Government as the Ultimate Risk Manager* (Cambridge, MA: Harvard University Press, 2002), p. 153.

17. Moss, *Socializing Security*, p. 176.

18. J. C. H. Emery, '"Un-American" or Unnecessary? America's Rejection of Compulsory Government Health Insurance in the Progressive Era', *Explorations in Economic History*, 47:1 (2010), pp. 68–81.

19. Emery, '"Un-American" or Unnecessary?'.

20. Rubinow, *Social Insurance*; B. N. Armstrong, *Insuring the Essentials: Minimum Wage, plus Social Insurance – A Living Wage Program* (New York: MacMillan, 1932); R. L. Numbers, *Almost Persuaded: American Physicians and Compulsory Health Insurance, 1912–20* (Baltimore, MD: Johns Hopkins University Press, 1978); S. Horrell and D. Oxley, 'Work and Prudence'; Hoffman, *The Wages of Sickness*.

21. Emery, '"Un-American" or Unnecessary?'. See also note 7 above.

22. This term is from B. Hoffman, *The Wages of Sickness*, p. 6.

23. Emery, '"Un-American" or Unnecessary?'. See also note 7 above.

24. Peebles, 'The State and Medicine'; P. Gosden, *The Friendly Societies in England 1815 to 1875* (Manchester: Manchester University Press,1961); B. B. Gilbert, *The Evolution of National Health Insurance in Great Britain*; E. Hopkins, *Working-class Self-help in Nineteenth-century England* (London: UCL Press, 1995); Horrell and Oxley, 'Work and Prudence'.

25. Horrell and Oxley, 'Work and Prudence', p. 54.

26. Hoffman, *The Wages of Sickness*, p. 9.

27. Lubove, *The Struggle for Social Security 1900–1935*, p. 17.

28. Rodgers, *Atlantic Crossings*, pp. 218–19.

29. J. E. Murray, *Origins of American Health Insurance: A History of Industrial Sickness Funds* (New Haven, CT: Yale University Press, 2007); J. C. H. Emery, 'Risky Business?

Nonactuarial Pricing Practices and the Financial Viability of Fraternal Sickness Insurers', *Explorations in Economic History*, 33:2 (1996), pp. 195–226; J. C. H. Emery, 'From Defining Characteristic to Vitiation of Principle: The History of the IOOF's Sick Benefit and its Implications for Studying American Fraternalism', *Social Science History*, 30:4 (2006), pp. 479–500; and Emery, '"Un-American" or Unnecessary?'.

30. I. M. Rubinow, 'Sickness Insurance', *American Labor Legislation Review*, 3 (1913), p. 166; J. P. Chamberlain, 'The Practicability of Compulsory Health Insurance in America', *American Labor Legislation Review*, 4 (1914), p. 53); I. Fisher, 'The Need for Health Insurance', *American Labor Legislation Review*, 7 (1917), pp. 9–23; B. B. Gilbert, *The Evolution of National Health Insurance in Great Britain*, p. 166; P. Johnson, *Saving and Spending* (Oxford: Clarendon Press, 1985); Hopkins, *Working-class Self-help*; J. Riley, *Sick, Not Dead: The Health of British Working Men During the Mortality Decline* (Baltimore, MD: Johns Hopkins University Press, 1997); G. Emery and Emery, *A Young Man's Benefit: The Independent Order of Odd Fellows and Sickness Insurance in the United States and Canada 1860–1929* (Montreal and London: McGill-Queen's University Press, 1999).

31. Rubinow, *Social Insurance*; Rubinow, 'Sickness Insurance'; Armstrong, *Insuring the Essentials*; P. Starr, *The Social Transformation of American Medicine, The Rise of a Sovereign Profession and the Making of a Vast Industry* (New York: Basic Books, 1982); 'US Social Security Administration', *Social Security Programs Throughout the World 1989*, Research Report #62 (1990).

32. J. E. Murray, 'Social Insurance Claims as Morbidity Estimates: Sickness or Absence?', *Journal of the Society for the Social History of Medicine*, 16:2 (2003), pp. 225–45; J. C. H. Emery, 'La Prevoyance volontaire aux Etats-Unis et la montee de l'assurance maladie publique et obligatoire avant 1920', *Revue Europeenne D'Histoire Sociale*, 16 (2005), pp. 8–19.

33. Emery and Emery, *A Young Man's Benefit*; Emery, 'From Defining Characteristic to Vitiation of Principle'; Murray, *Origins of American Health Insurance*.

34. Anderson, *The Uneasy Equilibrium*; Rodgers, *Atlantic Crossings*; Moss, *Socializing Security*.

35. Rubinow, 'Sickness Insurance'.

36. Fischer, 'The Need for Health Insurance', p. 15.

37. Canada and Australia would also be part of this laggard group at this time. F. G. Castles, in 'On Sickness Days and Social Policy', *Australian and New Zealand Journal of Sociology*, 28:1 (1992), pp. 29–44, challenges Australia's status as a laggard. Australia's first national health insurance law was not enacted until 1944, but after 1907 arbitrated wage awards stipulated that wages could not be reduced if a worker was absent from work due to sickness.

38. J. A. Lapp, 'The Findings of Official Health Insurance Commissions', *American Labor Legislation Review*, 10 (1920), pp. 27–40; Lubove, *The Struggle for Social Security 1900–35*, p. 67; Anderson, *The Uneasy Equilibrium*; Numbers, *Almost Persuaded*, p. 81; Moss, *Socializing Security*, p. 151; D. T. Beito, *From Mutual Aid to the Welfare State: Fraternal Societies and Social Services, 1890–1967* (Chapel Hill, NC: University of North Carolina Press, 2000); Hoffman, *The Wages of Sickness*, p. 2; Moss, *When All Else Fails*, p. 174.

39. Anderson, 'Health Insurance in the United States 1910–1920'.

40. Starr, *The Social Transformation of American Medicine*.

41. Anderson, 'Health Insurance in the United States 1910–1920', pp. 87, 387; I. M. Rubinow, *The Quest for Security* (New York: Henry Holt and Company, 1934), p. 214; Emery, '"Un-American" or Unnecessary?'.

42. American Association of Labor Legislation, 'Health Insurance – Tentative Draft of an Act', *American Labor Legislation Review*, 6 (1916), p. 239. See also Moss, *Socializing Security*.
43. A. Epstein, *Insecurity: A Challenge to America – A Study of Social Insurance in the United States and Abroad* (New York: Harrison Smith and Robert Hass, 1933), p. 469; Armstrong, *Insuring the Essentials*, p. 348.
44. Hoffman, *The Wages of Sickness*, pp. 54, 58.
45. M. R. Haines and A. C. Goodman, 'A Home of One's Own: Aging and Home Ownership in the United States in the Late Nineteenth and Early Twentieth Century', in D. I. Kertzer and P. Laslett (eds), *Aging in the Past: Demography, Society and Old Age* (Berkeley, CA: University of California Press, 1995).
46. M. P. Shanahan, 'The Distribution of Personal Wealth in South Australia 1905–1915', *Australian Economic History Review*, 35:2 (1995), pp. 82–111; P. H. Lindert, 'Three Centuries of Inequality in Britain and America', *Handbook of Income Distribution* (Amsterdam, New York and Oxford: Elsevier Science, North-Holland, 2000), pp. 167–216.
47. D. Costa, 'The Political Economy of State Provided Health Insurance in the Progressive Era: Evidence from California', NBER Working Paper Number 5328 (1995).
48. Hoffman, *The Wages of Sickness*, p. 58.
49. Rubinow, *Social Insurance*, pp. 28–9.
50. See Murray, *Origins of American Health Insurance*; and Emery, '"Un-American" or Unnecessary?' for Critical Appraisals of the AALL's Arguments.
51. Epstein, *Insecurity*, p. vii.
52. P. H. Douglas, *Social Security in the United States: An Analysis and Appraisal of the Federal Social Security Act* (New York: McGraw-Hill, 1936), pp. 3–4.
53. Rubinow, *Social Insurance*.
54. Ibid., p. 39. According to Moss, *Socializing Security*, p. 137, 'careful observers estimated that typical working families saved less than a single week's income per year'.
55. Rubinow, *Social Insurance*.
56. Epstein, in *Insecurity*, p. 101, asserts that 'the American standard assumes a normal family of man, wife, and two or three children, with the father fully able to provide for them out of his own income'. Rubinow in *Social Insurance*, p. 34, asserts that any financial accumulation that was gained by deploying women and children to work represented a 'vice of thrift'.
57. Rubinow, *Social Insurance*, p. 9.
58. See Moss, *Socializing Security*, p. 37; Hoffman, *The Wages of Sickness*; Moss, *When All Else Fails*, p. 7; and B. J. Glenn, 'Understanding Mutual Benefit Societies, 1860–1960', *Journal of Health Politics, Policy and Law*, 26:3 (2001), p. 640.
59. Rubinow, *Social Insurance*, p. 32.
60. Ibid., pp. 34–7.
61. Epstein, *Insecurity*, p. 102.
62. Rubinow, 'Public and Private Interests in Social Insurance', p. 185.
63. Fox, 'The Decline of Historicism'.
64. Rubinow, 'Sickness Insurance'; Lubove, *The Struggle for Social Security*, pp. 2–3. According to Fisher, 'The Need for Health Insurance', pp. 14–15, the logic of this claim that CHI was an 'un-American interference with liberty' meant that 'to remain truly American and truly free', was 'to retain the precious liberties of [the American] people to be illiterate, to be drunk, and to suffer accidents without indemnification, as well as to be sick without indemnification'.

65. For a discussion of these views, see Numbers, *Almost Persuaded*; Costa, 'The Political Economy of State Provided Health Insurance in the Progressive Era'; Hoffman, *The Wages of Sickness* and Quadagno, *One Nation Uninsured*.
66. Numbers, *Almost Persuaded*, p. 25.
67. Rodgers, *Atlantic Crossings*, p. 255.
68. Gilbert, *The Evolution of the National Health Service in Great Britain*.
69. Rodgers, *Atlantic Crossings*, p. 242.
70. Moss, *Socializing Security*, p. 157.
71. See also Anderson, 'Health Insurance in the United States 1910–1920'; Anderson, *The Uneasy Equilibrium*; Fox, 'The Decline of Historicism'; D. M. Fox, *Health Policies Health Politics: The British and American Experience, 1911–1965* (Princeton, NJ: Princeton University Press, 1986); Starr, *The Social Transformation of American Medicine*; Hoffman, *The Wages of Sickness*; and Quadagno, *One Nation Uninsured*.
72. Beito, *From Mutual Aid to the Welfare State*; Fox, *Health Policies Health Politics*, p. 13; and Kaufman, *For the Common Good?*.
73. Anderson, 'Health Insurance in the United States 1910–1920'; Anderson, *The Uneasy Equilibrium*; Numbers, *Almost Persuaded*; Fox, *Health Policies Health Politics*; and J. Engel, *Doctors and Reformers: Discussion and Debate over Health Policy, 1925–1950* (Columbia, SC: University of South Carolina Press, 2001).
74. Numbers, *Almost Persuaded*, p. 60. See Hoffman, *The Wages of Sickness*, ch. 6, for a discussion of the divided views of organized labour in the United States.
75. W. Sombart, *Why Is There No Socialism in the United States?* (New York: MacMillan Press, 1906; 1976).
76. Social insurance in Europe and England was intended to address 'social discontent' or 'socialist unrest' and ensure worker loyalty to the state rather than to Labour interests. In the absence of threat to political stability in the US, interest groups had no incentive to develop legislation through compromise. See Gilbert, *The Evolution of National Health Insurance in Great Britain*; Sombart, *Why Is There No Socialism in the United States?*; and Starr, *The Social Transformation of American Medicine*.
77. Rodgers, *Atlantic Crossings*, p. 258.
78. See Starr, *The Social Transformation of American Medicine*; Costa, 'The Political Economy of State Provided Health Insurance in the Progressive Era'; Moss, *Socializing Security*; and Beland and Hacker, 'Ideas, Private Institutions and American Welfare State "Exceptionalism" '.
79. Starr, *The Social Transformation of American Medicine*.
80. Beland and Hacker, 'Ideas, Private Institutions and American Welfare State "Exceptionalism"'.
81. Lapp, 'The Findings of Official Health Insurance Commissions', p. 32; Moss, *Socializing Security*.
82. Moss, *Socializing Security*, pp. 156–7.
83. Lubove, *The Struggle for Social Security 1900–1935*, p. 66.
84. Moss, *Socializing Security*; P. V. Fishback and S. E. Kantor, 'The Adoption of Workers' Compensation in the United States, 1900–1930', *Journal of Law and Economics*, 41 (1998), pp. 305–41.
85. Moss, *Socializing Security*, pp. 60–4.
86. Lubove, *The Struggle for Social Security 1900–1935*, p.76; Fishback and Kantor, '"Square Deal" or Raw Deal?'; Moss, *Socializing Security*.
87. According to Moss in *Socializing Security*, insurance and prevention were the main objectives of the AALL in the design of the legislation. Some AALL members (like Rubinow)

argued that social insurance was class legislation that should incorporate income redistribution as part of its design.

88. J. E. Ransom, 'Sickness Facts Indicate Urgent Need of Compulsory Health Insurance', *American Labor Legislation Review,* 10 (1920), p. 44; Lapp, 'The Findings of Official Health Insurance Commissions', p. 32; and Hoffman, *The Wages of Sickness,* pp. 96–100.
89. Emery, '"Un-American" or Unnecessary?'
90. Rodgers, *Atlantic Crossings,* p. 243.
91. Emery, '"Un-American" or Unnecessary?'.
92. These data are described in detail in M.R. Haines, 'Industrial Work and the Family Life Cycle, 1889–1890', *Research in Economic History,* 4 (1979), pp 289–356; also in B. Gratton and F. M. Rotondo, 'Industrialization, the Family Economy, and the Economic Status of the American Elderly', *Social Science History,* 15:3 (1991); also in Horrell and Oxley, 'Work and Prudence'. The survey gathered data on the demographic characteristics, occupations, incomes and expenditures of 8,544 families in twenty-four US states and five European countries who earned income from working in nine protected industries. Wage-workers from the US and the United Kingdom, cotton textile and iron-and-steel industries dominate the total number of observations, as do male-headed households according to Haines. While the survey does not constitute a random sample, Haines suggests (p. 294) that it is a representative sample of industrial wage-workers. Gratton and Rotondo (p. 342) suggest that the 1888–90 survey's inclusion of high-wage industries made the sample of households potentially more affluent than the wage-earning population, but the survey should be useful for representing the conditions of blue-collar workers in an industrializing economy. For my purposes of evaluating the need for CHI in the US, this sample is useful since the wage-workers represented in the survey would have been included in the compulsory health insurance arrangements. I would also expect that these data represent wage-earning Americans who were eligible to vote. See A. Keyssar, *The Right to Vote: The Contested History of Democracy in the United States* (New York: Basic Books, 2000). Despite the over-representation of higher-earning industrial households in these data, the data are useful for addressing the claims of the AALL reformers. For the 1889–90 sample, I calculate that only 22 per cent of American households in this sample had incomes high enough to meet Rubinow's 'minimum level of decency' in standard of living.
93. Gratton and Rotondo in 'Industrialization, the Family Economy, and the Economic Status of the American Elderly' report incomes and budget surpluses from the sample of American households in the 1888–90 cost of living survey and from another comparable sample of American households from the BLS 1917–19 cost of living survey. See also S. E. Kantor and P. V. Fishback, 'Precautionary Savings, Insurance, and the Origins of Worker's Compensation', *Journal of Political Economy,* 104:2 (1996), pp. 442–92; and C. M. Moehling, 'She Has Suddenly Become Powerful: Youth Employment and Household Decision Making in the Early Twentieth Century', *Journal of Economic History,* 65:2 (2005), pp. 414–38; for discussions of the 1917–19 data.
94. For 1888–90, Emery used information on earnings of household members, expenditures on food, rental costs, home and utilities, taxes, insurance, charity, vices and sickness and death. For 1917–19, Emery used information on earnings by household members, expenditures on food, clothing, housing rent, fuel and light, furniture, insurance, liquor and tobacco, medical expenses, cemetery expenses and 'miscellaneous'. Mortgage payments are not reported in the 1888–90 data so household expenditures of home owners are downward biased, which will increase the surplus measure (Gratton and Rotondo, 'Industrialization, the Family Economy, and the Economic Status of the American

Elderly'). To determine the potential size of the bias for the 1888–90 surplus measure, surpluses for 1917–19 are calculated with and without mortgage expenses. These calculations suggest that the median surplus of household heads in 1888–90 would be 1 percentage point lower if mortgage payments were to be included.

95. Emery, '"Un-American" or Unnecessary?'

96. Emery and Emery, *A Young Man's Benefit*.

97. Costa, 'The Political Economy of State Provided Health Insurance in the Progressive Era'.

98. According to Gilbert, in *The Evolution of National Health Insurance in Great Britain*, p. 164, English friendly societies opposed the introduction of contributory pension plans not because they competed with the friendly society benefits but because the contributory plan competed for the limited savings of the friendly societies' working class clientele. If the government plan forced the working man to divert his surplus savings into the government programme, the working man would no longer pay to belong to the friendly society.

99. Emery, '"Un-American" or Unnecessary?'.

100. See B. Gratton, 'The Poverty of Impoverishment Theory: The Economic Well-Being of the Elderly, 1890–1950', *Journal of Economic History*, 56:1 (1996), pp. 39–61, for a discussion of these developments in the US.

101. C. L. Weaver, 'On the Lack of a Political Market for Compulsory Old-Age Insurance Prior to the Great Depression: Insights from Economic Theories of Government', *Explorations in Economic History*, 20 (1983), pp. 294–328.

102. For large losses that occur infrequently, market insurance may be the preferred arrangement over self-insurance depending on the cost of the coverage, according to I. Ehrlich and G. S. Becker, 'Market Insurance, Self-Insurance, and Self-Protection', *Journal of Political Economy*, 80:4 (1972), pp. 623–48. In assessing an optimistic estimate that aggregate savings in the US amounted to $790 per family, Epstein, *Insecurity*, p. 115, asks, 'How adequate is such a sum for each family in the United States in meeting the different emergencies of modern life? ... How far will it go in case of a serious illness, an accident, or surgical operation?'

103. Rubinow, *The Quest for Security*.

104. Epstein, *Insecurity*, pp. 110–12.

105. Ibid., p. 100.

106. Emery, '"Un-American" or Unnecessary?'

107. Ibid.

108. Ibid.

109. Gilbert, *The Evolution of National Health Insurance in Great Britain*, pp. 180–1, 220–1.

110. Ibid., p. 219.

111. Murray, *Origins of American Health Insurance*.

112. Emery and Emery, *A Young Man's Benefit*; Beito, *From Mutual Aid to Welfare State*, pp. 29–31; Emery, 'From Defining Characteristic to Vitiation of Principle'; and Emery, '"Un-American" or Unnecessary?'.

113. Several studies seek to determine if self-insurance through savings was a substitute for voluntary insurance. M. G. Palumbo in 'Estimating the Effects of Earnings Uncertainty on Families' Saving and Insurance Decisions', *Southern Economic Journal*, 67 (2000), pp. 64–6; and Murray in *Origins of American Health Insurance*, provide some evidence from cross-sectional survey data from the 1890s that self-insurance (savings) was a substitute for insurance purchases. L. Di Matteo and J. C. H. Emery, 'Wealth and the Demand for Life Insurance: Evidence from Ontario, 1892', *Explorations in Economic History*, 39:4

(2002), pp. 446–69, find a negative correlation between the purchase of life insurance and the level of household wealth.

114. Rodgers, *Atlantic Crossings*, p. 243.

115. C. Lee, 'Life-Cycle Saving in the United States, 1900–90', *Review of Income and Wealth*, 47 (2001), pp. 165–79.

116. M. M. Davis, 'The American Approach to Health Insurance', *Millbank Memorial Fund Quarterly*, 12 (1934), pp. 201–17; Starr, *The Social Transformation of American Medicine*; and M. Thomasson, 'From Sickness to Health: The Twentieth-Century Development of U.S. Health Insurance', *Explorations in Economic History*, 39 (2002), pp. 233–53.

117. Armstrong, *Insuring the Essentials*, p. 334.

118. P. Gosden, *Self-help, Voluntary Associations in the Nineteenth Century* (London: B. T. Batsford, 1973).

119. Murray, *Origins of American Health Insurance*.

8 León-Sanz 'Medical Assistance Provided by *La Conciliación*, a Pamplona Mutual Assistance Association (1902–84)'

1. P. León-Sanz, 'Professional Responsibility and the Welfare System in Spain at the Turn of the 19th Century', *Hygiea Internationalis*, 5:1 (2006), pp. 75–90; F. Montero García and M. Estaban de Vega, 'Aproximación tipológica al mutualismo popular y obrero en España: el mutualismo asistencial', in S. Castillo (coord.), *La historia social en España: actualidad y perspectivas: actas del I Congreso de la Asociación de Historia Social, Zaragoza, septiembre, 1990* (Madrid: Siglo Veintiuno de España, 1991), pp. 457–69, at p. 462.

2. B. Harris, *The Origins of the British Welfare State: Society, State and Social Welfare in England and Wales, 1800–1945* (Basingstoke: Palgrave Macmillan, 2003), pp. 5–7; M. Gorsky, 'Friendly Society Health Insurance in Nineteenth-century England', in M. Gorsky and S. Sheard (eds.), *Financing Medicine: The British Experience Since 1750* (London; New York: Routledge, 2006), pp. 147–64.

3. About the introduction of the Obligatory insurance in Spain, see J. Cuesta Bustillo, 'El proceso de expansión de los seguros sociales obligatorios. Las dificultades, 1919–1931', in *Historia de la acción social publica en España: Beneficencia y previsión* (Madrid: Ministerio de Trabajo y Seguridad Social, 1990), pp. 287–317; I. Porras Gallo, 'Between the German Model and Liberal Medicine: The Negotiating Process of the State Health Care System in France and Spain (1919–1944)', *Hygiea Internationalis*, 6:2 (2007), pp. 135–49; S. Castillo (ed), *Solidaridad desde abajo: trabajadores y socorros mutuos en la España Contemporánea* (Madrid: UGT, 1994); J. Pons Pons and J. Silvestre Rodríguez (ed.), *Los orígenes del estado del bienestar en España, 1900–1945: los seguros de accidentes, vejez, desempleo y enfermedad* (Zaragoza: Prensas Universitarias de Zaragoza, 2010)

4. In Pamplona, apart from *La Conciliación*, during the first decades of the twentieth century similar entities were the *Sociedad de Artesanos* (Craftsmen's Guilds); the *Unión Productora*; the *Hermandad de la Pasión*; and two Unions (Local Federation of Workmen's Societies and the Free Catholic Union. See P. León-Sanz, 'The Mutual Benefit Societies' responses to the 1918–19 Influenza Pandemic in Pamplona', in M. I. Porras Gallo and R. A. Davis, *Emerging Infection, Emergent Meanings: The "Spanish" Influenza Pandemic of 1918–1919*, in press.

5. About this Society: P. León-Sanz, 'La concertación de la asistencia en la enfermedad en La Sociedad de Obreros *La Conciliación* (1902–1919)', in *Navarra: Memoria e Imagen* (Pamplona: Eunate, 2006), vol. 2, pp. 97–108; P. León-Sanz, 'Networking and interaction between a Mutual Assistance Association and other agencies (Pamplona,

1902–1919)'. *Hygiea internationalis*, 8:1 (2009), pp. 31–50; P. León-Sanz, 'The Strategies of Interrelations between Assistance Associations and Other Agencies in Pamplona, 1902–1936', in P. León-Sanz (ed.), *Health Institutions at the Origin of the Welfare Systems in Europe* (Pamplona: Eunsa, 2010), pp 167–92; P. León-Sanz, 'Private Initiatives against Social Inequalities and Health Vulnerabilities: the Case of *La Conciliación* (Pamplona, 1902–1920)', in P. Bourdelais and J. Chircop (eds.), *Vulnerabilities, Social Inequalities and Health* (Évora: Ediçoes Colibri, 2010), pp. 93–108.

6.   J. Andrés-Gallego, *Pensamiento y acción social de la Iglesia en España* (Madrid: Espasa-Calpe, 1984), pp. 287–95; J. Goñi Gaztambide, *Historia de los obispos de Pamplona* (Pamplona: Eunsa, 1999), pp. 561–99; J. M. Pejenaute Goñi, 'Las Sociedades de Socorros Mutuos en Navarra (finales del siglo XIX-Comienzos del XX)', in *Congreso de Historia de Euskal Herria* (Vitoria: Servicio Central de Publicaciones del Gobierno Vasco, 1988), vol. 6, pp. 279–81.

7.   Articles 10 and 22, respectively of the Regulations. General Archive of the University of Navarra, *La Conciliación* Archive (AGUN/LC), 10, General Register Book.

8.   AGUN/LC/3/*Minute Books*, 1920, vol. 9, p. 137.

9.   AGUN/LC/3/*Minute Books*, 1922, vol. 10, pp. 146–7. About these changes in *La Conciliación*'s structure: León-Sanz, 'Private initiatives against social inequalities', pp. 93–108.

10.   The main legislative issues that affected *La Conciliación* in the 1920s were: the administrative reforms of the Municipal Statute (March 1924); and the development of social-labour legislation: the non-voluntary unemployment benefit; the introduction of the Workers Obligatory Retirement and the so-called *Organización Corporativa Nacional* (decrees of 26 November 1926 and 12 May, 1928). See C. del Peso Calvo, *De la protección gremial al vigente sistema de Seguridad Social: apuntes históricos comentados* (Madrid: Talleres Gráficos Vda. de C. Bermejo, 1967); M. Vázquez de Prada, *Historia contemporánea de Navarra en sus documentos* (Barcelona: Ariel, 2001).

11.   This time it was the protectors who, in writing, at the meeting of the Mixed Board on 22 December 1925, expressed their displeasure as they had discovered that 'a commission composed of three workers only from the Mixed Board, has studied and presented for its approval a proposal on our well-thought-out and beloved regulations, which, according to authoritative sources, fundamentally discussed the internal constitution of *La Conciliación*'. AGUN/LC/3/*Minute books*, 1925, vol. 10, pp. 276–7.

12.   AGUN/LC/3/*Minute Books*, vol. 10, pp. 312–3.

13.   AGUN/LC/6/*Minute Books* General Meetings, vol. 1, p. 2–24.

14.   At that time the bishop was: Don Mateo Múgica Urrestarazu (1870–1968). Cf. G. Redondo, *Historia de la Iglesia en España 1931–1939* (Madrid: Rialp, 1993).

15.   This new modification of the Regulations was conditioned by the need to adapt to labour legislation, mainly the development of the non-voluntary unemployment benefit and the *Organización Corporativa Nacional*. Cf. 'La legislación social de la Dictadura' in J. Andrés-Gallego, *El socialismo durante la dictadura, 1923–1930* (Madrid: Tebas, 1977), pp. 193–216.

16.   'Balance del veintiséis aniversario de *La Conciliación*', AGUN/LC/U/7.

17.   AGUN/LC/3/*Minute Books*, 1928, vol. 11, pp. 144–5 and vol 12, pp. 9–10 (28 February).

18.   'Balance del veintiséis aniversario de *La Conciliación*', AGUN/LC/U/9.

19.   AGUN/LC/3/*Minute Books*, 1930, vol. 12, pp. 15–6. (12 January).

20.   Francisco Largo Caballero (1869–1946), was a Spanish politician and trade unionist. He was one of the historic leaders of the Socialist Party (PSOE) and of the Workers' General

Union (UGT). He was Minister of Labor Relations between 1931 and 1933, in the first governments of the Second Spanish Republic. He was Prime Minister (1936–1937).

21. *Gaceta de Madrid* (Madrid: Imprenta Real, 14 April 1932), n. 105, pp. 330–4.
22. Orden dando disposiciones para la efectividad de lo dispuesto en la Ley de 8 de Abril del año actual sobre Asociaciones Profesionales, *Gaceta de Madrid* (7 June 1932), n. 159, pp, 1738–1738; Orden disponiendo que el día 1º de Julio próximo los Gobiernos civiles hagan entrega a las Delegaciones provinciales de Trabajo de los Registros de Asociaciones Profesionales de Patronos y Obreros. *Gaceta de Madrid* (16 June 1933), n. 167, pp. 2030–1.
23. AGUN/LC/4/*Minute Books*, 1932, vol. 13, pp. 29–30. The Pamplona' bishop at that time was don Tomás Muniz Pablos. About this bisohp: J. Gorricho Moreno, 'La Diócesis de Pamplona en 1932: relación del obispo Muniz en su visita *ad Limina*'. *Príncipe de Viana*, 65, 231 (2004), pp. 53–86.
24. AGUN/LC/4/*Minute Books,* 1932, vol. 13, p. 21.
25. AGUN/LC/4/*Minute Books*, 1933, vol. 13, pp. 22–3.
26. Article 1 of the Regulations. AGUN/LC/10/General Register Book.
27. Article 2 of the Regulations. AGUN/LC/10/General Register Book.
28. Article 10 of the Regulations. AGUN/LC/10/General Register Book.
29. AGUN/LC/1/*Minute Books*, 1903, vol. 1, pp. 6–7.
30. AGUN/LC/1/*Minute Books*, 1903, vol. 1, pp. pp. 15–6.
31. AGUN/LC/1/*Minute Books*, 1903, vol. 1, p. 20.
32. AGUN/LC/1/*Minute Books*, 1903, vol. 1, p. 141.
33. Article 11 of the Regulations. AGUN/LC/10/General Register Book.
34. Article 16 of the Regulations. AGUN/LC/10/General Register Book.
35. AGUN/LC/1/*Minute Books*, 1902, vol. 1, pp. 6–7.
36. AGUN/LC/2/*Minute Books*, 1915, vol. 5, p. 141.
37. AGUN/LC/3/*Minute Books*, 1917, vol. 7, p. 5.
38. AGUN/LC/3/*Minute Books*, 1918, vol. 7, p. 302.
39. Article 8 of the Regulations. AGUN/LC/10/General Register Book.
40. Cf. for example: AGUN/LC/3/*Minute Books*, 1917, vol. 7, p. 44.
41. Between 1923 and 1930, 62 sick leaves were presented with delay.
42. AGUN/LC/2/*Minute Books*, 1914, vol. 5, pp. 147 and 149.
43. AGUN/LC/2/*Minute Books*, 1916, vol. 6, pp. 36.
44. AGUN/LC/3/*Minute Books*, 1928, vol. 13, pp. 13–4.
45. AGUN/LC/4/*Minute Books*, 1935, vol. 14, p. 32
46. In the records there are described several cases: AGUN/LC/2/*Minute Books*, 1914, vol. 3, p. 190; 1915, vol 4, p. 193; 1915, vol. 5, p. 140; 1916, vol. 6, p. 9; 1917, vol. 7, pp. 48–9.
47. Among 1923 and 1930 we have found 5 cases and 2 of these, later, they received the subsidies.
48. About the meaning of the hospital's assistance in these cases: cf. E. Rodríguez Ocaña, 'La asistencia médica colectiva en España, hasta 1936', in *Historia de la acción social pública en España: Beneficencia y previsión* (Madrid: Ministerio de Trabajo y Seguridad Social, 1990), pp. 321–61 (327).
49. Article 67, Regulations 1928. AGUN/LC/X.
50. Article 16 of the Regulations. AGUN/LC/10/General Register Book.
51. Article 11 of the Regulations. AGUN/LC/10/General Register Book.
52. AGUN/LC/1/*Minute Books*, 1904, vol. 1, pp. 149–50.
53. AGUN/LC/1/*Minute Books*, 1903, vol. 1, p. 25; 1904, vol 1, pp. 157–9; etc. Initially in the records figured the Visitors' name.

54. AGUN/LC/3/*Minute Books*, 1922.

55. AGUN/LC/2/*Minute Books*, 1917, vol. 6, p. 114.

56. AGUN/LC/2/*Minute Books*, 1915, vol. 5, p. 69; 1916, vol. 6, pp. 121 and 147.

57. AGUN/LC/3/*Minute Books*, 1918, vol. 7, pp. 140–1.

58. AGUN/LC/1/*Minute Books*, 1904, vol. 1, pp. 220–1 and 233–4.

59. AGUN/LC/3/*Minute Books*, 1918, vol. 6, p. 183.

60. AGUN/LC/3/*Minute Books*, 1917, vol. 7, p. 99.

61. AGUN/LC/4/*Minute Books*, 1935, vol. 14.

62. AGUN/LC/3/*Minute Books*, 1923, vol. 10, p. 333.

63. AGUN/LC/3/*Minute Books*, 1923, vol. 10, p. 320.

64. AGUN/LC/2/*Minute Books*, 1914, vol. 4, p. 188.

65. AGUN/LC/2/*Minute Books*, 1916, vol. 6, p. 115; 1917, vol. 6, pp. 363 and 356.

66. AGUN/LC/4/*Minute Books*, 1934, vol. 14, p. 76; when Sr. Casimiro Arrastia died, on May 1935, he was substituted.

67. AGUN/LC/4/*Minute Books*, 1934 vol. 14, p. 34.

68. AGUN/LC/4/*Minute Books*, 1935 vol. 14, p. 46.

69. AGUN/LC/4/*Minute Books*, 1937, vol. 15, p. 21.

70. AGUN/LC/4/*Minute Books*, 1935 vol. 14, p. 46.

71. AGUN/LC/4/*Minute Books*, 1936, vol. 15, p. 4.

72. AGUN/LC/2/*Minute Books*, 1915, vol. 5, p. 69

73. AGUN/LC/2/*Minute Books*, 1916, vol. 6, p. 71.

74. AGUN/LC/2/*Minute Books*, 1916, vol. 6, pp. 63, 71, 106.

75. AGUN/LC/6/*Minute Books* General Meetings, 1928, vol. 1, pp. 13–4.

76. AGUN/LC/6/*Minute Books* General Meetings, 1931, vol. 1, pp. 18–9. The Spanish Parlament approved the Illness Insurance Agreements for workers on 5 April 1932 (the Act was published on 4 November 1932).

77. General Archive of the University of Navarra, *Mutualidad Obrera Profesional* (AGUN/MOP), *Minute books*, 1932, p. 1.

78. I. Olabarri Gortazar, 'Las relaciones laborales (1841–1936). Balance y perspectivas de investigación', in J. Intxausti (dir.), *Euskal Herria. Historia y Sociedad* (San Sebastián: Caja Laboral Popular, 1985), pp. 279–97.

79. AGUN/MOP/*Minute Books*, 1934, pp. 25. And AGUN/LC/6/*Minute Books* General Meetings, 1932 and 1936.

80. A. Alvarez Rosete, *Elaborados con calma, ejecutados con prisa. El avance de los Seguros Sociales y la evolución del INP en España entre 1936 y 1958*, in Castillo and Ruzafa (coords.), *La previsión social en la historia*, pp. 201 and 261.

81. The Minutes mention references to the preliminary draft of a Law on Obligatory Insurance against the risks of illness, disability and death, which, from 1932 on, were the responsibility of the INP and would have a direct influence on the course of *La Conciliación*. AGUN/LC/4/*Minute Books*, 1933, vol. 13, pp. 29–30. Cf. also there are references on 24 January 1943 and AGUN/LC/4/*Minute Books*, 1944, vol. 16, pp. 61–5.

82. Letter to Sr. Don Julio San Gil, 2 August 1944. AGUN/LC/M.

83. J. Andrés-Gallego and D. Barba, *Acción Social Empresarial: 50 años de empresariado cristiano en España* (Madrid: Acción Social Empresarial, 2002).

84. E. Maza Zorrilla, 'El mutualismo en España, 1900–1941. Ajustes e interferencias', in Castillo and Ruzafa (coords.), *La previsión social en la historia*, p. 365.

85. The 1934 Catalonian Act was applied during a short period. Cf. C. Sarrias Cárdenes, 'Las Mutualidades de Previsión social en España 1939–2008', in Castillo and Ruzafa (coords.), *La previsión social en la historia*, p. 369.

86. Letter to Sr. Don Julio San Gil, 2 August 1944. AGUN/LC/M.

87. Letter to Sr. Don Julio San Gil, 2 August 1944. AGUN/LC/M.
88. Letter signed by Don Miguel María Troncoso (Provincial Delegate of the Central National Union), 3 October 1940, reference n. 5180. AGUN/LC/M.
89. AGUN/LC/4/*Minute Books*, 1940, vol. 15, pp. 51–4.
90. AGUN/LC/4/*Minute Books*, 1941, vol. 15, pp. 54–7; 1942, vol. 16, pp. 59–61.
91. AGUN/LC/4/*Minute Books*, 1941, vol. 15, pp. 54–7.
92. Letter from the *La Conciliacion*'s President to the Navarrese INP's Delegate (12 April 1944). The physicians were: Manuel Galán, José María Repáraz, D. Joaquín Ariz, D. Carlos Ciganda y D. José Alfonso. AGUN/LC/M.
93. AGUN/LC/4/*Minute Books*, 1943, vol. 16, pp. 61–5.
94. On 16 February 1945, the Reform of Articles 13, 15, 18, 19, 23, 27, 34, 67 and 74 was passed in order to 'adapt the Regulations of *La Conciliación* to the Regulations of Mutual Assistance Associations and Montepíos and to the Law on Obligatory Health Insurance'. AGUN/LC/4/*Minute books*, 1945, vol. 16, pp. 66–8.
95. 'Modificaciones al reglamento de la mutualidad obrera profesional *La Conciliación* de fecha 22 de octubre de 1941, inscrita en registro especial de montepíos y mutualidades, con el n. 432, acogidas en la asamblea general extraordinaria de 16 de febrero de 1945'. [Modifications of the *La Conciliación*'s Regulation, 22 October 1941; Association catalogued in the special registration of montepíos and mutualities, n. 432]
96. A. Redecillas López de Sabando, *El mutualismo laboral como medio de protección social: un estudio económico-financiero* (Madrid: Consejo Económico y Social, 2001), pp. 7, 319–21
97. AGUN/LC/4/*Minute Books*, 1944, vol. 16, p. 20.
98. In the archive there are abundance correspondence between *La Conciliación* and the 'Federación Mutualista del Norte' along the years.
99. The second category was that of the members 'whose daily basic wage or salary does not exceed 25 pesetas'; 'and those who earn more may, if they so wish, belong to the first category'. AGUN/LC/5/*Minute books*, 1949, vol. 17, pp. 75–6. 'Modificaciones al reglamento de la mutualidad obrera profesional *La Conciliación* de Pamplona inscrita en registro especial de montepíos y mutualidades con el n. 432, aprobadas en la asamblea general extraordinaria celebrada el día 17 de junio de 1949' [Modifications of the *La Conciliación*'s Regulation, 17 June 1949; Association catalogued in the special registration of montepíos and mutualities, n 432].
100. AGUN/LC/5/*Minute Books*, 1955, vol. 17, pp. 85–6.
101. J. Andrés-Gallego, 'El siglo XX', in *Historia de Navarra* (Pamplona: Gobierno de Navarra, 1995).
102. AGUN/LC/5/*Minute Books*, 1961, vol. 18, p. 8.
103. AGUN/LC/5/*Minute Books*, 1965, vol. 18, pp. 98–100.
104. 'Confidential Report', January 1967. AGUN/LC/P.
105. AGUN/LC/5/*Minute Books*, 1967, vol. 18, pp. 64–8, and 94.
106. AGUN/LC/5/*Minute Books*, 1968, vol. 18, pp. 76–8.
107. AGUN/LC/5/*Minute Books*, 1968, vol. 18, pp. 83, 88 and 93 (23 February; 19 June; 16 October). They sent to the Ministry's Department two more copies of the Regulations and the Extraordinary Board Meeting's record.
108. AGUN/LC/5/*Minute Books*, 1969, vol. 18, p. 96.
109. AGUN/LC/5/*Minute Books*, 1968, vol. 18, pp. 86–7, and 89–91.
110. AGUN/LC/5/*Minute Books*, 1968, vol. 18, p, 95.
111. AGUN/LC/5/*Minute Books*, 1972, vol. 19, pp. 36–7.
112. AGUN/LC/5/*Minute Books*, 1968, vol. 18, p. 86, and 1969, vol. 18, p. 3.
113. AGUN/LC/5/*Minute Books*, 1973, vol. 19, pp. 42–6.

114. AGUN/LC/5/*Minute Books*, 1971, vol. 19, p. 33.
115. AGUN/LC/5/*Minute Books*, 1972, vol. 19, p. 45.
116. AGUN/LC/5/*Minute Books*, 1972, vol. 19, pp 46 and 49. SURNE sent his Regulations and experiences to the *La Conciliación*.
117. AGUN/LC/5/*Minute Books*, 1972, vol. 19, p 38.
118. AGUN/LC/5/*Minute Books*, 1975, vol. 20, p. 12.
119. AGUN/LC/5/*Minute Books*, 1974, vol. 20, p. 8.
120. AGUN/LC/5/*Minute Books*, 1975, vol. 20, pp. 11–5.
121. AGUN/LC/5/*Minute Books*, 1976, vol. 20, p. 17.
122. AGUN/LC/5/*Minute Books*, 1977, vol. 20, pp. 24–5.
123. AGUN/LC/5/*Minute Books*, 1977, vol. 20, pp. 20–1.
124. AGUN/LC/6/Minutes' Book of *La Conciliación de Pamplona S. A.*, 1978–83.
125. AGUN/LC/6/Minutes' Book of *La Conciliación de Pamplona S. A.*, January 1979.
126. AGUN/LC/6/Minutes' Book of *La Conciliación de Pamplona S. A.*, January 1981.
127. AGUN/LC/6/Minutes' Book of *La Conciliación de Pamplona S. A.*, January 1983.
128. AGUN/LC/6/Minutes' Book of *La Conciliación de Pamplona S. A.*, 1978–83.
129. AGUN/LC/6/Minutes' Book of *La Conciliación de Pamplona S. A.*, January 1981.
130. Ley 6 de 1984, de 31 de marzo, de modificación de determinados artículos de los del Código Civil y de Comercio y de las Leyes Hipotecarias, de Enjuiciamiento Criminal y de Régimen Jurídico de la Sociedades Anónimas sobre interdicción [Law 6 of 31 March 1984 amending certain articles of the Civil and Commercial Code and the Mortgage Law, Criminal Procedure and Legal System of Corporations on interdiction].
131. J. Pons Pons, *El sector seguros en Baleares: empresas y empresarios en los siglos XIX-XX* (Palma de Mallorca: El Tall, 1998).
132. AGUN/LC/1/*Minute Books*, 1902, vol. 1, pp. 4–5.
133. León-Sanz, 'Private Initiatives Against Social Inequalities', pp. 93–108.
134. I. Olabarri Gortazar, *¿Lucha de clases o conflictos de intereses?: ensayos de historia de las relaciones laborales en la edad contemporánea* (Pamplona: Ediciones Universidad de Navarra, 1991), p. 161.

9 Vonk, 'In it for the Money? Insurers, Sickness Funds and the Dominance of Not-for-profit Health Insurance in the Netherlands'

1.   'Marktwerking voor zorg niet het toverwoord', *Het Financieele Dagblad*, 5 April 2005; 'Waarom ligt u hier? De markt smoort de moraal; Het onrecht van de markt in de zorg', *Trouw*, 29 mei 2010.
2.   M. H. D. van Leeuwen, *De eenheidsstaat. Onderlinges, armenzorg en commerciële verzekeraars 1800–1890* (Amsterdam/The Hague: Verbond van Verzekeraars/NEHA, 2000), p. 179.
3.   K. P. Companje, 'Ziekteverzekering volgens het Bismarckrecept?', in K .P. Companje (ed.), *Tussen volksverzekering en vrije markt. Verzekering van zorg op het snijvlak van sociale verzekering en gezondheidszorg 1880–2006* (Amsterdam: Aksant Uitgeverij, 2008), pp. 47–96, on p. 57.
4.   A. M. Brandt and M. Gardner, 'The Golden Age of Medicine?', in R. Cooter and J. Pickstone (eds), *Medicine in the Twentieth Century* (Amsterdam: Harwood Academic Publishers, 2000), pp. 21–37, on pp. 21–2; B. Hansen, 'New Images of a New Medicine: Visual Evidence for the Widespread Popularity of Therapeutic Discoveries in America after 1885', *Bulletin for the History of Medicine*, 73 (1999), pp. 629–78.

5. J. L. van Zanden, *The Economic History of the Netherlands 1914–1995. A Small Open Economy in the 'Long' Twentieth Century* (London and New York: Routledge, 1998), pp. 94–5; J. van Gerwen, *De ontluikende verzorgingsstaat. Overheid, vakbonden, werkgevers, ziekenfondsen en verzekeringsmaatschappijen 1890–1945* (Amsterdam/The Hague: Verbond van Verzekeraars/NEHA, 2000), p. 147.

6. 'Handelingen van de buitengewone vergadering van 2 en 3 mei 1918. Ziekteverzekering voor den middenstand', *Nederlands Tijdschrift voor Geneeskunde*, 3 (1918), pp. 193–4.

7. K. P. Companje, K. F. E. Veraghtert and B. E. M. Widdershoven, *Two Centuries of Solidarity. The Dutch, Belgian and German Health Insurance Funds During the 19 and 20 Century* (Amsterdam: Aksant, 2009), pp. 116–17.

8. K. P. Companje and R. A. A. Vonk, 'Ziektekostenverzekeringen en wettelijk geregelde arbeidsverhoudingen tot 1941', in Companje (ed.), *Tussen volksverzekering en vrije markt*, pp. 173–224, on pp. 185–90.

9. Companje and Vonk, 'Ziektekostenverzekeringen', pp. 193–4.

10. R. A. A. Vonk, 'Database particuliere ziektekostenverzekeraars in Nederland 1900–2006', Kenniscentrum Historie Zorgverzekeraars, at http://www.metamedicavumc.nl/KHZ/bronarchief/pdfs/Ziektekostenverzekeraars1900–2006.pdf [accessed 11 december 2010].

11. Companje en Vonk, 'Ziektekostenverzekeringen', pp. 194–7.

12. Rapport betreffende de resultaten van Fatum's zaken d.d. 13 mei 1927, ING Bedrijfsarchief, Amsterdam, Beleidsarchief Nationale Nederlanden, inv. nr. A32 (0301412027).

13. Centraal Bureau voor de Statistiek, *Verzekering tegen de kosten van ziekenhuisverpleging op 1 januari 1940* (The Hague: Albani, 1940), p. 7; W. W. Katz, 'Theorie en praktijk der ziektekostenverzekering', *Het Verzekeringsarchief*, 20 (1939), pp. 61–72, on p. 63.

14. 'Maatschappij-berichten', *Algemeen Assurantieblad*, 5:24 (1938), pp. 510–11.

15. J. C. W. Duncker, 'De Toekomst der Ziekteverzekering', *Het Verzekeringsblad voor Nederland en België*, 31 (1941), pp. 36–7, on p. 36; M. A. Thomasson, 'From Sickness to Health: The Twentieth-Century Development of U.S. Health Insurance', *Explorations in Economic History*, 39 (2002), pp. 233–53, on pp. 233–5.

16. Brief van de minister van Sociale Zaken aan de directie van de MVZ, 29 juni 1936, Nationaal Archief, Den Haag, 2.15.37 – afdeling Volksgezondheid (Hereafter NA VGZ), inv. nr. 866; Brief van de SG aan de DG van volksgezondheid, d.d. 22 augustus 1936, NA VGZ, NA, 866.

17. 'Ziekteverzekering en de gevaren van het onderlinge en coöperatieve stelsel! III', *De Vraagbaak*, 8:26 (1935), pp. 1–4, on p. 3.

18. Companje, 'Het Ziekenfondsenbesluit en de gevolgen voor de verzekering van zorg 1940–1986', *Tussen volksverzekering en vrije markt*, pp. 477–536, on pp. 507–11.

19. F. T. Schut, 'Competition in the Dutch Health Care Sector' (PhD Dissertation, Erasmus University Rotterdam, 1995), pp. 137, 157; Companje, 'Het Ziekenfondsenbesluit', pp. 502–4.

20. Companje, 'Het Ziekenfondsenbesluit', p. 513.

21. Brief van G. Ady aan M. Rost van Tonningen d.d. 21 februari 1942, Nederlands Instituut voor Oorlogsdocumentatie, Amsterdam, Archief van het departement voor Bijzondere Economische Zaken (Hereafter NIOD BEZ), V36; E. Fraenkel-Verkade (ed.), *Correspondentie van Mr. M.M. Rost van Tonningen. Deel I: 1921-mei 1942* (The Hague: Nijhoff Uitgeverij, 1969), p. 738.

22. Companje, 'Het Ziekenfondsenbesluit', pp. 504–6.

23. Notulen van de vergadering van den Raad van Bijstand der Ondervakgroep Ziekenhuiskostenverzekering Vaste Premie d.d. 1 november 1943, Nationaal Archief, Den Haag,

2.06.082 - archief van het Directoraat-Generaal voor de Prijzen (hereafter NA PZ) inv. nr. 234.

24. Ibid.

25. Companje, 'Het Ziekenfondsenbesluit', pp. 504–6.

26. Brief van de ondervakgroep Ziektekostenverzekering aan de Gemachtigde voor de Prijzen d.d. 27 oktober 1943, NA PZ, inv. nr. 234.

27. Companje, Veraghtert and Widdershoven, *Two Centuries*, pp. 252–3.

28. Ibid., pp. 253–4.

29. Brief van de directeur-generaal van de prijzen aan de secretaris van de bedrijfsgroep schadeverzekering d.d. 4 augustus 1947, NA PZ, inv. nr. 1184

30. 'De ziektekostenverzekering', *Het verzekeringsblad*, 38 (1949), pp. 44–7, at p. 44.

31. H. L. Kunneman, *De Ziektekostenverzekering* (Zeist: Sint Gregoriushuis, 1951), p. 35.

32. Rapport van de commissie ter bevordering van de oprichting van instellingen voor Gezondheidszorg 1946, Stichting HiZ, Amsterdam, Archief Stichting Utrechts Ziekenhuisverplegingsfonds, inv. nr. 9.

33. Notulen van de vergadering van het bestuur 9 maart 1950, Stichting HiZ, Archief Permanente Commissie van Overleg, inv. nr. 7.

34. Schut, 'Competition', p. 139; Companje, 'Het Ziekenfondsenbesluit', pp. 516–18.

35. Schuurmans Stekhoven, *Het nieuwe ziekenfondsrechthandboek voor de pracktijk* (Deventer: uitgeverij KLuwer, 1942), pp. 228–333.

36. 'Ziektekostenverzekering, steeds actueel', *Het verzekeringsblad*, 46 (1957), pp. 77–9, at p. 77.

37. Notulen vergadering bestuur d.d. 29 maart 1950, Stichting HiZ, Amsterdam, Archief Federatie VVZ, inv. nr. 20.

38. Brief van VZVZ aan de Nederlandse Unie van Schadeverzekeraars d.d. 10 mei 1953, Verbond van Verzekeraars, Den Haag, Archief van de NVOZ (Hereafter VvV NVOZ), s19/Z.416.

39. Schut, 'Competition', p. 140. 'Het Wit-Blauwe Kruis lanceert de onvervalbare oppeil-verplegingsverzekering', *Het Verzekeringsblad*, 45 (1957), pp. 214–15; Concept Jaarverslag van de NVOZ over het jaar 1967, VvV NVOZ, S.19/Z.1149,

40. Companje, 'Het Ziekenfondsenbesluit', p. 519. Schut, 'Competition', p. 141.

41. Voorwaarden en lijst van verzekerde risico's van de Verzekeringsgroep voor Bijzondere Risicio's 1957, VvV NVOZ, S19/Z.418.

42. 'Ziektekostenpolis voor Bijzondere Risico's', *Het Verzekeringsblad*, 46 (1957), pp. 45–8, on p. 45–6; A. de Bruin, 'De toestand bij de stichting A.Z.R.', *Verenigde Verzekeringspers*, 30 (1959), p. 461.

43. Aantekeningen van de bespreking d.d. 19 oktober 1951, Stichting HiZ, Amsterdam, Archief Permanente Commissie van Overleg, inv. nr. 21.

44. Schut, 'Competition', pp. 139–42.

45. Mededeling van P.A. Zeven over zijn gesprek met enkele specialisten d.d. 13 oktober 1965, VvV NVOZ, s19/Z.333; Brief van de minister van EZ aan de minister van BiZa d.d. 31 maart 1947, NA PZ, inv. nr. 1196.

46. CBS, *Kosten en financiering van de gezondheidszorg in Nederland 1968* (The Hague: Staatsuitgeverij, 1972), p. 53 and p. 67.

47. Notulen van de vergadering van het bestuur van de NVOZ d.d. 18 februari 1965, VvV NVOZ, s19/Z.421.

48. Companje, 'Het Ziekenfondsenbesluit en de verstrekking van zorg', *Tussen volksverzekering en vrije markt*, pp. 649–708, at pp. 682–4.

49. Companje, 'Het Ziekenfondsenbesluit', p. 519.

50. Companje, 'Verzekering van zorg 1943–2007: gezondheidszorg of sociale zekerheid?', *Tussen volksverzekering en vrije markt*, pp. 559–628, on pp. 572–3.

51. Notulen van de vergadering van het bestuur van Sectie II van de NVOZ d.d. 10 augustus 1965, VvV NVOZ, S19/Z.421.

52. M. Kerkhoff and W. P. M. Dols, 'De Algemene Wet Bijzondere Ziektekosten. Debatten en ontwikkelingen tot 1987', *Tussen volksverzekering en vrije markt*, pp. 709–94, on p. 728–9.

53. Ibid., pp. 728–9.

54. Verslag van de bespreking van de KLOZ met de GOZ van vrijdag 18 maart 1966, VvV NVOZ, s19/Z.415.

55. Notulen vergadering bestuur d.d. 25 oktober 1966, Stichting HiZ, Amsterdam, Archief KLOZ

56. Notulen van de vergadering van het bestuur van de NVOZ d.d. 26 oktober 1966, VvV NVOZ, S19/Z.1588.

57. Schut, 'Competition', p. 142.

58. Ibid., p. 143.

59. Ibid., p. 142.

60. Companje, Veraghtert and Widdershoven, *Two Centuries*, pp. 258–9.

61. Van der Zanden, *The Economic History*, pp. 158–70.

62. Schut, 'Competition', pp. 143–5.

63. Ibid., pp. 140–4.

64. Notulen van de vergadering van het bestuur van de NVOZ d.d. 22 november 1966, VvV NVOZ, S19/Z.189; Notulen vergadering bestuur d.d. 31 mei 1966, Stichting HiZ, Amsterdam, Archief KLOZ

65. Consumentenbond, 'Ziektekostenverzekering 2', *Consumentengids*, 26 (1968), pp. 484–93.

66. Companje, 'Het Ziekenfondsenbesluit', pp. 510–11.

67. Companje, 'Verzekering van zorg', p. 579

68. P. A. Zeven, F. Schrijver and J. A. Boogman, *Zeven Pijlers voor een nieuwe structuur van gezondheidszorg. Naar een nieuwe opzet voor de financiering van de Nederlandse gezond-heidszorg* (The Hague: NVOZ, 1972).

69. Companje, 'Verzekering van zorg', p. 580.

70. Ibid., pp. 581–4.

71. Kerkhoff and Dols, 'De Algemene Wet Bijzondere Ziektekosten', pp. 760–8.

72. Ibid., p. 760–8.

73. G. H. Okma, 'Studies on Dutch Health Politics, Policies and Law' (PhD Dissertation, University of Utrecht, 1997), p. 107.

74. Ibid.

75. Kerkhoff and Dols, 'De Algemene Wet Bijzondere Ziektekosten', pp. 760–8.

76. Companje, Veraghtert and Widdershoven, *Two Centuries*, pp. 270–1.

77. Ibid., pp. 273–81.

78. R. A. A. Vonk, 'database particuliere ziektekostenverzekeraars'.

10 Rigter, 'Belgian Mutual Health Insurance and the Nation State'

1. K. P. Companje, K. F. E. Veraghtert and B. E. M. Widdershoven, *Two Centuries of Soli-darity. German, Belgian and Dutch Social Health Insurance 1770–2000*, (Amsterdam: Aksant, 2009), p. 311; P. Lindert, *Growing Public. Social Spending and Economic Growth since the Eighteenth Century*, 2 vols (Cambridge: Cambridge University Press, 2004), vol.

1, pp. 197, 202–3; 'Eco-Santé OCDE 2010, Comment la Belgique se positionne', April 2010, at http://www.oecd.org/dataoecd/45/22/38980735.pdf [accessed 11 December 2010]; Dexia, 'Vergrijzing: impact en uitdaging voor de lokale besturen', p. 25, at http://www.dexia.be/nocms/election/Vieillisssement_nl.pdf [accessed 11 December 2010] and Total expenditure on health. As a percentage of gross domestic product, 12 July 2011, at http://www.oecd-ilibrary.org/social-issues-migration-health/health-key-tables-from-oecd_20758480 [accessed 3 October 2011].

2.   Companje, Veraghtert and Widdershoven, *Two Centuries of Solidarity*, p. 311.

3.   Dexia, 'Vergrijzing: impact en uitdaging voor de lokale besturen', p. 5, at http://www.dexia.be/nocms/election/Vieillisssement_nl.pdf [accessed 11 December 2010].

4.   Companje, Veraghtert and Widdershoven, *Two Centuries of Solidarity*, pp. 34–5 and 40; L. van der Valk, 'Zieken- en begrafenisfondsen in de negentiende eeuw', *NEHA-JAAR-BOEK 1996* (Amsterdam: Aksant, 2009), pp. 162–210, at www.neha.nl/publications/1 996/1996_10vandervalk.pdf [accessed 11 December 2010].

5.   Datasets – Journeymen's Organizations/Caisses de Secours et de Prévoyance – The Netherlands at http://www.collective-action.info/datasets_guilds_caisses_netherlands_report [accessed 27 December 2010].

6.   Companje, Veraghtert and Widdershoven, *Two Centuries of Solidarity*, pp. 40, 49.

7.   L. van der Valk, 'Overheid en de ontwikkeling van het verzekeringswezen 1500–1815', in J. van Gerwen and M. H. D. van Leeuwen, *Studies over zekerheidsarrangementen. Risico's, risicobestrijding en verzekeringen in Nederland vanaf de Middeleeuwen*, (Amsterdam/ Den Haag: Verbond van Verzekeraars/NEHA, 1998), p. 41 and van der Valk, 'Zieken-en begrafenisfondsen in de negentiende eeuw'.

8.   B. E. M. Widdershoven, *Het dilemma van solidariteit. De Nederlandse onderlinge ziekenfondsen*, (Amsterdam: Amsterdam University Press, 2005), pp. 39–40.

9.   van der Valk, 'Zieken- en begrafenisfondsen in de negentiende eeuw', pp. 167, 172.

10. Ibid., p. 171; Companje, Veraghtert and Widdershoven, *Two Centuries of Solidarity*, p. 52.

11. Companje, Veraghtert and Widdershoven, *Two Centuries of Solidarity*, pp. 49, 52.

12. van der Valk, 'Zieken- en begrafenisfondsen in de negentiende eeuw', pp. 172–3.

13. Ibid., pp. 168, 175–6.

14. Ibid., pp. 166, 175, 194, n. 76.

15. Ibid., pp. 173–6.

16. Companje, Veraghtert and Widdershoven, *Two Centuries of Solidarity*, p. 48.

17. van der Valk, 'Zieken- en begrafenisfondsen in de negentiende eeuw', pp. 165, 187.

18. E. H. Kossmann, *De Lage Landen 1780–1940* (Amsterdam/Brussel: Elsevier, 1984), p. 107; R. Rezsohazy, *Geschiedenis van de kristelijke mutualistische beweging in België*, (Antwerpen/Amsterdam: Standaard-Boekhandel, 1957), p. 64; M. A. Visschers, *Over de maetschappijen van onderlingen bijstand in België*, (Brussel: Drukkery van G. Stapleaux, 1854), p. 8; S. Gerkens and S. Merkur, *Belgian Health system review, Health Systems in Transition*, 12:5 (2010) at http://www.euro.who.int/__data/assets/pdf_file/0014/120425/E94245.PDF. [accessed 20 December 2010].

19. van der Valk, 'Zieken- en begrafenisfondsen in de negentiende eeuw', pp. 184–6; Companje, Veraghtert and Widdershoven, *Two Centuries of Solidarity*, p. 53.

20. M. Vermote, *Gezondheid. 75 jaar Nationaal Verbond van Socialistische Mutualiteiten 1913–1988*, (Gent: Amsab, 1988), pp. 17, 18, 42; *Enquête sur la condition des classes ouvrières et sur le travail des enfants* (Brussel 1846–1848), 3 vols. M.A. Visschers was a driving force behind this inquiry.

21. Companje, Veraghtert and Widdershoven, *Two Centuries of Solidarity*, p. 79.

22. R. Rezsohazy, *Geschiedenis van de kristelijke mutualistische beweging in België*, pp. 65–6.

23. Ibid., pp. 67–70.
24. Document no. 48 Chambre des Représentants, Projet de loi relatif aux sociétes de secours mutuels. Rapport fait, au nom de la section centrale (1), par M. 'T Kint de Naeyer. 21 Janvier 1851, at http://www3.dekamer.be/digidoc/DPS/K2269/K22691908/K22691908.PDF [accessed 11 December 2010], p. 4.
25. Rezsohazy, *Geschiedenis van de kristelijke mutualistische beweging in België*, p. 68. See also N. Broten, 'From Sickness to Death: The Financial Viability of the English Friendly Societies and Coming of the Old Age Pensions Act, 1875–1908', *LSE working papers*, no. 135/10 (2010).
26. Document No. 48 Chambre des Représentants, p. 2.
27. Ibid., p. 2, note 2, and Document No. 272 Chambre des Représentants, Projet de loi relatif aux société de secours mutuels. 11 Mai 1850, at http://www3.dekamer.be/digidoc/DPS/K2268/K22682037/K22682037.PDF [accessed 11 December 2010], pp. 18–40 ; Visschers, *Over de maetschappijen van onderlingen bijstand in België*, pp. 20–1.
28. Document No. 48 Chambre des Représentants, p. 3, Document No. 272 Chambre des Représentants; Companje, Veraghtert and Widdershoven, *Two Centuries of Solidarity*, pp. 51, 80; G. van Meulder, 'Mutualiteiten en ziekteverzekering in België (1886–1914)', *Belgisch Tijdschrift voor Nieuwste Geschiedenis*, 27 (1997), 1–2, at http://www.flwi.ugent.be/btng-rbhc/pdf/BTNG-RBHC, 27, 1997, 1–2, pp 083–134.pdf, pp. 83–134, on p. 86.
29. Document No. 48 Chambre des Représentants, p. 2.
30. The total population of Belgium at that time was 4,5 million. See http://nl.wikipedia.org/wiki/Bevolking_van_België [accessed 11 December 2010].
31. Document No. 48 Chambre des Représentants, p. 3.
32. Document No. 272 Chambre des Représentants, pp. 16–17.
33. Ibid., p. 18.
34. Ibid., p. 18.
35. Ibid., pp. 6–26.
36. Ibid., pp. 6–10.
37. Ibid., p. 11; Visschers, *Over de maetschappijen van onderlingen bijstand in België*, p. 6.
38. Document No. 272 Chambre des Représentants, p. 16.
39. Ibid., p. 11.
40. Ibid., pp. 20–2 and 36.
41. Ibid., p. 28.
42. K. Veraghtert and B. Widdershoven, *Twee eeuwen solidariteit: de Nederlandse, Belgische en Duitse ziekenfondsen tijdensde negentiende en de twintigste eeuw* (Amsterdam: Askant, 2002), p. 78.
43. Visschers, *Over de maetschappijen van onderlingen bijstand in België*, pp. 8 and 22, Rezsohazy, *Geschiedenis van de kristelijke mutualistische beweging in België*, p. 72; van Meulder, 'Mutualiteiten en ziekteverzekering in België (1886–1914)', p. 86.
44. Visschers, *Over de maetschappijen van onderlingen bijstand in België*, pp. 9–10.
45. Ibid., p. 10.
46. Ibid., p. 10.
47. Ibid., p. 11.
48. Ibid., pp. 12–16.
49. Kamerstuk, 'Projet de loi relatif aux société de secours mutuels', pp. 27–8.
50. Companje, Veraghtert and Widdershoven, *Two Centuries of Solidarity*, pp. 80–1.
51. Document No. 48 Chambre des Représentants, pp. 18–40; Visschers, *Over de maetschappijen van onderlingen bijstand in België*, pp. 20–1.
52. Visschers, *Over de maetschappijen van onderlingen bijstand in België*, p. 14.

53. A. de Swaan, *Zorg en de staat. Welzijn, onderwijs en gezondheidszorg in Europa en de Verenigde Staten in de nieuwe tijd* (Amsterdam: Bert Bakker, 1989), pp. 205–6; E. Reidegeld, *Staatliche Sozialpolitik in Deutschland. Von den Ursprungen bis zum Untergang des Kaiserreiches 1918*, 2nd rev. edn, 2 vols (Wiesbaden: VS Verlag für Sozialwissenschaften, 2006), vol. 1, p. 163.

54. Visschers, *Over de maetschappijen van onderlingen bijstand in België*, pp. 6–7.

55. Ibid., pp. 7–8.

56. 'De kiemen van sociale zekerheid', https://securitesociale.be/CMS/nl/about/displayThema/about/ABOUT_1/ABOUT_1_2.xml [accessed 11 December 2010]. In Parliament there was some fear that the state would not be able to guarantee this savings fund. K. Van Acker, J. Deferme and L. Vandeweyer, *Hoeders van de volksgezondheid. Artsen en mutualiteiten tijdens het interbellum: het Antwerpse voorbeeld* (Gent: Amsab, 2005), p. 19.

57. G. Souvereyns, *Solidair in gezondheid. 100 jaar christelijk mutualisme in de Kempen*, (Leuven: CM Turnhout/KADOC-Leuven, 2001), p. 72; Document No. 272 Chambre des Représentants, p. 28.

58. Companje, Veraghtert and Widdershoven, *Two Centuries of Solidarity*, pp. 81–3, 88.

59. Ibid., pp. 82, 87.

60. Ibid., pp. 85–8.

61. van Meulder, 'Mutualiteiten en ziekteverzekering in België (1886–1914)', pp. 105, and 120; Companje, Veraghtert and Widdershoven, *Two Centuries of Solidarity*, pp. 88–9, 92.

62. Document No. 152 Chambre des Représentants, Sociétés mutualistes. Revision de la loi du 3 Avril 1851. Exposé des motifs. 24 Avril 1894, at http://www3.dekamer.be/digidoc/DPS/K2328/K23280771/K23280771.PDF [accessed 11 December 2010], p. 5.

63. Document No. 176 Chambre des Représentants, Rapport, fait, au nom de la commission, par M. 'T Kint de Roodenbeke. Revision de la loi du 3 avril 1851. Exposé des motifs. 18 May 1894, at http://www3.dekamer.be/digidoc/DPS/K2328/K23280987/K23280987.PDF [accessed 11 December 2010], p. 20.

64. Document No. 176 Chambre des Représentants; Companje, Veraghtert and Widdershoven, *Two Centuries of Solidarity*, p. 92.

65. van Meulder, 'Mutualiteiten en ziekteverzekering in België (1886–1914)', pp. 108–9; Companje, Veraghtert and Widdershoven, *Two Centuries of Solidarity*, pp. 88–9, 92.

66. Ibid., pp. 107–8.

67. Ibid., pp. 108–9; Companje, Veraghtert and Widdershoven, *Two Centuries of Solidarity*, pp. 88–9, 92.

68. S. H. Scholl (ed.), *150 jaar katholieke arbeidersbeweging in West-Europa 1789–1939* (Brussel: Arbeiderspers, 1961), p. 72.

69. 'Like most nineteenth-century voluntary associations, mutual insurance companies were grounded in principles of both democracy *and* exclusionary elitism'. Non-discriminatory policies towards applicants or egalitarian and redistributative forms of allocation of revenues and premiums 'were often only enforced and distributed by the intervention of state authorities'. M. Lengwiller, 'Insurance and Civil Society: Elements of an Ambivalent Relationship', *Contemporary European History*, 15 (2006), pp. 397–416, on pp. 414–16.

70. G. van Meulder, 'Mutualiteiten en ziekteverzekering in België (1886–1914)', pp. 117–18; Companje, Veraghtert and Widdershoven, *Two Centuries of Solidarity*, p. 90.

71. Companje, Veraghtert and Widdershoven, *Two Centuries of Solidarity*, p. 92.

72. Souvereyns, *Solidair in gezondheid. 100 jaar christelijk mutualisme in de Kempen*, pp. 309–10.

73. Handelingen Tweede Kamer der Staten-Generaal 1916–1917. 15 Mei 1917, p. 2581, at www.statengeneraaldigitaal.nl [accessed 11 December 2010].

74. Companje, Veraghtert and Widdershoven, *Two Centuries of Solidarity*, p. 95; Kamerstuk 265 van de Belgische Kamer van Volksvertegenwoordigers, Ontwerp van wet tot verzekering tegen ziekte, vroegtijdige invaliditeit en ouderdom. 6 Mei 1914, at http://www3.dekamer.be/digidoc/DPS/K3063/K30631142/K30631142.PDF [accessed 11 December 2010].

75. Document No. 261 Chambre des Représentants, Proposition de loi relative à l'assurance en vue de la maladie, d'invalidité prématurée et de la vieillesse. 21 Mai 1913, at http://www3.dekamer.be/digidoc/DPS/K3058/K30582149/K30582149.PDF [accessed 11 December 2010], pp. 8–9.

76. Document No. 261 Chambre des Représentants, p. 19.

77. K. Van Acker, J. Deferme and L. Vandeweyer, *Hoeders van de volksgezondheid. Artsen en mutualiteiten tijdens het interbellum: het Antwerpse voorbeeld* (Gent: Amsab, 2005), pp. 47–75.

78. Ibid., p. 95.

79. Companje, Veraghtert and Widdershoven, *Two Centuries of Solidarity*, p. 145.

80. S. H. Scholl (ed.), *150 jaar katholieke arbeidersbeweging in West-Europa 1789–1939*, p. 81.

81. Companje, Veraghtert and Widdershoven, *Two Centuries of Solidarity*, pp. 145–7 and 243.

82. Van Acker, Deferme and Vandeweyer, *Hoeders van de volksgezondheid*, pp. 96–7; Companje, Veraghtert and Widdershoven, *Two Centuries of Solidarity*, pp. 148–52.

83. Companje, Veraghtert and Widdershoven, *Two Centuries of Solidarity*, pp. 152–5.

84. On the strength of Belgianness see M. Conway, 'Belgian's Mid-Century Crisis: Crisis of an Nation State?', *Belgisch Tijdschrift voor Nieuwste Geschiedenis*, 35 (2005), pp. 573–96, at http://www.flwi.ugent.be/btng-rbhc/pdf/BTNG-RBHC,%2035,%20 2005,%204,%20pp%20573–596.pdf [accessed 11 December 2010] and Kamerstuk 572 van de Belgische Kamer van Volksvertegenwoordigers, Wetsontwerp tot instelling en organisatie van een regeling voor verplichte ziekte- en invaliditeitsverzekering, 8 Maart 1963, http://www3.dekamer.be/digidoc/DPS/K2104/K21043875/K21043875.PDF [accessed 11 December 2010], p. 2.

85. Companje, Veraghtert and Widdershoven, *Two Centuries of Solidarity*, p. 224.

86. Ibid., pp. 221–2.

87. Ibid., p. 225.

88. Document No. 572 Chambre des Représentants; Companje, Veraghtert and Widdershoven, *Two Centuries of Solidarity*, pp. 224–45.

89. Companje, Veraghtert and Widdershoven, *Two Centuries of Solidarity*, pp. 232–46.

90. Gerkens and Merkur, *Belgian Health System Review, Health Systems in Transition*, p. 204.

91. Companje, Veraghtert and Widdershoven, *Two Centuries of Solidarity*, pp. 239–6.

92. Ibid., p. 245.

93. E. Schokkaert en C. Van de Voorde, 'Defederalisering van de Belgische gezondheidszorg?', (Leuven 2007), at http://www.econ.kuleuven.be/ces/les/LES119.pdf [accessed 11 December 2010], pp. 1–29, on pp. 3–5; D. Corens, *Belgian Health System Review, Health Systems in Transition*, vol. 9, No. 2, 2007 at http://www.euro.who.int/__data/assets/pdf_file/0007/96442/E90059.pdf [accessed 27 December 2010]; Gerkens and Merkur, *Belgian Health System Review, Health Systems in Transition*.

94. Companje, Veraghtert and Widdershoven, *Two Centuries of Solidarity*, pp. 310–11, 324 and 362–3.

95. Lindert, *Growing Public*, vol. 1 and *Eco-Santé OCDE 2010*. Comment la Belgique se positionne.
96. Companje, Veraghtert and Widdershoven, *Two Centuries of Solidarity*, p. 312.
97. Ibid., pp. 313–18.
98. Ibid., p. 320, and 'Beroep ingesteld op 25 januari 2010 – Europese Commissie/Koninkrijk België (Zaak C–41/10)', at http://curia.europa.eu/jurisp/cgi bin/gettext.pl?lan g=nl&num=79899687C19100041&doc=T&ouvert=T&seance=REQ_COMM [accessed 11 December 2010]
99. Companje, Veraghtert and Widdershoven, *Two Centuries of Solidarity*, p. 321.
100. Ibid., pp. 320–3.
101. Schokkaert and Van de Voorde, 'Defederalisering van de Belgische gezondheidszorg?', p. 9.
102. Companje, Veraghtert and Widdershoven, *Two Centuries of Solidarity*, pp. 323–5.
103. Ibid., pp. 321–5.
104. Ibid., pp. 325–6; Schokkaert and Van de Voorde, 'Defederalisering van de Belgische gezondheidszorg?'.
105. Medinews, 'Vlaamse Huisartsen Willen Splitsing Gezondheidszorg', 1 April 2010, at http://www.medinews.be/full_article/detail.asp?aid=16271 [accessed 11 December 2010].
106. G. Messiaen, 'Uitdagingen Ziekteverzekering', at https://www.wlz.be/jsp/content. jsp?l=Nl&r=112&d=1120&o=Mut400 [accessed 11 December 2010].
107. Nieuw Pierke, 'Organisatie gezondheidszorg: federaal of per gemeenschap?', 25 November 2008, at http://www.nieuwpierke.be/forum_voor_democratie/nl/node/366 [accessed 11 December 2010].
108. F. Daue, 'Mutualiteiten: wat zijn de nieuwe kansen op lange termijn?', 3 December 2009, at http://www.itinerainstitute.org/nl/bibliotheek/_paper/ what-are-the-new-challenges-for-sick-funds-for-the–30-years-to-come-what-are-their-strengths-and-weaknesses-how-do-we-translate-this-into-opportunities-and-concrete-projects-and-how-do-we-initiate-change/ [accessed 27 December 2010]; Gerkens and Merkur, *Belgian Health system review, Health Systems in Transition*; M. De Vos and B. Van Damme, 'De Gezondheidseconomie: uitdagingen, opportuniteiten en pistes voor hervorming', (2010), http://www.itinerainstitute.org/upl/1/default/doc/health_12_ NL.pdf [accessed 27 December 2010]; *De Standaard*, 22, 25, 28 November and 2 December 2010; E. Schokkaert and C. Van de Voorde, 'Belgium's Health Care System: Should the Communities/Regions Take it Over? Or the Sickness Funds', (2001), at http://www.itinerainstitute.org/nl/bibliotheek/_paper/a-new-institutional-design-for-belgium-healthcare-system/ [accessed 9 February 2011]. In this last paper Schokkaert en Van de Voorde state that shifting positions on solidarity are a greater challenge to the system than affordability.
109. *Nieuwsblad*, 'Koning looft Van Rompuy en Damiaan', 24 December 2009, at http:// www.nieuwsblad.be/Article/Detail.aspx?articleID=DMF20091224_02 [accessed 11 December 2010]. According to C. Strikwerda, Belgium has been the quintessential Western European state. C. Strikwerda, 'If All of Europe Were like Belgium: Lessons in Politics and Globilization From one Country', *Belgisch Tijdschrift voor Nieuwste Geschiedenis*, 35:4 (2005), pp. 503–22, on p. 503, at http://www.flwi.ugent.be/btng-rbhc/archive/2005–04/pp 503–522.html [accessed 20 December 2010].

INDEX

Act for the Encouragement and Relief of
  Friendly Societies 1793 (UK), 89–90
Albert II, king of Belgium, 205
Aldaba, Andrés José, 142
American Association for Labor Legislation
  (AALL), 121, 122–3, 124, 241n87
  compulsory health insurance, 122–3,
    124–5, 127, 129, 239n42
American Federation of Labor, 128
American Medical Association, 128
Ancient Order of Foresters, 4–5, 89, 90, 91,
    94, 95
  and Foresters' courts, 96, 99, 111–12,
    112, 235n2
  and insolvency, 94, 107, 116–17, 118,
    119, 236n37
  membership data, 110, 111, 113, **114**, 115
  and national health insurance, 103
  and old age pensions, 101
Anderson, O. W., 121, 125, 237n5, 237n7
Ansell, Charles, 91, 231n8
Antediluvian Order of Buffaloes, 89
Armstrong, B., 135–6, 238n20, 239n31,
    239n43
Arnabat Mata, R., 226n53
Asociacionismo en España contemporánea, 66
Atkinson, J. J., 210n31
Atlantic Charter, 173
Australia, national health insurance, 239n37

Barcelona, 69, 74, 80, **81**, 82, 84, 227n66
Barnsley Chronicle, 23–4
Bavarian *Knappschaften*
  membership, 33–4, **33**
  mergers and closures, 36, **36**
  number of KVs, 32
  size of KVs, 34, *35*
  statistics, 31–2, *32*

Bavarian mining law (1869), 29
Beland, D., 129, 237n10, 238n13
Belgium
  Belgian Constitution (1831), 192
  Belgian independence (1830), 192
  Catholic Congresses Liège, 196
  child labour inquiry (1846–8), 192
  compulsory health insurance, 189, 190,
    192, 199
  compulsory pension law, 198
  General Annuity Fund (Lijfrentekas),
    193, 195
  German occupation, 171, 172, 186, 198
  Ghent mutual funds, 191, 196
  government intervention and legislation,
    193–4
  guilds and mutual aid funds, 190, 191
  health care costs, 189, 202–3, 204
  health insurance funds, 203
  health insurance system, 204–5
  Le Chapelier Law (1795–1866), 190,
    192
  Mutuality Law (1851), 194, 195
  Mutuality Law (1894), 196
  Old Age, Sickness and Disability Insur-
    ance Act (1914), 197–8
  Pension Law (1900), 197
  pensions, compulsory pension law, 198
  Poor Relief, 191–2
  population, 189, 190, 202, 254n30
  Prévinaire study of funds, 191–2
  provincial register (1849), 192
  relief and welfare funds survey (1812),
    190, 253n5
  Rogier mutual relief funds (1848), 192
  Royal decree (1820), 191
  social security system, 200, 204

state pensions, 192
statutory health insurance, 6
Visschers report (1849), 193, 195
voluntary and supplementary health
 insurance, 201–2
widows and orphans funds, 191, 192
Belgium Flanders, 198, 202, 203, 204
Belgium and mutual societies
 Alliance of Liberal Health-Insurance
  Funds (LLM), 198
 competition with commercial insurers,
  203
 European Commission and health insur-
  ance funds, 203
 government subsidies, 199
 growth in number, 196–7
 and health care, 189, 199
 Institute of Medical Control, 200
 Leburton Act (1963), 200
 local authority supervision, 192
 membership, 193
 National Alliance of Christian Mutuali-
  ties (LCM), 198, 201, 203
 National Alliance of Occupation-Related
  Mutualities (LLBBOZ), 198, 201
 National Alliance of Socialist Mutualities (MVSM), 198, 203
 National Christian Alliance, 200
 National Fund for Insurance against
  Sickness and Disability (RVZI),
  199–200
 National Institute for Health and Dis-
  ability Insurance (RIZIV), 200–1
 national mutualist alliances formation, 198
 national and regional federations, 196–7
 National Savings Fund (ASLK), 196
 OMNIO and MAB systems and co-
  payments, 201
 and pension funds, 194–5, 196
 Petit Report (1975), 201
 sickness and funeral funds, 191, 192
 socialist insurance funds, 198
 socialist mutualities, 198–9, 201, 203
 supplementary services, 203
Belgium and social welfare
 Demotte reforms (2005), 204
 National Pension Fund, 194, 195, 196, 197
 national pension plan, 192

National Social Security Office, 199
 regional health care, 204
Belgium Wallonia, 198–9, 200, 202, 204
Benson, John
 coalmining history, 10, 209n13,
  209n16–18, 210n24, 212n82
 specialist funds for miners, 2, 208n2
Bergamo, 47, 48, 50, 53, 62, 217n3, 219n10
Berger, Stefan, coalmining, 10, 209n14
Bertillon, Jacques, 95, 232n34
Beveridge Report, 173
Billington, Edward, 19
Bismarck's social insurance, 27, 38, 128, 195
 health insurance coverage, 33
 invalidity pension, 38
  and sick pay rates, 40
 sickness insurance law (1883), 30
Blackley, Canon W. L.
 statutory health insurance, 102,
  233n44–5
 statutory old age pension, 97, 98
Blond, Philip, 1, 207n1, 230n2
Boer War, 99
Booth, Charles, non-contributory state pen-
 sion, 97–8, 109, 233n47
Brabrook, Edward, 93, 94, 232n22, 233n52
Brandt, A. M., 250n4
Brescia, 47, 48, 50, 52, 53, 62, 217n3
Bretton Woods monetary system, 180
Britain
 Ancient Order of Foresters, 4–5, 89, 90,
  91, 94, 95
 and Foresters' courts, 96, 99, 111–12,
  112, 235n2
 and insolvency, 94, 107, 116–17, 118,
  119, 236n37
 membership data, 110, 111, 113, **114**, 115
 and national health insurance, 103
 and old age pensions, 101
 Antediluvian Order of Buffaloes, 89
 Charity Organisation Society, 101
 compensation and industrial accidents,
  211n40–3
 Friendly Societies Act (1875), 110
 Grand United Order of Oddfellows,
  90, 111
 Independent Order of Oddfellows, 90, 91
 Institute of Actuaries, 93–4, 99

Manchester Unity of Oddfellows, 90,
    92, 95
  age distribution, **100**
  sickness claims, 96, **96**, 99
Old Age Pensions Act (1908), 107, 109,
    110, 117, 120
Royal Commission on Friendly Societies
    (1875), 90, 94, 97, 101
Royal Commission into the Operation of
    the Poor Laws (1832), 94
Royal Statistical Society, 94, 95
Select Committee on National Provident
    Insurance, 95, 102
Workmen's Compensation Act, 94–5
British friendly societies, 89
actuarial analysis, 3, 110, 115–16, **117–19**
'affiliated orders', 90, 95, 111
age longevity problem, 112
age and sickness rates, 91, **91**, 97, 100
age-specific morbidity, 4, 91, 105
assets/investments, 116
census (1861) data, 114
Chief Registrar of Friendly societies, 94,
    95, 110, 111
data for research analysis, 111, 113–14,
    114, 115
duplicate membership, 94
Friendly Societies Act (1793), 89–90
Friendly Societies Act (1875), 110
  and funeral/burial insurance, 89, 104
growth of societies, 95, 108, 113
health care, 104
Highland Friendly Society, 91
honorary members, 92, 108
insolvency, 94, 107, 109, 110, 112,
    116–17
insurance the primary function, 90–1
  and medical profession, 104, 115
members' contributions, 108
membership, 107, 109, 111, 113, 115
membership in 19th century, 90
national health insurance, 4, 97, 101–2,
    103, 104
occupations of members, 95, 113, 115
and old age pensions, 4, 5, 89, 97, 98
  contributory pensions, 101, 109
  non-contributory pensions, 98, 101,
    109, 120

patronized societies, 90
poor law returns data, 113
poor relief, 16–17, 90, 94, 97–8, 102, 108
private insurance companies, 104
record keeping, 112, **112**
Royal Commission on Friendly Societies,
    90, 94, 97, 101
sickness claims, 95, 96, **96**, 104, 109
sickness rates, 91, *91*, 92, 95, 97, 100, 105
sickness rates urban and rural compari-
    son, 92, *93*
superannuation schemes, 100
British National Insurance Act (1911), 197
British welfare state
  growth of, 89
  and medical profession, 104, 115
  national health insurance, 97, 101, 104
  old age pensions, 97
  private insurance companies, 104
  statutory old age pension, 109, 120
Broten, Nicholas
  actuarial risk, 44
  and Ancient Order of Foresters, 4–5, 99
  British friendly societies and old age pen-
      sions, 4, 5, 234n53
  and insolvency risk, 99
  LSE Discussion Paper, 99, 234n53
Brown, John, 94, 232n29

Calder, R. F., 103, 234n73
Campbell, Alan, 10, 209n10
Canada, 204, 239n37
Castillo, Santiago, 66, 208n10, 221n5,
    222n10–11, 223n19-20, 224n25
Castles, F. G., 239n37
Catalonia, 69, 223n17, 227n64
  Barcelona, 69, 74, 80, **81**, 82, 84, 227n66
  Catalan Autonomy Statute, 80
  Catalan Federation of Mutual Provident
      Societies (1896), 80, 230n92
  Catalan Federation of Mutual Provident
      Societies (1944), 87
  Catalonia Law on Mutual Assistance
      Associations (1934), 80, 155
  Federation of Friendly Societies of the
      Province of Barcelona (1918), 80
  Law of Catalan Mutual Societies (1935),
      230n92

number of friendly societies, 82
number of mutual insurance funds, 80, **80**
Challinor, R., 209n8
Chamberlain, Joseph, 97–8
Le Chapelier Law (1791), 190, 192
Chaplin, Sid, and coalmining villages (UK), 19
charitable institutions, in Spain, 67, 71–4,
   72, 73
charity
   in Belgium, 194
   in Italy, 48, 58
   in Spain, 73, 74, 225n30
   in United Kingdom, 101, 125
   see also Poor Relief
Charles IV, king of Spain, 71
child labour
   in Belgium, 192
   in Italy, 57, 219n16
Church, Roy, 15, 21, 208n3
   *Strikes and Solidarity: Coalfield Conflict
      in Britain 1889–1966*, 10, 209n15
Civil War in Spain, **72**, 85, 137, 138, 153
   and Mutual Assistance Associations, 153
   and workers' societies, 154
coalfields in Britain *see* North Staffordshire
   (Potteries) coalfield; Northumberland
   and Durham coalfield
Companje, Karel-Peter, 187, 205, 253n1–2
La Conciliación de Pamplona S. A.
   (1978–84), 163
   medical service cancelled, 163
   membership decline, 163
   self-liquidation, 164, 165
   see also Sociedad Protectora de Obreros
      La Conciliacíon (1902–84)
Cordery, Simon, 89, 96, 207n5
Costa, D., 125, 130–1, 240n47, 240n65
Croll, Andy, 10, 209n14
Crossick, G., 209n5
Cuesta Bustillo, J., 221n4, 244n3, 228n79

Daunton, Martin, 10, 21, 209n12, 212n73
Deadman, E. B., 103, 234n76
Dekker, Wisse, and Dekker-plan, 184
Demotte, Rudy, 204
Den Uyl, Joop, 182
Derbyshire Miners' Association, 18, 211n54
Digby, A., 235n81

disease and insurance, 13, 129
   in Italy, 55, 220n18–19
   in Spain, 72, 73, 74, 77, 144
Dlabačová, Anna, 187
Doorn, T. van, 205
Douglas, P. H., 126, 240n52
Drion, F. J. W., 197
Durham Coal Owners' Association, 14, 21,
   212n81
Durham Miners' Association, 17–18, 20, 23,
   211n52, 212n80, 213n87
Dutch Medical Association (NMG), 168,
   169, 171, 173

Eden, Frederick Morton, 90
Emery, George, 5, 44, 110, 117, 130, 208n13
Emery, J. C. Herbert, 44, 110, 117, 187,
   208n13
   and compulsory health insurance, 5, 129,
      238n18–19
   data from US Department of Labor, 5,
      130
   household income and surpluses, **132**,
      242n94
   and voluntary health insurance, 123, 129,
      130–2
Employers' Liability Act 1880 (UK), 18, 23
Employers' Liability Assurance Corporation
   (UK), 25
Epstein, A., American standard of living,
   127, 131, 240n56, 243n102
Estado, protesta y movimientos sociales (Cas-
   tillo & de Orruño), 66
Esteban de Vega, M., 222n7–8, 224n29,
   225n30, 244n1
European Commission, 203
Evison, J., 210n30

Finlaison, Alexander Glen, 91, 92, 231n17
The First National Congress of Public
   Health 1934 (Madrid), 138
Fisher, I., 124, 240n64
Fisk, Audrey, 96
Flanders, 204
   Flemish Health Care Fund, 204
   Flemish mutualities, 198, 202, 203
   German occupation, 198

Social-Democrats and social security system, 204

Fleming, Sir Alexander, 77

Foresters' Miscellany, 102, 232n27, 232n29–30

Fox, D. M., 122, 237n3

France, 123, **132**, 133, **134**, 193, 194, 195

Franco, Francisco, Franco regime, 5, 67, 86–7, 88, 153

Frederick II, king of Prussia, 29

Friendly Societies Act 1793 (UK), 89–90

Friendly Societies Act 1875 (UK), 110

friendly societies in Belgium *see* Belgium and mutual societies

friendly societies in Italy *see* Societàs di Mutuo Soccorso

friendly societies in Spain *see* Sociedad Protectora de Obreros *La Conciliacíon*

friendly societies in United Kingdom *see* Britain; British friendly societies

Fullana, P. 227n55, 230n93

García Checa, A., 222n9, 223n17

Gardner, M., 250n4

Garibaldi, Giuseppe, 219n10

General Annuity Fund (Lijfrentekas) in Belgium, 193, 195

Ghent, 191, 196

Gilbert, Bentley, 4, 99, 100, 128, 207n6, 208n12, 233n49–50
    contributory pension scheme, 98, 243n98
    insolvency in friendly societies, 107, 109, 111, 119
    membership profile, 119–20
    and national health insurance, 102, 241n76
    and statutory pension scheme, 119, 128, 134
    structure of friendly societies, 108

Girón, José Antonio, 153

Glasman, Maurice, 1, 207n2, 230n2

Gompers, Samuel, 128

Goodman, A. C., 125, 239n45

Gorsky, Martin, 26, 89, 105, 115, 207n5
    British friendly societies, 4, 209n6–7
    growth of friendly societies, 9, 26, 113

Gosden, Peter, 90, 108, 111, 113, 209n19, 230n5–6

Grand United Order of Oddfellows, 90, 111

Gratton, B., 242n92–3, 243n100

Great Depression, 82

Guinnane, Timothy, 2–3, 30, 40, 41, 215n10–11, 216n26

Guntupalli, Aravinda, 4, 105, 221n3

Hacker, J. S., 129, 237n10, 238n13, 241n78

Haines, M. R., 125, 239n45, 241n92

Hardy, George Francis, 92, 99, 233n52

Harris, Bernard, 4, 91, 105, 221n3, 231n11, 236n32

Harrison, Royden, 10, 209n9

Health Insurance Act 2006 (Netherlands), 6, 167

Hiltrop, Julius, 30, 31, 215n12

Hinde, Andrew, 4, 105, 221n3, 233n41

Hoffmann, B., 36, **37**, 125–6, 237n1, 237n4

Hookham, R. P., 97, 233n46

Hopkins, Eric, 89, 209n5, 230n1

Hudson, Samuel, 94, 232n30

Independent Collier (ed. Harrison), 10, 209n9–11

Independent Order of Odd Fellows (IOOF), 90, 91, 129, 208n13, 216n28, 238n29

industrialization
    in the Basque Country, 82
    in Britain, 113
    Second Industrial Revolution in Spain, 70, 79, 82
    and SMSs in Northern Italy, 3, 48, 49, 61
    in United States, 126

Institute of Actuaries (UK), 93–4, 99

International Conference on Sickness Insurance (1927), 83

International Labour Office (1919), 82

International Social Security Association (1927), 82

Italy
    child labour regulation, 219n16
    country savings banks (Casse Rurali), 57
    creation of welfare state, 61
    fascism and the SMSs, 62
    government relationship with SMSs, 52, 60–1
    labour law and female workers, 219n14

limited social security and pensions, 57
National Fund for Insurance (1883), 60
National Fund for the Maternity Insurance and Leave (1910), 62
National Fund for Social Security (1898), 60
provision of welfare assistance, 62, 63
state pensions for officials and soldiers, 51, 62
suffrage for men, 54, 62, 219n13
tax concessions for cooperatives, 57
trade unions, 52, 62, 219n11
Italy Eastern Lombardy
accidents in the workplace, 220n21
agricultural accident insurance, 220n20
Bergamo, 47, 48, 50, 53, 62, 217n3, 219n10
Brescia, 47, 48, 50, 52, 53, 62, 217n3
censuses, 216n2
development of welfare state, 220n22
increase in SMS numbers, 218n6–8
pellagra, 58, 220n19
population, 217n3
Second Italian War of Independence, 216n1
SMSs (societàs di mutuo soccorso), 3, 216n1–2, 217n4–5, 220n17–18
suffrage for men, 219n13
trade unions, 219n11
see also Societàs di Mutuo Soccorso (SMS) in Eastern Lombardy

Jaffe, J. A., 212n71
Jevons, H. S., 210n36
Johansson, S. R., 232n40
Jopp, Tobias, 2–3, 44, 216n29

Karwehl, Harry, 30, 31, 215n15
Knappschaft law (1854), 27, 29
Knappschaft law reform (1906), 29, 32, 38
Knappschaften, 1, 2–3, 28–9, 45
actuarial risk, 3, 27–8, 31, 42, 44, 45
claim costs and deficits, 42, 43, **43**
closures and mergers, 42, 43, **43**
compensation for loss of earnings, 3
compulsory contributions, 27
contributions to sick pay from employers, 41, 42, 45
health and pension insurance, 28, 30, 31, 46
legislation and sick pay rates, 40–1

membership variation, 45
mergers of small KVs, 42, 43, **43**, 45
moral hazard, 3, 27, 31, 39, 45
moral hazard measurement, 40, 41
mutual associations, 45
old-age pension insurance, 44, 214n2
optimal size of KVs, 3, 30–1, 44, 45
primary functions, 27
Reich regulations (1887, 1905) and sickness, 41, 42
Reichsknappschaft, 3, 30, 45
research on sick days and claims, 41–2
small KVs and discipline, 40
small KVs and sick days, 39
social insurance, 29–30
of sub-optimal size, 3
Knappschaften in Bavaria
Bavarian KV statistics, 31, *32*
membership, 33–4, **33**
mergers and closures, 36, **36**
mining law (1869), 29
number of KVs, 32
size of KVs, 34, *35*
Knappschaften in Prussia, 28
actuarial risk in small KVs, 45
advantages of small KVs, 39
average financial data for KVs, 36, *37*
average membership and claims, 38
average sick days per KV member, *39*
contributions from mine owners, 38
local mining codes, 28–9
membership, 33–4, **33**
mergers and closures, 36, **36**
mergers and economies of scale, 45
moral hazard, 39
number of KVs, 32
Prussian KV statistics, 31, *32*
Prussian miners' social insurance, 27
Prussian mining reform, 27
size of KVs, 34, *35*, 45
statutory workmen's insurance, 38
voluntary contributions, 28
Koch, Robert, 77

Lancashire and Cheshire Miners' Federation, 25, 211n56
Lancashire and Cheshire Miners' Permanent Relief Society (1872), 11, 210n23

Laporte, Norman, 10, 209n14
Lapp, J. A., 239n38, 241n81, 241n88
Largo Caballero, Francisco, 85, 141, 245n20
Laslett, J., 209n9
Leburton Act 1963 (Belgium), 200
Lee, C., 135, 243n115
Leo XIII, Pope, 138
León Sanz, Pilar, 244n1, 244n4–5
    and Sociedad Protectora de Obreros *La Conciliación*, 5, 208n11, 223n17, 245n9
Linden, Marcel van der, 207n4, 208n9–10, 208n1
    editor *Social Security Mutualism*, 1
Lindert, Peter, 122, 237n8, 237n11
Little Sisters of the Poor, 162
Lloyd-George, David Lloyd George, 1st earl, 102, 103, 104–5
Logan, Roger, 112, 236n27
London School of Economics, Discussion Paper (Broten), 99, 234n53
Lubbers, Ruud, 182
Lubove, R., 122, 124, 129, 237n3
Ludlow, John, 95

Macnicol, John, 99, 100, 101, 232n40, 233n52
    The politics of retirement in Britain, 99, 232n40, 233n52
Majorca
    development of societies, 224n22, 230n93
    Montepío de la Caridad, 77, **78**, 229n82
Manchester Unity of Oddfellows, 90, 92, 95, 96, **96**, 99, **100**
Marimón, A., 227n55, 230n93
Maza Zorrilla, E., 222n6, 221n5
miners and insurance *see Knappschaften*; North Staffordshire (Potteries) coal-field; Northumberland and Durham coalfield
Mitchell, B. R., 15, 16, **16**, 113, 210n27, 210n34
Moffrey, R., 111, 236n16
Montepío de la Caridad, 77, **78**, 229n82
montepíos (mutual fund societies) in Spain, 67, 70, 86, 153, 155, 224n26
    employers' montepíos, 227n59
    and medical fees, 227n55

Montero García, F., 222n7
Morecroft, C. W., 94, 103, 232n27, 234n72
Moss, D. A., 240n54, 241n87
    compulsory health insurance, 128, 129
    concept of security in US, 122, 241n84–6
Murray, J. E., 134, 136, 238n29, 239n32, 243n113
mutual aid societies in Italy *see* Societàs di Mutuo Soccorso
Mutuality Laws (Belgium), 19, 195, 196

Napoleon III, 195
Narlborough, C. W., 103, 234n74
National Health Law 1963 (Spain), 153
National Insurance Institute (INP), Spain 137
Navarre, 152, 158
    Navarrese Provincial Delegation of Trade Union Unity, 156
    Obligatory Healthcare Insurance population covered, 158
    Official College of Physicians in Navarre, 156, 157
    Programme for Industrial Promotion (1964), 158–9
Neave, David, 89, 108, 230n1, 230n5–6, 235n3
Neison, Francis, Jr, 92
Neison, Francis, Sr
    rates of mortality, **100**, 231n9, 231n13
    sickness rates, 91, 92, 93, 231n9
Netherlands
    AWZ (national insurance scheme for long-term care), 178
    amended and renamed AWBZ, 180
    inclusion of hospitalization, 179
    opposition from private insurance sector ,179
    bovenbouwers (superstructures), 174–5
    bankruptcy of bovenbouwer AZR, 176
    competition with commercial insurers, 175, 186
    deductibles, 181, 182
    Dekker-plan, 184
    dual system social and private health insurance, 176
    mergers with sickness funds, 184
    opposition to AWZ-plan, 179

proposed merger with sickness funds, 183
BVV (compulsory health insurance
    scheme), 178–9
Central Institute for Hospital Charges
    (COZ), 177
and private health insurance, 177
commercial health insurance, 167, 169, 175
ANPZ-policy, 175–6
competition with bovenbouwers, 175,
    181, 186
disadvantages indemnity-based plans,
    185
expansion in health care sector, 176
formation of cartel, 175
opposition to AWZ-plan, 179
opposition to Dekker-plan, 184
premium-differentiation, 182, 186
sale of health insurance portfolios, 185,
    187
and WTZ reform, 186
development of health policy, 6
Directorate-General of Price-Control,
    and health insurance premiums, 172
Dutch economy and Bretton Woods
    collapse, 180
Dutch government plan for social secu-
    rity, 173
Dutch Medical Association (NMG),
    168–9, 171
and Sickness Fund Council, 173
government and health care cuts, 182
government and national health insur-
    ance, 182
Health Insurance Act (2006), 6, 167
Health Insurers Netherlands, 185
interdependence of private and commer-
    cial health insurance, 186
KLOZ (Committee for National Organ-
    izations of Private Health Insurers),
    177, 178, 182
merged with VNZ into Health Insurers
    Netherlands, 185
NOZ (national risk-pool) established, 179
voluntary cross-subsidization, 182–3
Ministry of Social Affairs
    and private health insurance, 171, 178
    and Sickness fund Council, 173
    and sickness fund insurance, 171

supervision of health insurance, 172
mono-line insurers, 169, 170
MOOZ (Act on the co-funding Over-
    representation Elderly Sickness Fund
    Insured), 183–4
multiple-line insurance companies, 170,
    185, 186
mutual aid societies origins, 192
mutual insurance companies, 256n69
national health insurance, 182
non-profit sickness funds, 6
not-for-profit hospital insurance funds,
    170, 172
not-for-profit (mutual) health insurance,
    167, 169, 171, 181
NOZ (Dutch Mutual Reinsurance Insti-
    tute for Health Insurance), 179–80
Poor Law, 178
Price-Control and Social Affairs, 172, 173
private health insurance, 180–1
    (1910–30), 168–9
    (1930–40), 170–1, 173
    (1945–50), 173–4
recession, 182
Sickness Fund Council, 173, 175, 185–6
Sickness Fund Decree, 171, 172, 173, 185
sickness funds, 168, 174, 175, 183, 184,
    185, 186
    and supplementary insurance schemes,
    172–3
Simons decision, 184, 186–7
Social Health Insurance, 177
Social Health Insurance (1940–5), 171, 172
social justice versus profit-making (1945-
    50), 173–5
Standard Insurance Policy (SPP), 183
Van der Reijden plan, 182, 183
Van Rijn's system, 173
Veldkamp and health care systems, 178,
    179, 180
voluntary health insurance, 171–2, 182,
    183
WTZ (Act on the Access to Health
    Insurance), 183, 184, 186
non-profit sickness funds, in Netherlands, 6
North Staffordshire Coal and Ironworkers
    Permanent Relief Society (1869), 2, 11,
    12, 25, 210n29

colliery owners' payments, **24**
North Staffordshire Miners' Federation, 18, 20
North Staffordshire (Potteries) coalfield, 10, 11
  charity and poor law guardians, 16–17
  Coal and Ironworkers' Permanent Relief Society (1869), 2
  commercial insurance policies, 19–20
  compulsory subscription to pit clubs, 22–3
  Disaster Funds, Mossfields and Talke, 17
  employers and employees relationship, 21, 26
  friendly society membership, 9–10
  industrial accidents, 14, 18
  miners' earnings, 14–16, **16**
  occupational risk, 13–14, **14**
  trade-unions, 18
Northumberland and Durham coalfield, 2, 10–11, 19
  charity and poor law guardians, 16–17
  collections for colleagues, 20
  commercial insurance policies, 19–20
  Disaster Funds, Hartley and Seaham, 17, 20
  employers
    accident assistance, 21, 22
    payment of smart money, 22
    permanent relief fund, 23–4
    relationship with employees, 21
  friendly society membership, 9–10
  industrial accidents, 14, 18, 21
  miners' earnings, 14–16, **16**
  Miners' Permanent Relief Fund (1862), 2
  occupational risk, 13–14, **14**
  trade unions, 17–18
Northumberland and Durham Miners' Permanent Relief Fund (1862), 2, 11, **12**, 20, 23, 213n94–5
  owners' payments, **24**
  subscriptions deducted at source, 24–5
Northumberland Miners' Mutual Confident Association, 17, 23
  funeral fund and non-fatal accident fund, 20
  legal action Withymoor colliery deaths, 18
Northumberland Steam Collieries Defence Association, 21–2
Nottingham Ancient Imperial Order of Oddfellows, 90

Numbers, R. L., and AALL movement, 128, 238n20, 239n38, 240n65

Obama, Barack, 5
Oddfellows Magazine, 92, 231n16
Olabarri, Professor, 166
Old Age Pensions Act 1908 (UK), 107
Old Age, Sickness and Disability Insurance Act 1914 (Belgium), 197–8
Orruño, José M. Ortiz, 66, 221n5, 224n25
Outram, Quentin
  and British coal owners, 21, 212n70
  Strikes and Solidarity: Coalfield Conflict in Britain 1899-1966, 10, 209n15

Palumbo, M. G., 243n113
Pasteur, Louis, 77
Pease, Sir J. W., 23
Peebles, A., 237n1, 238n24
pellagra, 58, 220n19
Pension Law 1900 (Belgium), 197
The politics of retirement in Britain (Macnicol), 99, 232n40, 233n52
Pons Pons, Jerònia, 3–4, 222n5, 224n22, 226n45
Poor Law
  in Belgium, 191–2
  in Netherlands, 178
  in United Kingdom, 16–17, 90, 94, 97–8, 102, 108, 113
Pratt, John Tidd, 94
Prévinaire, E. J., Belgian Poor Relief, 191, 192
La Previsión social en la Historia (2009), 66
Primo de Rivera, José Antonio, 85, 141, 153
Prudential (insurance), 19–20
Prussian *Knappschaften*, 28
  actuarial risk in small KVs, 45
  advantages of small KVs, 39
  average financial data, 36, **37**
  average membership and claims, 38
  average sick days per member, *39*
  contributions from mine owners, 38
  local mining codes, 28–9
  membership, 33–4, **33**
  mergers and closures, 36, **36**
  mergers and economies of scale, 45
  miners' social insurance, 27
  mining reform, 27

moral hazard, 39
number of KVs, 32
size of KVs, 34, *35*, 45
statistics for KVs, 31, *32*
statutory workmen's insurance, 38
voluntary contributions, 28

Quadagno, J., 237n1, 237n3-4, 237n11

Ransom, J. E., 241n88
Ratcliffe, Henry, 92, 231n9
Rea, P. M., 94
Reijden, Joop van der, 182, 183
Rerum Novarum (1891)
    and Catholic mutualism in Spain, 67,
        138, 226n49
    and decline of Catholic SMSs in Italy, 52
Rhijn, Aart van, 173
Rigter, Danièle, 6, 187
Rio Tinto mine (Huelva), 79
Rodgers, D. T., 237n1, 237n9
    compulsory health insurance (US), 122,
        128, 130, 135
    voluntary mutual aid, 124
Rogier, Charles, 192
Roman Catholic Church
    Catholic Congress Liège, 196
    and Catholic SMSs in Italy, 52
    and friendly societies in Spain, 67, 138,
        140, 142-3
Roolvink, Bouke, 180
Rotondo, F. M., 242n92-4
Royal Commission on Friendly Societies
    1875 (UK), 90, 94, 97, 101
Royal Commission into the Operation of
    the Poor Laws (1832), 94
Royal Statistical Society (UK), 94, 95
Rubinow, I. M., 124, 237n2, 239n31,
    239n41
    compulsory health insurance, 127-8,
        241n87
    standard of living (US), 126-7, 242n92
    wage-earners' savings (US), 126, 131,
        240n56
Ryan, G. H., 93-4, 95

savings United States and Europe, 132-3,
    132, 134, **134**
Schokkaert, E., 257n93, 257n101, 258n108
Schouten, R., 205
Second Industrial Revolution in Spain, 70,
    79, 82
Second Italian War of Independence, 216n1
Select Committee on the Poor Laws (UK), 90
Sickness Fund Decree 1941 (Netherlands),
    172, 173, 185
Simons, Hans, 184, 186-7
social insurance
    compulsory sickness insurance, 82, 83
    international legislation, 82
Social Sciences and Humanities Research
    Council (SSHRC), 136
Social Security Mutualism (ed. van der
    Linden), 1
Sociedad Protectora de Obreros *La Concili-
    ación* (1902–84), 5, 137-9, 244n4-5,
    248n94-5
    actuarial assessment, 159, 160
    Aid Fund Commission, 143, 144
    La Asociación Protectora de Obreros de
        Pamplona La Conciliación, 140
    Association of Employers, 139
    Association of Workers' Societies, 142
    average wages, **152**
    benefit control, 147-8
    Casa de Misericordia, 144
    Chronic Fund (1914), 139, 143
    and the Civil War, 153
    Commission for Reform of the Regula-
        tions, 160
    effect of Social Security, 159
    financial difficulties, 161
    formation of La Conciliación Ltd
        (1978), 162, 163
    foundation and evolution, 137, 138, 164
    General Board of Insurance, 157
    and guilds, 138, 139, 140
    Illness Fund, 156
    income and expenditure, 159, 161, *162*
    influenza pandemic (1918), 149, 150
    Instituto Obrero de Seguros sociales de
        Barcelona, 152
    labour legislation, 245n15
    labour mediation, 139, 154

Law on Labour Accidents, 155
legislative issues, 245n10
liquidation of the society, 161–2
medical service, 143, 156, 164
membership, 5, 138, 144–5, 159–60,
   160, 161
  contributions, 151, 160
  regulations, 144, 157
midwifery service (1914), 139
Mixed Board (employers and employees),
   139, 140, 143, 245n11
Mixed Services Society, 144
morbidity rates, 149
Mutual Benefit fund, 140
Mutual Insurance Society, 141, 164
Mutualidad Obrera Profesional, 148, 152
National Corporative Organization, 140
National Health law (1963), 153
Navarrese Provincial Delegation of Trade
   Union Unity, 156
Northern Mutual Federation, 158
Obligatory Healthcare Insurance, 154,
   156, 157
Official College of Physicians of Navarre,
   156, 157–8
pharmaceutical service (1914), 139
physicians and benefit control, 147, 149
post-mortem aid, 139, 144, 151, 157, 160
re-definition of the society (1941), 155
reforms (1933), 141–2
Regulations (1926), 140
Regulations (1928), 140, 141
Regulations (1933), 142–3
Regulations (1941, 1943), 154–5
Savings Bank, 139
services provided, 139
sick leave
  benefit, 143, 144, 149, 150–1, 152, 164
  costs, 150–151, *151*
  rate, 149, 150, 157
  regulations, 145–6, 148, 149
social-labour legislation, 164
structural changes (1902–36), 139–40
Superior Management Board, 140
trade unions, 156, 165
worker members and benefit control,
   146–7, 248n99
workers' guilds, 138

Workers Protection Association, 140
workers' societies disbanded, 154
Societàs di Mutuo Soccorso (SMSs) in Eastern Lombardy, 47, 48, 51, 52–3
  benefits of membership, 54–5
  in Bergamo and Brescia, 47, 48, 50, 53, 62
  Catholic bank contributions and loans, 56
  Catholic SMSs, 4, 47, 49, 50, 51, 52
  contributions from owners/employers,
     51, 53
  cooperatives for goods and services, 56–7
  economic and social relevance, 59–60
  employers' liability insurance, 54, 62
  funeral expenses, 55
  government interference, 52, 60–1
  honorary members, 53, 56, 60
  illnesses recorded by SMSs, 58
  income and expenditure, 54, **54**, 58, **59**
  maternity benefits, 55
  membership, 47–8, 50, **50**, 51
  National Federation of the SMS (1901), 61
  number of SMSs in region, 48–9, *49*, 50
  pension payments, 54, 55, 56, **59**, 61, 62
  Provincial Federation of Catholic SMSs,
     53, 56
  rural SMSs, 53–4
  social activities, 56
  socialist SMSs, 50, 51, 56
  and the State, 47
  subsidies for illnesses, 58, 62
  trade unions, 52, 62
  unemployment payments, 54, 58, 62
  war veterans' SMSs, 51–2
  welfare system of the SMSs, 57–8
  work conditions and wages, 52
Societàs di Mutuo Soccorso (SMSs), 3
  Catholic societies, 3, 47, 48, 49
  closures due to 'public policies', 49
  definition of, 48–9
  and Fascist regime, 3
  growth due to industrialization, 3
  mutual financial support, 49–50
  socialist societies, 3, 49
  types of SMS, 50–1, 52–3
  unemployment benefits, 3
  wages and working conditions, 3
Solidaridad desde abajo (ed. Castillo), 66

Sombart, Werner, socialism and American
workers, 128, 241n75–6
Spain
actuarial studies, 226n45
Biscay province, 79, **80**, 224n25, 225n35,
227n59
Central National Union, 156
Civil War, **72**, 85, 138, 153, 154
establishment of the liberal state, 71
Falangists, 153
First National Health Congress (1934), 138
Franco regime, 4, 5, 67, 86–7, 88, 153,
229n87
General Instruction of Public Health
legislation (1904), 73
General Instructions for Charity (1885,
1889), 71
General State Budget, 83
infectious diseases, 72–3, 74
Institute for Social Reform, 67
insurance companies (private), 74–5
insurance coverage of Montepío de la
Caridad, 77
labour disputes repression, 86–7
maternity insurance (1929), 85, 86
medical care, 73, 227n57
National Conference on Sickness,
Disability and Maternity Insurance
(1922), 84, 228n79–80
National Health Service, 153
National Institute for Social Security
(INP), 153
National Sickness Insurance Fund, 87
National Welfare Institute, 87
Obligatory Healthcare Insurance, 137,
138, 154, 157, 158, 165
the Old Regime, 68, 69, 70, 71
poverty, 74
Second Republic (1931–6), 85, 86, 153,
155, 165
sickness insurance project (1931–3), 85
social and political history studies, 66
Social Security system, 137, 154, 158
state compulsory sickness scheme, 4, 5,
83, 85, 86, 87
state and health care failings, 83, 84
state intervention in welfare, 86
state social insurance programmes, 68

state subsidies/subventions (1880s),
228n75
tax system, 84
workers' societies disbanded, 154
see also Catalonia
Spain Navarre, 152, 158
Navarrese Provincial Delegation of Trade
Union Unity, 156
Obligatory Healthcare Insurance population covered, 158
Official College of Physicians in Navarre,
156, 157
Programme for Industrial Promotion
(1964), 158–9
Spanish Civil War (1936-39), 137, 138, 153
and Mutual Assistance Associations, 153
and Workers' societies disbanded, 154
Spanish friendly societies, 66, 67, 68, 69,
70, 75
actuarial rigour, 65, 74, 76
agricultural friendly societies, 75–6
burial societies, 86
Catalan Federation of Mutual Provident
Societies (1896), 80, 87
Catholic mutualism, 66–7
charitable institutions, 71, 72, **72**, **73**, 74
charitable medical care, 73
charity (public), 74, 225n30
confraternities of Old Regime, 65, 70, 75
contributions deducted at source, 79
contributions from patrons, 75
draft law and the state, 85
effect of state scheme, 88
employers' contributions, 79
employers' liability, 68
employers' societies, 70, 78, 79, 86, 87
expenditure of societies in Barcelona, **81**
Federation of Friendly Societies of the
Province of Barcelona (1918), 80
Franco regime and friendly societies, 4, 5, 67
funeral expenses, 77
guilds, 65, 66, 67, 70, 138, 139
and health care, 4, 68, 76, **76**, 77
health care and private insurance companies, 74–5, 83
industrial welfare practices, 79
industrialization and growth of friendly
societies, 69, 70

Instituto Nacional de Previsión (INP), 137
Labour Accident Mutual Societies, 154
Law on Mutual Assistance Associations
    and Montepíos (1941), 156
legislation, 84, 86, 87
medical igualas/igualatorios, 73, 86, 87,
    225n35
membership, 75, 76, 77, 86
mining companies and health care, 79
Montepío de la Caridad, 77, **78**, 229n82
montepíos (mutual fund societies), 67,
    70, 86, 153, 155, 224n26
  employers' montepíos, 227n59
  and medical fees, 227n55
mutual aid insurance societies, 68, 87, 137
Mutual Assistance Societies regulations,
    154–5
mutual benefit societies in Pamplona, 244n4
mutual insurance coverage, 80
mutual insurance funds, **80**
and National Welfare Institute, 87
number registered after legislation
    (1941), 86
number of societies (1887), 69
old age/retirement pensions, 68, 70
paternalism, 70, 79
patronage, 66
private insurance companies, 74–5, 83, 86
protected societies (sociedades asisten-
    ciales), 66
in province of Barcelona, 82
sickness cover, 68, 70, **81**, 85, 86, 229n88
Sociedad Protectora de Obreros *La
    Conciliación*, 5, 137–8
solidarity in rural areas, 69–70
state subsidies, 83–4
SURNE insurance mutual association, 161
trade unions, 67, 75
unemployment, 68
widows' and orphans' pensions, 70
Spanish legislation
  Central Health Office (1925), 80–1
  charity laws (1822 and 1849), 71
  compulsory sickness insurance law
    (1942), 86
  Corporative Organization of Labour
    (1926), 164
  Dato Law (1900), 68

and friendly societies, 67
General Instruction of Public Health
    legislation (1904), 73
General Instructions for Charity (1885
    and 1889), 71
insurance law (1908), 67
labour accident insurance (1932), 150
Law of Agricultural Trade Unions
    (1906), 226n51
Law of Associations, 226n50
Law of Associations (1887), 84
Law of Catalan Mutual Societies (1935),
    230n92
Law on Labour Accidents, 155
Law on Mutual Assistance Associations
    and Montepíos (1941), 156
Law on Mutual Societies (1941), 67, 86,
    87, 154–5
Law on Obligatory Insurance, 247n81
Law for the Ordering of Private Insur-
    ance (1984), 166
Law on Professional Associations (1932),
    164
Law on Trade Union Unity, 156
Madoz legislation (1855), 71
Mon-Santillán reform (1845), 84
National Health law (1963), 153
Obligatory Healthcare Insurance, 156,
    157
Regulation (1852), 71
statutory scheme (1942), 4, 5
Spaven, Pat, 10, 209n11
Spierings, R., 205
Staffordshire Sentinel, 13, 25, 210n25,
    211n44–5
Starr, Paul, 125, 129, 239n31, 241n76, 241n78
Stead, J. Lister, 101, 103–4, 232n27
Steam Collieries Defence Association, 23,
    213n88, 213n92–3
Streb, Jochen, 2–3, 30, 40, 41, 215n10–11
*Strikes and Solidarity: Coalfield Conflict
    in Britain 1889–1966* (Church and
    Outram), 10
suffrage
  in Italy, 54, 62, 219n13
  in United States, 129
SURNE insurance and pensions, Spain, 161
Sutton, William, 91

Switzerland, 5, 123, **132**, 133, **134**, 194, 228n68

Tedeschi, Paolo, 3
Tomassini, L., 208n9, 218n5, 219n11
trade unions
    in British mining areas, 17–18, 23
    and friendly societies, 4, 67, 68
    in Northern Italy, 52, 56, 62, 217n5, 219n11
    in Spain, 80, 154, 156, 165, 226n51
Tranter, E. B., 103, 234n75
Treaty of Versailles (1919), 82
Treble, James, 98–9, 100, 101, 103, 233n43

UK Economic and Social Research Council, 1, 105
La Unión mine (Cartagena), 79
United Coal Trade Association, 23, 212n81
United States
    American Association for Labour Legislation (AALL), 121, 122–3, 124, 125, 127
    average earnings, 125, 126, 127, 128
    compulsory health insurance, 121, 122–3, 125, 132, 135
    employers' liability, 129
    historical background, 123–4
    and labour organizations opposition to levies, 128
    medical profession, 128
    opposition to, 125, 127–8, 129, 132
    rejection, 127, 134
    cost of living and wages, 126, 130
    decentralization of political power, 129
    friendly societies decline, 124
    household income and surpluses, **132**
    incomes and savings compared to Europe, 132–3, **132**, 134, **134**
    Independent Order of Odd Fellows (IOOF) sickness insurance, 129
    National Civic Federation, 125
    national health insurance, 5, 121
    occupational hazards, 126
    public old-age insurance, 122
    reformers and social insurance, 126
    voluntary health insurance, 123–4, 129, 131–2, 134–5

wage-earners' savings, 126, 129, 130–1, 132
Workers Compensation, 121, 122, 129, 241n84
University of Southampton, Insurance, Sickness and Old Age (2009), 1
Usui, C., 228n69

Veldkamp, Gerard, 178, 179, 180
Vilar Rodríguez, Margarita, 3–4, 222n5, 224n25, 226n52, 229n86
Visschers, M. A., 193, 195, 254n18, 254n20, 254n27
Vonk, Robert, 6, 205, 250n10
Voorde, C. Van de, 257n93, 257n101, 258n108

Wallonia, 198, 204
    Walloon Christian Federation, 200
    Walloon mutualities, 198–9, 202
Washington Conference (1921), 82
Watson, Alfred, 96, 231n10, 232n26, 234n52
    age distribution, **100**
    sickness claims, 94, 95
    sickness rates, 91, 92, 93, **96**
Watson, Reuben, 102
Weardale Coal and Iron Company of Durham, 21
Weaver, C. L., 131, 243n101
Weinbren, Daniel, 89, 92, 207n5, 213n94
West Riding of Yorkshire Miners' Permanent Relief Fund (1877), 11, 210n23
women, membership of friendly societies, 197
women workers
    in Italy, 217n3, 219n14
    maternity benefits in Italy, 55, **59**
    midwifery service in Spain, 85
    pensions in Spain, 120
    in United States, 127, 240n56
Workers' Compensation (US), 121, 122, 129, 241n84
Workmen's Compensation Act 1897 (UK), 94–5
World Economic History Congress (2009), 1
World War I
    effect of, 82, 112, 127–8
World War II, 6, 77, 199, 205

Yeo, S., 207n7, 235n84

Milton Keynes UK
Ingram Content Group UK Ltd.
UKHW031145141024
449569UK00024B/1053

9 781138 661615